GLOBAL HORROR

HYBRIDITY AND ALTERITY IN TRANSNATIONAL HORROR FILM

FIRST EDITION

GLOBAL HORROR

HYBRIDITY AND ALTERITY IN TRANSNATIONAL HORROR FILM

Edited by Samirah Alkassim and Ziad El-Bayoumi Foty

George Mason University

cognella®

SAN DIEGO

Bassim Hamadeh, CEO and Publisher
Kaela Martin, Project Editor
Celeste Paed, Associate Production Editor
Emely Villavicencio, Senior Graphic Designer
Alexa Lucido, Licensing Manager
Natalie Piccotti, Director of Marketing
Kassie Graves, Senior Vice President of Editorial
Jamie Giganti, Director of Academic Publishing

Copyright © 2021 iStockphoto LP/francescoch.
Copyright © 2017 iStockphoto LP/Sjo.
Copyright © 2021 iStockphoto LP/imaginima.

Printed in the United States of America.

3970 Sorrento Valley Blvd., Ste. 500, San Diego, CA 92121

Contents

Acknowledgments

Much appreciation and thanks go to our editors Kaela Martin and Susana Christie for bearing with us through the transformations of this project. We'd also like to thank all our contributors for the generosity of their time, expertise, and labor in the chapters they've written for this book. Not least, of course we thank our families for sharing this endeavor with us, particularly Dr. Dina Alkassim for her intellectual support, and Dr. Soheir Morsy and Mr. Amr El-Bayoumi for their generous advice and consulting on Reading 2.1 "The Hollywood Terrorist and Counter-Hegemonic Self-Representation." We would also like to thank professors Giovanna Chesler and Tommy Britt of George Mason University for encouraging this book project at its incipient stage.

Introduction

This textbook was written for an undergraduate class in global horror film. Although there are many excellent sources on the subject, from books that focus on specific regions like *Korean Horror Film* edited by Alison Peirse and Daniel Martin or *Horror to the Extreme: Changing Boundaries in Asian Cinema* edited by Jinhee Choi and Mitsuya Wada-Marciana, to anthologies like *Horror: The Film Reader* edited by Mark Jankovich, *The Horror Reader* edited by Ken Gelder, or *The Dread of Difference: Gender and the Horror Film* edited by Barry Keith Grant, every other decade there seems to be a compelling need to produce a new anthology or focus on the genre. Perhaps this is because real global horror continues to grow and flourish in ways that command our attention, presenting us with provocative existential questions about humanity, difference, progress, and the future of life on this planet.

We begin with certain assumptions about what constitutes cinematic horror. Using the vehicle of narrative, often rooted in a culture's folklore, horror film presents cautionary tales that express our greatest fears, sometimes involving extreme violence and excessive displays of blood and bodily fluids and mentally and/or morally unstable characters, occurring in precarious environments or situations that are subject to sudden upheaval caused by real or imagined forces. We also proceed from assumptions about what constitutes a cinematic genre, relying on the idea that a film genre, as explained by Thomas Schatz,[1] is a complex set of rules that are tacitly understood by both filmmakers and audiences, and that are defined by the sociocultural context in which the genre is produced. These rules, furthermore, determine narrative structure and elements of a story, whether a western, horror, crime drama or comedy, through the coding of character, mise en scene and cinematography. When societies change, genres reflect these changes.

As a film genre, horror has endured through time, markets, and cultural contexts, and has had widespread influence on artists, filmmakers, audiences, students, and

---

1 Thomas Schatz, "Film Genre and the Genre Film" in *Hollywood genres: formulas, filmmaking, and the studio system*. (New York: McGraw Hill, 1981).

cultural producers. It is indeed a global genre with local and very specific manifestations, both as an industrial product and independent cinema, an expression of popular culture and art cinema, and an exploitation film and cult movie. Horror film has always involved the piercing of boundaries (both literally and figuratively), infinite adaptations of recognizable tropes and patterns, and great success, even if at times arriving too late for the directors. These factors are no doubt part of the reason for its popular appeal.

When we study horror films, we are often concerned with how horror distorts and engages excess through, as Gelder observes the "rhetorics of horror," which articulate what is understood as evil, horrific, or monstrous in a given social context. He situates horror as both archaic and modern, figured as both otherworldly and emergent from real, modern horror.[2] But horror's association with modernity must also factor in, as Grant observes, the intersection of material horrors with gendered, racial, and ethnic oppression, as well as the oppression of governing regimes against people. Jancovich relies on James Naremore's observations that neither genre films nor film genres are fixed fields and that films can change the characteristics of a genre. He points out that horror film calls for analysis not only of culture but of the policies that govern culture, and the necessity of situating this analysis in relation to "specific contexts of production, mediation, and consumption."[3] This book expands on these arguments by examining expressions of the genre produced in different cultural contexts, some of which prompt us to consider how it has been used to subvert hegemonic representations and address the traumas of colonialism and racism. As such, we challenge the idea of what it means to be inside or outside of a film cannon, while affirming the transformative and adaptive nature of the horror genre across geographic borders.

Because this book does not offer a totalizing study of the subject, there are certain developments and areas that have been left out. These include the early silent horror such as the fantasy/horror films of Georges Méliès, the Hollywood creature feature films of the 1930s, the pre-Hays code films of the early 1930s, Hitchcock films, the British Hammer films of the 1950s and 60s, the Italian *giallo* films of the 1960s and 70s, the Hong Kong extreme cinema of the 1980s, and the American grindhouse films of the 1960s to 80s.

Instead, this book connects known figures, tropes, and areas of scholarship in horror film studies (in Unit I) with understudied and new explorations of horror film produced in "far-away" geographies (in Unit II). This study clarifies the genre's breadth and complexity as an international art form while prompting students to consider questions about difference, kinship, humanity, power, oppression, and more existential issues through our readings of classic horror films, cult horror films, and "other" expressions of horror that inform us about the world we inhabit. In so doing, it offers a framework to consider what it means to study

---

2   Ken Gelder, ed., "Introduction" in *The Horror Reader*. (Oxfordshire: Routledge, 2000), 3.

3   Mark Jancovich, ed., "Introduction" in *Horror, A Film Reader*. (Oxfordshire: Routledge, 2002), 2.

horror film in the twenty-first century of transnational cinemas, in the space of screens and constantly evolving technologies of mediation, and at a moment when contemporary global politics require a radical reappraisal of the racialized and gendered Othering that has become the bedrock of so much horror, real and fictional.

Filmography

READING 1.1

Das Cabinet des Dr. Caligari [The Cabinet of Dr. Caligari] by Robert Wiene (1920)

Der Golem, wie er in die Welt kam [The Golem] by Carl Boese and Paul Wegner (1920)

Der Student von Prag [The Student from Prague] by Paul Wegner (1913)

Der Student von Prag [The Student from Prague] by Henrik Galeen (1926)

Metropolis by Fritz Lang (1927)

Nosferatu, eine Symphonie des Grauens [Nosferatu: A Symphony of Horrors] by F.W. Murnau (1922)

READING 1.2

A Girl Walks Home Alone at Night by Ana Lily Amirpour (2014)

Bram Stoker's Dracula by Francis Ford Coppola (1992)

Dracula by Todd Browning (1931)

Nosferatu, eine Symphonie des Grauens [Nosferatu: A Symphony of Horrors] by F.W. Murnau (1922)

The Addiction by Abel Ferrara (1995)

The Hunger by Tony Scott (1983)

What We Do in the Shadows by Taika Waititi (2014)

READING 1.3

28 Days Later by Danny Boyle (2002)

Dawn of the Dead by George A. Romero (1978)

House of the Dead by Uwe Boll (2003)

Night of the Living Dead by George A. Romero (1968)

Resident Evil by Paul W. S. Anderson (2002)

The Walking Dead by Michael Curtiz (1936)

Some titles in this list were taken from: Elisabeth Scherer, Selection from "Well-Travelled Female Avengers: The Transcultural Potential of Japanese Ghosts," *Ghost Movies in Southeast Asia and Beyond: Narratives, Cultural Contexts, Audiences*, ed. Peter J. Bräunlein and Andrea Lauser, pp. 81–82. Copyright © 2016 by Brill Academic Publishers. Reprinted with permission.

The White Zombie by Victor Halperin (1932)

READING 1.4

Blade Runner by Ridley Scott (1982)

Code 46 by Michael Winterbottom (2004)

District 9 by Neill Blomkamp (2009)

Metropolis by Fritz Lang (1927)

Monsters by Gareth Edwards (2010)

Sleep Dealer by Alex Rivera (2008)

Star Wars by George Lucas (1977)

The Phantom Menace by George Lucas (1999)

READING 1.5

Alien by Ridley Scott (1979)

Dressed to Kill by Brian De Palma (1980)

Repulsion by Roman Polanski (1965)

Silence of the Lambs by Jonathan Demme (1991)

The Brood by David Cronenberg (1979)

Videodrome by David Cronenberg (1983)

READING 1.6

Abby by William Girdler (1974)

Blackenstein by William A. Levey (1973)

Blacula by William Crain (1972)

Candyman by Bernard Rose (1992)

Ganja and Hess by Bill Gunn (1973)

Get Out by Jordan Peele (2017)

Horror Noire: A History of Black Horror by Xavier Burgin (2019)

Sugar Hill by Paul Maslansky (1974)

Us by Jordan Peele (2019)

Them by Little Marvin (TV series, 2021)

READING 2.1

Feature films:

Bearwalker by *Shirley* Cheechoo (2001)

BeDevil by Tracey Moffat (1993)

Blood Quantum by Jeff Barnaby (2019)

Cinema Red: Natives and Horror by Mike J. Marin (2019)

Rhymes for Young Ghouls by Jeff Barnaby (2013)

Spout by Alex Munôz (2009)

The Dark Place by Kodie Bedford, Perun Bonser, Rob Braslin, Liam Philips, and Bjorn Stewart (2019)

The Darkside by Warwick Thornton (2013)

The Dead Can't Dance by Rodrick Pocowatchit (2013)

The Dead Lands by Toa Fraser (2015)

The Smudging by Mike J. Marin (2016)

Violet by Mark D. Williams (2015)

Short films:

Beyond the Fear by Joe Singh (2019)

Blood Sky by LaRonn Katchia (2017)

Bloodland by Elle-Maija Tailfeathers (2011)

Cherry English by Jeff Barnaby (2003)

Corn Husk by Jaiden Mitchell (2018)

Crosser by Jennifer Varenchik (2019)

Demon by Mike J. Marin (2019)

Etlinisigu'niet [Bleed Down] by Jeff Barnaby (2018)

?E?Anx [The Cave] by Helen Haig-Brown (2009)

File Under Miscellaneous by Jeff Barnaby (2010)

Future Nation by Kent Monkmen (2005)

Ghost Food by Amanda Strong (2017)

He Can't Be Caught by James Luhan (2007)

Missing Indigenous by LaRonn Katchia (2017)

Night Cries by Tracey Moffat (1990)

O For a Thousand Tongues by Nathaniel Vass (2017)

Sacred by LaRonn Katchia (2019)

Savage by Lisa Jackson (2009)

Shadow Dancer by LaRonn Katchia (2017)

The Amautalik by Niel Christopher (2014)

The Black Case [Le mallette noire] by Carolin Monnet (2014)

The Burden of Being by Rodrick Pocowatchit (2014)

The Candy Meister by Cowboy Smithx (2014)

The Colony by Jeff Barnaby (2007)

The Moogai by Jon Bell (2020)

The Party's Downstairs by Mike J. Marin (2018)

The Vampire Upstairs by Joe Singh (2019)

These Walls by Doreen Manuel (2012)

You Are a Lesbian Vampire by Thirza Cuthand (2007)

READING 2.2

Babel by Alejandro G. Inarritu (2006)

Back to the Future by Robert Zemeckis (1985)

Black Sunday by John Frankenheimer (1977)

Hurt Locker by Kathryn Bigelow (2008)

Kiss Me Deadly by Robert Aldrich (1955)

Paradise Now by Hani Abu Assad (2005)

Ramy by Ramy Youssef (tv series, 2019–), season 1, episode 4 "Strawberries"

Sleeper Cell by Ethan Reif and Cyrus Voris (tv series, 2005)

24 by Jon Cassar (TV series, 2005, 2006)

Syriana by Stephen Gaghan (2005)

True Lies by James Cameron (1994)

The War Within by Joseph Castelo (2005)

Valentino's Ghost by Michael Singh (2012)

READING 2.3

À Meia-Noite Levarei Sua Alma [At Midnight I'll Take Your Soul] by José Mujica Marins (1964)

Cronos by Guillermo del Toro (1993)

El espinazo del diablo [The Devil's Backbone] by Guillermo del Toro (2001)

El laberinto del fauno [Pan's Labyrinth] by Guillermo del Toro (2006)

El misterio de Kharisiri [The Mystery of the Kharisiri] by Henry Vallejo (2005)

El páramo [The Squad] by Jaime Osorio Márquez (2011)

El vampiro [The Vampire] by Abel Salazar (1957)

Habitaciones para turistas [Rooms for Tourists] by Adrián García Bogliano (2004)

Hasta el viento tiene miedo [Even the Wind Is Afraid] by Carlos Enrique Taboada (1968)

Juan de los muertos [Juan of the Dead] by Alejandro Brugués (2011)

KM 31 by Rigoberto Castañeda (2006)

La Llorona by Jayro Bustamante (2019)

Pura sangre [Pure Blood] by Luis Ospina (1982)

Qarqacha. El demonio del incesto [Qarqacha: The Demon of Incest] by Melitón Eusebio (2002)

Sudor frío [Cold Sweat] by Adrián García Bogliano (2011)

Vampiros en la Habana [Vampires in Havana] by Juan Padrón (1985)

READING 2.4

1920 by Vikram Bhatt (2008)

Bandh Darwaza [The Closed Door] by Tulsi and Shyam Ramsay (1990)

Bhoot [The Ghost] by Ram Gopal Varma (2003)

Cheekh [The Scream] by Mohan Bhakri (1985)

Dahshat [The Panic] by Tulsi and Shyam Ramsay (1981)

Do Gaz Zameen Ke Neeche [Beneath Two Yards of Earth] by Tulsi Ramsay (1972)

Ek Nanhi Munni Ladki Thi [There Was a Young Girl] by Vishram Bedekar (1970)

Ghost by Puja Jatinder Bedi (2012)

Ghutan [Suffocation] by Shyam Ramsay (2007)

Hatyarin [The She-Vampire] by Vinod Talwar (1991)

Haunted 3D by Vikram Bhatt (2011)

Hotel by Tulsi and Shyam Ramsay (1981)

Kaali Khuhi [The Black Well] by Terrie Samundra (2020)

Kaun [Who's There?] by Ram Gopal Varma (1999)

Khooni Shaitan [Bloody Devil] by Kanti Shah (2002)

Raat [The Night] by Ram Gopal Varma (1992)

Purana Mandir [The Old Temple] by Tulsi and Shyam Ramsay (1984)

Raaz [The Secret] by Vikram Bhatt (2002)

Rise of the Zombie by Devaki Singh and Luke Kenny (2013)

Sannata [The Silence] by Tulsi and Shyam Ramsay (1981)

Shaitani Ilaaka [Satan's Circle] by Kiran Ramsay (1990)

Shaapit [Cursed] by Vikram Bhatt (2010)

Veerana [Vengeance of the Vampire] by Tulsi and Shyam Ramsay (1988)

The Zee Horror Show by Ramsay Brothers (1993)

READING 2.5

Gakkō no kaidan [School Ghost Stories] (TV series, 1994)

Gakkō no kaidan [School Ghost Stories] by Hirayama Hideyuki (1995)

Ghost Dance by Ken McMullen (1983)

Honogurai mizu no soko kara [Dark Water] by Hideo Nakata (2002)

Jaganrei [Psychic Vision] by Ishii Teruyoshi (1988)

Joyū-rei [Don't look up] by Hideo Nakata (1996)

Kairo [Pulse] by Kiyoshi Kurosawa (2001)

Kwaidan [Ghost Stories] by Kobayashi Masaki (1965)

Ringu by Hideo Nakata (1998)

Saam gaang [Three] by Kim Jee-woon, Nonzee Nimibutr, and Peter Ho-Sun Chan (2002)

Shutter by Banjong Pisanthanakun and Parkpoom Wongpoom (2004)

Suwīto Hōmu [Sweet Home] by Kiyoshi Kurosawa (1989)

The Changeling by Peter Medak (1980)

Yee do hung gaan [Inner Senses] by Chi-Leung Law (2002)

READING 2.6

Bando [Peninsula] by Yeon Sang-ho (2020)

Busanhaeng [Train to Busan] by Yeon Sang-ho (2016)

Cheonnyeon ho [The Thousand Year Old Fox] by Shin Sang-ok (1969)

Gisaengchung [Parasite] by Bong Joon-ho (2019)

Gokseong [The Wailing] by Na Hong-jin (2016)

Gwoemul [The Host] by Bong Joon-ho (2006)

Hanyeo [The Housemaid] by Kim Ki-young (1960)

Janghwa, Hongryeon [A Tale of Two Sisters] by Kim Ji-woon (2012)

Oldeuboi [Old Boy] by Park Chan-wook (2003)

READING 2.7

122 by Yasir Al-Yasiri (2019)

Achoura by Talal Selhami (2017)

Akher Wahed Fina [The Last of Us] by Ala Eddine Slim (2017)

Al Fil Al-Azraq 2 [Blue Elephant 2] by Marwan Hamed (2019)

Anyab [Fangs] by Mohamed Shebl (1981)

Atlal [The Last Man] by Ghassan Salhab (2007)

Bab al-Hadid [Cairo Station] by Yousef Chahine (1959)

Blind Sun by Joyce Nashawati (2015)

Bloodline by Rami Yasin (2020)

Djinn by Toby Hooper (2018)

In Vitro by Larissa Sansour and Soren Lind (2020)

Kandisha by Jerome Cohen-Olivar (2008)

Kindil al-Bahr by Damien Ounouri (2016)

Manivelle: The Last Days of the Man of Tomorrow by Fadi Baki (2017)

READING 2.8

Aal by Bahram Bahramian (2010)

A Girl Walks Home Alone at Night by Ana Lily Amirpour (2014)

Ānhā [Them] by Mehdi Aghājāni, Milād Jermūz (TV series, 2021)

Asiri [Yoruba for Secrets] by Mohammad Ali Sajjadi (2002)

Cherk-nevis [The Drafts] by Ali Janab (2014)

Ehzār [Seance] by Ramin Abbasi Zadeh (TV series, 2018–2019)

Ehzār [Seance] by Alireza Afkhami (TV series, 2021)

Ezhdeha Vāred Mishavad [A Dragon Arrives] by Māni Haghighi (2015)

Faryād-i Nimeh-shab [The Midnight Terror] by Samuel Khachikian (1961)

Dastforūsh [The Peddler] by Mohsen Makhmalbaf (1986)

Dāyereh-ye Minā [The Cycle] by Dāriush Mehrjui (1975)

Ghazieh Shekl-e Aval, Shekl-e Dovvom [First Case, Second Case] by Abbas Kiarostami (1979)

Gräns [Border] by Ali Abbasi (2018, Sweden)

Heivān [Animal] by Bahman Ark and Bahrām Ark, (2017)

Hol Dān [Hold On] by Mehdi Aghajani (TV series, 2018)

Hojūm [Invasion] by Shahram Mokri (2017)

Khābgāh-i Dokhtarān [Girls' Dormitory] by Mohammad Hossein Latifi (2004)

Khāneh Siāh Ast [The House Is Black] by Forough Farrokhzād (1963)

Khesht va Āyeneh [Brick and Mirror] by Ebrahim Golestan (1964)

Mādar-e Ghalb-e Atomi [Atomic Heart] by Ali Ahmadzadeh (2014)

Māhi va Gorbeh [Fish and Cat] by Shahram Mokri (2013)

Mashgh-e Shab [Homework] by Abbas Kiarostami (1989)

Parināz by Bahrām Bahrāmian (2010)

Persepolis by Marjane Satrapi and Winshluss (2007, France)

Poost [Skin] by Bahman Ark and Bahrām Ark (2018)

Sahereh [The Sorceress] by Davūd Mir-bagheri (1998)

Shab-i Bist-o-nohom [The 29th Night] by Hamid Rakhshani (1989)

Shatranj-i Bād [The Chess of the Wind] by Mohammad Reza Aslani (1976)

Sheitān Vojūd Nadārad [There Is No Evil] by Mohammad Rasoulof (2021)

Soghūt-e Yek Fereshteh [Fall of An Angel] by Bahram Bahramian and Hamid Bahramian (TV series, 2011)

Telesm [The Spell] by Dariush Farhang (1987)

Ān Shab [The Night] by Kourosh Āhāri (2021)

Two and Two by Babak Anvari (2010)

Under the Shadow by Babak Anvari (2016, UK)

Yek Ettefāgh-i Sādeh [A Simple Event] by Sohrāb Shahid-sāles (1973)

Zālāvā by Arsalān Amiri (2020)

Zanghā [Rings] by Mohamad Reza Honarmand (1986)

Zār by Nimā Farāhi (2016)

Known Tropes and Subgenres

The following six readings present a curated selection of reprinted essays that chart major horror tropes, subgenres, and scholarship that have become canonical to horror film studies.

In reading 1.1, Ian Roberts discusses the German expressionist film *Nosferatu* and how it presents the threat of the other through ambiguity and the *unheimlich/* uncanny. In reading 1.2, Dale Hudson explores the ways in which vampire films present fears of miscegenation, migration of bodies, transformation of borders, and, in American films, anxieties over American exceptionalism. Kristine Larsen traces, in reading 1.3, the scientific causes of zombification explored in the history of zombie films—frequently at the expense of ethical rights for sentient life forms—and the fears of science they reveal. In reading 1.4, Everett Hamner examines contemporary science fiction films that thematize immigration and other forms of border crossing as "a rebellion against techno-scientific imperialism," an example of which can be seen in *Sleep Dealer*. Barbara Creed, in reading 1.5, focuses on male monsters and how they trouble the traditional differentiation of the sexes, implying gender ambivalence in their embodiment of feminine characteristics and affinities between monster and woman. Finally, Robin Means Coleman, in reading 1.6, focuses on the American Blaxploitation horror films of the 1970s where the critiques of Black horror films and the representations of Black characters in horror films, however reflective of damaging stereotypes, converge in interesting ways.

Each reading includes the following features: key terms and figures, recommended films, introduction to the reading, post-reading/post-screening questions, and bibliography. Many of the key terms can be found in the glossary at the end of the book where definitions are provided.

Demons Without and Within

F.W. Murnau's *Nosferatu*

By Ian Roberts

KEY TERMS AND FIGURES

German expressionism

Max Reinhardt

F.W. Murnau

Robert Wiene

Fritz Lang

Unheimlich

Uncanny

Psychological horror

Supernatural horror

Dystopian horror

RECOMMENDED FILMS

Das Cabinet des Dr. Caligari [The Cabinet of Dr. Caligari] by Robert Wiene (1920)

Der Golem, wie er in die Welt kam [The Golem] by Carl Boese and Paul Wegner (1920)

Der Student von Prag [The Student from Prague] by Paul Wegner (1913)

Der Student von Prag [The Student from Prague] by Henrik Galeen (1926)

Metropolis by Fritz Lang (1927)

Nosferatu, eine Symphonie des Grauens [Nosferatu: A Symphony of Horrors] by F.W. Murnau (1922)

INTRODUCTION

The roots of horror cinema are located in folklore from around the world and European and American literary genres that trace back at least to the fifteenth century. Studies of the subject tend to begin with the "silent" films produced in Germany during the Weimar republic of the 1920s, which belong to the genre of German expressionism. Influenced by the intimate character-based narratives of the *kammeraspiele* genre (chamber drama) initiated by theatre pioneer Max Reinhardt, and the visual style and themes found in German expressionist paintings, German expressionist cinema is split between horror and social realism. The latter exploited the possibilities of realism afforded by the camera to convey tales of social and economic hardship experienced by Germans in the wake of the First World War, which corresponded to social malaise if not actual horror. The horror films, however, exploited the possibilities of imagination afforded by the camera, and established three strains that persist to this day: psychological horror, supernatural horror, and dystopian science fiction horror. These strains are respectively represented in *Das Cabinet des Dr. Caligari (The Cabinet of Dr. Caligari), Nosferatu: eine Symphonie des Grauens (Nosferatu: A Symphony of Horrors)*, and *Metropolis*. For psychological horror, *The Cabinet of Dr. Caligari* expresses anxieties about mind control, mental illness, and authoritarian power. Supernatural horror takes the form of a foreign and racialized vampire, *Nosferatu*, who is driven by lust and brings plague to a quaint Bavarian town. Representative of science fiction horror, *Metropolis* provides a dystopian view of economic apartheid and the gulf between rich industrial overlords and exploited workers. These prevalent subgenres often overlap.

In this chapter, Ian Roberts focuses on *Nosferatu* for its ability to bring audiences into the world of the film through visual techniques. As a result, it significantly departed from films like *The Cabinet of Dr. Caligari,* illustrating new possibilities of how cinema could transcend the medium of theatre. These include the forward movement of actors toward the camera, dramatic use of high-contrast lighting and shadows, sped-up action shots, the use of negative film, and stop motion cinematography. Roberts also discusses how cinematography enhances a sense of the *unheimlich*, or uncanny, particularly in the landscape shots. The unheimlich, meaning "unhomely," was theorized in Freudian psychology as the strange familiarity within the unfamiliar, something that creates unsettling feelings of dread. In Roberts's discussion of the use of arches, window frames, and doorways that both contain and connect the characters of Hutter, Ellen, and the vampire, he observes how the film's ambiguity accompanies the production of the unheimlich/uncanny, which delivers a horror tale about sexuality/death (*eros/thanatos*) and fear of the other. The latter was not only in an imagined sense, but a result of the collapse of centuries-old empires (Astro-Hungarian, Russian, Ottoman) and increasing nationalist sentiments in early twentieth-century Europe, as the lands east of Germany were considered a threat.

This fear of the other is shown to be both internal and external through the dynamic between Nosferatu and Ellen. Roberts concludes his chapter by observing that this dual threat of the other allows for the film to transcend time and appeal to modern viewers. To this we can add a long list of "othering" representations that have been used to inspire fear in various (targeted) audiences, thus ensuring the longevity of both *Nosferatu* and the vampire subgenre that persists in the representational field among many other subgenres of horror.

Demons Without and Within

F. W. Murnau's *Nosferatu*

By Ian Roberts

Its unusual *mise-en-scène* notwithstanding, the success of *The Cabinet of Dr Caligari* can be attributed in great measure to the air of abnormality which permeated its imagery. The sense of unease, of a creepy, uncanny Atmosphere intruding into quotidian life is summed up by the German term *unheimlich,* a concept which has a long literary and artistic tradition in German culture. The well-known Grimm brothers' *Kinder- und Hausmärchen* (*Children's and Household Tales*) of 1812, for instance, seem to confirm that the stories most beloved of the Germans are those which are filled with ghouls and witches, threatening to abduct, boil, eat or otherwise do harm to the human characters. Such well-known tales as Little Red Riding Hood or Hansel and Gretel (just two of those recorded by the brothers), amply demonstrate how the nation's dark forests go hand-in-hand with tales of horror and the paranormal.

Following on from the military defeat of Germany in 1918, the young Weimar Republic suffered an inauspicious start. Not only had millions died as a result of the conflict, but thousands more were killed in three outbreaks of Spanish influenza which swept across Europe between 1917 and 1919.[1] Furthermore, the reparations forced upon Germany by the victorious Allies at Versailles in June 1919 extended the misery: short-lived revolutions, the French occupation of the Ruhr and street fighting between rival factions became part of the daily struggle to survive. Hyper-inflation and mass-unemployment followed, resulting in individuals wheeling around barrow-loads of cash in the search for a loaf of bread, and unemployed former soldiers standing in line for a bowl of soup. Little wonder, then, that narratives of foreboding, images of ghouls and

---

1   Among the victims of the deadly virus was the Austrian Secessionist artist Egon Schiele, who died of Spanish flu on 31 October 1918. Most commentators agree that the epidemics together killed more of the planet's population than had been killed in World War One.

Image 1.1.1 The epitome of horror: F. W. Murnau's 'nosferatu' monster

other horrors, and psychological studies of the beast within struck a nerve with a population which was, metaphorically at least, still glancing over its shoulder in fear, uncertain of its future in a period of chaos.

As Lotte Eisner illustrated admirably in her work *The Haunted Screen* German art and literature offered ample images of horror for the citizens of the Republic, images which filmmakers were quick to appropriate. The Romantics' celebration of the *unheimlich* and the supernatural lent German film what Siegfried Prawer calls the 'rich heritage of demonic folklore, Gothic fiction, and black Romanticism' (1980: 32) which seemingly lies at the heart of German culture.

In Expressionism there was a mixed reaction to the supernatural, since many in the movement were more concerned with invisible terrors than the inner conflicts and emotions of the individual. Edvard Munch's *The Scream* (1893) perfectly encapsulates the expressionist belief that horror is not solely the result of external terrors. Even so, the expressionist filmmakers quickly discovered that there was a lucrative market for fear in postwar Germany.

Even though it would be entirely misleading to claim that the paranormal and the supernatural were the only themes in early German film, the number of surviving films and titles do suggest that this was a popular genre in the years before and after World War One.[2] Thus *Das Todestelephon* (*The Telephone of Death,* Oskar Messier, 1912), *Die Insel der Seligen* (*The Island of the Dead,* Max Reinhardt, 1913) or *Der Andere* (*The Other,* Max Mack, 1913), to mention just three, all dealt with themes of terror and the paranormal to a certain extent: *The Other,* for instance, was a Jekyll and Hyde tale of one man's struggle to contain his alter ego and the ensuing fight between good and evil. It became apparent that horror was able to pay its way, establishing a generic expectation which, when coupled with a renowned director and/or a star lead, could reasonably expect to make a profit both in Berlin and elsewhere.

---

2   For further reading see, for example, Kessler & Warth (2002).

PAUL WEGENER: 'THE FATHER OF CALIGARI'

An early success in this genre came with *Der Student von Prag* (*The Student of Prague*, 1913), a script written and directed by the young Reinhardt actor Paul Wegener, co-directed with Stellan Rye. Produced by Deutsche Bioscop (which was later responsible for *The Cabinet of Dr Caligari*), it was based on Goethe's archetypally Germanic version of the *Faust* legend, as well as material by E. T. A. Hoffmann. The film was a chilling tale of one man's descent into madness. More importantly, it paved the way for a series of horror movies in Germany and laid down the marker for a visual style which we would now consider typical of expressionist film. As Paul Cooke claims: 'If *Caligari* is the father of [cinematic] Expressionism, *Der Student von Prag* can be seen as the father of *Caligari*' (2002: 20).

In the film, Balduin, the eponymous student of Prague (played by Wegener), has crippling debts, and develops an infatuation with the noblewoman Countess Margit (Grete Berger). In desperation he turns to the satanic wizard Scapinelli (John Gottowt) who agrees to solve all the young man's woes, in return for anything in Balduin's possession. Balduin accepts and Scapinelli claims the young student's reflection as payment. Although the young man's fortunes in life and love do indeed improve, he is tormented by his *Doppelgänger* (who, in the classic psychoanalytical sense, can be viewed as Balduin's repressed desires made incarnate), until his alter ego eventually implicates him in murder. The desperate student attempts to shoot his evil double, but instead succeeds only in shooting himself. As he dies, Scapinelli mocks him, scattering the torn pieces of their contract over his body. In the final scene Balduin's tormenting alter ego stands over the unfortunate's grave. A lacklustre remake of *The Student of Prague* in 1926[3] shows just how quickly the genre developed in the first decades of the industry's history, quickly becoming a staple part of a moviegoer's diet.[4]

Buoyed by the success of *The Student of Prague*, Wegener returned to the world of horror and the supernatural to produce and star in *Der Golem* (*The Golem*, Henrik Galeen, 1915). Again based on a mixture of sources and drawing heavily on Jewish mythology, the story of the Golem was one of man's desire to exert control over others, on the one hand, and of a mistrust of artificial lifeforms, on the other. These are of course themes which recur regularly throughout the Weimar period (see the section on *Metropolis* in the next chapter, for instance), and indeed continue to be popular to this day. This film, too, was remade just a few years later as *Der Golem, wie er in die Welt kam* (*The Golem, How He Came Into the World,* Paul Wegener and Carl Boese, 1920). The earlier version is now lost, but the remake, which is still available, reveals just how neatly this story fits into the overall pattern of supernatural films.

---

3   This remake was directed by Henrik Galeen. Galeen's writing credits include *Der Golem* (*The Golem*, writer and director, 1915), *Nosferatu* and *The Waxworks*. He also directed *Alraune* (*Mandrake*, 1928), an experimental film which contains extravagant expressionistic dream sequences.

4   We should not discount the influence of horror movies which were appearing elsewhere in Europe and the US at this time, such as Carl Theodor Dreyer's *Blade af Satans bog* (*Leaves from Satan's Book,* 1921); see Prawer 1980: 8–9.

The Golem is a clay automaton, created to meet a specific need at a time of testing. The Lord of a medieval German city intends to banish the Jewish population, so old Rabbi Low (Albert Steinrück) turns to cabbalistic texts in his search for a solution. From these texts he learns how to create a magical homunculus, a clay statue which will carry out the rabbi's wishes without hesitation. Initially all goes well and the Golem is instrumental in restoring the fortunes of the Jews. Later, however, the Golem abducts the rabbi's daughter Miriam (Lyda Salmonova), and then rampages through the city streets. Only an encounter with a little girl eventually stays his hand. Thus beguiled, the Golem cannot prevent the girl from removing the life-giving key from his chest, whereupon he reverts to clay and the terror is ended.[5] A series of six films in Germany, the first part entitled *Homunculus* (Otto Rippert, 1916) likewise took up the theme of the clay monster with great success.

But not only does the success of such films suggest that the topic was one dear to the hearts of the German audience, it is also clear that the *unheimliche Stimmung*, or unsettling atmosphere of these tales provided creative impetus to filmmakers still seeking to establish the cinema as a legitimate art form. Furthermore, such films were equally successful from a commercial point of view. Wegener himself later explained how the genre established itself for both commercial and technical reasons:

> After a few failed films, about which I would rather remain silent, I had the idea of the Golem, this strange, mythical clay figure of the Rabbi Low from the legends of the Prague ghetto, and with this I moved still further into the territory of the purely filmic—here everything is presented on the screen, in a flowing together of a fantasy world of previous centuries with present-day life. (Quoted in Scherber 1990: 27)

Thus the screen became the perfect medium to combine elements of Romanticism, the Gothic novel and other artistic influences with the population's day to day fears over the volatile political situation in Weimar Germany. Utilising expressionist effects to the full, filmmakers succeeded in articulating a sense of existential angst before psychoanalysis had reached the popular consciousness. Artistic integrity and box-office success seemed to go hand-in-hand and the genre flourished. Still more significant from the point of view of this study was Wegener's realisation that the medium allowed for new narrative possibilities, particularly in the area of lighting, which could be utilised to enhance the sense of foreboding in the audience, sitting as

---

5   Note how often these themes reoccur in later films: the monster which abducts the beautiful girl features repeatedly, in *Dr Caligari* of course, but also in *Metropolis* and most famously in *King Kong* (Merian Cooper, 1933). The motif of innocence facing terror becomes the core of *Frankenstein* (James Whale, 1931) and countless imitations. Siegfried Prawer, in his study *Caligari's Children*, runs through the key motifs of horror—drawn from the earliest examples—in his chapter 'The Making of a Genre' (1980: 8–47).

it was in a darkened room: 'Rhythm and tempo, light and dark all play a role in film just like in music' (ibid.). The fantastic, the subconscious, the dream world and the horrific—all summed up in one way or another by the term *unheimlich*—discovered a natural home in early cinema. Siegfried Kracauer goes so far as to suggest that this theme was particularly apt for the early filmmakers since it presented them with technological challenges which would serve to set the cinema apart from other artistic media (1947: 28f).

F. W. MURNAU AND NOSFERATU

Of all the films which sought to depict the pervasive fear of the German people as the Republic lurched from one crisis to the next, the 'symphony of horror' called *Nosferatu* is surely the best known. Its director, F. W. Murnau was described by Lotte Eisner as 'the greatest film-director the Germans have ever known', claiming that in his films 'cinematic composition was never a mere attempt at decorative stylization. He created the most overwhelming and poignant images in the whole German cinema' (1969: 97).

Murnau was born Friedrich Wilhelm Plumpe on 28 December 1888, into a respectable middle-class family in Kassel. Whilst at university in Berlin and Heidelberg, and in defiance of his father's plans for him, he fell in with a group of young, avant-garde artists, including the poet Else Lasker-Schuler, who had contributed greatly to the expressionist scene in Berlin, and Franz Marc, the founder of the 'Blue Rider' group in Munich [...]. Inspired by these vivacious young people he changed his name to Murnau, after the Bavarian spa village where they vacationed together, and pursued his real love of acting. He was discovered by Max Reinhardt and began his theatrical training at the *Deutsches Theater* in Berlin, where he became acquainted with the likes of Emil Jannings, Werner Krauss and, a particular friend, Conrad Veidt.

Murnau volunteered for military service in 1914 and served, first as an infantry officer on the Eastern Front, then as an observer in a *Luftwaffe* squadron in France, where he reputedly survived a number of crashes. In 1917 he and his pilot are supposed to have inadvertently flown across the Swiss border, where they landed and were interned by the neutral authorities there. Murnau saw out the rest of the war in relative comfort, even directing some stage plays to general acclaim from local critics. Murnau later recalled that he was also approached by the German Embassy in Switzerland to produce propaganda films for the German war effort. Nothing remains of them today to confirm Murnau's anecdote.

After repatriation Murnau renewed his association with the Reinhardt actors. Instead of returning to the stage, however, he founded a film production company with Conrad Veidt called the *Murnau Veidt Filmgesellschaft* and began making films. Significantly, the supernatural and the uncanny seem to have been staple motifs of much of Murnau's early film production. His first film *Der blaue Junge* (*The Blue Boy*, 1919) depicts a nobleman's struggle to rid himself of a curse, which centres on a portrait of the eponymous blue boy hanging in the familial home. Later films continue the theme: *Der Januskopf* (*The Head of Janus,* 1920) is a variation on the Jekyll and Hyde story, and supernatural elements can be observed too in *Schloss Vogelöd* (*The Haunted Castle,* 1921) and *Phantom* (1922). Murnau's international breakthrough came in 1925 with the release of *The Last Laugh.* In this film of social status and degradation, the senior porter of a metropolitan hotel (played by Emil Jannings) is demoted and loses his standing and self-respect as a result. The film charts his steady decline until, in a curious—and barely credible—reversal of fortune, a millionaire bequeaths him a fortune and he returns to the hotel, this time as a guest where he can exact revenge of a sort by treating his best friend to a marvellous meal whilst his former manager is forced to wait upon him hand and foot (the last laugh of the film's English-language title).

Murnau's reputation as one of the true innovators of the early film industry is due in no small measure to his use of the *entfesselte Kamera* (unchained camera) in his films. Although the camera had not been entirely motionless beforehand, this concept became associated with Murnau and his cameraman Karl Freund after the release of *The Last Laugh* because of the innovative solutions Murnau and his team found to various challenges presented to them by the narrative. Thus the camera was variously placed on the front of a bicycle (for the opening long take of travelling down the hotel lift and out of the hotel lobby), on an elaborate platform and pulley/cable contraption (for the representation of sound flying out of the bell of a trumpet) as well as on what were by that time more conventional dollies and trolleys for a range of sequences. Murnau became the acknowledged master of this technique because he seems to have been the first to use movement as a narrative device, helping to develop the story. So great was the acclaim over the images in *The Last Laugh* that the film enabled Murnau to break into the lucrative American market—touring there himself in late 1925/early 1926—and eventually to land a plum contract with Fox.

Towards the end of his career in Germany, Murnau returned to the portrayal of the *unheimlich* when he directed Ufa's flagship production of *Faust* (1927). Murnau had a startlingly clear vision of how to depict the story. Drawing upon a number of versions of the *Faust* legend, in the script by Hans Kyser, Mephisto (Emil Jannings) taunts the archangel Gabriel into a wager over the soul of the learned scientist Faust (Gosta Ekman). The ensuing battle sees Faust's hometown ravaged by the plague. In desperation, Faust accepts Mephisto's offer of unlimited power and eternal youth. Only when he falls in love with the beautiful Gretchen (Camilla Horn) and loses her as a consequence of Mephisto's infernal meddling, does Faust renounce his pact with the devil and choose to burn with Gretchen at the stake. Some of the scenes demonstrate a total mastery of the medium in both composition and technical innovation. Murnau deploys his full range here—the use of *chiaroscuro* to heighten tension in the plague-ridden town, the dissolve shots which reveal rejuvenated versions of Faust and Mephisto, the exhilarating magic-carpet ride over the Altdorfer-inspired representation of the German countryside, and the post-production addition of rings of fire which surround Faust as he invokes the name of the devil (predating Lang's more celebrated use of the technique to film the Maria-robot transformation in *Metropolis*) all demonstrate Murnau's complete mastery of the medium of film.

In many ways *Faust* stands as an allegory of Weimar cinema, hinting at the price the filmmaker must pay to create such beautiful images. Frustrated by the demands of Ufa's studio system, which was already in decline, Murnau accepted an offer from Fox studios in Hollywood. By the time *Faust* premiered, Murnau had emigrated to America, and was never to return to Germany. Murnau directed three films for William Fox, including Sunrise: *A Song of Two Humans* in 1927, the only film ever to be granted an Academy Award 'For Unique Artistic Contribution'.[6] Ever restless, Murnau's last film was the independently produced *Tabu* (1930), shot in the Polynesian islands with the acclaimed documentary-maker Robert Flaherty.[7] Shortly before its premiere, however, he was fatally injured in a car accident near Santa Barbara in California. He died on 11 March 1931, aged 43, already viewed by many as one of the greatest directors of Weimar cinema, maybe even of the silent era. Charlie Chaplin is said to have described him as 'the best director Germany ever sent to Hollywood' (quoted in Prinzler 2003: 7), while Fritz Lang, who gave an oration at Murnau's graveside in Berlin, stated effusively 'film can be thankful that he has given it its very foundations. ... His entire work was ballads in pictures' (quoted in Becker & Albrecht 1981: 110–11).

NOSFERATU: EINE SYMPHONIE DES GRAUENS

Murnau's 'Symphony of horror' *Nosferatu* stands as the pre-eminent expressionist horror film of the Weimar period. The conflation of a musical term in the film's subtitle with the supernatural motif epitomises Weimar's curious relationship with the *unheimlich,* for it suggests both approbation and fear of the unknown, as well as indicating the artistic portrayal of horror so common in German culture. This is most apparent when regarding the central figure, the vampire Count Orlok, otherwise known as Nosferatu.

The origins of the film are particularly illuminating. The co-scriptwriter and producer of the film, Albin Grau, had developed a fascination with the paranormal. He claimed to have heard stories of vampires whilst serving in the German army in eastern Europe during World War One, which inspired the film (see Eisner 1973:109). The local name for such creatures was the

---

6   This award was bestowed at the very first ceremony held in the Roosevelt Hotel, Hollywood on 16 May 1929. It was given the unusual title because Academy members could not decide whether to give the Best Picture award to a commercially successful film, *Wings* (William A. Wellmann), or to recognise the artistry of *Sunrise*. For one time only they compromised and recognised both films as 'best pictures' in their own right. Janet Gaynor, who played the City Woman in *Sunrise*, was awarded Best Actress as a result of her work on several films in the preceding period.

7   For a fuller account of Murnau's life and career, see Roberts (2007).

'nosferatu'. Grau founded his own production company, Prana Film, in 1921 with the ambitious aim of producing a programme of films dealing exclusively with supernatural themes, although *Nosferatu* was the only project which came to fruition. It was intended to be an adaptation of Bram Stoker's celebrated Gothic novel *Dracula* (1897), an example of the transnational nature of cinema even in its early days, but legal complications led Grau and fellow scriptwriter Henrik Galeen to adapt the screenplay in an attempt to disguise the film's origins.[8]

The storyline is very familiar to modern audiences: Thomas Hutter (Gustav von Wangenheim) works as an estate agent in the German town of Wisborg. As a result of his aspirations, perhaps, Hutter accepts a curious commission to travel to the Transylvanian residence of the mysterious Count Orlok,[9] who wishes to buy a property in Wisborg, directly opposite Hutter's house. His wife, Ellen (Greta Schröder) experiences dark premonitions and begs her husband not to go. Upon reaching Orlok's homeland, *far in the* East, strange events occur. The locals tell of evil legends, and wolves prowl the nighttime landscape. The mood of foreboding increases when Hutter is conveyed to Orlok's castle on a supernatural carriage journey through an eerie wood. It transpires that the Count is in fact a vampire, and Hutter falls victim to his demonic attentions. Worse still, when Orlok—the dreadful Nosferatu—glimpses a portrait of Ellen, he sets off to Wisborg, enthralled by her beauty. Hutter races after him to try to prevent the calamity which threatens.

Wherever Nosferatu goes, pestilence and disaster follow: the crew of his ship all die, and plague ravages Wisborg upon his arrival. Ellen in the meantime anticipates Nosferatu's arrival, and appreciates that only by keeping him in her bedroom until dawn can the town be saved. Hutter is powerless to prevent the tragedy unfolding. Ellen, now in Nosferatu's thrall, invites the monster into her bedroom. He enters her chamber, claiming his transfixed victim, and sates himself upon her blood all night long. Only as the cock crows does Nosferatu realise his folly in lingering too long, and disappears in a puff of smoke at dawn: Wisborg is safe.

Contemporary audiences and critics alike were reportedly gripped by the film. A sophisticated publicity campaign had preceded the film's launch, including rumours (no doubt initiated by the studio) that Schreck was a real vampire. And then the premiere itself, on 4 March 1922 at the Berlin Zoological Gardens, was followed by a lavish costume party. Critics were suitably impressed: 'an interesting (if not to say sensational) work', declared one (see Prinzler 2003:130). The noted Hungarian film critic and theorist Bela Baldzs went as far as to

---

8   These efforts proved unsuccessful. Following the release of the film Stoker's widow won a court case preventing the further distribution and screening of *Nosferatu*. All existing copies were ordered seized and destroyed and for many years the film, at least in its original form, was considered lost. Eisner investigates a re-released version of 1930, which has some synchronised sound, under the title *Die zwölfte Stunde: Eine Nacht des Grauens* (*The Twelfth Hour: A Night of Horror*). It is worth speculating that the protracted legal action may well have led to the financial ruin of Prana Film even before the case was found in favour of Mrs Stoker, thus explaining why Prana failed to produce any further films. For further reading on the subject of the film's alternative versions, and eventual restoration, see 'The Riddle of Nosferatu' in Eisner 1973: 108–19.

9   Orlok was played by the wonderfully monikered Max Schreck, whose surname means 'fright' in German.

assure his readers: 'The images were all taken from nature. But a frosty breath of wind from beyond the grave blew through them all' (ibid.). Later, Lotte Eisner recognised how the sense of fear and foreboding in the film had been enhanced by the unusual techniques employed by Murnau during the shooting:

> Murnau created an atmosphere of horror by a forward movement of the actors towards the camera. The hideous form of the vampire approaches with exasperating slowness, moving from the extreme depth of one shot towards another in which he suddenly becomes enormous. Murnau had a complete grasp of the visual power that can be won from editing, and the virtuosity with which he directs this succession of shots has real genius. (1969: 102–3)

Indeed, many of the visual tricks, as well as some apparently conventional *mise-en-scène* lend the film a modernity which can surprise audiences today. In the scene where Hutter first encounters Nosferatu, for instance, the coach in which he is conveyed travels at abnormal speed through a forest of brilliantly white trees. This was achieved by cranking the camera at half the standard speed, then using a negative image of the scene in the finished film in order to unsettle the viewer. The carriage itself was painted white for the shoot, so that in a negative print it would appear black, as the audience might expect, against the eerie white backdrop of the forest. Stop-motion, too, is employed to show the canvas cover of the ship's hold rotting back by unseen agency when the vampire emerges from the bowels of the ship to terrorise Wisborg.

It is easy to see why the film is still a staple of expressionist film festivals today and is celebrated as one of the most important establishing works of the horror genre. Max Schreck's gestures, costume and make-up are directly inherited from the expressionist stage,[10] but this is purely a tool to enhance the uneasy, oppressive mood of the film through the portrayal of the Dracula character, since other characters' acting styles are largely conventional for the day. Lighting plays a key role, unsurprisingly, with many scenes being shot in a half-light which renders the edge of the frame almost totally black, but this again is perhaps to be expected of a film which is centred upon a hideous creature of the dark. Where *Nosferatu* comes into its own as an expressionist film is in its setting: although on the surface everything seems a realistic portrayal of the protagonists' world, in fact much is manipulated to underscore the supernatural element central to the plot. Even scenes which do not contain an ostensibly supernatural component, such as the views of landscapes, add to the sense of the uncanny here. Murnau had already been acknowledged as a director with a keen eye for the filmed landscape; contemporary reviews of his films frequently attest to this, even when the reviewer was perhaps otherwise

---

10   Compare with the characters in *The Cabinet of Dr Caligari*, for instance, but note also the photograph of Heinrich George in Eisner 1973:117 for a theatrical precedent.

unimpressed by the film as a whole. What is significant, though, is how such images enhance the sense of the *unheimlich* throughout the film: the mountains glower with an ethereal light which makes it difficult to place the time of day. Images of wooded slopes and rocky peaks are frequently intercut with shots of the main action to draw clear parallels between landscape and story. 'As always,' wrote Eisner in her monograph of this director, 'Murnau found visual means of suggesting unreality' (1973: 118).

Of great significance is the use of the arch, and of frames, in Murnau's *mise-en-scène*, particularly when combined with *chiaroscuro* lighting effects. When Hutter arrives at the castle, the sequence of him meeting Orlok is framed by the multi-layered arches of the castle keep. This signifies the location where Hutter's fate is sealed in a series of shots which reinforce the inevitability of the young couple's doom, revealing that they are trapped in much the same way as the fly offered to the Venus fly trap in the sequence featuring Professor Bulwer. Window frames, too, enhance subjectivity in the film, either cutting across the faces of the protagonists to act as imprisoning bars or to impede a view of one of the characters. They force the audience to share the point of view of the protagonists, often concealing as much as they reveal. The window (and its frame) becomes especially significant in the relationship between Ellen and Nosferatu, evidence of what David Robinson calls 'Murnau's uncompromisingly individual approach to Expressionism' (1973: 95). Firstly, when Orlok has reached Wisborg and the plague is claiming its dead, the viewer shares the point of view of Ellen when she looks out of her window at the pall bearers carrying the coffins to internment. Here, the cross-pattern of the frame hinders her (and our own) view of the townspeople below, suggesting that she is already isolated from the rest of society by her decision to offer herself to the vampire for the sake of her husband. As she turns away from the street she is drawn to the book wherein she learns that she must sacrifice herself to counter the vampire's malevolence. Later we see the Count himself, having taken up residence in buildings opposite the Hutter household, waiting for Ellen to call him. He is filmed behind the window, hands wrapped around the strong horizontal and vertical bars which demonstrate that the vampire is as much a prisoner, as much a victim, as Ellen and the others. The shadow of one of the bars falls across his face, holding him captive until Ellen's gesture will liberate him. She has been lying restlessly on her bed when she becomes aware of Orlok's vigil. She grips her breast, supernaturally aware of the vampire's intent, before walking to the window. With a brief, tender glance at her husband, asleep in a chair, she turns to the window. The moonlight filters through her diaphanous nightgown, revealing the body beneath which she is now prepared to sacrifice, as she flings open the window, her arms outstretched in an approximation of crucifixion. Immediately, Nosferatu begins the final leg of his journey to her. This latent sense of foreboding is further reinforced by Murnau's use of *chiaroscuro* shadows in the film. Here shadows quite clearly enhance the narrative, as Nosferatu's enlarged shadow is famously seen climbing the stairs to Ellen's room. As she shrinks back to her bed, the shadow of his clawed hand reaches across her body and clenches her breast in triumph: only then do we see the vampire himself, feeding on the limp body of the victim. Thus *thanatos* (death) and *eros* (sexuality)—both regarded as frightening to a society still bound by strict Wilhelminian values—are united in an orgasmic sequence: as sunlight floods into the room the next morning, Nosferatu, who has slept with his head on Ellen's body, shrinks from the sun's rays then arches his back and disappears in a wisp of smoke.

Image 1.1.2 Into the monster's lair: Hutter arrives at Count Orlok's castle

Much of the film's success lies in its multiple readings, many of which play on the notion of a threat to ordered society, either from without or from within. The former idea is perhaps the most apparent, with Nosferatu presenting a very real threat to the Hutters and to the town where they live. The war on the Eastern front had been particularly unforgiving (as it was to prove again in the Second World War) and had served to reinforce the long-standing belief that the lands to the East of Germany were a threat to the Germans' existence. Nosferatu, an Eastern Count who travels to Germany to claim Hutter's wife, and

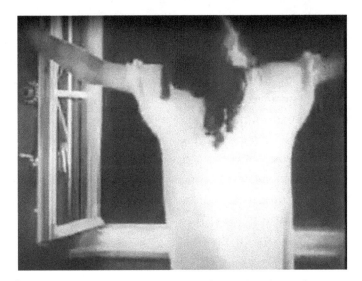

Image 1.1.3 Sacrifice and sensuality: Ellen invites the nosferatu to her bedroom

who brings death and pestilence with him, conforms perfectly to these racial stereotypes, thus enhancing the thrill of fear generated by the film's images. When Nosferatu loads his earth-filled coffins for the journey westwards, and when the crew of the *Empusa* die in turn aboard the rat-infested ship, the audience shudders in unspoken acknowledgement of this xenophobia. For John Sandford, Count Orlok's ratlike appearance reinforces the sense of society overrun, citing the rat-infested ship which bears the vampire to Germany: 'Rats, and the plague that they bring with them, are, historically and in folk-memory, not native to northern Europe, but an invasive, "foreign" force from the East' (1995: 318). This association of rats, pestilence and invasion from the East, as well as Nosferatu's rat-like teeth and long fingernails, draws upon long-standing anti-Semitic prejudice, even before the Nazis began their concerted campaign against the Jews.[11]

Then there is the threat from within, which in this case centres on Hutter's wife. It should be noted that Weimar Germany was a society of rapid change, with the values of Wilhelminian Germany fighting a rearguard action against the progressive, amoral values of the new, decadent order. Ellen is portrayed as a chaste, morally upright middle-class young woman, for whom marriage has little to do with love or fulfilment. She is very much the plaything of Hutter and the patriarchal society within which her repressed self is trapped, much as the ball she dangles before the kitten is used to tease and taunt the creature. Almost from the outset Ellen exhibits a supernatural understanding of the events which are unfolding at the count's castle. Here, again, Murnau's careful *mise-en-scène* suggests that, however much concern Ellen may have for her husband, in reality she is fascinated by the menace and virility of Nosferatu. Eyeline matches link the young bride with the vampire even when they are separated by great distances, and once Orlok has begun his voyage to Wisborg it is significant that Ellen goes to wait beside the sea, even though her husband is clearly travelling to her 'rescue' by land. In the scene where Ellen, dressed in black, waits among the dunes, the intertitles state only that she is 'pining for her beloved', without revealing the identity of the lover she awaits. As she sits and gazes out to sea, surrounded by the simple crosses of a sailors' graveyard, the sense of premonition, which has been present throughout, reaches new levels. It would seem that she is torn, subconsciously at least, between a sense of duty to her husband and the promise of fulfilment offered by the Count. As the film proceeds towards its dreadful conclusion, it becomes clear that the drive for personal sexual satisfaction prevails over the restrictions of societal mores. The restless sea (a favourite image of Murnau's and one which establishes a now-familiar trope in cinema) speaks figuratively of the complex undercurrents of desire and repression which torment the young woman. Thus, when Ellen lumbers to the window (her gait recalling that other somnambulist, Cesare, who is in Caligari's thrall), it is clear that she is already under the spell of the vampire: her shiver as she throws open the window is not simply due to the chill night air, but also highlights the frisson of anticipation with which she awaits her liberation. Although we might now see Nosferatu as the subconscious alter-ego of the sexually-repressed Hutter, in much the same way as the student of Prague was haunted by his double, the concept of a threat to the balance of society is startlingly clear.

---

11 Such imagery was, of course, exploited to terrible effect by the Nazis just a decade later in *Der ewige Jude* (*The Eternal Jew*, Fritz Hippier, 1940).

Nosferatu has influenced successive generations of film makers, and Max Schreck's vampire has inspired many screen monsters. Indeed, there have been a number of screen tributes to Murnau's creation, including Werner Herzog's compelling remake *Nosferatu: Phantom der Nacht* (*Nosferatu: Phantom of the Night,* 1979). Then American author Jim Shepard published a semi-fictitious biographical novel about Murnau, entitled *Nosferatu in Love* (1998). This follows the director's career

Image 1.1.4 Supernatural connection: The eyeline match between Orlok and Ellen

utilising a careful blend of established fact and creative fiction, including a fictitious diary of the shooting of *Nosferatu* itself. One entry reads: 'We look for the fantastic within ourselves' (1998:102), Shepard suggesting an autobiographical, psychological impulse to Murnau's films of imperilled lovers. Later, E. Elias Merhige's film *Shadow of the Vampire* (2000) plays on the rumours of Max Schreck's vampirism to produce an amusing homage to Murnau's masterpiece, where the director (played by John Malkovich) offers Schreck (Willem Dafoe) the lives of minor crew members to sate his bloodlust, with the promise of Greta Schröder as his great reward at the end of shooting.

In an essay written by Murnau in 1928 he outlined the principles which underpinned his approach to filmmaking. As one of the true pioneers of the Weimar period he brought a painter's eye and a technician's understanding of the new medium which produced some of the freshest and most beautiful films of the era. 'Real art is simple', he began,

> but simplicity requires the greatest art. The camera is the director's sketching pencil. It should be as mobile as possible to catch every passing mood, and it is important that the mechanics of the cinema should not be interposed between the spectator and the picture. ... Everything is subordinated to my picture[s]. (2004: 68)

In the case of *Nosferatu,* Murnau took a simple scenario and, thanks to cinematic innovation and the subtle use of expressionist devices, greatly enhanced the sense of a supernatural threat. But the success of the film lies in its ability to subvert the medium to the story, thus ensuring that the chilling images of the vampire Nosferatu abide and chill audiences even today. *Nosferatu: A*

Symphony of Horror thus stands for many at the pinnacle of Weimar cinema, with its perfect blend of story and technique. The notion of threat, of demons which can be seen as both an external and an internal danger, and the underlying sense of the *unheimlich* which pervades virtually every frame of the film have guaranteed that this early horror film has remained in the canon of great Weimar cinema ever since. If Dr Caligari was Kracauer's prototype for Hitler and the hypnotic power he wielded over the German people, then we should perhaps develop his approach still further and acknowledge that the fear engendered in audiences by the vampire Nosferatu surely prefigures the terror of the National Socialists' victims a few years later. Thus the film gains added poignancy for the modern viewer since the vampire represents both the anti-Semitic fear of the Jewish/Eastern threat, as well as the sinister terror of the Nazis, at one and the same time. More apposite is the realisation that in the dreadful gaze of Count Orlok, Weimar audiences were both thrilled and repelled in equal measure, and along with the film's commercial success, in producing *Nosferatu* the young film industry took a huge step towards artistic legitimacy.

BIBLIOGRAPHY

Becker, Klaus and Gerd Albrecht. *Friederich Wilhelm Murnau: ein grosser Regisseur der 20er Jahre*. Kassel: Stradtsparkasse Kassel, 1981.

Cook, Paul. *German Expressionist Films*. Harpenden: Pocket Essentials, 2002.

Eisner, Lotte. *The Haunted Screen: Expressionism in the German Cinema and the Influence of Max Reinhardt*. London: Thames and Hudson, 1969.

Eisner, Lotte. *Murnau*. London: Secker and Warburg, 1973.

Kessler, Frank and Eva Warth. "Early Cinema and its Audiences" in *The German Cinema Book* ed. by Tim Bergfelder, Erica Carter and Deniz Gokturk. London: British Film Institute, p. 121–8, 2002.

Kracauer, Siegfried. *From Caligari to Hitler: A Psychological History of the German Cinema*. Princeton: Princeton University Press, 1947.

Murnau, F. W. "The Ideal Picture Needs No Titles" (1928) in *German Essays on Film* ed. by Richard McCormick and Alison Guenther-Pal. New York: Continuum, p. 66–8, 2004.

Prawer, Siegfried. *Caligari's Children: The Film as Tale of Terror*. Oxford: Oxford University Press, 1980.

Prinzler, Hans Helmut (ed.). *Friedrich Wilhelm Murnau: ein Melancholiker des Films*. Berlin: Bertz, 2003.

Roberts, Ian. "Friedrich Wilhelm Murnau, transatlantic thresholds and transcendental homelessness." *Studies in European Cinema*, 4, 3, p. 223–33, 2007.

Robinson, David. *World Cinema: A Short History*. London: Methuen, 1973.

Sandford, John. "Chaos and Control in the Weimar Film" in *German Life and Letters*, 48, 3, p. 311–23, 1995.

Scherber, Jurgen. *Damals in Neubalbesberg: Studios, Stars und Kinopalaste*. Leipzig: Edition Leipzig, 1990.

Shepard, Jim. *Nosferatu in Love*. London: Faber and Faber, 1998.

POST-READING QUESTIONS/POST-SCREENING QUESTIONS

Directions: Use what you learned from reading this chapter and watching the film to respond to the questions.

1. What are some of the historical circumstances of Weimar Germany and the aftermath of WWI that may have affected the narrative in F.W. Murnau's film Nosferatu?

2. Explain the concept of the unheimlich or uncanny as Roberts defines it in relation to the film.

3. Describe how the supernatural horror of Nosferatu is visualized (in terms of lighting, camera techniques, special effects, costume, and the appearance of the characters) and expressed thematically (in terms of ideas).

4. Aside from visual style and intended effects, how does this film operate as a tale of horror?

Blood, Bodies, and Borders

By Dale Hudson

KEY TERMS AND FIGURES

Gothic folklore

Transnational borders

Migratory vampires

Ottoman Empire

British Empire

Bram Stoker

Francis Ford Coppola

Ana Lily Amirpour

Feminist vampire

Veiling

Iran

Middle East

Hollywood dream factory

RECOMMENDED FILMS

A Girl Walks Home Alone at Night by Ana Lily Amirpour (2014)

Bram Stoker's Dracula by Francis Ford Coppola (1992)

Dracula by Todd Browning (1931)

Nosferatu by F.W. Murnau (1922)

The Hunger by Tony Scott (1983)

INTRODUCTION

This chapter allows us to look at vampires beyond the classic tropes of consumerism, sexuality, addiction, death, and pestilence, but also as generative of new understandings of our interconnected modern world. Ever since its introduction in gothic folklore, the vampire has been a symbol of human despair and existential dread intersecting with issues surrounding the human form in sexual, social, cultural and gendered contexts. In this chapter, Dale Hudson addresses the transnational migratory nature of vampires by which they have been defined since their origins in Bram Stoker's 1897 novel *Dracula*. He traces how this view evolved as Hollywood developed in the twentieth century and extended beyond North America into Eastern European and Asian outposts of production. While Stoker's vampire appears at the intersection of late nineteenth-century empires just before their respective and rapid declines in the early twentieth century (Astro-Hungarian, British, and Ottoman), the vampire crosses geographies from east to west (Romania on the western-most side of the Ottoman empire to London), as those borders were shifting.

Hudson begins by tracing the evolution of the vampire from its origins in 17th century European folklore to 18th and 19th century European literature and the 20th century screen, crossing from folkloric contexts to aristocratic settings and mobility. During this evolution women acquired more rights as citizens, immigration waves arrived from Europe and the Global South, western European world power transformed from a territory-bound colonial relationship to post-colonial economic hegemony, and the US rose as a military and economic world power leading in the thirst for oil and other minerals on which the economies and communications industries of the 21st century depend. While Stoker's Count Dracula was based on Lord Ruthven in John Polidori's *The Vampyre* (1819), and female vampires were based on Countess Karnstein in Joseph Sheridan LeFanu's *Carmila* (1872), it wasn't until Stoker's *Dracula* that vampires acquired the characteristic of "deadly outsiders" traveling across the contradictions of universal human rights and humanism by which the European states distinguished themselves while "enslaving, indenturing, and dispossessing on a scale hitherto unimagined" their colonial subjects.

Hudson observes that vampire stories always involve the mixing of blood, migration of bodies, transformation of borders, and, in the case of American films, anxieties over American exceptionalism, even in the form of a European blood sucker. He contrasts the classic film vampires with the modern-day Edward Cullen of the *Twilight* television series. Cullen is a non-violent native-born white male from the American mid-west, whose white male privilege gives him the power of belonging, mobility, and passing as human within white American culture, while Bela Lugosi's Dracula (in *Dracula* by Todd Browning,1931) may sometimes pass as a citizen (of London), whereas Max Schrek's Count Orlock (in *Nosferatu* by F.W. Murnau, 1920) can do neither. Both Count Dracula and Cullen signal different transitional moments in US immigration history: where the former represents a period of unregulated immigration during the 1920s, the latter represents a longer period of transnational economic integration.

This chapter calls on us to attend to two levels of analysis in our study of the vampire film: one based on elements of narrative and form (of stories, characters, styles, and performance); and the other on the political economies that determine production, distribution, and exhibition. Hudson models this on his comparative study of Francis Ford Coppola's *Bram Stoker's Dracula* and Ana Lily Amirpour's *A Girl Walks Home Alone at Night*, two films separated by 20 years. He describes the former as refashioning Dracula in the form of "Vampire Ayatollah" and parodying the early 1990s era of reactionary (American) politics in the wake of post-Cold War dissolution, in which the new enemy was to be found in the Middle East. By contrast, *A Girl Walks Home Alone at Night* is set entirely in a fictionalized Middle Eastern context, with its opening shot of oil pumps evoking not only the "parasitic relationship of humans to the planet," but also US interests in the region. Hudson further invites us to consider what it means when the classic female-victimizing figure of abject horror has turned into a chador-wearing feminist vampire riding a skateboard and cleaning up Bad City of its exploitative evil men. This vampire's chador evokes many things for viewers: both the Western fascination with veiling as something understood to oppress women in Muslim countries, and as a signifier (for Iranians and other Middle Easterners) of history, identity, and geography. In addition to asking us to reconsider our assumptions about the chador/veil, it also expands our assumptions about a genre that is continually re-inventing itself, and as such, forces us to consider the porous borders of the Hollywood dream factory and its images of the East, from the vantage point of "a world that has mutated due to human migrations," in which "vampires appear where histories meet."

Lastly, Hudson's reading of the vampire and its importance in Hollywood illuminates its continuity as it transforms and expands across different geographies, cultures, media forms, and audiences. This power of adaptation links the vampire to other creatures of abjection like zombies or werewolves. But what most distinguishes vampires as unique is the way in which they resemble us, while their cinematic history has projected anxieties over racial and cultural purity, or alternative visions of belonging and resistance.

Blood, Bodies, and Borders

By Dale Hudson

Ana Lily Amirpour's black-and-white *A Girl Walks Home Alone at Night* seduced audiences with a skateboard-riding, feminist hijabi vampire. It reimagined the socially and emotionally isolated female vampires in classical Hollywood's *Dracula's Daughter* and later art-house films, such as Michael Almereyda's *Nadja* and Abel Ferrara's *The Addiction*. Amirpour promoted her film as "the first Iranian vampire western," playfully reworking national and generic assumptions. She purposefully confuses and deliberately fuses spaces of national histories, identities, and geographies into transnational ones. She challenges nationalist certainties within the political theatrics by US and Iranian leaders, which extend from the US-backed Pahlavi monarchy (1925–79) through the Iranian Revolution and hostage crisis (1979–81) into political disagreements between Iranian president Mahmoud Ahmadinejad (2005–13) and US president George W. Bush (2001–9) over nuclear programs that resurface today in debates on lifting the US trade embargo and normalizing relationships. *A Girl Walks Home Alone at Night* asks us to think about—and to feel—what it is like to inhabit this history across space. Amirpour's film does not tell the story of a vampire, who migrates from one place to another, infecting humans with vampirism, so they mutate into vampires. Instead, she tells a story of a world that has mutated due to human migrations, where things might not be what they appear—and where systems of human relations may themselves be vampire-like. Vampires appear where histories meet.

Like classical Hollywood's first vampire films, Amirpour's film raises questions about immigration and belonging through motifs of blood, bodies, and borders. These motifs can be traced both to literary sources, such as Bram Stoker's novel *Dracula* (1897), and to cinematic ones, such as early films on immigration and assimilation. The figure of the vampire accumulates meaning, as it moves from folklore and literature to theatrical stage and cinematic screen. Supernatural qualities in vampire stories allow social assumptions to find overt expression, whereas other kinds of stories demand that they remain hidden in covert agendas. Vampire hunters murder vampires—and are seldom arrested. Although scenes of violence, sexuality, and interspecies coupling were discreetly hidden behind the vampire's black cape—yet exploited in stills for advertising and promotion—Béla Lugosi's portrayal of Count Dracula excited imaginations with his sexually predatory and socially destabilizing suggestiveness in *Dracula*. He departs from the animalized-cadaverous vampire in *Nosferatu, eine Symphonie des Grauens/Nosferatu: A Symphony of Horror* (Germany 1922; dir. F. W. Murnau). Count Orlok looks and moves like a cadaver. Murnau's close-ups of his rat-like teeth and long shots of shadows cast by his talon-like hands as they grasp the tender throats of victims were abandoned for classical Hollywood's medium shots of fangless vampires in tuxedos. Over nearly nine decades, Hollywood's stars become increasingly recognizable as *sexually desirable* even when portraying vampires stigmatized as *socially undesirable*.

Hollywood's most humanized and domesticated vampire, *Twilight*'s Edward Cullen, is nonviolent until sexual. He is a native-born American from the Midwest. He does not wear a black cape like Count Dracula because he does nothing to hide. Nor does he wear a black chador like Amirpour's vampire because he embodies white-male privilege. Count Dracula is deathly pale under his whiteface makeup, but Edward is positively sparkly under his glamour lighting and special effects. If Count Dracula passes as human in ways that Count Orlok cannot, then Edward passes as a citizen in ways that Count Dracula—and many people of color today—cannot. Count Dracula and Edward Cullen represent different moments in a transnational US history. One vampire encounters the first decade of regulated immigration and border; the other, several decades in transnational economic integration. In Stoker's novel, Count Dracula can only rest peacefully in a box lined with soil from his native Transylvania, a convention that remains in countless vampire films. His mobility is limited. Edward does not require sleep but nonetheless has bedrooms inside a family house in the Pacific Northwest and a holiday-getaway home in Brazil. He can come and go where and when he pleases. His mobility is virtually unlimited. He claims access to powers of belonging unimaginable to earlier generations of Hollywood vampires.[1] Count Dracula and Edward, however, are able to pass as white, male, human, and perhaps even as citizens. It is precisely this recognizable—if not legally recognized—quality of Hollywood's vampires that makes them evocative of shifting perceptions of national belonging in the United States. Edward Cullen's uncontested right to feel American suggests a different configuration of history, identity, and geography than the contested rights of vampires in Amirpour's film or Stoker's novel.

---

1 Only Native America, configured as a pack of werewolves/shape-shifters, perceives Edward's passing as trespassing. From the perspective of indigenous nations, the very concept of native-born American suggests systemic trespassing-as-passing.

Despite their differences, vampire stories generally involve *bloods* that mix, *bodies* that migrate, and *borders* that mutate. Vampires drain lives by sucking blood and reanimate bodies by giving blood. They pollute or contaminate bloodlines and transform identities. They take multiple wives and reproduce endemically. They are sometimes seen as nonproductive in terms of capital but over-reproductive in terms of children. Vampires resist control and containment by loving outside social norms, yet must rest in coffins lined with soil from their homeland and cannot enter a house without the owner's invitation. They might be deathly pale but are not quite white. They seduce and frighten us with erotically charged spectacles of mixed blood, unruly bodies, and ever-shifting borders—all of which move alongside shifting definitions for the "us" in the United States. The erotically and nationally charged spectacle of vampires has been interpreted in relation to sexually transmitted diseases (syphilis and HIV) and the ascendancy of secularism and modern technologies over religion and superstition. It can also be contextualized in relation to social and legal discourses of blood (e.g., quantum theories, anti-miscegenation, *jus sanguinis*), bodies (e.g., phenotypes, skin color, biometrics), and borders (e.g., *jus soli*, criminalized vagrancy, illegal immigration) that define citizenship and territory. Vampires "pass" as one of us—and sometimes "trespass" against us. Vampire stories facilitate critical examination of nativism that targets immigrant and indigenous groups with outrageous claims that they "drain" the economy and should "go home" or, in the case of indigenous nations, should "disappear."

Vampires also question US national exceptionalism that can delegitimize and discredit dissenting voices in democratic debate, especially ones of minoritized groups who may identify as women, LBGTQ, disabled, homeless, or stateless. In social life, citizenship is performed and contested along intersecting vectors of difference—race/ethnicity, sex and gender, sexuality, class, religion, nationality/nativity, ability, and species, among other "styles of the flesh," as Judith Butler (1986: 48) might call them. The figure of the vampire unearths these buried dimensions of history identity and geography through tropes of blood, bodies, and borders. This book argues that vampires are not necessarily feared or desired because they will drain the blood of nation; instead, they may be feared or desired because they threaten or promise to populate the nation with progeny of so-called mixed blood. The constant and unpredictable shape-shifting and flight of vampires point to unresolved anxieties over, and unrealized aspirations about, America. Since vampires are often nonhuman characters, vampire films and series push us to think beyond interracial communities to interspecies ones. Because they transcend rational and empirical categories of knowledge, supernatural species become apt figures for showing us something about our relationship with others, including nonhuman animals and nonanimal species. Supernatural species like vampires, zombies, and werewolves dare us to look beyond the visual and auditory evidence, beyond technologies of vision and hearing that record audiovisual images in ways that seem invisible, silent, and unbiased.

THE MOMENT OF COUNT DRACULA

Developed in eastern European folklore during the seventeenth century, the term *vampire* was appropriated into western European literature.[2] Folkloric vampires were reanimated corpses who stayed close to home and familiar, but literary vampires became aristocratic antiheroes who travelled afar to embrace the foreign and faraway. They passed as human and transgressed social norms in poetry by Samuel Taylor Coleridge and Charles Baudelaire, stories by John Polidori and James Malcolm Rymer, plays by James Planché and Charles Nodier.[3] Abbreviated, the term *vamp* designated sexualized women including the earliest cinematic vampires played by Theda Bara and Musidora.[4] Most cinematic vampires follow conventions of aristocratic Lord Ruthven from Polidori's *The Vampyre* (1819), who served as a prototype for Count Dracula. Countess Karnstein from Joseph Sheridan LeFanu's *Carmilla* (1871–2) produced a model for female vampires, including Amirpour's. Unlike Ruthven, Carmilla was bound to her father's colonial property and, like European women, could not travel freely or even count as a citizen. Bram Stoker's *Dracula* reconfigured vampires from intimate friends into the deadly outsiders that dominate what we think about vampires (Auerbach 1995).

The moment of Count Dracula is one of social contradictions and transformations. European states expanded overseas empires while announcing democratic principles at home. They championed universal rights and humanism while enslaving, indenturing, and dispossessing on a scale hitherto unimagined. Science allegedly confirmed and visualized prejudices that criminalized deviances from invented norms. Vampires emerge within this moment. Stoker narrates anxieties and aspirations that anticipate US experiences. *Dracula* consolidates conventions that lend themselves to adaptation for stage and screen. Ordinary props like crucifixes and coffins become extraordinary objects to injure or protect vampires. There may be no literal connections to race and immigration, but there are affective ones. Audiences *feel* that they cannot see or know enough. The world is not what it may have once seemed.

The novel supports a range of interpretations. Carol Senf (1982) saw *Dracula* as a reactionary response to the New Woman, who claimed independence and sometimes autonomy from men. During the HIV panic, Christopher Craft (1997) related vampirism to sexually transmitted diseases such as syphilis and gonorrhea. Other critics read *Dracula* in relation to Darwin's theory of evolution and Freud's theory of the unconscious. Still others understand the novel

---

2   First documented use in 1734/1745, the *OED* suggests *vampire* enters from French and Magyar. For etymology, see Wilson [1985] (1998) and Murgoci [1927] (1998). McClelland argues Slavic word *vampir* "was a shorthand (and probably pejorative) label for an individual who either belonged to a specific group or practiced a particular belief or ritual" (2008: 31), organizing around a triad of Jews, Pagans, and heretics (47).

3   On plays, see: Stuart 1994.

4   Theda Bara was Hollywood's transformation of Theodosia Goodman from "nice Jewish girl" into epitome of male anxieties over female agency in *A Fool There Was* (USA 1915; dir. Frank Powell). Her stage name was allegedly an anagram for "Arab Death." As Musidora, Jeanne Roques portrayed Irma Vep in *Les Vampires* (France 1915–1916; dir. Louis Feuillade). Her name an anagram for the word *vampire*, Irma Vep is herself a scrambled character—part victimizer, part victim.

as a critique of modernity and of capitalism.[5] Stephen Arata finds reactionary panic in fears of "reverse colonialism" via vampires invading "the space of their knowledge" before bodies or land (1997: 470). "[Count] Dracula imperils not simply his victims' personal identities, but also their cultural, political, and racial selves," he explains; "miscegenation leads, not to the mixing of the races, but to the biological and political annihilation of the weaker race by the stronger" (465–6). He situates *Dracula* in relation to England's occupation of Ireland, which was later reproduced around the world.

In recent decades, the novel is understood less literally. Joseph Valente reads it as social satire of British culture, explaining Stoker was "an interethnic Anglo-Celt and hence a member of a conquering and conquered race, a ruling and a subject people, an imperial and an occupied nation" (2002: 4). For David Glover, *Dracula* is an Irish novel about Ireland rather than an English one about England. Faraway Transylvania is described in terms of nearby Ireland, and vampire-hunting protagonists are not heroes (1996: 33). Stoker was himself Anglo-Irish—part of the colonizing English, who often felt like the colonized Irish. Feeling foreign as a son of a Catholic Italian within Protestant England, Polidori's relationship to nation is also vexed.[6] Given their ambivalent experiences of British colonialism, their interpretation of the figure of the vampire lends itself to both postcolonial and posthuman critique. Rather than internalizing racism to become model colonial subjects—or ignoring it altogether to pose as cosmopolitan citizens, Polidori and Stoker imagined vampires to contest racism, sexism, and speciesism within humanism.

Dracula opens questions on mobility in relation to history, identity, and geography. Part travelogue and part mystery, it foregrounds historical intersections of blood, bodies, and borders upon which contemporary ones develop. Vampire stories concern travellers, responses to whom are riddled with curiosity and apprehension. Initially recounted through epistles by individual characters, *Dracula*'s narrative coheres as a relay of different accounts of crossing borders; disciplining undisciplined bodies with taxonomies (e.g., race/ethnicity, class, gender and sex, species); fretting and fighting over blood's overdetermined meaning. The plot concerns different migrations that precede the mutations of humans into vampires—and vampires in any number of other forms: (1) Jonathan Harker relocates temporarily from England to Transylvania to work for Count Dracula, (2) Count Dracula attempts to relocate permanently from Transylvania to England, (3) Harker returns to England after being nursed to health by Christian nuns, (4) Count Dracula flees England for Transylvania after being targeted by bloodthirsty vampire hunters,

---

5   For analyses of scholarship, see: Carter 1988: 1–6, Davison 1997, and Gordon and Hollinger 1997.

6   Polidori describes conflicts between Italian nationality and English citizenship: "I, although born in England, am not an Englishman" (cited in MacDonald 1991: 20). Entangled in Anglo-French relations, the Alien Bill (1793) deported foreigners, including Catholics, "on suspicion that they were concerned in practices dangerous to the state" (80).

(5) vampire hunters chase Count Dracula to Transylvania, where they assassinate him, and (6) Harker returns to visit Transylvania with his wife after vanquishing vampires.

The moment of Count Dracula suggests a reconfiguring of social relations through emerging mobilities. Before immigrating to England, Count Dracula purchases property and acculturates himself to its foreign society. He hires Harker to prepare legal documents. The exact reason for his emigration is unknown. He is the only major character whose voice is excluded. Incomplete evidence becomes reason for the vampire hunters' irrational suspicions that find expression in terms of blood, bodies, and borders. The novel's epistolary form shifts between letter and newspaper stories to diary entries that evoke conventions of travel writing. We learn what characters *feel* as they travel between different geopolitical contexts. In the first diary entry, "3 May Bistritz," Harker records a memo to get a recipe for "*paprika hendl*" (1997: 9) for his fiancée Mina. Travel writing conveys a sense of ownership, notes Mary Louise Pratt, even in "anti-conquest" forms, by engaging "strategies of representation whereby European bourgeois subjects seek to secure their innocence in the same moment as they assert European hegemony" (2008: 3, 9). Harker's personal profiteering parodies this hegemony through his colonial arrogance and ignorance evident. He legally facilitates Count Dracula's mobility, but Count Dracula financially facilitates his mobility.

Like travel writing, *Dracula*'s characters convey ownership of land through the possessive language of military, religious, and economic campaigns over foreign lands. Although not mentioned in its epistles, part of the novel's broader historical context was the so-called scramble for Africa, culminating in the Berlin Conference (1884–5). European colonization of Africa coincided with the US colonization of the western plains (1825–80). Territory was visualized on illustrated maps and narrativized in exploration stories in images of primitivized and animalized female bodies, awaiting colonizers to conquer their unruly and assumed natural ways (Shohat and Stam 1994). Count Dracula appears suspicious for having three wives and for seducing men and women alike. In addition to prejudices against Muslims as polygamists with harems of sex slaves, Count Dracula's too-many wives parody colonizers' displaced awareness of their own avarice in annexing so many foreign lands. While the deranged English character of Renfield might quote Christian biblical verse—"the blood is the life"—other characters imply that the possession of land is the only kind of life worth living.

The hyper-visibility of bloods mixing in Stoker's novel lampoon anxieties over distinct racial/ethnic and national types, which legitimized regulation of immigration while obscuring its economic and political causes. Stoker parodies associations of blood with soil—two key elements in determining rights to citizenship according to *jus sanguinas* (right of blood) and *jus soli* (right of soil). Blood becomes more than a vessel for diseases such as syphilis. It allegedly confirms faith that identities are bound to geographies. Blood's significance moves from biological and medical to cultural and political. Describing a conversation on the "story of his race," Harker records that Count Dracula identifies as Székely, one of the "four distinct nationalities" in Transylvania. He is "descended from Attila and the Huns" (Stoker 1997: 10), adding that Székelys have veins inside of which "flows the blood of many brave races" within the "whirlpool of European races" (33). He claims that "there is hardly a foot of soil in all this region that has not been enriched by the blood of men, invaders and patriots" (27) within a tumultuous history of battles among Wallachians, Saxons, and Turks to control Transylvania. The soil with which Count Dracula travels—his "earth-boxes," usually rendered as coffins—is presumably sodden with Balkanism's divisive violence, an antithesis to unifying purity and coherence of the modern nation-state and a terrifying omen that geopolitical borders cannot tame and contain historical borderlands.

For Britons, the Balkans existed as a site for cultural conflicts between a so-called Christian civilization and its Islamic orient, replete with nomadic Jews and Roma (i.e., gypsies or "counterfeit Egyptians"). Cultural differences are mapped onto geopolitical divisions of land and remapped onto bodies and behaviors. Vampires evoke an orientalized Europe that bordered on becoming Asia or—perhaps worse in British minds—an Islamic world. The Balkans may not have been important as a terrestrial passage from Britain to its most important colony India, but they were important within larger geopolitics. The Treaty of Berlin (1878) decided the fate of the Balkans with Britain's effort as "maintaining the Ottoman presence in Europe as a counterbalance to Russia," which it saw as "a possible threat to Britain's control of India" (Gibson 2006: 71). As borderlands between European Christianity and European Islam, they posed a problem for Enlightenment conceptions of secular modernity. Vampire hunters act in the name of rationality and humanity but combine spiritual and political concepts, not unlike practices that Partha Chatterjee (1993) finds among anticolonial nationalists in British India. In *Dracula*, Christian civilization is no longer able to mask itself as secular. Its basis in religion emerges in highly visible ways, notably crucifixes as weapons against vampires. The novel asks us to notice blind spots.

Stoker parodies nativist anxieties as Britain became increasingly less homogeneous than the nation-state's imaginary amalgamation of nation and state demands. At the turn of the century, London became not only metropolitan, but multinational. Fears of cultural submersion and possible racial/ethnic or national extinction abounded. Jews from eastern Europe became second only to the Irish as the largest immigrant community in England.[7] Nineteenth-century laws collapsed racialized groups, notably Roma, into what David Mayall describes as the "larger vagrant problem" within the "context of the needs of an industrialising urbanising society" wherein "itinerancy served merely as a cloak for a deviant range of predatory, parasitic and criminal activities," thereby defining "the superiority of the settled over the nomadic culture"

---

7   Halberstam questions Stoker's friendship with Burton, author of a "tract reviving the blood libel against Jews in Damascus" and statements against writers for not being "good Christians" (1995: 86).

and facilitating fears and prejudices against "immigrants, nomads, and other minority groups" (1992: 8). Laws sustained illusions of racial superiority of settled over nomadic peoples.[8] Bodies became legally visible; borders, legible; blood, territorialized. Itinerant and nomadic bodies were criminalized or stigmatized as premodern, savage, and animalistic, all of which was mapped anatomically onto the figure of the vampire. For readers today, vampires are more often emancipatory. Novelist Anne Rice allowed them to speak in *Interview with the Vampire* (1976).

Count Dracula's immigration is portrayed not only as what he might *take* from, or *diminish* within, England but also as what he might *bring* to, or *augment* within, England. Fears over his draining the national body of blood do not produce nativist anxieties; fears over his blood mixing into the national body—changing its composition and appearance—do. Count Dracula's body becomes an obsession, with Harker repeatedly noting the "very marked physiognomy" of his Transylvanian host. Maria Todorova argues that it was not until the late eighteenth century that "an awareness that the European possessions of the Ottoman Empire had a distinct physiognomy of their own that merited separate attention" took place, shattering the "unitary character of the oriental world" (1997: 62). The terrifying idea of orientalized Europeans suggests why Stoker's characters describe Count Dracula's body in terms of animals and corpses. "[Count] Dracula is seen as a metaphor for the Balkan condition and for the Western rejection of Balkan Europeanness as 'impure'," explains Vesna Goldsworthy; he "is threatening precisely because he is European," and the Balkans are perceived as "a contagious disease, an infectious sore in the soft underbelly of Europe, best left to fester in isolation" with its conflicts as "revolting departures from the ideal of cosmopolitanism" (1998: 83, xi).[9] Her analysis evokes stories about Janissaries, young Christian men who were kidnapped and enslaved to the Ottoman Sultan, which circulated as Europe began to imagine itself as a separate continent, rather than mere subcontinent of Asia.[10]

The novel's tropes of blood, bodies, and borders raise questions about territory-bound identities. The concept of nation-states made sovereignty territorial after the Peace of Westphalia in 1648. Empires, however, made sovereignty extraterritorial through colonialism and imperialism. Access to citizenship is infinitely deferred or abridged for racialized citizens. Some bodies are discursively bound to land, appearing as rightful occupants; others, discursively unbound, criminalized as illegal immigrants. Bodies are marked when they cross borders or are perceived to have crossed them even generations earlier. The etymology of territory from *terra* (earth) and *terrere* (to frighten) points to why Count Dracula's immigration and purchase

---

8   Restrictions were minimal since 1783's repeal of the 1530 anti-Gypsy Act, threatening Roma with execution. Laws preventing immigration begin early twentieth century, targeting Russian and Polish Jews, and expelling Jewish, Chinese, Italian, and German communities.

9   Goldsworthy finds British and US economic interests in the Balkans were minor during the 1920s and 1930s. A nineteenth-century "narrative colonisation," she argues, begins with Lord Byron as "its Columbus" (1998: x).

10   See: Lewis and Wigen 1997 on Europe's continental self-invention.

of fifty properties (i.e., plots of English land) represents terrorism to vampire hunters. He is required to repose in, and travel with, "earth-boxes" filled with soil from his native land. They pathologize his "earth-home," "coffin-home," and "hell-home" (212). Isomorphic notions of restricted movement—place moving with people—evoke the nineteenth-century German expression "blood and soil" (*Blut und Boden*) to suggest "blood and soil become mixed in national perceptions," implying unchanging notions of descent within a homeland that has existed since time immemorial (Connor 1999: 205).[11]

If Count Dracula's blood drinking is an indirect way of describing sexual relations, then it promises to manifest itself in subsequent generations of so-called mixed-blood children. Vampirism spreads by infection and contagion, producing impure thoughts and progeny, altering perceptions of social coherence and demographic statistics that allegedly confirm it and legitimize political representation. Count Dracula becomes a radical figure in disrupting primordial notions of nation in an era of nation-states. Blood functions in discourses on racial purity and public health, which are mapped onto bodies to locate them within geopolitical systems of relational power. Miscegenation and degeneration are visualized in caricatures with animalistic features and behaviors, reflecting social and institutional prejudices—or in cadaverous creatures, reflecting fears of illness. Angela Smith argues that eugenics replaced superstitions about stillbirths, difficult births, and birth defects with genetic determinism (2011: 40). The pseudoscience maintained irrational fears of "illegitimate offspring of two illegitimate persons," she argues, citing a phrase from Emily Gerard's study on folklore, which Stoker read as part of his research. Count Dracula's blood mixes into the English bodies of Renfield, Lucy, and Mina, destabilizing their gender, sexuality, and allegiance. Their blood becomes impure; their bodies and minds, unstable and degenerate. Once-white bodies are racialized when vampirized, as are once-all-white bodies politic. It is not until 1864, a few years after Charles Darwin's *On the Origin of Species* (1859), that the term "miscegenation" replaced amalgamation for "the fertile fusion and merging of two races," notes Robert Young, with constructions of race functioning according to evolutionary structures with "computation of normalities" and "degrees of deviance" measured against an idealized white norm with none more demonized than "mixed race" (1995: 7, 170).[12] Vampires, however, refuse all forms of racism. For Donna Haraway, the vampire "insists on the nightmare of racial violence behind the fantasy of purity in the rituals of kinship" (1996: 322–3). Considered more monstrous than partially assimilated immigrants were native-born persons whose racial/ethnic identities could not be fully determined. If conservative British readers got chills over images of blood, bodies,

---

11   Drawing upon Foucault's arguments that European modernity produces blood and race as biological entities through clinical descriptions and mappings onto an "anatomical atlas," Linke argues the body is attributed with strategic importance, a "strategy for political power" upon which "a new system of legal justice is imprinted" (1999: 157–159).

12   Southern Democrats coin the term to discredit Lincoln and Republicans; Ku Klux Klan was founded two years later (Gross 2010: 74–75).

and borders affected by vampires, then so too did Hollywood's conservative US audiences. Others, however, took comfort in seeing imperial patriarchy contested.

Stoker's novel questions ambivalence about nativist notions that some immigrants never fully assimilate because they might incite a degeneration of nation. It contests these violent epistemologies, something that Hollywood largely continues. Universal's *Dracula* and *Drácula* were adapted from staged versions of Stoker's novel—Hamilton Deane's in London in 1924 and John L. Balderston's in New York in 1927—rather than the novel directly. By maintaining the narrative's location in England, the immigrant-vampire negotiates contradictions within US representational democracy without directly implicating nativism and colonialism. The year 1924 marks significant changes in policy: indigenous nations and their territories were involuntarily absorbed into the republic under the Indian Citizenship Act, European immigration was regulated according to national quotas under the Johnson-Reed Act, and border crossings from Canada and México were regulated by the Border Patrol. Like vampires, immigrants were suspected of multiple allegiances and diminished patriotism.[13] Fears of submersion ignited xenophobia and racism, evident in Henry James's description of Jewish ghettos as evidence of the "Hebrew conquest of New York" ([1907] 1968: 132). Power largely was concentrated in the universalized particular of so-called natural persons, specifically "free white persons," from the Naturalization Act of 1795 until 1952.[14]

The moment of Count Dracula coincides with the apex of US imperialism, when blood served as pseudoscientific yet legally binding confirmation of race/ethnicity, determining degrees of personhood and entitlement to land allotments.[15] Abridged or deferred citizenship becomes waiting forever at the threshold of political representation. The notorious one-drop rules did not involve analysis of blood samples but relied upon appearance, color, and association. Legal definitions of race were sometimes determined by imagined blood quantum to distinguish persons (citizens and free noncitizens) from property (slaves). The United States systematically dismantled indigenous nations through the Dawes Commission's policies of forced assimilation, tribal enrollment, and land allotment beginning in 1893. It overthrew the Hawai'ian monarchy

---

13   Theodore Roosevelt demanded "100 percent Americans" over "hyphenated Americans." The 1917 Immigration Act required English-language literacy to discourage immigration from Italy, Poland, and Hungary and bar it from Asia except China, Japan, and Philippines (Hing 2004: 54; Daniels 2002: 278).

14   "Natural person" recognizes corporate personhood as "legal persons." Three-fifths Compromise (1787) determined "all other persons" counted as three-fifths of whole persons.

15   England's *jus soli* came to the United States, yet birthright citizenship excluded racialized nationals (Haney López 1996: 39–40). The first naturalization law (1790) limited eligibility—"fitness for self-government"—to "free white persons" (Jacobson 1998: 7). Only post-Civil War did citizenship became *national*. "Servile blood" of "an ancestor once held in involuntary servitude" was imagined to "contaminate and pollute the Indian blood and render such a person incapable of taking land under a treaty with the United States" (Gross 2010: 163). Mexican American organizations opposed classification as *race* (versus *nationality* or *white ethnicity*) along with prejudices informed by eugenicists like Madison Grant who feared "peon blood" of *mestizaje* (Spanish-Indian-African) produced "race bastards," "amazing racial hybrids," and "ethnic horrors that will be beyond the powers of future anthropologists to unravel" (Foley 2012: 62).

during the same year—and later annexed Guam and Puerto Rico and invaded the Philippines in 1899. To assassinate Count Dracula, English vampire hunters rely upon the brute force of Texan adventurer Quincey P. Morris, who embodies the spirit of the Republic of Texas, which occupied Mexican lands, dispossessed populations, and annexed territory before dissolving into the United States.[16] An ever-shifting nexus of definitions of blood, bodies, and borders determined what territories could be incorporated into the republic and who could own property and therefore count as a full citizen.[17]

The moment of Count Dracula announces the postcolonial condition in the heart of empire, affecting both colonizer and colonized with an impurity and instability brought by empire (cf. Said 1993). The supernatural qualities of Stoker's vampire allow for multiple readings, including contradictory ones. Since sweeping social changes continue to affect our lives, vampire stories often demand inconclusive and speculative models for analysis and interpretation. The figure of the vampire's meaning is highly unstable. Some are associated with exploitation, corruption, and theft, evident in Karl Marx's characterization of capitalism as "vampire-like" and "werewolf-like," which David McNally describes as not "mere rhetorical flourishes" but "means of depicting the actual horrors of capitalism" from child-labor and factory systems to genocides and slavery (2012: 13). Such associations travel widely and sometimes return in critiques of colonialism and capitalism, imperialism and neoliberalism. In her study of rumor and history in colonial Africa, Luise White examines a transnational genre of African stories about people hired by Europeans to capture East Africans and take their blood, calling them "vampire stories" since "no other term conveys the racial difference encoded in one group's need for another's blood" (2000: 9). Updated for a neoliberal moment, such associations reappear in *Laal Rang* (India 2016; dir. Syed Ahmad Afzal), based on events about human blood mafias in the northern Indian state of Haryana and featuring a top blood thief who uses the nickname "Dracula." Other vampires are figures of resistance, empowerment, and generosity, evident in the multitude of responses to vampire film and television, including anticolonial, feminist, postcolonial, queer, and posthumanist appropriations of their stories to challenge power to reclaim both history and dignity. Minoritized writers from Octavia Butler (1976) to Jewel Gomez (1991) employ vampires to critique US colonialism from indigenous, black, and queer perspectives—and speculate fictions about other scenarios for America. Comparably, Amirpour's appropriation of the figure of the vampire speculates about transnational histories and feminisms in ways anticipated by Stoker in the moment of Count Dracula.

---

16   Texas was populated with 35,000 whites, who seceded from México to declare Independent Lone Star Republic of Texas in 1836. Annexed in 1845, the United States gained of 55% of Mexican territory with 80,000 inhabitants.

17   Puerto Rico and Philippines were not envisioned for "settler citizens"; New Mexico and Hawai'i were whitened for incorporation as states (Gómez 2007: 7).

COUNT DRACULA REFASHIONED AS "VAMPIRE AYATOLLAH"

Produced and directed by Francis Ford Coppola, Columbia Pictures' *Bram Stoker's Dracula* features a vampire so outrageously costumed and performed that one critic described it as a "vampire ayatollah," referencing not what the Islamic Revolution meant to Iranians, whether supporting or opposing it, but what it meant to certain Americans. Coppola simultaneously ignites and parodies reactionary politics. Count Dracula is refashioned as a thinly veiled throwback to US foreign policy during the 1970s, which saw challenges to its ability to influence domestic policy in foreign states. The film conjures Christian anxieties over Islam as a supernatural conquest over western ascendancy. It seems to illustrate ways that nationalism and national exceptionalism mask relationships between immigration and globalization through contrivances of Hollywood genre and cinematic citation. Vampires evoke unspeakable frights over erosions to the American Dream by the founding of the Organization of the Petroleum Exporting Countries (OPEC) in 1960, US military defeat in Southeast Asia in 1975, and deposition of the US-backed Iranian monarchy of Reza Shah Pahlavi in 1979. At the same time, the film's outlandish costumes and performances, like Stoker's novel, offer space to critique imperialism.

Bram Stoker's Dracula reflects its moment of production, as Cold War geopolitics crumbled. Count Dracula is orientalized almost as a textbook illustration of Edward Said's landmark study *Orientalism* (1978) on how Europe invented itself as a civilization by inventing an Orient that conflated different historical and cultural aspects of the Middle East, North Africa, South Asia, East Asia, Southeast Asia, Central Asia, and the Balkans into a monolithic and unchanging Other. In Coppola's film, Count Dracula looks Turkish, Japanese, Chinese, Hungarian, and Russian, yet none of these identities entirely. His appearance and performance are explicitly heterogeneous, so as to be anti-mimetic, yet gain power through reality effects of their irreconcilable details more than special effects of supernatural flight and physical transmogrifications.

Figure 1.2.1 Gary Oldman as an orientalized Count Dracula welcomes Keanu Reeves as Jonathan Harker at the start of another excellent adventure. *Bram Stoker's* Dracula (USA 1992; dir. Francis Ford Coppola).

The film's satire buries reactionary politics beneath lavish sets and costumes. Its elaborate and bejeweled costumes even helped hoist orientalist design back onto fashion runways. For audiences inclined towards xenophobia, Count Dracula becomes a new post-Cold War threat that migrated from geopolitics to religion, evoking the vitriol and furor of the Christian Crusades against the Ottomans during the Middle Ages. Vampire hunters appear heroic, like cowboys in classical Hollywood Westerns. For other audiences, the vampire hunters become emotionally insecure and violence-prone patriarchs—and Count Dracula, an object of desire or identification.

The film also demonstrates Hollywood's vampire-like qualities by revealing its dependency on drawing talent and labor from across the globe before sending products and images into the world. Hollywood acts like a vampire. "Can a vampire resist fresh blood?" asked a journalist about how "Hollywood was destined to discover Hong Kong" in "the rapidly shrinking world of global entertainment" (Ansen 1996: 66). Rather than a vampire unable to resist the *new* (for Hollywood at the time) blood of Hong Kong martial arts and pyrotechnics, the film casts Hollywood as a vampire unable to resist the *vintage* blood of classical and avant-garde European and East Asian film-making through copious and conspicuous references to Jean Cocteau, Sergei Eisenstein, and Kurosawa Akira that often overwhelm pretentions of literary faithfulness and historical verisimilitude—and aestheticize its politics. Count Dracula triggers anxieties of Coppola's generation over the US colonial defeat in Southeast Asia, lamented in his *Apocalypse Now* (1979), and the so-called oil crisis, also during the 1970s, that announced the twilight of an American Century. Critics were quick to notice the film's Islamophobia during US military invasions in the MENASA regions (Sinclair 1993: 15; Sharrett 1996: 265–6). The film seemed to restage Stoker's novel as the 1991 invasion of Iraq like the "scripts replayed unrevised" that Pratt observed about the 2003 invasion in relation to European imperialism (2008: xiii). For younger audiences, the vampire hunters' earnestness could only be social satire.

The film's refashioning of Count Dracula allows audiences to speculate about alternative meanings. Its sympathetic vampire might encourage us to temper patriotic impulses to invade foreign states in search of weapons of mass destruction and cheap oil. Count Dracula (Gary Oldman) is in many ways a better partner for Mina Murray (Winona Ryder) than her fiancé Jonathan Harker (Keanu Reeves), whose occasional ineptitude is annoying. Coppola allows Mina to take command and drive a stake through Count Dracula's heart, releasing him from vampirism. She does not sacrifice her own life, as the female protagonist does in Murnau's *Nosferatu*. Coppola's vampire hunters seek to destroy Count Dracula and a sense of deep historical, transnational connection that he resurrects through love, visualized as Vlad Țepeș and wife Elisabeta in an eastern orthodox mosaic.

Coppola mobilizes *affect* and *spectacle*, more than *ideology* and *narrative*, to structure meaning, suggesting why audiences interpret the film differently. Coppola's Count Dracula becomes a "vampire ayatollah," evoking the terror of the hostage crisis, and conflating the Iranian ayatollah Khomeini with Iraqi president Saddam Hussein, thereby naturalizing the US invasion of Iraq in a continuum from Christian Crusades to Manifest Destiny. At the same time, Count Dracula becomes a satire of nationalist xenophobia. Coppola emphasizes what he calls the "John Ford Western finale" (Schumacher 1999: 449) by which a transnational brigade of vampire hunters travels from England to Transylvania, where they assassinate the local ruler, much like the so-called Coalition of the Willing assassinated Hussein. Count Dracula does not need to signify Hussein through direct correspondence or resemblance; instead, the figure of the vampire evokes affective responses to universalized villains identified along a so-called axis of evil. Count Dracula is less a signifier of Hussein and Khomeini than the vampire hunters are one of US military intervention in the MENASA regions framed as universalized good (e.g., saving women, promoting democracy) along the emotional register of the white-savior myth that emerged earlier in Westerns. Schatz describes the Western as "America's foundational ritual," suggesting the symbolic rather than the historical accuracy of the genre's "values, attitudes, and ideals associated with westward expansion and the taming and civilizing of the West" in films that "do not celebrate the past itself, but rather our contemporary idealized version of the past" (1981: 46, 63).[18] *Bram Stoker's Dracula* could be said to present an idealized version of the present as the past for some audiences—and an imaginative critique of such certainty for others. It also raises questions about the effects of history on the present. Genre conventions cannot fully erase or silence the presence of transnational history. The film conveys a story of two-way migrations: a vampire migrates to England, and vampire hunters migrate to Transylvania; moreover, some hunters migrated to England from Holland and Texas. *Bram Stoker's Dracula*'s meanings exceed conventional frameworks for Hollywood, US history, and horror. It is not a film that evokes primal or archetypal fears and desires. It is one that is very much about a particular experience of America.

AN IRANIAN AMERICAN FEMINIST SCREENS A VAMPIRE FILM AT SUNDANCE

Screened at the Sundance Film Festival in 2014, *A Girl Walks Home Alone at Night* examines effects of geopolitical relationships on Iranians and Iranian Americans. She recovers feminist potential in LeFanu's *Carmilla* and abandons masculine insecurities in Stoker's *Dracula*. Her central characters are types. She provides no backstory for their circumstances. They simply exist in Bad City.[19] The film opens with Arash (Arash Marandi), costumed in white T-shirt and blue jeans, stealing a cat (Masuka), who becomes his primary companion in an isolating town. He lives with his father, Hossein "The Junkie" (Marshall Manesh), who pays for the company of Atti "The Prostitute" (Mozhan Marnò) and goes into debt buying heroin from Saeed "The Pimp"

---

18   Turner describes the frontier as a site for productions of Americanness (1920: 1). US national exceptionalism "fails as a useful tool for assessing the current moment because it reads the national past solely from a national perspective" (Rana 2010: 6).

19   Amirpour's graphic novels (2014/2015) tell the Girl's story of wandering through desert in search of death before returning home.

(Dominic Rains). Arash loses his prized possession, a 1957 convertible Ford Thunderbird, to pay his father's debts, then steals excess jewelry from Shaydah "The Princess" (Rome Shadanloo), who has recently had her nose reshaped and still wears the trendy bandage of plastic surgery.

Known only as the Girl (Sheila Vand), the vampire's solitary strolls do not make her vulnerable. Her chador is open, flapping like a cape. Whereas male vampires lure and attack women beneath the street lamps, she protects herself in dimly lit desolate streets to evaluate men by their behavior. She asks "The Street Urchin" (Milad Eghbali) whether he is good and tells him that she is watching him. He runs away, and she takes his skateboard, enhancing her mobility. Her constrained appetite for blood erupts into violence only against men who enact physical or psychological violence against others. After witnessing Saeed's humiliation of Atti, she seduces him by sucking his finger suggestively—mimicking fellatio, as she has previously seen Atti do; then, she severs his finger with her teeth—evoking castration, as she knows Atti is not free to do. She removes Saeed's severed finger from her mouth and traces the contours of his lips with it, parodying conventions from pornography. She bites his neck, drinks his blood, steals his jewelry, and explores his CD collection. By killing him, she enables Arash to recover the car for which he has worked years as a gardener for Shaydah's family.

Arash is different from the other men who the Girl meets as she walks alone at night. In their initial encounter, he is shot to emphasize physical beauty without the violent exhibitionism of Saeed, who had unzipped his tracksuit to showcase his taunt abdominal muscles and elaborate tattoos. The English word "SEX" appears on his chest; the Farsi expression "سک شک" (*koskesh*, vulgar slang for pimp), on his head.[20] His body is ornamented with gold chains, Mohawk haircut, and Fu Manchu mustache. Arash wears a vampire costume that he sewed himself. After failing to seduce Shaydah at a costume party, he wanders alone into a neighborhood that he does not recognize. Transfixed in a cloud of ecstasy and too tired to stand, he is harmless as a male predator. The Girl pushes him home on a skateboard. There, he moves slowly across the frame towards her. His high-collared cape follows behind him in a long take. The scene undercuts conventions of male vampires rapidly attacking female victims. The Girl does not bite Arash. Instead, the scene enfolds as one of intimacy between two lonely characters as the chorus to the song "Death" conveys mixed feelings of attraction and fear.

The film mobilizes music affectively to convey emotional registers of belonging to two places with strained political relations—and also belonging to neither place. Music reveals mutations and migration impelled by political events. Tracks by underground Iranian rock bands Radio Tehran and Kiosk, Armenian-Lebanese-US fusion Bei Ru from Los Angeles's Little Armenia, post-punk White Lies from London, the Spaghetti Western-inspired music of Federale from Portland (United States), and a ballad by Iranian singer and songwriter Daruish (aka Daruish Eghbali), whose career began in the 1970s, play over carefully choreographed scenes with

---

20   I thank Chani Gatto Bradshaw for contacting the film's producer about this term.

Figure 1.2.2 The Girl (Sheila Vand) encounters Arash (Arash Marandi), lost under a streetlamp and dressed like a classical Hollywood vampire. *A Girl Walks Home Alone at Night* (USA 2014; dir. Ana Lily Amirpour).

little or no dialogue. Unlike classical Hollywood's vococentrism, as Michel Chion calls dialogue's prioritization (1994: 5, 1996), the film allows auditory and visual images to produce equivocal meanings. They evoke moods, rejecting explicit causality that typically structures Hollywood films. The love scene is followed by one in which drag queen Rockabilly (Reza Sixo Safai) dances with a child's balloon. The fringe of her cowboy-style shirt sways like the balloon's string. The figure of the vampire becomes a means to understand loneliness, isolation, and forgetting what one wants from life within exploitative social conditions. Characters turn to drugs like heroin, cocaine, and ecstasy for refuge.

Amirpour's film explores how emotions develop within broader political and economic conditions informed by international relations. The film was largely shot in Taft (California), a small town that existed exclusively for petroleum and natural gas production. In a vampire film, shots of oil pumps, moving mechanically to extract petroleum from below the earth's surface, evoke the parasitic relationship of humans to planet. Oil becomes earth's blood and sustenance for materialistic human desires, such as Arash's fancy sports car. Oil also powers escape from exploitative conditions. Bad City defines a bleak world, structured by vampire-like social relations. Saeed exploits Hossein's addiction, which in turn exploits Arash's ability to earn money. Informal economies supplement state failures to provide for citizens. Whether cisgender or transgender, women are particularly vulnerable. There appears little work apart from prostitution, which, like drug addiction, is not uncommon in modern Iran, as documented in Mahnaz Afzali's *Zananeh/The Ladies' Room* (2003). Saeed and Hossein exploit Atti's vulnerable circumstances; a nameless man physically abuses Rockabilly in a scene deleted from the final cut. It is a world where humans have forgotten why they are living and how to dream of something better. It is a also dystopic take on the American Dream—and not only for Iranian Americans, who escaped or whose parents escaped the 1979 revolution, but for Americans who dream of cheap products and lifestyles made from petroleum.

Bad City mixes feelings of estrangement and dislocation along with ones of community and relocation. The film's black-and-white cinematography and uncluttered visual style evoke the look of classical Hollywood's vampire films and the social content of the Iranian new wave, including Farrokh Ghaffari's *Jonoub-e Shahr/South of the City* (1958) and Forough Farrokhzad's *Khanen siah ast/The House Is Black* (1962), whose images of modern Iran contradicted state discourses of modernization in "the American way" by showing evidence that industrialization and oil did not benefit everyone (Sadr 2006: 90–129). Amirpour evokes Dariush Merhju'i's *Gaav/The Cow* (1969), a critique of single-commodity national economies under Mohammad Reza Pahlavi (aka Shah of Iran) that was praised by ayatollah Khomeini (Naficy 2011: 160) for its implicit critique of the Pahlavi monarchy. Amirpour's film acts like its transnational sequel: both are set in remote villages where the precarity of life within petroleum-based economies is palpable. Shots of oil wells also visually evoke David Lynch's experimentation with digital cameras and photo-manipulation software in *Industrial Soundscape* (2002), which animates still photographs into disquieting figures of nightmares. Oil pumps feel like giant creatures from another realm that drain the planet of its vitality and announce the ascension of humans as top predators during the Anthropocene. We might learn something from other species.

Amirpour's film does not minimize difference but points to unequal ways that globalizing forces affect people, particularly Muslim women. She re-contextualizes conventions from classical Hollywood vampire films for post-revolutionary Iran and its diaspora. Rather than a horse-drawn carriage, the Girl rides a skateboard. Rather than a black cape, she wears a black chador. The significance of such props is multilayered. While images of girls in hijab on skateboards are hardly unusual—girls participate in the Skateistan NGO's events in Afghanistan to bypass the ban on girls riding bicycles—they might seem unexpected to Hollywood audiences, much like images of Palestinians practicing *parkour* in the ruins of abandoned Israeli settlements in Gaza or videos of Saudis practicing joyriding and drifting in Riyadh. Skate parks are common meeting places for female and male Iranian street artists, such as Icy and Sot, and underground bands such as The Yellow Dogs, featured in Bahman Ghobadi's *Kasi az gorbehaye irani khabar nadareh/No One Knows about Persian Cats* (2009), about Tehran's skater-artist-musician scene. Modernity remains "at large," as Arjun Appadurai (1995) argues. Modernity is not unified or singular but dis-unified and multiple. It can startle and frighten. If "one of the few privileges that accrue the latecomer [to modernity]" is the "license to play with form and refigure function according to the exigencies of the situation" (Gaonkar 2001: 21), then one of the many obligations of early adopters is understanding the effects of modernity and accepting internal and external critique. Amirpour's film evokes the playfulness of vampire media in unsettling assumptions.

Iran remains ominous for many US audiences. Hollywood profited from Iran's uneasy relationships with the United States in reactionary melodrama *Not Without My Daughter* (1991), Ben Affleck's *Argo* (2012), set during the Islamic Revolution of 1979, and Jon Stewart's *Rosewater* (2014), set during the Green Movement of 2009. Perhaps more than during the hostage crisis, US audiences are habituated by post-9/11 Islamophobia and anti-terrorist/anti-immigrant discourses to see hijab exclusively as women's oppression or menace. Indeed, Said's title *Covering Islam* (1981) evokes "covering" as simultaneously *revealing* through making visible and *concealing* through translating into foreign terms of understanding (Said 1997). Lila Abu-Lughod (2013) argues that US obsessions with "veiling" enable popular support for US military invasions in the name of rescuing women *from* Islam. Amirpour's vampire suggests that things are more complex.

For Iranian exiles, chadors evoke compulsory hijab, visualized in Marjan Satrapi's graphic novel *Persepolis* (2000) and its film adaptation (2007), but chadors do not foreclose feminist agency. Veiling's history in Iran includes Reza Shah's banning of chadors and headscarves on 7 January 1936, resulting in the forceful unveiling of women in public. Veiling in prerevolutionary Iran came to signify political resistance to programs of accelerated modernization, urbanization, and industrialization based on Turkish president Mustafa Kemal Atatürk's western-modeled programs (both of which had disastrous effects on the lives of rural and minoritized populations), along with religious identity and modesty. The Girl's chador asks audiences to reflect upon their assumptions about people based on their appearance, particularly Muslim women's clothing. For many Muslim women, hijab and modest dressing offer protections from unsolicited attention, including the sadistic and fetishistic male gaze around which most Hollywood films continue to be structured.

The chador serves as an occasion to think about history, identity, and geography. Çagla Hadimioglu argues that the term chador's Persian etymology can be traced to the Turkish *chadir*, translating as *tent*. The chador becomes "an extended boundary that assures that she always occupies a private space" (2011: 216). She explains that a "chador is another skin, a place of inhabitation such as a home," so that the garment literally "alters geography" (2011: 134). Noting the accumulations of meanings imposed upon the chador by Muslims and non-Muslims—feminist or otherwise, Hadimioglu suggests that black chadors differ from the veils-as-screens in the orientalist imagination of subjugated women; however, it is not a garment altogether without meaning. "Perhaps," she suggests, "the black of the chador should be considered not as a void but as the result of an accumulation of inscriptions or projections so dense that they become solid—and an ostensible black 'hole' that is in fact saturated with intention, memory, and meaning" (2011: 130). Amirpour's relationship to chadors is simultaneously involuntary and liberating.

Chadors evoke experiences by Iranian emigrants when they return to Iran as Iranian Americans. Iran is a place where they may have never lived or even been born. In interviews, Amirpour describes her idea for a vampire in a chador as inspired by a visit to Iran with her family. Intrigued by the garment, its weight and fabric, she noticed that she did not disappear into the so-called faceless crowds of women wearing obligatory hijab. She felt self-conscious of her difference but also a sense of familiarity with hearing Farsi spoken everywhere, as at home with her family. Drawing on her own experience as part of a 1.5 generation, who feels out of place in both places, she reworks the vampire as a misunderstood figure like the physically disfigured Joseph Carey Merrick in Lynch's *The Elephant Man* (1980), a film she claims among her favorites. While Sundance journalists found a hijabi vampire on a skateboard to be a "quirky twist" to the longsuffering of "teen vampires" in *Twilight* and *The Vampire Diaries*, the film concerns different configurations of experience that often get erased, silenced, marginalized.

Amirpour establishes relationships of kinship and intimacy, something Auerbach defined as significant to vampires before Stoker's novel shifted meaning to foreignness and violence (1995: 113). The film encourages relationships between the isolated, dispossessed, and marginalized, much like the figure of the vampire. It does not celebrate heroism of colonial and imperial military interventions as a means of saving women and children, typically from the very tyrants installed in power by the United States. Nor does it hide the alienating effects of a global petroleum economy, which Timothy Mitchell (2011) links to possibilities and limitations of democracy. It creates a cinematic space for Iranians and Iranian Americans that is not made exotic but fairly mundane. As a Hollywood film for the current moment, it provides a model for de-exoticizing veiling by considering chadors as clothing whose meaning is as unstable and subject to migration and mutation as Stoker's figure of Count Dracula. The film asks us to look again or look closely, to listen again or listen more closely, to what we might have missed, rather than looking and listening only to what confirms what we think we already know.

THE FIGURE OF THE VAMPIRE AS OBJECT AND METHOD

Comparing *A Girl Walks Home Alone at Night* with *Bram Stoker's Dracula* establishes a range of difference in stories about the United States told as vampire stories. Some convey an emotional sense of debates over political representation for minoritized and often criminalized groups; others critique minoritizing and criminalizing discourses and policies that limit political representation. Most concern shifting relationships between history, identity, and geography— visualized in blood, bodies, and borders. Part of the context of thinking about vampires as both object and method responds to enduring blind spots in universalizing approaches. This book draws upon interventions and interruptions in film, television, and media studies that unsettle the field's critical concepts, historiographical methodologies, and theoretical concerns, based exclusively on Hollywood and European films. It engages comparative, often transnational or transcultural, approaches (Gopalan 2002; de la Mora 2006; Gerow 2010; Ganti 2013) that draw extended critiques (Bogle 1973; García Espinosa [1969] 1983; Rocha [1965] 1983; Solanas and Getino [1968] 1983; Diawara 1993) of nationalist frameworks for conceptualizing film (Bazin [1958–62] 1971; Sarris [1968] 1996; Kracauer [1960] 1997). As both object and method, vampires render Hollywood unbound, though not severed, from its heroic self-invention as privately funded dream factories that thrive within free-market economies. Hollywood produces vampire media outside the territorial United States in the mythical homeland in Europe and the largely unacknowledged former US colony of the Philippines—the imaginary origins and lost frontiers of empire. At the same time, Hollywood vampire films and television series complicate assumptions about the promise of America to provide equitable political representation of all citizens and fair treatment of all noncitizens with the nation-state's territories.

Vampires challenge us to think beyond an uncritical and ostensibly secular faith in realism by displacing the representational with the affective (cf. Majithia 2015). They help us to understand relationships between race/ethnicity and political representation, within relationships between political economy and cinematic representation. The preponderance of Hollywood films that receive theatrical release in parts of Africa, Europe, Latin America, and Southeast Asia during much of the twentieth century cannot be detached from US state support for Hollywood. Like emigration, film distribution is not always entirely voluntary. Critical conventions reproduce what Shohini Chaudhuri calls the "inequities of global film distribution" (2005: 4). Box-office power is maintained indirectly through military power or directly through international policy like the Bretton Woods Agreement (1944) and the General Agreement on Trade and Tariffs (1947).[21] Audiences sometimes love Hollywood films because there are no alternatives due to conditions of trade, recovery, and even independence agreements.

For this reason, it is unsurprising that anticolonial and postcolonial critics (Memmi 1957; Fanon 1961; Mbembe 2003), along with critics of capitalism (Deleuze and Gattari 1987; Marx [1867] 1990; Hardt and Negri 2004), frequently evoke supernatural figures like vampires to describe experiences of dislocation, self-estrangement, and reinvention.[22] Vampires appear and reappear in writing by intellectuals to recover forms of knowledge that have historically been marginalized and delegitimized. Much as the transnational does not elide the continuing relevance of the national, the postcolonial does not elide the continuing relevance of the colonial and the imperial, which are articulated in terms of structural adjustments and proxy wars. Since colonialism and imperialism involve "the subjection of one people by another," Robert

---

21   Criticisms by Hollywood lobbyists overstate subsidies for film industries elsewhere ignore how Hollywood benefits from "a vast array of state, regional and city film commissions," offering "hidden subsidies to the film industry (via reduced local taxes, free provision of police services, and the blocking of public thoroughfares)" (Miller et al. 2005: 96).

22   The Founding Fathers are considered neither immigrant nor indigenous, but somehow naturally—or perhaps supernaturally—"American" (cf. Daniels 2002: 3–4).

Young argues: "so long as oppressive power of that kind continues, then analysis of the forms and practices of colonialism and imperialism remains relevant to the problems we face today" (2015: 2). Vampire film and television becomes a location where amnesia over US colonialism and imperialism—and, moreover, repression of US postcolonial condition—finds expression in supernatural form.

Vampires emerge where inequalities abound. The myths of America and the realities of the United States function as a *contact zone* between indigenous, colonial, immigrant, imperial, and national histories. Pratt defines contact zones as "social spaces where disparate cultures meet, clash, and grapple with each other, often in highly asymmetrical relations of domination and subordination" (2008: 7), that is, "where peoples geographically and historically separated come into contact with each other and establish ongoing relations" (8). The *postcolonial condition* informs our transnational moment. Her analysis provides a model whose relevance has only amplified in the twenty-first century since postcolonial studies, in Gauri Viswanathan's words, examines "cultural interaction between colonizing powers and the societies they colonized, and the traces that interaction left on literature, arts, and human sciences in both societies" (cited in Bahri and Vasudeva 1996: 54). These interactions continue to affect different people in different ways. Amirpour's family did not just happen to immigrate from Iran to the United States any more than Coppola's family immigrated from Italy to the United States. Hollywood's vampire films carry the mark of immigration, past and present.

Contact zones are also useful when thinking about films and series in which humans come into contact with supernatural species. To grapple with contact zones when species meet, Donna Haraway uses the term *figure* because "figures are not representations or didactic illustrations, but rather material-semiotic nodes or knots in which diverse bodies and meanings coshape one another" (2008: 4). Vampires can seem like intruders or emancipators; vampire hunters, like vigilantes or freedom fighters. Globalizing forces, particularly colonialism, imperialism, free trade, and war, figure in ways that are often obscured by extant critical conventions. Early scholarship on vampire films often focused on them as lowbrow entertainment that tapped into so-called archetypal fears and desires, thereby legitimizing them as objects for critical study.[23] Rather than assume a universalized Other met with an equally universalizing response in a dread of difference, this book explores how Hollywood's stories about vampires have been shaped by histories of immigration and globalization that inform films as aesthetically and politically different as Amirpour's *A Girl Walks Home Alone at Night* and Coppola's *Bram Stoker's Dracula*. Like past scholarship that located feminist and queer moments in vampire stories, this book looks for immigrant and indigenous moments—afterlives of race, which have less systematically been explored.

23 Early studies include Kracauer 1947, Eisner 1952, Butler 1967, Clarens 1967, Pirie 1972 and 1977, Silver and Ursini 1975, Prawer 1980, Twitchell 1985, Carroll 1990, and Coates 1991.

At a point where commerce and migration converge, sometimes around policy, vampire films and series contribute to developments in critical methodologies that do not segregate *textual meaning* of stories, characters, styles, and performance from *political economies* that determine production, distribution, and exhibition. These two axes of analysis comingle and contaminate each another. Although the vampire's migrations and mutations are framed as supernatural, the films and series are remarkably consistent for their explicit or implicit preoccupation with everyday lived experiences of globalization through immigration. Globalization allows some groups to pass as global citizens, others languish as stateless; it also allows films to travel across national borders with some arriving on the other side as art, others as trash. Immigration recruitment and regulation thus share something with film production and distribution in their entanglements with broader shifts within globalization. Everyday market economies of stereotypes of race/ethnicity, sex and gender, class, religion, nationality and nativity, ability, and species reflect the effects of globalization on film production, distribution, and exhibition. Hollywood defends its home and foreign markets by creating illusions of the inferiority of films produced elsewhere, often reinforcing social stereotypes that Mexican films are cheap like Mexican labor. Vampires allow us to see Hollywood—and America—as transnational in ways that other films often obscure.

Hollywood's reliance on professional standards to discredit competition extends discourses of national exceptionalism that diminishes the contributions of, and contestations by, immigrant and indigenous communities to US history. Assumptions that foreclose certain questions about Hollywood can benefit from self-reflection in other fields. "US policymakers depended upon the fantasy of American exceptionalism to authorize their practices of governance," explains Donald Pease, "but historians and literary scholars turned the beliefs imbedded within the fantasy into the principles of selection through which they decided what historical events they would allow representation within the historical record and which literary works they would include within the US canon" (2009: 11). Radway et al. focus on "ways that racialization and gender and sex discrimination have been fundamental to the construction of the American national subject" (2009: 1–6). Whether in textbooks in a university classroom or in clickbait "best films of all time" lists circulated through social media, canonization invariably consolidates historical distortions and misrepresentations. Vampire film and television becomes a site where omissions within national/nationalist discourse resurface within contradictory and inassiminable aspects of a postcolonial United States (cf. Singh and Schmidt 2000), suggesting reasons for the appearance of a vampire riding a skateboard in hijab alongside one refashioned as a poster boy for orientalism.

BIBLIOGRAPHY

Abu-Lughod, Lila (2013), *Do Muslim Women Need Saving?*, Cambridge, MA: Harvard University.

Ansen, David (1996), "Movies: Chinese takeout," *Newsweek* (19 February), p. 66.

Appadurai, Arjun (1995), *Modernity at Large: Cultural Dimensions of Globalization*, Minneapolis: University of Minnesota.

Arata, Stephen D. [1990] (1997), "The Occidental tourist: Dracula and the anxiety of reverse colonization," in Bram Stoker, *Dracula: A Norton Critical Edition*, ed. Nina Auerbach and David J. Skal, New York: W. W. Norton, pp. 462–70.

Auerbach, Nina (1995), *Our Vampires, Ourselves*, Chicago: University of Chicago.

Bahri, Deepika and Mary Vasudeva (1996), "Pedagogical alternatives: Issues in post-colonial studies: Interview with Gauri Viswanathan," in Deepika Bahri and Mary Vasudeva (eds), *Between the Lines: South Asians and Postcoloniality*, Philadelphia: Temple University, pp. 54–63.

Bazin, André [1958–62] (1971), *What is Cinema?*, trans. Hugh Gray, Berkeley: University of California.

Bogle, Donald (1973), *Toms, Coons, Mulattos, Mammies, and Bucks: An Interpretive History of Blacks in American Films*, New York: Viking.

Butler, Octavia E. (1976), *Fledgling*, New York: Grand Central.

Butler, Judith (1986), "Sex and gender in Simone de Beauvoir's *Second Sex*," *Yale French Studies* 72, pp. 35–49.

Carroll, Noël E. (1990), *The Philosophy of Horror, or Paradoxes of the Heart*, New York: Routledge.

Carter, Margaret L. (1988), *Dracula: The Vampire and the Critics*, Ann Arbor: UMI Research.

Chatterjee, Partha (1993), *The Nation and Its Fragments: Colonial and Postcolonial Histories*, Princeton: Princeton University.

Chaudhuri, Shohini (2005), *Contemporary World Cinema: Europe, Middle East, East Asia, South Asia,* Edinburgh: Edinburgh University.

Chion, Michel [1990] (1994), *Audio-vision: Sound on Screen*, trans. Claudia Gorbman, New York: Columbia University.

Chion, Michel [1982] (1999), *The Voice in Cinema*, trans. Claudia Gorbman, New York: Columbia University.

Clarens, Carlos (1967), *An Illustrated History of the Horror Film*, New York: Capricorn.

Coates, Paul (1991), *The Gorgon's Gaze: German Cinema, Expressionism, and the Image of Horror*, Cambridge: Cambridge University.

Connor, Walker (1994), "Man is a rational animal," in *Ethnonationalism: The Quest for Understanding*, Princeton: University of Princeton, pp. 195–209.

Craft, Christopher [1984] (1997), "'Kiss me with those red lips': Gender and inversion in Bram Stoker's *Dracula*," in Bram Stoker, *Dracula: A Norton Critical Edition*, ed. Nina Auerbach and David J. Skal, New York: W. W. Norton, pp. 444–66.

Daniels, Roger [1990] (2002), *Coming to America: A History of Immigration and Ethnicity in American Life*, 2nd edn, New York: Perennial/HarperCollins.

Davison, Carol Margaret (ed.) (1997), *Bram Stoker's Dracula: Sucking Through the Century, 1897–1997*, Toronto: Dundurn.

de la Mora, Sergio (2006), *Cinemachismo: Masculinities and Sexuality in Mexican Film*, Austin: University of Texas.

Deane, Hamilton and John L. Balderston (1993), *Dracula: The Vampire Play* [1927], in David J. Skal (ed.), *Dracula: The Ultimate, Illustrated Edition of the World-famous Vampire Play*, New York: St. Martin's.

Deleuze, Gilles and Félix Guattari [1980] (1987), *A Thousand Plateaus: Capitalism and Schizophrenia*, trans. Brian Massumi, Minneapolis: University of Minnesota.

Diawara, Manthia (1993), "Black American cinema: The new realism," in Manthia Diawara (ed.), *Black American Cinema*, New York: Routledge, pp. 3–25.

Eisner, Lotte H. (1952), *L'Ecran démoniaque: les influences de Max Reinhardt et de l'expressionnisme*, Paris: E. Losfeld.

Fanon, Frantz (1961), *Les Damnés de la terre*, Paris: François Maspero.

Foley, Neil (2012), "Becoming Hispanic: Mexican Americans and whiteness," in Paula S. Rothenberg (ed.) (2012), *White Privilege: Essential Readings on the Other Side of Racism*, 4th edn, New York: Worth, pp. 55–65.

Ganti, Tejaswini (2013), *Bollywood: A Guidebook to Popular Hindi Cinema*, 2nd edn, London: Routledge.

Gaonkar, Dilip Parameshwar (2001), "On alternative modernities," in Dilip Parameshwar Gaonkar (ed.), *Alternative Modernities*, Durham: Duke University, pp. 1–23.

García Espinosa, Julio [1969] (1983), "For an imperfect cinema," trans. Julianne Burton, in Michael Chanan (ed.), *25 Years of the New Latin American Cinema*, London: British Film Institute, pp. 28–33.

Gerow, Aaron (2010), *Visions of Japanese Modernity: Articulations of Cinema, Nation, and Spectatorship, 1895–1925*, Berkeley: University of California.

Gibson, Matthew (2006), *Dracula and the Eastern Question: British and French Vampire Narratives of the Nineteenth-Century Near East*, New York: Palgrave Macmillan.

Glover, David (2012), *Vampires, Mummies and Liberals: Bram Stoker and the Politics of Popular Fiction*, Durham: Duke University.

Goldsworthy, Vesna (1998), *Inventing Ruritania: The Imperialism of the Imagination*, New Haven: Yale University.

Gomez, Jewel (1991), *The Gilda Stories*, Ann Arbor: Firebrand.

Gómez, Laura (2007), *Manifest Destinies: The Making of the Mexican American Race*, New York: NYU.

Gopalan, Lalitha (2002), *Cinema of Interruptions: Action Genres in Contemporary Indian Cinema*, London: British Film Institute.

Gordon, Joan and Veronica Hollinger (eds) (1997), *Blood Read: The Vampire as Metaphor in Contemporary Culture*, Philadelphia: University of Pennsylvania.

Gross, Ariela (2010), *What Blood Won't Tell: A History of Race on Trial in America*, Cambridge, MA: Harvard University.

Hadimioglu, Çagla (2011), "Black tents" in Zoya Kocur (ed.), *Global Visual Cultures: An Anthology*, Chichester: Wiley-Blackwell, pp. 126–35.

Halberstam, Judith (1995), *Skin Shows: Gothic Horror and the Technology of Monsters*, Durham: Duke University.

Haney López, Ian F. (1996), *White by Law: The Legal Construction of Race*, New York: NYU.

Haraway, Donna J. (1996), "Universal donors in a vampire culture: It's all in the family: Biological kinship categories in the twentieth-century United States," in William Cronon (ed.), *Uncommon Ground: Rethinking the Human Place in Nature*, New York: W. W. Norton, pp. 321–66.

Haraway, Donna J. (2008), *When Species Meet*, Minneapolis: University of Minnesota.

Hardt, Michael and Antonio Negri (2004), *Multitude: War and Democracy in the Age of Empire*, New York: Penguin.

Hing, Bill Ong (2004), *Defining America through Immigration Policy*, Philadelphia: Temple University.

Jacobson, Matthew Frye (1998), *Whiteness of a Different Color: European Immigrants and the Alchemy of Race*, Cambridge, MA: Harvard University.

James, Henry [1907] (1968), *The American Scene*, Bloomington: Indiana University.

Kracauer, Siegfried (1947), *From Caligari to Hitler: A Psychological History of the German Film*, Princeton: Princeton University.

Kracauer, Siegfried [1960] (1997), *Theory of Film: The Redemption of Physical Reality*, Princeton: Princeton University.

Lewis, Martin W. and Kären E. Wigen (1997), *The Myth of Continents: A Critique of Metageography*, Berkeley: University of California.

McClelland, Bruce (2008), *Slayers and Their Vampires: A Cultural History of Killing the Dead*, Ann Arbor: University of Michigan.

MacDonald, D. L. (1991), *Poor Polidori: A Critical Biography of the Author of The Vampyre*, Toronto: University of Toronto.

McNally, David (2012), *Monsters of the Market: Zombies, Vampires and Global Capitalism*, London: Haymarket.

Majithia, Sheetal (2015), "Rethinking postcolonial melodrama and affect with Deepa Mehta's *Earth*," *Modern Drama* 58:1, pp. 1–23.

Marx, Karl [1867] (1990), *Capital: A Critique of Political Economy*, trans. Ben Fowkes, Harmondsworth: Penguin.

Mayall, David (1992), "British Gypsies and the state," *History Today* 42:6, p. 6.

Mbembe, Achille (2000), *De la Postcolonie, essai sur l'imagination politique dans l'Afrique contemporaine*, Paris: Karthala.

Memmi, Albert (1957), *Portrait du colonisé, précédé par Portrait du colonisateur*, Paris: Buchet/Chastel.

Miller, Toby, Nitin Govil, John McMurria, and Richard Maxwell (2005), *Global Hollywood 2*, London: British Film Institute.

Mitchell, Timothy (2011), *Carbon Democracy: Political Power in the Age of Oil*, London: Verso.

Murgoci, Agnes [1927] (1998), "The vampire in Roumania," in Alan Dundes (ed.), *The Vampire: A Casebook*, Madison: University of Wisconsin, pp. 47–56.

Naficy, Hamid (2011), *A Social History of Iranian Cinema, Volume 2: The Industrializing Years, 1941–1978*, Durham: Duke University.

Pease, Donald E. (2009), *The New American Exceptionalism*, Minneapolis: University of Minnesota.

Pirie, David (1972), *A Heritage of Horror: The English Gothic Cinema, 1946–1972*, London: Paul Hamlyn.

Pirie, David (1977), *The Vampire Cinema*. London: Paul Hamlyn.

Pratt, Mary Louise (2008), *Imperial Eyes: Travel Writing and Transculturation*, 2nd edn, New York: Routledge.

Prawer, S. S. (1980), *Caligari's Children: The Film as Tale of Terror*, Oxford: Oxford University.

Radway, Janice A., Kevin K. Gaines, Barry Shank, and Penny von Eschen (2009), "Introduction," in Janice A. Radway et al., *American Studies: An Anthology*, Malden: Wiley-Blackwell, pp. 1–6.

Rice, Anne (1976), *Interview with the Vampire*, New York: Alfred A. Knopf.

Rocha, Glauber [1965] (1983), "An aesthetics of hunger," trans. Burnes Hollyman and Randal Johnson, in Michael Chanan (ed.), *25 Years of the New Latin American Cinema*, London: British Film Institute, pp. 13–14.

Sadr, Hamid Reza (2006), *Iranian Cinema: A Political History*, London: I. B. Tauris.

Said, Edward W. (1978), *Orientalism*, New York: Vintage.

Said, Edward W. (1993), *Culture and Imperialism*, New York: Vintage.

Said, Edward W. [1981] (1997), *Covering Islam: How the Media and the Experts Determine How We See the Rest of the World*, new edn, New York: Vintage.

Sarris, Andrew [1968] (1996), *The American Cinema: Directors and Directions 1929– 1968*, New York: De Capo.

Schatz, Thomas (1981), *Hollywood Genres: Formulas, Filmmaking, and the Studio System*, New York: McGraw-Hill.

Schumacher, Michael (1999), *Francis Ford Coppola: A Filmmaker's Life*, New York: Crown.

Senf, Carol A. (1982), "*Dracula*: Stoker's response to the new woman," *Victorian Studies* 26, pp. 33–49.

Sharrett, Christopher (1996), "The horror film in neoconservative culture," in Barry Keith Grant (ed.), *The Dread of Difference: Gender and the Horror Film*, Austin: University of Texas, pp. 253–76.

Shohat, Ella and Robert Stam (1994), *Unthinking Eurocentrism: Multiculturalism and the Media*, New York: Routledge.

Silver, Alain and James Ursini (1975), *The Vampire Film*, South Brunswick: A. S. Barnes and Company.

Sinclair, Ian (1993), "Invasion of the blood," *Sight and Sound* 3:1, p. 15.

Singh, Amritjit and Peter Schmidt (2000), "On the borders between US studies and post-colonial theory," in Amritjit Singh and Peter Schmidt (eds), *Postcolonial Theory and the United States: Race, Ethnicity, and Literature*, Jackson: University of Mississippi, pp. 3–71.

Smith, Angela (2011), *Hideous Progeny: Disability, Eugenics, and Classic Horror Cinema*, New York: Columbia University.

Solanas, Fernando and Octavio Getino [1968] (1983), "Towards a third cinema: Notes and experiences from the development of a cinema of liberation in the third world," trans. Julianne Burton and Michael Chanan, in Michael Chanan (ed.), *25 Years of the New Latin American Cinema*, London: British Film Institute, pp. 17–28.

Stoker, Bram [1987] (1997), *Dracula: A Norton Critical Edition*, ed. Nina Auerbach and David J. Skal, New York: W. W. Norton.

Stuart, Roxana (1994), *Stage Blood: Vampires of the Nineteenth-century Stage*, Bowling Green: Bowling Green State University.

Todorova, Maria (1997), *Imagining the Balkans*, Oxford: Oxford University.

Trinh, T. Minh-ha (1992), *Framer Framed*, New York: Routledge.

Turner, Frederick Jackson (1920), *The Frontier in American History*, New York: Henry Holt.

Twitchell, James B. (1985), *Dreadful Pleasures: An Anatomy of Modern Horror*, Oxford: Oxford University.

Valente, Joseph (2002), *Dracula's Crypt: Bram Stoker, Irishness, and the Question of Blood*, Urbana: University of Illinois.

Vishwanathan, Gauri [1990] (2015), *Masks of Conquest: Literary Study and British Rule in India*, New York: Columbia University.

White, Luise (2000), *Speaking with Vampires: Rumor and History in Colonial Africa*, Berkeley: University of California.

Wilson, Katharina [1985] (1998), "The history of the word vampire," in Alan Dundes (ed.), *The Vampire: A Casebook*, Madison: University of Wisconsin, pp. 3–34.

Young, Robert J. C. (1995), *Colonial Desire: Hybridity in Theory, Culture, and Race*, London: Taylor and Francis.

POST-READING QUESTIONS/POST-SCREENING QUESTIONS

Directions: Use what you learned from reading this chapter and watching the film to respond to the questions.

1. What are one or two examples of historical events, provided by Dale Hudson, that parallel the release of specific vampire films in the history of Hollywood?

2. In your own words, explain how the author defines Hollywood and its geographic scope.

3. Hudson compares *A Girl Walks Home Alone at Night* with Bram Stoker's *Dracula.* Do you agree with the basis of his comparison? Explain why or why not.

4. How do you see the iterations of vampires changing over time, and how is this reflected in these two films?

"Nightmare Horrors and Perils of the Night"

Zombies and Modern Science

By Kristine Larsen

KEY TERMS AND FIGURES

Zombie

Post-enlightenment individualism

Gothic horror literature

Corrective science

Haitian voodoo

Slavery

Biopower

George A. Romero

RECOMMENDED FILMS

28 Days Later by Danny Boyle (2002)

Dawn of the Dead by George A. Romero (1978)

House of the Dead by Uwe Boll (2003)

Night of the Living Dead by George A. Romero (1968)

Resident Evil by Paul W. S. Anderson (2002)

The Walking Dead by Michael Curtiz (1936)

The White Zombie by Victor Halperin (1932)

INTRODUCTION

The zombie as a figure of abject horror has acquired several meanings since its first appearance in the 1932 film *The White Zombie*. But throughout its different forms of monstrous othering, it has steadfastly embodied our deepest fears of oppression and societal dissolution as human-created, if not engineered, processes. The pervasiveness and persistence of this particular monster attests to an awareness of human failure, as it is always humanity's actions, whether through rituals or mad science, that have resulted in a zombie infestation. As zombies and zombie scholarship have evolved over time and across widening media platforms, the most common representation points to the dangers of biopolitics when servicing Darwinian capitalist goals, warning us that nature and science's "corrective" in the twentieth and twenty-first centuries require a rethink, if not dismantling, of post-Enlightenment individualism. Most current scholarship dwells on the intersection of biopolitics and horror, drawing on Foucault's study of biopower, where large groups of humanity are controlled by various systems and regimes, which are then threatened and overcome by a viral zombie outbreak.

In this chapter, Kristin Larsen discusses the scientific causes of zombification explored in recent films, and the fears of science they reveal, tracing an evolution from the early cinematic zombies who still retained some human elements, to the present "post-human" figure, which emerged in the wake of WWII. Just as persistent as the zombie is the representation of the mad scientist, for which Larsen surveys films spanning six decades, from *The Walking Dead* to the *House of the Dead*, with special emphasis on zombie films from the 1980s until the early 2000s. The most notorious mad scientist she argues, is Herbert West in the *Re-animator* comedy film series (starting in 1985), whose motivation to defeat death by developing a re-animator serum led to flagrant disregard for the common ethical concerns meant to distinguish medical doctors from snake oil merchants.

In the 1980s, zombie films were frequently concerned with the violation of the sanctity of the human body, especially insofar as body parts are treated as commodities (in the 1985 *Return of the Living Dead*). Larsen points out we begin to see this in Romero's 1978 film *Dawn of the Dead*. While in the opening scene zombies in the housing project are given last rites, by the middle of the film once the group of survivors are living in the shopping mall, zombies are treated as objects devoid of any human trace, which must be disposed of as quickly as possible. She points out that where scientists objectify and treat the zombie body in the same way they treat lab rats, and soldiers treat the zombie as the enemy, other characters often ponder whether the zombie retains any human elements and is deserving of human rights, which pits them in direct opposition to the military industrial complex (and its scientific institutions). Fear of the unholy tryst between corporations and science, which results in the creation of zombies or their use "to control society as a whole" is often reflected in zombie films. Larsen reminds us that this is not exclusively the subject of fiction, as we know from the documented evidence of Nazi, Chinese, and US military and National Institute of Health (NIH) experiments on human subjects, to name a few, who were seen "as something other than human." All this has contributed to general mistrust among the public of science and scientific officials. Scientists in zombie films, Larsen argues, tend to differentiate zombies from humans, as other and inhuman, which she connects to the historical treatment by scientists of zombies as the underclass to domesticate them, reminiscent of the slave origins of the Haitian zombie.

Larsen repeatedly points out the influence of real-life transgressions of scientists (and science) on depictions of the zombie, from documented cases of illegal organ harvesting by coroners' offices and funeral homes for sale on the black market (*The Mad Ghoul* from 1943 and *The Chilling* from 1989) to the use of biochemical warfare on humans, evident in the long history of zombie films. The intersection of animal cloning, genetically modified food, and biochemical agents (as seen in *Resident Evil*) corresponds to real-life documented instances of the use of biochemical and biological warfare by armies to neutralize their enemies (WWI, Vietnam War, Iran/Iraq war, among others), a practice that Larsen dates back to the Tartar jettisoning of plague-ridden bodies over city walls in 1346 to infect the city of Kaffa. She concludes by reminding us that zombie media, like classic gothic horror literature, warn us about the potential abuse of science for personal, corporate, and political enrichment at the expense of ethical rights for humans and others.

| Figure 1.3.1 Still from *White Zombie* (1932)

| Figure 1.3.2 Image from Mumbai Film and Comic Con 2014

If there is any question why zombie horror has until recently belonged to the midnight B-movie category, the films Larsen describes should leave no doubt as to why. Zombies are neither organized nor charismatic monsters, and their promises do not include greater equity, better living conditions, or more humane social systems, but rather death, cannibalism, and an "existence" more abject than the most subaltern life. They illuminate unpredictability, against which the predictability of zombies seems far more benign. The persistent message is that humans are their own worst enemy.

Figure Credits

Fig. 1.3.1: Source: https://commons.wikimedia.org/wiki/File:White_Zombie_1932.jpg.

Fig. 1.3.2: Copyright © by Elroy Serrao (CC BY-SA 2.0) at https://commons.wikimedia.org/wiki/File:M-FCC_2014_-_Zombie_(15903954407).jpg.

"Nightmare Horrors and Perils of the Night"

Zombies and Modern Science

By Kristine Larsen

Science (so noble in origin and original purpose) has produced in alliance with sin nightmare horrors and perils of the night before which giants and demons grow pale. [1]

—J.R.R. Tolkien

In the second half of the twentieth century, the zombie has increasingly become the poster child for the collection of cinematic monsters that have captivated the imaginations of film directors and their audiences. From multiple encyclopaedic compendia and myriad graduate student theses to articles in *The Economist*, *Popular Mechanics*, and *Newsweek*, popular culture pundits and academics from across the disciplines are pondering the increasing popularity of these unlikely cinematic darlings. Zombies are devoid of social skills, aesthetic properties, and basic hygiene. They lack the eroticism of the vampire, and never ask their victims if they want to be "turned." Rather, they are usually portrayed as part of a mindless, marauding hoard driven by the single-minded primeval urge to feed on human flesh. But this has not always been the cinematic vision of the undead. In the first few decades of the zombie's film history, it was still recognizable as human, a silent, lumbering slave who often menaced rather than killed, and would never think (if they thought at all) of eating their victims. These early cinematic zombies were created using some semblance of traditional Haitian rituals, and even if their creator was a scientist, science had very little to do with it.

Then the world changed. On 16 July 1945, American scientists tested the first nuclear bomb, and less than a month later used this terrifying weapon on Japanese civilians in order to end World War II. At that first test in Alamogordo, New Mexico, lead physicist J. Robert

---

1 Verlyn Flieger and Douglas A. Anderson, *Tolkien on Fairy-stories* (London: Harper Collins, 2008), p. 269.

Oppenheimer recalled a quotation from the Hindu scripture, *The Bhagavad Gita*: "Now I am become death, the destroyer of worlds."[2] While Oppenheimer later admitted that he was "a little scared of what I had made,"[3] and tried (in vain) along with many of his Manhattan Project colleagues to prevent the development of the even more destructive hydrogen "super" bomb, he hid behind the party line of scientists in claiming that he (and they) could not be held accountable for the misuse of their discoveries. "If you are a scientist," he argued, "you believe that it is good to find out how the world works; that it is good to find out what the realities are; that it is good to turn over to mankind at large the greatest possible power to control the world. …"[4] Some scientists may earnestly believe that the situation is so clearly black and white, but as the arts have shown us, the world is filled with fascinating shades of grey. Science does not exist in a vacuum; rather, it is the vocation of *scientists*, who, as humans, are certainly not infallible. While, as Tolkien noted, the goal of science may be noble in principle, scientists as individuals cannot be expected to be any nobler than the general public, especially when their funding is provided by large military complexes or global corporations (whose motivations are certainly considered less than noble in the eyes of the general public).

Enter the stereotype of the mad scientist, overstepping the bounds of what is "natural" and falling into the trap of "playing God." Since the publication of Mary Shelley's *Frankenstein* in 1818, some in the general public have looked at the scientific establishment with suspicious eyes. Modern marvels such as genetic engineering, nuclear energy, and nanotechnology only further their mistrust of science, as they see the modern equivalent of a genie released from its bottle with little thought as to the possible outcomes. A significant percentage of the general public worries, based on what surveys demonstrate is an incomplete understanding of the basic science,[5] if the Large Hadron Collider will create a black hole that could destroy the earth. They question why the US military stockpiles smallpox and anthrax in high security laboratories, and question the wisdom of changing the genetic structure of bacteria, crops, and livestock. It appears that with each scientific advance there seems to be yet another theoretical opportunity for the world to destroy itself, whether through nuclear holocaust, pandemic, or deadly material returned to our planet through some space mission. The modern zombie can therefore be thought of as the bastard child of science, a metaphor for the horrors—both real and perceived—that may unintentionally befall humanity as a result of cutting-edge scientific research. The methods of zombification portrayed in films in recent decades reflect the general public's fears about what many believe modern science has (or has the potential

---

2   "J. Robert Oppenheimer Interview," *A.J. Software and Multimedia*, http://www.atomicarchive.com/Movies/Movie8.shtml, accessed 3 January 2011.

3   Gerard J. De Groot, *The Bomb* (Cambridge, MA: Harvard University Press, 2005), p. 112.

4   Ibid.

5   The National Science Board has been tracking the public's attitudes towards and knowledge of science for several decades. *Science and Engineering Indicators: 2010* can be found at http://www.nsf.gov.statistics/seind10.

to) become, especially in partnerships with military and corporate institutions—the so-called "military industrial complex." This essay will explore examples of some of the most widely-used "scientific" causes of zombification, and illustrate how these films reflect real-world concerns of science and ethics.

The number of zombie films which feature archetypal mad scientists is legion. Two representative examples separated by six decades are *The Walking Dead* (1936) and *House of the Dead* (2003). In the former, Boris Karloff stars as an executed prisoner who is resurrected by an unscrupulous scientist obsessed with the secrets of life and death. The more recent film centres on college students who attend an ill-fated rave on a mysterious island and become the prisoners of an evil scientist who has developed an immortality serum which he has not only used on himself, but also has used to create zombies. Some works openly embrace the Frankenstein comparison, as in the case of George A. Romero's *Day of the Dead* (1985), where the mentally unbalanced scientist Dr. Logan is openly referred to as "Frankenstein" by both his fellow scientists and the military personnel sharing their bunker. In Robin Becker's 2010 novel *Brains: a Zombie Memoir*, the scientist who develops the zombie-creating biochemical agent is named Dr. Howard Stein. Former English professor-turned-zombie Dr. Jack Barnes refers to Stein as "my creator. Our father, Mad Scientist Extraordinaire. God in the Garden of Evil."[6] Like Shelley's protagonist, Howard Stein spurns his creation, explaining to Jack that he and the other still-cognisant zombies are "a mistake. Something out of *Frankenstein*."[7]

Perhaps the most (in)famous mad scientist of zombie films is Herbert West of the *Re-animator* series. Loosely based on a short story by H.P. Lovecraft, the original film introduced audiences to the megalomaniac young scientist West and his glow-in-the-dark green reanimating reagent. With a complete disregard for both the ethical mores of the medical establishment and the Miskatonic Medical School student handbook, West conducts his reanimation experiments on both animals and humans—seen by him as simply objects on which to test his serum—without seeming concern for either the wishes of those experimented on or the unpredictable and unstable results of these experiments. "I've conquered brain death," he boasts to roommate and fellow medical student Dan Cain. "We can defeat death. We can even achieve every doctor's dream and live lifetimes."[8] While it can be debated whether or not West was right about physicians' aspirations, the viewer can certainly interpret the film as a cautionary tale against unrestricted, profit-driven medical research, especially such experiments in which the unwilling participants have not given their informed expressed consent.

---

6   Robin Becker, *Brains: A Zombie Memoir* (New York: Eos, 2010), p. 4.

7   Becker, *Brains*, p. 178.

8   Dennis Paoli, William J. Norris, and Stuart Gordon, *Re-animator*, directed by Stuart Gordon (1985; Troy, MI: Anchor Bay Entertainment, 2007), DVD.

In *Film, Horror, and the Body Fantastic*, Linda Bradley sees *Re-animator* and similar works from the 1980s as reflecting not only on the objectification but the intentional commoditisation of the human body, both as a whole and as a semblance of pieces. For example, in *Re-animator* West injects the head and decapitated corpse of rival scientist Hill, noting with enthusiasm "Yes, parts. I've never done whole parts."[9] In *The Return of the Living Dead* (1985) the reanimating gas causes individual body parts and dogs sliced in half for medical school demonstrations to move on their own. In Bradley's words, "the horror and the real monster had become the body itself."[10] The zombie horrifies us not only because it wants to eat our flesh, but because it violates the presumed sanctity of the body, and robs us of the promise of a peace after death—so much for "rest in peace." In the early scenes of *Dawn of the Dead*, corpses are not objectified, but initially humanised, given last rites and covered in shrouds before being locked into a low-income housing unit's basement storage cage, despite the fact that the next-of-kin know what their family members will become. "Why do these people keep them here?" Roger asks. Fellow SWAT team member Peter explains, "because they still believe there's respect in death."[11] As long as one considers zombies as human, there is an emotional attachment, and disposing of the bodies in a violent and callous way (beheading or burning) becomes difficult. However, as the epidemic spreads and the main characters (the two SWAT team members and two television journalists) barricade themselves in a shopping mall, the zombies are increasingly seen as (and treated like) objects, an admittedly dangerous form of trash that must be unceremoniously disposed of. The zombies—useless commodities—stand in stark opposition to the riches of the mall's stores and restaurants which sustain the characters over several months.

Similar to *Dawn of the Dead*'s mall dwellers, cinematic scientists have no compunctions about dispatching zombies, often after having conducted vivisection or other experiments upon them. These scientists are portrayed as logical, detached, and mechanical. Just as they can inflict pain on a lab rat in the name of science, or disembowel a cadaver with clinical precision, scientists in zombie movies are above thinking of zombies as human. Similarly, a soldier thinks of the zombie as the enemy, a target to be eliminated. But in many zombie films, some characters openly consider whether or not zombies actually retain some of their humanity, and therefore are still deserving of basic human rights. This way of thinking puts these characters in direct opposition to the military and scientific perspectives depicted in the films. For example, in the 2006 Canadian dark comedy *Fido*, Jon Bottoms, a nefarious former Zombie Wars hero and ZomCon head of security, visits a school classroom. Young Timmy Robinson asks if zombies are dead or alive. Bottoms warns Timmy and the other children that although

---

9   Ibid.

10   Linda Bradley, *Film, Horror, and the Body Fantastic* (Westport, CT: Greenwood Press, 1995), pp. 73–74.

11   George A. Romero, *Dawn of the Dead*, directed by George A. Romero (1978; Troy, MI: Anchor Bay Entertainment, 2004), DVD.

"to some people zombies might seem human," they are in fact "creatures [with] only one goal, and that is to eat your flesh."[12] In *Night of the Living Dead*, Dr. Grimes dispassionately describes an experiment in which a cadaver whose four limbs had been amputated came back to life. He calmly instructs people to dispose immediately of all corpses through burning, and that "the bereaved will have to forgo the dubious comfort that a funeral service will give. They're just dead flesh, and dangerous."[13] While corpses are only seen as dangerous in works of art such as film and literature, corpses themselves are sometimes seen by some *as* works of art, or more basely as cash-generating commodities to be bought and displayed, for example in exhibits of plastinated corpses and body parts such as *Bodies Revealed* and *Human Body Worlds*. In the case of at least one such exhibit, *Bodies: the Exhibition*, there have been allegations that the bodies were those of Chinese prisoners procured from the black market.[14]

Not only are entire bodies procured without the consent of the deceased or their kin (as was done in past centuries in the case of grave robbers supplying cadavers to medical schools), but individual body parts can likewise be illegally obtained. The infamous "Travellers Beware" viral email from 1997 purported to tell the true story of business travellers waking up in a bathtub of ice and missing a kidney. This urban legend is possibly based on a 1989 news story out of London about a Turkish citizen who claimed he was lured to London under false pretence and had a kidney stolen. However, it turned out that he had in fact advertised his kidney for sale in a Turkish newspaper.[15] There have been a number of large-scale black market organ rings broken up across the world in the past few decades, in which profit-driven doctors prey on poor, uneducated people as the unwilling (or at least uninformed) donors, and rich and desperate Westerners as the recipients of the ill-gotten organs. For example, the World Health Organization estimates than a fifth of the 70,000 transplanted kidneys each year are illegally procured.[16] But shadowy black markets are not the sole illegal source of human body parts and tissues. In 1997 it was disclosed that the Los Angeles County Coroner's Office was harvesting corneas from corpses and selling them to tissue banks without the next-of-kin's consent.[17] Unscrupulous funeral home and crematorium directors, as well as employees at one noted

---

12   Robert Chomiak, Andrew Currie, and Dennis Heaton, *Fido*, directed by Andrew Currie (2006; Santa Monica, CA: Lionsgate, 2007), DVD.

13   George A. Romero and John A. Russo, *Night of the Living Dead,* directed by George A. Romero (1968; New York: The Weinstein Company, 2008), DVD.

14   Brian Ross, Rhonda Schwartz, and Anna Schecter, "N.Y., China Investigating Black Market in Bodies," *ABC News* (15 February 2008), http://abcnews.go.com/id=4296982, accessed 3 January 2011.

15   Barbara Mikkelson and David P. Mikkelson, "You've Got To Be Kidneying," (12 March 2008), http://www.snopes.com/horrors/robbery/kidney.asp, accessed 3 January 2011.

16   Janeen Interlandi, "Not Just an Urban Legend," *Newsweek* (10 January 2009), http://www.newsweek.com/2009/0109/not-just-urban-legend.html, accessed 3 January 2011.

17   Karen Brandon, "Mortician Accused of Selling Body Parts," *Chicago Tribune* (25 February 2002), http://articles.chicagotribune.com/2002-02-25/news/0202250134_1_michael-francis-brown-corneas-body-parts, accessed 3 January 2011.

medical school, have succumbed to the high prices which pharmaceutical companies, surgical instrument companies, and tissue banks are willing to pay for human tissues and body parts.[18]

Zombie films have long capitalised on the public's fears about illegal organ harvesting. For example, in *The Mad Ghoul* (1943), mad scientist Dr. Morris uses fresh human hearts (and an ancient Egyptian poison) to reanimate corpses, while in *Doctor Blood's Coffin* (1960) the eponymous medical student transplants hearts cut from the chests of still-living donors into dead bodies in order to reanimate them. The zombie film *Monstrosity* (1963) tells the story of a mad scientist who aids an elderly woman in her plot to transplant her brain into a more youthful body. New York police follow a trail of missing body parts and mutilated corpses to a zombie-creating mad scientist in *Dr. Butcher, M.D.* (1980), while in *The Chilling* (1989) the president of a cryogenics laboratory sells the organs of those he is supposed to be protecting in cold storage, until a freak storm turns the frozen patients into zombies. In the misuse of human tissues and organs, profit is the underlying motivation. There is money to be made, and there are those in the medical community who ignore both morality and legality in order to profit from such activities.

While capitalism is generally favoured over other economic systems by most Americans, the general public is all-too-aware of the inherent dangers of large corporations insinuating themselves into our lives (at the cost of all other competition). For example, there are those who refuse to shop at Walmart and refer to Microsoft as the "Evil Empire," choosing to use other computer products whenever possible just on principle. In several recent zombie films, the intersection of science and profit plays a central role, in the guise of unethical super-corporations whose activities either create the zombies, or use the zombies as an excuse to control society as a whole. The first film in the *Resident Evil* series (2002) begins with a confidential file on the Umbrella Corporation, outlining the scope of its influence. It is described as a ubiquitous commercial enterprise that is funded by the military and specialises in genetic experimentation and viral technology.[19]

As Alice, the heroine of the series, slowly regains her memory throughout the film, the viewer learns that she had planned to steal the Umbrella Corporation's bio-engineered T-virus from the subterranean Hive laboratory in order to bring down the all-powerful unethical corporation (whose trademark can be found on everything from bullets to wedding rings in the film). Spence (like Alice, a security officer who was supposed to be guarding the mansion entrance to the Hive) actually steals the virus and antivirus for monetary gain. Despite the damage the T-virus does to the planet once it escapes from the Hive, the Umbrella Corporation

---

18   Alan Zarembo and Jessica Garrison, "Profit Drives Illegal Trade in Body Parts," *LA Times* (7 March 2004), http://articles. latimes.com/2004/mar/07/local/me-parts7, accessed 3 January 3, 2011.

19   Paul W.S. Anderson, *Resident Evil*, directed by Paul W.S. Anderson (2002; Culver City, CA: Sony Home Entertainment, 2008), DVD.

continues to experiment with its deadly product in the remaining films in the series. Their goal is not to cure what remains of humanity, but instead to control both the zombies and the human survivors, and therefore rule the world. In *Resident Evil: Afterlife* (2010), Umbrella Corporation chief Albert Wesker injects Alice with a serum which neutralises the T-virus, thus deactivating the telekinetic and extrasensory powers, superhuman strength, extreme agility, and seemingly limitless healing ability the virus had granted her. "Umbrella Corporation is taking back its property," he sneers. "You didn't work out, so you're being recalled."[20] Although Alice is clearly being referred to as a product, a thing, she actually thanks Wesker for returning her humanity to her. In the eyes of the corporation, their exclusive virus (with which they had intentionally infected her) had turned her into a commodity; hence she is often referred to as "Project Alice" by Umbrella scientists and executives throughout the series. Alice recognises that she has been dehumanised by this process, by the experiments that were done upon her without her knowledge or consent, and therefore welcomes the chance to be cured of what she considers to be a disease.

A less overtly evil (but equally manipulative) science-based corporation is *Fido*'s ZomCon. The film opens with a black and white newsreel extolling the virtues of ZomCon and its role in winning the Zombie Wars, as well as its centrality in securing the safety of the suburban way of life. ZomCon controls not only the zombies, but every aspect of society, from burials to school curricula, and the ZomCon logo appears on items from cars to caskets. The society of *Fido* is reminiscent of George Orwell's *1984* and similar dystopias in the way that information is controlled and spun for public consumption. In one of the more disturbing references in the film, Ray and Stan, the school bullies, are uniformed "ZomCon Cadets," an organisation which appears to owe more to the Hitler Youth than the Boy Scouts (including violence against those who do not follow the ZomCon party line).

One cannot raise the spectre of the Nazi Party without considering the horrors they propagated on humanity. One class of atrocities in particular was done with the help of science, namely human experimentation. Although a complete examination of the barbaric experiments perpetrated on concentration camp victims is certainly beyond the scope of this work[21] (as is a detailed exploration of a subgenre of zombie films that feature Nazis), it should be noted that they included (but were not limited to) the intentional infliction of gangrene and mustard gas wounds; infecting victims with malaria and typhus; simulations of high altitude (low oxygen) conditions; freezing experiments; forcing victims to drink sea water; and Josef Mengele's infamous experiments on twins. However, despite the fact that the Nazi experiments are

---

20   Paul W.S. Anderson, *Resident Evil: Afterlife*, directed by Paul W.S. Anderson (2010; Culver City, CA: Sony Home Entertainment, 2010), DVD.

21   A more detailed study of Nazi human experiments can be found in Vivien Spitz, *Doctors from Hell: the Horrific Account of Nazi Experiments on Humans* (Boulder, CO: Sentient Publications, 2005) and Lucette Matalon Lagnado and Sheila Cohn Dekel, *Children of the Flames: Dr. Josef Mengele and the Untold Story of the Twins of Auschwitz* (New York: Morrow, 1991).

perhaps the most well-known (thanks in part to the Nuremberg Trials), they are by no means isolated cases in the twentieth century. For example, during the Second Sino-Japanese War (1937–1945) and World War II, Japan's Unit 731 did their own experiments on the effects of freezing conditions on the human body (using Chinese prisoners of war) and studied the effects of plague and other diseases on the human body through the vivisection of both living and dead Chinese victims (some of the former without the benefit of anaesthesia).[22]

Nor was the United States above conducting secret (and not-so-secret) human experiments without the informed consent of the participants. Between 1950 and 1975 the US Army conducted experiments on nearly 7,000 human subjects which studied the effects of nerve gas, psychotropic chemicals, and pain killers as incapacitating agents for use in warfare.[23] But by far the most infamous example of American human experimentation is the "Tuskegee Study of Untreated Syphilis in the Negro Male," a forty-year study conducted by scientists associated with the US Public Health Service of the effects of syphilis on over 400 African-American men in Alabama who were not even told that they had the disease. What is perhaps most alarming about this event is that it was not concealed, but in fact was openly discussed in medical journals and conferences. It was not until the media caught wind of the study that it was quickly ended in the 1970s.[24] A lingering side effect of this study is a distrust of the medical establishment by a segment of the African-American community, including a persistent urban legend that AIDS was created by the US government specifically to infect African-Americans.[25] In 2010, medical historian and Tuskegee experiment expert Susan Reverby of Wellesley College uncovered an eerily similar experiment in Guatemala funded by the US National Institutes of Health. Between 1946 and 1948 nearly 700 Guatemalan prisoners and mental hospital patients were infected with syphilis in order to test the effects of penicillin on disease prevention.[26]

Psychologists have studied these instances of institutionalised abuse and have found that perpetrators often justify the abuse by visualising and referring to the victims as something other than human, or as humans of somehow less intrinsic value than him or herself. For example, Japanese researchers in Unit 731 not only viewed the Chinese prisoners as intrinsically inferior to Japanese citizens, but in documents referred to the Chinese prisoners as "research material," "monkeys," or even "logs."[27] Similarly Nazi scientists viewed the concentration camp victims (Jews, Roma, homosexuals, and other marginalised and oppressed groups) as less than

---

22   Gerhard Baader, Susan E. Lederer, Morris Low, Florian Schmaltz, and Alexander V. Schwerin, "Pathways to Human Experimentation, 1933–1945: Germany, Japan, and the United States," *Osiris* 20 (2005), p. 221.

23   Jonathan D. Moreno, *Undue Risk* (New York: W.H. Freeman, 2000), p. 251.

24   James H. Jones, *Bad Blood*, rev. ed. (New York: Free Press, 1993), p. 7.

25   Jones, *Bad Blood*, pp. 220–21.

26   Donald G. NcNeil, Jr., "US Apologizes for Syphilis Tests in Guatemala," *New York Times* (1 October 2010), http://www.nytimes.com/2010/10/02/health/research/02infect.html, accessed January 3, 2011.

27   Baader et al., "Pathways to Human Experimentation," p. 223.

human, for example referring to the female inmates at the Ravensbrück concentration camp as "rabbit girls."[28]

As previously noted, in a number of zombie films, scientists are depicted as accentuating the differences between humans and zombies (in a clearly hierarchical schemata), labelling them as "other" and inhuman. This opens the door to all manner of gruesome scientific experimentation on zombies (and other humans) in the name of science. For example, in *Dawn of the Dead*, the scientist character known in popular culture circles as "Patchy" explains without emotion that zombies are not cannibals because cannibalism occurs within a species. "These creatures cannot be considered human," he explains. "They prey on humans. They do not prey on each other."[29] As previously noted, in the *Resident Evil* series, Alice is clearly viewed as a commodity, Umbrella Corporation property, and an experiment. Not only does she lack control over what is done to her own body, but over her very genetic code as well. In *Resident Evil: Extinction* (2007), Dr. Isaacs creates dozens (if not hundreds) of Alice clones, who one by one die during the course of experiments he runs upon them. When one particular clone fails to survive the test (a series of battles against mutants and machines), Isaacs instructs his assistants to "get rid of that," and the clone is unceremoniously dumped into a cement ravine along with innumerable other clones.[30] The visual similarity to photographs of the disposal of concentration camp victims is certainly intentional. The Alice clones are perceived to be expendable laboratory materials, akin to bacteria being studied in a petri dish, and can therefore be discarded like ordinary trash.

Similarly, much of *Day of the Dead* centres around Dr. "Frankenstein" Logan's experiments on the zombies. Although Logan explains that "they are us," his treatment of his "specimens" (referred to as "dumb-fucks" by the military in this subterranean research facility) is less than humane.[31] In one experiment he has severed all the vital organs in a zombie's torso, leaving it basically just limbs and a brain. In another he has removed the head with the exception of the brain. A fellow scientist, Sarah Bowman, criticises Logan for what she considers pointless experiments, and is further horrified to learn that the zombie whose skull and face were removed is not a "wild" zombie but in fact the former military commander of the facility, who had recently died from a zombie attack.

While the experiments conducted on zombies reflect the general inhumanity of human experimentation in the twentieth century,[32] a number of these experiments have a particular goal—to domesticate and control the zombies as one might an animal or a slave. The potential

---

28   Baader et al., "Pathways to Human Experimentation," p. 230.

29   Romero, *Dawn of the Dead.*

30   Paul W.S. Anderson, *Resident Evil: Extinction*, directed by Russell Mulcahy (2007; Culver City, CA: Sony Home Entertainment, 2008), DVD.

31   George A. Romero, *Day of the Dead*, directed by George A. Romero (1985; Troy, MI: Anchor Bay Entertainment, 2003), DVD.

32   Animal experimentation and animal rights is, of course, an important related topic which is not considered here except in passing simply due to considerations of the essay's length.

for zombies to serve as a slave underclass harkens back to the original Haitian zombie, who had lost his will and personality and was under the complete control of the voodoo master. Early zombie films relied heavily on this archetype, for example *White Zombie* (1932), generally considered the first film of the genre. *Day of the Dead*'s Dr. Logan justifies his experiments as searching for a way that a zombie could be "domesticated. It can be conditioned to behave, the way we want it to behave."[33] Indeed, he succeeds in getting the zombie he nicknames Bub to mimic shaving and telephone usage, and Bub even remembers how to use a gun (much to the chagrin of the vicious Captain Rhodes). Logan's experiments mirror B.F. Skinner-type conditioning experiments done on rats and pigeons, with an added twist—to reinforce Bub's good behaviour he rewards the zombie with his favourite food, pieces of human flesh.

The domestication of zombies is also the stated goal of some of Dr. Isaacs' experiments in *Resident Evil: Extinction*. Isaacs injects zombie subjects with a special serum which is meant to return some intelligence and memories to the zombies and suppress their desire for human flesh. He explains to the Umbrella Corporation Board that the zombies are "animals, essentially. We can train them, if we can take away their baser instincts. They'll never be human"; however they would provide the "basis for a docile workforce."[34] He successfully tests the intelligence and problem-solving skills of zombie subjects, such as using a camera and cell phone; however, one becomes frustrated by the task of trying to fit a square peg into a round hole and attacks the lab technicians.

Zombies are used as mindless (literally) menial labourers in two other recent films, *Fido* and *Shaun of the Dead* (2004). In the former, the ubiquitous ZomCon corporation uses science and technology to solve the zombie problem through the domestication collar, which contains the zombies' desire for human flesh, "making the zombie as gentle as a household pet."[35] Zombies are used as gardeners and household servants, to entertain children, and to deliver newspapers. Some are treated like pets (for example, being kept on a leash), and the title character (named by Timmy Robinson, his owner's son) is actually chained outside and taunted like a neglected dog. At the end of *Shaun of the Dead*, fictional television reports and programming demonstrate how the subdued zombie population is being used to collect shopping carts in parking lots and other simple tasks, and for entertainment (for example, as easily-ridiculed targets on reality shows). Shaun keeps his best friend Ed (now a zombie) chained in the backyard shed to have someone to play video games against. The objectification of zombies (and the accompanying loss of basic human rights) is a central theme in S.G. Browne's 2009 novel *Breathers: A Zombie's Lament*, in which zombies not only lose their social security numbers, but the rights to surf the internet, ride public transportation, and be seen alone in public. The main zombie character,

---

33　Romero, *Day of the Dead.*

34　Anderson, *Resident Evil: Extinction.*

35　Chomiak, Currie, and Heaton, *Fido.*

Andy Warner, spends much of the novel being picked up and caged by Animal Control for his civil disobedience, and is frequently threatened by his mortified parents with being given to zoos, medical schools, "plastic surgery chop shops," or crash test dummy facilities.[36] Once again, the comparison between zombies and lab animals is intentional. A connection can also be drawn to the 2002 British film *28 Days Later*. Here the source of the zombie (or at least zombie-like behaviour) outbreak is the so-called Rage virus, which is accidently unleashed when animal rights activists try to liberate animals from a laboratory in which the virus is being tested.

Animals have been front and centre in another of the twentieth century's controversial scientific achievements, genetic engineering. From the cloning of Dolly the sheep to the production of strains of mice genetically engineered to exhibit such human traits as baldness, obesity, and propensities for various cancers, and even the creation of a glow-in-the-dark rabbit, scientists have been able to modify the genetic code of myriad plants and animals for the perceived benefit of society. Disease-resistant wheat and vitamin-enriched rice may reduce starvation and malnutrition in Third World countries, but in many industrialised nations such genetically modified foods are viewed with suspicion at best, and through conspiracy theory lenses at worst. One of the most vocal opponents has been Britain's Prince Charles, who accused genetic engineering of taking us into "realms that belong to God and God alone."[37] A 2010 poll of 3,000 Americans found that 93% felt that genetically modified food should be labelled as such and only 38% expressed a willingness to eat genetically modified meat products.[38] Such uncertainties are reflected in the 2005 film *Severed: Forest of the Dead*, in which the sap from genetically-engineered lumber trees creates zombies.

The public's concerns regarding another specific application of genetic engineering—cloning—has also been measured by pollsters. For example, in a 2004 Opinion Research Corporation poll 84% of those surveyed opposed the commercial cloning of pets.[39] Two years later, the Genetic Savings and Clone company stopped taking orders for cloning cats after only six years in operation. The National Science Foundation's *2010 Science and Engineering Indicators* surveys found that 78% of Americans oppose genetically engineering or cloning humans.[40] In addition to the charge that such experiments are tantamount to "playing God," opposition to human modifications centres around such ethical and theological issues as whether clones have souls, whether they deserve the same basic rights as other humans, whether clones could be

---

36   S.G. Browne, *Breathers: A Zombie's Lament* (New York: Three Rivers Press, 2009), p. 81; p. 181.

37   Jeff Randall, "Prince Charles warns GM crops risk causing the biggest-ever environmental disaster," *The Telegraph* (August 12, 2008), http://www.telegraph.co.uk/earth/earthnews/3349308/Prince-Charles-warns-GM-crops-risk-causing-the-biggest-ever-environmental-disaster.html, accessed 3 January 2011.

38   "National Survey of Healthcare Consumers: Genetically Engineered Food," *Thomas Reuters* (October 2010), http://www.factsforhealthcare.com/pressroom/NPR_report_GeneticEngineeredFood.pdf, accessed 3 January 2011.

39   "Animal and Pet Cloning Opinion Polls," *Center for Genetics and Society* (4 April 2005), http://www.geneticsandsociety.org/article.php?id=470, accessed 3 January 2011.

40   National Science Board, *Science and Engineering Indicators*, pp. 7–41.

used as organ banks for the wealthy, and if such technologies could be used to develop a race of perfect soldiers. A number of countries, including the United States and United Kingdom, have banned the cloning of adult humans,[41] and bioethicist Arlene Judith Klotzko notes that "any scientist who actively engages in cloning humans in order to create a new human being risks being branded a 'mad scientist'."[42]

Such a label certainly fits Dr. Isaacs and the other scientists of the *Resident Evil* series. In the first film, the holographic Red Queen explains that the Umbrella Corporation's bio-engineered T-virus has both "medical and military applications."[43] Renegade security officer Spence is killed by the mutant creature known as the Licker, called one of the Hive's "early and unstable experiments." Once the Licker feeds on Spence, it incorporates his DNA and mutates once again into a "better, faster hunter." When Matt, an activist who is also trying to bring down the Umbrella Corporation, is scratched by the Licker, he too begins to mutate, and the Umbrella Corporation Clean Team takes him away to become part of the "Nemesis program."[44] In the second film, *Resident Evil: Apocalypse* (2004) Matt has completely transformed into a grotesque monster, and is made to fight Alice, whose own exposure to the T-virus has mutated her in a different manner, but one which the Umbrella scientists realise might be militarily as valuable. When Alice successfully appeals to the last shred of humanity left in Matt/Nemesis, he is killed by the Umbrella forces.[45]

As described above, Isaacs continues to experiment on the T-virus and the zombies it creates, under the guise of domesticating them for the Umbrella Corporation. His true motivations are to recapture Alice at any cost after she is allowed to escape, and to use his serum and her DNA to create a species of super-zombies under his control. As he explains to an Umbrella bureaucrat who questions the aggression of his zombies, "some aggression has its uses." His new tests focus on clones of Alice, which he treats like lab rats, forcing them to negotiate a maze of mortal dangers. When clone number 87 momentarily appears successfully to reach the final stage of the test, Isaacs gloats that his research "will change the face of everything,"[46] only to be faced with yet another failure. When Isaacs is bitten by one of his super-zombies, he injects himself with an overdose of the anti-virus, and mutates into a grotesque physical form worthy of his inner monstrosity. He taunts Alice with the fact that even though he used to think she was the future, he has come to understand that his new form is the true realisation of that goal. In the next film in the series (2010's *Resident Evil: Afterlife*), the nefarious Andrew Wesker has become

---

41   Cloning of embryonic stem cells is also regulated to varying degrees, and is a controversial subject in its own right.

42   Arlene Judith Klotzko, *A Clone of Your Own? The Science and Ethics of Cloning* (Cambridge: Cambridge University Press, 2000), p. xxi.

43   Anderson, *Resident Evil.*

44   Ibid.

45   Paul W.S. Anderson, *Resident Evil: Apocalypse*, directed by Alexander Will (2004, Culver City, CA: Sony Home Entertainment, 2008), DVD.

46   Anderson, *Resident Evil: Extinction.*

a mutant through exposure to the T-virus, and seeks to "ingest" Alice in order to regain control over the virus within his body. In keeping with the Umbrella Corporation's patent disregard for human dignity, the tanker ship Arcadia sails the Pacific coastline kidnapping uninfected survivors in order to have fresh specimens for their scientific experiments.[47]

Biochemical agents and genetic engineering are used to create an army of zombie soldiers in a number of other films. For example, in *Shock Waves* (1977), the legendary Peter Cushing plays a Nazi officer who was responsible for a band of indestructible undead storm troopers called the Death Corps. Dr. Hill's ultimate plan in *Re-animator* is to use West's reagent and his own laser lobotomy procedure to create an army of zombies who will give him "undreamed of power."[48] A group of teenagers attempt to rescue a friend from Hybra Tech's experiments with Trioxin 5 in *Return of the Living Dead: Necropolis* (2005), and discover the corporation's plot to create an army of zombie soldiers. The creation of zombie soldiers by the US Army during the Vietnam War is central to the plotline of *Automaton Transfusion* (2006), and *Flight of the Living Dead: Outbreak on a Plane* (2007) featured a genetically engineered mutation of malaria (incorrectly referred to as a virus) which was intended to produce soldiers who could continue to fight even after dying.

While one can argue whether or not the general public's fear of possible military misuses of genetic engineering are well-founded or not, there is no doubt that the possibility of biochemical agents being used either against soldiers or civilians is a very real threat in the twenty-first century. From the use of mustard gas in World War I to napalm in the Vietnam War and Sarin in the war between Iran and Iraq in the 1980s, chemicals have been used to kill, disfigure, and incapacitate both on the battlefield and beyond. But biological warfare is older still, dating back to the Tartars' catapulting of plague-ridden corpses over the city walls into the city of Kaffa in 1346. The plague was also used in biological warfare in World War II, when Japan's Unit 731 dropped canisters containing plague-infected fleas on the Chinese countryside.[49] In the years since the end of the Cold War, information has slowly come to light concerning the United States and Soviet biological warfare programs, including the possible genetic engineering of bacterial strains which are antibiotic resistant and target specific ethnic groups.[50] In addition to these artificial biological weapons, the Centre for Disease Control has identified approximately sixty pathogens which have the potential for use in biological warfare, including anthrax, typhoid fever, plague, Ebola, and smallpox.

Any thoughts that biological warfare or bio-terrorism could be prevented in the United States were quashed in the fall of 2001, when anthrax-laden letters killed five people and sickened

---

47   Anderson, *Resident Evil: Afterlife*.

48   Paoli, Norris, and Gordon, *Re-animator.*

49   Committee on Homeland Security, *Engineering Bio-Terror Agents: Lessons From the Offensive US and Russian Biological Weapons Programs* (Washington D.C.: US Government Printing Office, 2005), p. 18.

50   Committee on Homeland Security, *Engineering Bio-Terror Agents*, p. 22.

seventeen others. After a lengthy investigation, the attacks were traced back to a scientist, Dr. Bruce Ivins, who committed suicide before he could be indicted for the crime. According to the FBI investigation final report, Ivins had access to the specific strain of anthrax used in his job at the Fort Detrick, Maryland bio-defence laboratories, and his motivation was the possible cancellation of his anthrax vaccine program (due to criticism of the vaccines after the Gulf War), exacerbated by reported long-term mental health issues.[51]

If a real-life scientist and government employee could "crack" and use biochemical weapons on innocent citizens, it is certainly no surprise that similar scenarios have been dramatised in a number of zombie films. In *The Earth Dies Screaming* (1964), alien robots (rather than human scientists) use chemical warfare to kill the majority of the human race, and reanimate some human corpses in order to terrorise the survivors. The fictional experimental World War II gas Gamma 693 is the cause of a zombie outbreak in *Gamma 693* (1981), and an experimental AIDS vaccine creates a zombie outbreak in *Zombie '90: Extreme Pestilence* (1990). In the Japanese films *Biozombie* (1998) and *Junk* (2000), biochemical warfare agents cause corpses to reanimate, and Umbrella Corporation's bio-engineered T-virus was the source of the infection in the *Resident Evil* series.

The *Return of the Living Dead* series adds an interesting twist to references of military biochemicals in zombie films. The first movie in the series begins with a written disclaimer that the "events portrayed in this film are all true."[52] According to the story recounted by Frank, one of the employees at the Uneeda Medical Supply warehouse, Trioxin was developed by the Darrow Chemical Company for the military, in order to "spray on marijuana or something."[53] The chemical was accidentally spilled at a VA Hospital in Pittsburgh and reanimated corpses in the morgue. According to Frank, *Night of the Living Dead* was a fictionalisation of this actual event, and in order to convince Freddy, his new assistant, of the veracity of the tale, shows him the barrels of Trioxin (and zombies) accidentally shipped to their warehouse, resulting in the accidental release of Trioxin and the start of a new zombie outbreak. *Planet Terror* (2007) plays on widespread stories of Gulf War syndrome (possibly caused by exposure to chemical warfare). A platoon of soldiers stationed in Afghanistan stumbles upon Bin Laden's hiding place and for some reason is sprayed with the chemical DC-2 (known as "Project Terror"). The chemical turns humans into zombies, and the platoon has only managed to remain human by procuring a supply of the chemical from an unscrupulous biochemist who claims that "science comes first, but business comes a close fucking second."[54] When the chemical is released, it turns a

---

51   "Amerithrax Investigative Summary," *United States Department of Justice* (19 February 2010), http://www.justice.gov/amerithrax/docs/amx-investigative-summary.pdf, accessed 3 January 2011.

52   Dan O'Bannon, *The Return of the Living Dead*, directed by Dan O'Bannon (1984; Beverly Hills, CA: Twentieth Century Home Entertainment, 2007), DVD.

53   Ibid.

54   Robert Rodriguez, *Planet Terror*, directed by Robert Rodriguez (2007; New York: The Weinstein Company, 2007), DVD.

small town into a zombie hoard, and a doctor examining one of the early victims compares the horrible lesions and other symptoms to those he has previously seen in returning Iraqi veterans. "The shit they spread around there you just wouldn't believe," he explains to the concerned patient.[55] The DuPont Chemical Company may have once promised "Better Things for Better Living … Through Chemistry,"[56] but the lesson of numerous zombie films is that chemical discoveries are not always used for the betterment of society.

In the end, zombie media deliver a fresh vision of the classic Frankenstein trope, providing another venue for the creation of cautionary tales against historical and, more importantly, potential future abuses of scientific discoveries. For example, in *Brains: A Zombie Memoir*, zombie and former college professor Jack Barnes explains the ultimate genius of George A. Romero:

> His initial trilogy […] was prescient in the grand tradition of science fiction becoming fact. First you have to imagine a man on the moon, then you can put one there. Imagine an atom-splitting bomb, and then build one. Imagine a virus that turns corpses into the walking dead, and someone, somewhere, will develop the virus.[57]

This is the ultimate lesson of modern science—if something can be imagined by the human mind, some scientist will seek to discover how to make it a reality. Conversely, whatever science can create, some human mind (either fictional or all-too-real) will conceive how to misuse it for personal, financial, or political gain.

The scientific advances of the twentieth century have brought about increased economic prosperity, medical miracles, and forms of leisure and entertainment previously only considered in works of fiction. But with new discoveries come new ethical challenges, and questions as to whether all possibilities in the laboratory must be realised. Zombie films offer us a chance to ponder difficult questions at the intersections of science, technology, and ethics. Kenneth Bainbridge, director of the Trinity atom bomb test, called the test a "foul and awesome display" and later remarked to fellow scientist J. Robert Oppenheimer "Now we are all sons of bitches."[58] Other scientists and engineers may have certainly thought the same after seeing the results of their work. For example, Alfred Nobel is widely said to have bequeathed his fortune to set up what became the Nobel Prizes out of a sense of regret over the uses of dynamite and the other explosives he had developed. These geniuses of science ultimately concluded that they

---

55 Ibid.

56 "Better Things: … 1939," *Dupont*, http://www2.dupont.com/Heritage/en_US/1939_dupont/1939_indepth.html, accessed 3 January 2011.

57 Becker, *Brains*, p. 4.

58 "The Manhattan Project: An Interactive History—The Trinity Test," *US Department of Energy Office of History and Heritage Resources*, http://www/cfp/doe.gov/me70/manhattan/trinity.htm, accessed 3 January 2011.

had given birth to something truly monstrous. And as in the case of Shelley's classic tale, one must ask, who is the real monster—the scientist or what he or she creates? Therefore *Day of the Dead*'s Dr. Logan appears to have been correct when he said of zombies, "they are us," for when we look into the heartless, decaying face of the undead, driven by the unreflecting need to consume (albeit human flesh rather than scientific knowledge), one can ask whether that face is being held up as a mirror into which all of us—especially scientists—must gaze.

BIBLIOGRAPHY

Anderson, Douglas A., and Verlyn Flieger. *Tolkien on Fairy-Stories.* London, U.K.: Harper Collins, 2008.

Anderson, Paul W. S. *Resident Evil.* DVD. United States: Sony Pictures Releasing, 2002.

Anderson, Paul W. S. *Resident Evil: Afterlife.* DVD. United States: Sony Pictures Releasing, 2010.

Anderson, Paul W. S. *Resident Evil: Apocalypse.* DVD. United States: Sony Pictures Releasing, 2004.

Anderson, Paul W. S. *Resident Evil: Extinction.* DVD. United States: Sony Pictures Releasing, 2008.

"Animal and Pet Cloning Opinion Polls." Center for Genetics and Society, April 4, 2005. https://www.geneticsandsociety.org/internal-content/animal-and-pet-cloning-opinion-polls.

Baader, Gerhard, Susan E. Lederer, Morris Low, Florian Schmaltz, and Alexander V. Schwerin. "Pathways to Human Experimentation, 1933-1945: Germany, Japan, and the United States." *Osiris* 20 (2005): 205–31. https://doi.org/10.1086/649419.

Badley, Linda. *Film, Horror, and the Body Fantastic.* Westport, CT: Greenwood Press, 1995.

Becker, Robin M. *Brains: A Zombie Memoir.* New York, NY: Eos, 2010.

"Better Things: ... 1939." Dupont. Accessed January 3, 2011. http://www2.dupont.com/Heritage/en_US/1939_dupont/1939_indepth.html.

Brandon, Karen. "Mortician Accused of Selling Body Parts." Chicago Tribune, February 25, 2002. https://www.chicagotribune.com/news/ct-xpm-2002-02-25-0202250134-story.html.

Browne, S. G. *Breathers: A Zombie's Lament.* New York, NY: Three Rivers Press, 2009.

Chomiak, Robert, Andrew Currie, and Dennis Heaton. *Fido.* DVD. Canada: TVA Films, 2006.

Committee on Homeland Security. Engineering Bio-Terror Agents: Lessons From the Offensive US and Russian Biological Weapons Programs. Washington, D.C.: US G.P.O., 2005.

DeGroot, Gerard J. *The Bomb: A Life.* Cambridge, MA: Harvard University Press, 2005.

Interlandi, Janeen. "Not Just an Urban Legend." Newsweek.com. Newsweek, January 10, 2009. https://www.newsweek.com/organ-trafficking-no-myth-78079.

"J. Robert Oppenheimer Interview." A.J. Software and Multimedia. Accessed January 3, 2011. http://www.atomicarchive.com/Movies/Movie8.shtml.

Jones, James H. *Bad Blood: The Tuskegee Syphilis Experiment.* New York, NY: Free Press, 1993.

Klotzko, Arlene Judith. *A Clone of Your Own?: The Science and Ethics of Cloning*. Oxford: Oxford University Press, 2004.

"The Manhattan Project: An Interactive History—The Trinity Test." Manhattan project: The Trinity Test, July 16, 1945. US Department of Energy Office of History and Heritage Resources. Accessed January 3, 2011. http://www/cfp/doe.gov/me70/manhattan/trinity.htm.

McNeil, Donald G. "US Apologizes for Syphilis Tests in Guatemala." The New York Times. The New York Times, October 1, 2010. http://www.nytimes.com/2010/10/02/health/research/02infect.html.

Mikkelson, David P., and Barbara Mikkelson. "You'Ve Got To Be Kidneying." Snopes.com. Accessed January 3, 2011. http://www.snopes.com/horrors/robbery/kidney.asp.

Moreno, Jonathan D. *Undue Risk: Secret State Experiments on Humans*. Routledge, 2000.

"National Survey of Healthcare Consumers: Genetically Engineered Food." Thomson Reuters, October 2010. http://www.justlabelit.org/wp-content/uploads/2011/09/NPR_report_GeneticEngineeredFood-1.pdf.

O'Bannon, Dan. *The Return of the Living Dead*. DVD. United States: Orion Pictures, 1985.

Paoli, Dennis, William J. Norris, and Stuart Gordon. *Re-Animator*. DVD. United States: Empire International Pictures, 1985.

Randall, Jeff. "Prince Charles Warns GM Crops Risk Causing the Biggest-Ever Environmental Disaster." The Telegraph. Telegraph Media Group, August 12, 2008. http://www.telegraph.co.uk/earth/earthnews/3349308/Prince-Charles-warns-GM-crops-risk-causing-the-biggest-ever-environmental-disaster.html.

Rodriguez, Robert. *Planet Terror*. DVD. United States: Dimension Films, 2007.

Romero, George A. *Dawn of the Dead*. DVD. United States: Anchor Bay Entertainment, 2004.

Romero, George A. *Day of the Dead*. DVD. United States: United Film Distribution Company, 1985.

Ross, Brian, Rhonda Schwartz, and Anna Schecter. "N.Y., China Investigating Black Market in Bodies." ABC News. ABC News Network. Accessed January 3, 2011. https://abcnews.go.com/Blotter/ny-china-investigating-black-market-bodies/story?id=4296982.

Russo, John, and George A. Romero. *Night of the Living Dead*. DVD. United States: Continental Distributing, 1968.

United States Department of Justice. "Amerithrax Investigative Summary." US Department of Justice, February 19, 2010. https://www.justice.gov/archive/amerithrax/docs/amx-investigative-summary.pdf.

Zarembo, Alan, and Jessica Garrison. "Profit Drives Illegal Trade in Body Parts." Los Angeles Times. LA Times, March 7, 2004. http://articles.latimes.com/2004/mar/07/local/me-parts7.

POST-READING QUESTIONS/POST-SCREENING QUESTIONS

Directions: Use what you learned from reading this chapter and watching the film to respond to the questions.

1. What are the characteristics of the zombie that differentiate it from other monsters in the horror genre?

2. What is Larsen's main argument about the intersection of science and zombie media?

3. How do zombie films amplify or exploit public mistrust of science?

4. In the sixty-year history of zombie films discussed in this chapter, what do you find the most interesting representation and why?

Virtual Immigrants

Transfigured Bodies and Transnational Spaces in
Science Fiction Cinema

By Everett Hamner

KEY TERMS AND FIGURES

Global South

Techno-capitalism

Virtual immigrants

Globalization

Biotechnology

Cyborgification

Alex Rivera

Gareth Edwards

Michael Winterbottom

RECOMMENDED FILMS

Blade Runner by Ridley Scott (1982)

Code 46 by Michael Winterbottom (2004)

District 9 by Neill Blomkamp (2009)

Metropolis by Fritz Lang (1927)

Monsters by Gareth Edwards (2010)

Sleep Dealer by Alex Rivera (2008)

Star Wars by George Lucas (1977)

The Phantom Menace by George Lucas (1999)

INTRODUCTION

S cience fiction horror tends to be understood as one of techno-horror, conjuring images from *Metropolis*, American B-movies from the 1950s, Japanese monsters, and other films in a genealogy that unites film histories across geographies. It often highlights the impotence of science in confrontation with colossal human-made existential problems, raising disturbing questions about humanity's place in a world it attempts to conquer and tame. In this chapter, Everett Hamner turns to a very contemporary issue that is also very old, that of immigration in a world of increasingly policed borders. While inviting us to rethink assumptions about geopolitical boundaries and transitional spaces, he examines films that depict worlds where techno-capitalism's tendency to divide humanity against itself is turned on itself, illustrating what he calls the *evasion* of national boundaries. Evasion, he explains, occurs alongside the fusion of human bodies with alien forms and cybernetic biotechnologies. This functions in more than one sense, suggesting the ability of science fiction to reduce the significance of borders, as well as to redraw them in a way that acknowledges painful historical injustices and reconceives alternative futures.

Hamner begins by briefly reviewing Ridley Scott's *Blade Runner* and three of the twenty-first-century descendants, *Sleep Dealer*, *Code 46*, and *District 9*, which he considers immigration narratives. This provides an additional entry point to exploring *Monsters* in conversation with *Sleep Dealer*'s unique story of cyborgification at the US–Mexico borderlands. While in reality these borders have become ever more imposing and sealed off, films like *Sleep Dealer* treat them as increasingly porous, particularly at the US-Mexico boundary. Hamner points out that the evasion of said borders occurs simultaneously with the increasing cyborgification of the human body. But *Sleep Dealer* also offers the possibility of hope when the contemporary border crossers are able to harness the forces that are intended to oppress them and use them to their own advantage, turning techno-capitalism against itself.

The chapter makes some key distinctions in situating twenty-first-century science fiction. Hamner mentions "old" science fiction, which links technologically modified bodies with "shifts in race, class, and politics," an example of which can be seen in Fritz Lang's *Metropolis*. By contrast, contemporary science fiction films often thematize immigration and other forms of border crossing as "a rebellion against techno-scientific imperialism," an example of which can be seen in *Sleep Dealer*. What is clear is that in this rebellion, twenty-first-century films are more about the present than they are about the future. He also distinguishes between the science fiction films of Hollywood (*Blade Runner*, *Star Wars*) and lower-budget independent films (*Monsters*), which could afford to be more thematically risky.

Twenty-first-century films are preoccupied with epidemics, infection, and contamination (*District 9*, *Monsters*), which border crossers threaten to bring, echoing age-old fears of immigrants. Those who make the journeys rely on often unethical coyotes who are powerful figures in the political economies of the borderlands. Hamner argues that *Sleep Dealer* contrasts with *District 9* in appealing both to the marginalized potential immigrant and those who benefit from the privilege of US citizenship and residence north of the US–Mexico border. He notes the film sends a cautionary message about "bioengineered abuses" at the border, but also suggests the possibility for this technology to be used toward progressive politics, imagining a world where Latin Americans can maintain strong ties their homeland, and still safely and legally cross borders.

In sum, Hamner reconceptualizes Hollywood blockbusters such as *Star Wars* and *Blade Runner* as representations that can be immigration narratives, distinct from twenty-first century science fiction films, and that take into account the effects of techno-capitalism across borders, while momentarily allowing us to dream of overcoming them. We can see this in the generation of filmmakers influenced by the Hollywood classics, who went on to produce films like *Sleep Dealer*, *Code 46*, and *District 9*. This is particularly clear in *Sleep Dealer*, which reimagines the horrors of the past and present, while suggesting possibilities for the future. Ultimately Hamner reframes science fiction cinema within a global context by repositioning the popular genre into a broader network of production, distribution, and exhibition. In so doing, he invites discussion and critique of the perils of globalization, as they intersect with technologies of policing and subversion across borders.

Virtual Immigrants

Transfigured Bodies and Transnational Spaces in
Science Fiction Cinema

By Everett Hamner

In the director's commentary for his feature-length debut, *Sleep Dealer* (2008), Alex Rivera interprets the first film he ever saw, *Star Wars* (George Lucas, 1977), as an immigration narrative. As he points out, Luke Skywalker is a peasant farmer living in a desert landscape whose home is destroyed by an imperial army. This leaves him little choice but to head toward the realm of his oppressors, not unlike many immigrants today. Although sharing in the mass love affair with this space opera, Rivera is struck that Luke is perceived so heroically.

> When he flees his home and tries to get past the border guards, essentially we're all rooting for him. We want him to break the law, we want him to get through, to get to the other side. And yet in our society and in our political culture, there is a massive movement and cultural energy toward sealing borders, toward stopping people's movements.

That incongruity inspired a film echoing some elements of *Star Wars,* but also exploring the consequences when contemporary border-crossers triumph less fully than young Jedi knights. Indeed, *Sleep Dealer* joins a growing body of twenty-first-century science fictional immigration narratives that are rethinking assumptions about geopolitical boundaries and transnational spaces. With gargantuan and miniscule budgets alike, such films are emerging from and being set in increasingly diverse locations, especially in the Global South. Often spawning controversy, they challenge depictions of stable divides between the haves and have-nots. Even as the physical barriers between nations and socioeconomic groups grow more visually imposing, those represented on-screen—even if initially impressive—are more and more likely to be exposed as superficial, porous, and unsustainable.

Strikingly, this penetration and evasion of national boundaries increasingly appears in SF cinema alongside imagined fusions of human bodies with alien and cybernetic biotechnologies. The boundaries erected between people groups are being traced and extended to the cellular and digital levels, so that ostensible differences between self and other become tangible simultaneously at societal and microscopic scales. Returning to *Star Wars,* consider the more recent prequel, *The Phantom Menace* (George Lucas, 1999), in which another peasant boy (Luke's future father) is uprooted from his desert home. In the original film (1977's *A New Hope*), we watched an elderly Obi-Wan Kenobi recruit his protégé on the basis of intuition and personal history, but two decades of film history later, Obi-Wan's younger self and a Jedi partner must first analyze the "midi-chlorians" in Anakin Sky-walker's bloodstream. For Lucas's more recent installments, biometrics allows precise measurements of leadership, courage, and awareness; it is only after such authentication that the Jedi can offer to serve as Anakin's escorts (coyotes?) through enemy space. This practice of utilizing micro biological testing to confirm personal characteristics and justify opportunities to reach beyond traditional geopolitical and socio-economic limits has grown increasingly common in the new millennium. But SF cinema is also becoming bolder in its Foucauldian critiques of these assessments: the *Star Wars* universe may affirm their ease and reliability, but other films like *Gattaca* (Andrew Niccol, 1997) warn that they could exacerbate the new caste systems emerging under global capitalism.

In probing this entanglement of biotechnology and immigration, this chapter begins with brief looks at Ridley Scott's *Blade Runner* (1982) and two of its early twenty-first-century descendants, *Code 46* (Michael Winterbottom, 2003) and *District 9* (Neill Blomkamp, 2009). Using *Monsters* (Gareth Edwards, 2010) as an additional entry point, the chapter then concentrates upon *Sleep Dealer*'s unique story of cyborgification in the US–Mexico borderlands. Twenty-first-century SF films are more regularly taking advantage of the genre's capacity to interrogate the physiological methods by which nation-states and various neoliberal entities maintain absolutist geographical boundaries, but Rivera's work in particular exposes the corporate ideology by which otherwise successful immigrants may be denied individual and communal agency. Yet with all of its dystopian imagery and its condemnation of abuses, *Sleep Dealer* ends up far from hopeless: it also shows how, upon recognizing their status as puppets, contemporary border

Figure 1.4.1 Alex Rivera's *Sleep Dealer* (2008) rethinks portrayals of the US–Mexico borderlands that feature only green fields to the north and dusty shantytowns to the south.

crossers sometimes find new opportunities to turn techno-capitalism against itself, utilizing virtual networks to reconceive transnational spaces and to uncover the material conditions that foreground some narratives and suppress others.

Although aiming to uncover new dimensions of science fiction cinema, the methodology employed by this chapter is hardly unprecedented. My working hypothesis is that SF is uniquely well suited as a mode of thinking to concurrently acknowledge painful historical injustices (often via allegory) and to conceive alternative futures wherein human beings make different choices. There are many worthy definitions of the genre along these lines, but I emphasize its capacity to render tangible techno-cultural forces that are often so ubiquitous as to go unrecognized in our daily lives. As Istvan Csicsery-Ronay Jr. explains, "[The technological empire] is so pervasive a force of social gravitation that it feels like nature. ... Sf must be counted as the primary institution of art that makes this new regime habitable by the imagination."[1] Of course we must also remember that this capacity did not first emerge in the twenty-first century. Whenever a genre mutates, some antecedents of its current traits usually can be found in earlier textual expressions. One can look at least as far back as *Metropolis* (Fritz Lang, 1927) to find SF cinema linking technologically modified bodies with shifts in race, class, and politics. What is relatively new in the genre, though, is the visual predominance of immigrants and borders within stories about our increasingly digitalizable, microscopically legible selves. Filmmakers are now thematizing unsanctioned immigration and other crossings of political boundaries as a rebellion against techno-scientific imperialism, so that early twenty-first-century SF film explicitly connects national identity and emerging forms of biotechnology in ways only incipient in earlier works.

To better appreciate both contemporary SF's inheritance and its innovations, take Scott's film noir classic, *Blade Runner,* and Winter bottom's unjustly neglected tale of unbridled genetic testing, *Code 46,* which appeared two decades later. Like *Star Wars,* Scott's masterpiece is rarely described as an immigration narrative, yet the freedom (or lack thereof) to move across political boundaries—even if located between planets rather than nations—is central to its premise. When organic android Roy Batty dies a preprogrammed death in the climactic scene, his defiant last words culminate an escape from off-world colonial enslavement; he succumbs only after confronting those who would deny his personhood and convincing the bounty hunter played by Harrison Ford that his "artificial" kind is worthy of existence. Ultimately, Rick Deckard (Ford) renounces his role as a type of Immigration and Naturalization Services (INS) agent, departing with a female replicant into an undefined future and arguably recognizing his own "illegal" status. If Jonathan Auerbach observes that film noir has long been a preeminent genre for filmic expositions upon national loyalty, even claiming that "there could be no film

---

1   Istvan Csicsery-Ronay Jr., "Empire," in *The Routledge Companion to Science Fiction,* ed. Mark Bould et al. (New York: Routledge, 2009), 371.

noir without the FBI,"[2] *Blade Runner* witnesses SF cinema's similarly enduring interest in the surveillance practices of groups like the INS, Homeland Security, and transnational corporations.

As the core narrative of Scott's dark classic is recycled by the brighter *Code 46*, both the repetitions and the modifications testify to the growing interplay of biotechnology and immigration issues. Following Katherine Hayles's logic wherein we are already posthuman, Winterbottom envisions an Earth invaded not by replicants but by bio-tech security entities with names like "The Sphinx." In many ways, this is an expansion of the power housed in the similarly Egyptian pyramids of *Blade Runner*'s Tyrell Corporation: instead of producing a limited number of cyborgs who tug upon the definitions of human and nonhuman, the bio-surveillance industry of *Code 46* reengineers and monitors everyone. Winterbottom's protagonist must find the source of a Shanghai production center's problem with "cover" (or visa) stealing, but he follows Deckard's lead in switching sides, abandoning his blade-running responsibilities—as well as those as husband and father—in favor of an ill-fated romance. The main difference, and a rather bleak one, is that he clearly fails to escape, crashing his getaway car and returning to his family (perhaps even his role as corporate tool) after a seemingly routine memory wipe.

At the same time, *Code 46* foregrounds the border fence and the geographic expanse between privilege and oppression in a manner absent from Scott's film. Shifting from a noir Los Angeles into a washed-out, glaring cityscape in which information about personal identity is all too readily available (William uses one of Maria's hairs to acquire a genome scan in mere hours), the film's future includes an impressive wall between its absolutely separated "first" and "third" worlds, with miles of barren desert creating a permanent divide. This is not the Flat Earth of Thomas Friedman, but a world whose obsession with correct *papeles* (papers) and absolute compartmentalization of the rich and poor is greater than ever (a divide stretched even further by 2013's *Elysium,* in which upper-crust society literally removes itself to Earth's orbit). Yet as Yosefa Loshitzky recognizes, "*Code 46*'s message is that it is not the future which is so frightening, but the present."[3] We are not really looking at a future Shanghai, but a collage of shots taken in contemporary Shanghai, Dubai, Hong Kong, and elsewhere, as if to remind us that specific locations and cultures matter little under global capitalism. Whereas *Blade Runner* famously deleted the green wilderness of its theatrical version's "happy ending" in the director's cut and subsequent editions—thus removing any geographical distance the film originally envisioned between life within and outside social protections—*Code 46* uses its aerial shots and long takes to emphasize the physical gap between developed sophistication and under-developed invisibility. As Maria concludes in overdubbed narration that we learn has been offered throughout the film from a state of exile, "They don't care what you think if

---

2   Jonathan Auerbach, *Dark Borders: Film Noir and American Citizenship* (Durham, N.C.: Duke University Press, 2011), 24.

3   Yosefa Loshitzky, *Screening Strangers: Migration and Diaspora in Contemporary European Cinema* (Bloomington: Indiana University Press, 2010), 128.

you're afuera [outside]. Why bother? To them it's as though we don't exist." Appropriately, even as the film portrays global elites' assimilation of select non-English terms into a single dialect, most former speakers of "foreign" languages are rendered inaudible.

Some critics have been frustrated by this muting of the disadvantaged Other, observing with Kathy-Ann Tan that "*Code 46* ultimately fails to offer a satisfactory alternative realm from which the subaltern can speak."[4] However, this is not necessarily the goal of Winterbottom's film. The dystopian realms created by SF cinema need not be understood mimetically. Rather, I would encourage consideration of *Code 46*'s massive border checkpoint and the surrounding desert emptiness as a lament for the many Marias forced into idealized but abandoned Madonna roles by seemingly unquestionable financial measurements of individual and social value. Still, Tan and others are right that this film does not yet envision the border as a dynamic space; for the poor, its checkpoints provide daily opportunities for hawking wares to travelers, but not places where anyone can live. That sense of the physical landscape around geopolitical demarcations as a realm in which individuals and communities actually play and work, are born and die, must be found elsewhere.

It might be objected that *District 9* features an urban ghetto rather than a true international border, but this film is just as concerned as *Code 46* with the inextricability of immigration and biopolitical manipulation. Whatever one may think of Blomkamp's grotesque humor, the film initially treats the division between haves and have-nots just as directly and starkly as does Winterbottom's film. In this case, the humans have all the guns and the alien "prawns" are imprisoned in a Johannesburg shantytown with massive walls; the real difference, though, is that ultimately these barriers prove surprisingly porous. When the new camp supervisor, a blithely insensitive employee of "Multi-National United (MNU)," accidentally sprays himself with an alien oil-like substance and begins turning into a human–prawn hybrid, he is able to escape MNU's medical personnel and vast paramilitary force long enough to sneak back into the sequestered zone, the one place in the sprawling city where he has a chance of hiding. As his genetic mutation from human to partially alien DNA foments his transformation from tormentor to alien sympathizer, he gradually recognizes that the neoliberal corporation he has blithely served is willfully ignoring the personhood of those it designates illegal.

Many reviews and essays have noted the problemic nature of the film's racial politics, not least in its treatment of the Nigerian immigrant. John G. Russell compares *District 9* to *Avatar* (James Cameron, 2009) in its reliance on "a new kind of racial performativity in which actors of color assume a guise more palatable to whites than their true form and provide white film-makers an opportunity to play with issues of race in a more 'entertaining' and less controversial

---

4   Kathy-Ann Tan, "'If You're Not on Paper, You Don't Exist': Depictions of Illegal Immigration and Asylum in Film—on Michael Winterbottom's *In This World* (2002) and *Code 46* (2003)," in *Multi-Ethnic Britain 2000+: New Perspectives in Literature, Film and the Arts,* ed. Lars Eckstein et al. (New York: Editions Rodopi, 2008), 313.

manner while providing themselves plausible deniability should it prove otherwise."[5] That is, twenty-first-century SF film is finding a way to have its aliens and eat them too, employing irony and satire to such a degree that it gets away with ridiculing the ethnic Other because no one knows when to take it seriously. John Reider's view is that therefore "even *District 9*'s critical impulses have to become its parasites,"[6] while Andrea Hairston concludes the film is "caught in the colonial impulse it seeks to disrupt."[7] Perhaps the most forgiving approach is Eric D. Smith's insistence that

> holding together in *impossible* accord the incommensurable realities of slum city and gated suburb, human and alien, black and white, salaried professional and abject refugee under the monstrous sign of global class struggle, *District 9* outlines the emergent political subjectivity of the *real* state of exception, a solidarity without essence and without borders in which we are all refugees, in which we are all monsters.[8]

But does the film actually achieve this unity "without borders," or does it simply render its boundaries more permeable than SF traditionally does, trusting that extreme differences in physical appearance will maintain the necessary categorical differences between species (and by analogy, races)?

This question about the visibility of difference invites attention to a less-commented-upon aspect of *District 9*, the exigencies of the production location itself. We learn from the director's commentary that the main shooting site (the shantytown inhabited by the prawns) was an impoverished "suburb" of Johannesburg, one whose residents were permanently relocated to a new neighborhood with brick structures, as Blomkamp somewhat proudly explains. Throughout this alternative soundtrack, in fact, he ruminates about living in one of the city's richer suburbs during shooting, each day descending into the muck of impoverished South Africans' existence in order to film. One assistant producer is lauded for her ability to turn up as many rotting animal carcasses as needed at a moment's notice, and Blomkamp repeatedly notes how revolting he found the shantytown. By contrast, he ruminates, "You have these gated communities that have all the money in the world and electric fences and biometric fingerprinting devices to open the gate. And outside of these gated communities you have

---

5   John G. Russell, "Don't It Make My Black Face Blue: Race, Avatars, Albescence, and the Transnational Imaginary," *Journal of Popular Culture* 46, no. 1 (2013): 213–14.

6   John Rieder, "Race and Revenge Fantasies in *Avatar*, *District 9* and *Inglourious Basterds*," *Science Fiction Film and Television* 4, no. 1 (Spring 2011): 55.

7   Andrea Hairston, "Different and Equal Together: SF Satire in *District 9*," *Journal of the Fantastic in the Arts* 22, no. 3 (2011): 342.

8   Eric D. Smith, *Globalization, Utopia, and Postcolonial Science Fiction: New Maps of Hope* (New York: Palgrave Macmillan, 2012), 158.

poverty that doesn't exist anywhere really except Africa and parts of India." On one hand Blomkamp cannot emphasize starkly enough the split he observes—"It's the elite get richer and richer and the masses get poorer and poorer until finally you end up in a place where you have a city or a country that's got five percent of the population controlling all of the wealth and everybody else lives in abject poverty"—but on the other, his film portrays the slim hope that the most oblivious and exploitative of bureaucratic functionaries could become infected with genuine empathy for those he has afflicted.

Indeed this plot depends on conversion by epidemic, a motif also evident in the public health fears explored by Emily Maguire's chapter on zombies in this volume. The division between "us" and "them" is not just geopolitically but also biologically determined, and thus it is subject to sudden and dramatic shifts when one is bitten (or in *District 9*'s case, sprayed) by a new and different source of contagion. In fact, much the same process is at work on the other side of the Atlantic in *Monsters* (2009). Relying upon the lowest budget of the films I examine here, this B-movie romantic comedy/horror flick appears as if it were rushed through production in hopes of capitalizing upon *District 9*'s box office draw. Presupposing that NASA has discovered other life within our solar system, Gareth Edwards's film explains that a probe bringing back samples broke up during reentry over Mexico, thus relocating the contamination crisis. Unfortunately, because the spaceship scattered organic material over the northern half of the country, the entire region has to be sequestered as an "infected zone." With the US and Mexican militaries having spent years attempting to contain the squid-like aliens spawned from this disaster—the allegory does not attempt subtlety—the main characters are a media mogul's adventurous daughter and a photographer in southern Mexico, a peon the boss entrusts with escorting his "little girl" to a ferry ride home. Of course the irresponsible photographer gets drunk, their passports are stolen, and they have to take the tougher route via land, traversing alien-infested paths and rivers with guidance from former coyotes. When they miraculously reach the border, our hero and heroine find a monumental but broken wall, one they contemplate at length before passing. Soon after being collected at an abandoned gas station, the travelers and their military escorts are assaulted by "the creatures." Unsurprisingly, neither the immigrant stand-ins nor the aliens end well; as one realizes upon reviewing the story-concluding but film-opening title sequence, the woman is apparently killed, while the alien creatures are last seen fighting soldiers.

As the main characters reflect upon first seeing the border wall, "It's different looking at America from the outside," which may be understood as the film's central insight. Undoubtedly, whether imagined as literal aliens or human beings treated as aliens, would-be immigrants have too rarely felt welcome at the US's southern border, and even a hastily constructed thriller like *Monsters* can effectively interrogate that history. In the process, though, it also has something to tell us about the relationship between US and Latin American filmmaking. At first, Edwards's disaster tale might seem to illustrate the kind of tripartite distinction between Hollywood, Mexican, and Latino film-making offered by Camilla Fojas. She argues that

> Mexican border films are strongly nationalist, discouraging northerly migration and debunking the myth of the "American Dream." They thematize the entanglements of cultural contact and the experience of displacement and economic exile, whereas Hollywood border films tend to focus on the heroic mission of the Texas Rangers, border guards, DEA agents, or other police personnel.[9]

However, SF films outside of the Hollywood studio system, like *Monsters,* sometimes complicate this binary paradigm, neither rejecting the promised land outright nor merely celebrating those who defend it. Instead, much twenty-first-century SF better fits the third category Fojas identifies, the "Latino border films" that "challenge the presumptions of US nationalism and subsequent cultural attitudes about immigrants and immigration and often critically reconstruct their Hollywood kin,"[10] but still find some appeal in life north of the Río Bravo. As we will see, *Sleep Dealer* particularly epitomizes this third category insofar as its critique aims at north *and* south, challenging non-Latino US audiences as well as Latinos and Latin Americans. In a sense, this is a lower-budget *District 9* that has something to say to those who identify with the prawns as well as those who find themselves uncomfortably aligned with the MNU.

Some of *Sleep Dealer*'s innovations as transnational SF cinema have already been outlined by Lysa Rivera. She urges greater attention to "an under-examined history of Chicano/a cultural practice that employs science-fictional metaphors to render experiences of marginalization visible and to imagine alternative scenarios that are at once critically informed and imaginative."[11] Seeing NAFTA and the neoliberalism it enabled as a galvanizing force for increasingly transnational science fiction, she argues that "post-NAFTA borderlands science fiction ... is the *formal* articulation of a specific historical narrative: namely the history of US/Mexico capitalist labor relations in the region and militant fights for an alternative framework."[12] In this sense, SF film functions not only as post-factual allegory but as active intervention, fleshing out borderlands by insisting upon their dynamic possibilities as much as their static barriers. Of course, as she notes, the "future" of our stories can become "not so much a site of progress and humanistic harmony as a return to the colonial past,"[13] so that "cyborg labor" serves as "nothing more than a politically-charged symbol for real life labor practices under late

---

9   Camilla Fojas, *Border Bandits: Hollywood on the Southern Frontier* (Austin: University of Texas Press, 2008), 4–5.

10   Ibid., 2.

11   Lysa Rivera, "Future Histories and Cyborg Labor: Reading Borderlands Science Fiction after NAFTA," *Science Fiction Studies* 39, no. 3 (November 2012): 415.

12   Ibid., 417.

13   Ibid., 418.

capitalism."[14] Therefore in her reading, *Sleep Dealer* exposes the irony by which biotechnology may lead not to Latin American liberation, but more thorough slavery.

This is also the main argument offered by Luis Martín-Cabrera, who demonstrates that the film shows "how technology and cognitive labor may actually reproduce forms of colonial exploitation and oppression rather than leading to automatic liberation from the shackles of physical labor."[15] As with Rivera's interpretation, I think this is undeniable. However, my assessment of the film's transnational and biotechnological vision is more mixed. *Sleep Dealer* certainly sounds a strongly cautionary note about bioengineered abuses; there is little doubt that the film laments Memo's treatment at the hands (wires?) of Cybertek, the virtual reality sweatshop where he finds employment upon arriving in Tijuana. And Rivera's film could hardly be more biting in attacking a *cybracero* future in which the United States extracts all of its southern neighbors' labor while caring for none of the laborers. But even as it powerfully laments the exploitation of Latin Americans, *Sleep Dealer* also suggests the potential for some forms of technology to serve a progressive politics. The apparent key is that immigrants gain relative mastery over biotechnology rather than merely becoming its organic slaves, a self-reproducing source of battery power like that envisioned by *The Matrix* (Andy Wachowski and Lana Wachowski, 1999) and its sequels. Ultimately, this is a dream in which immigrants, legal and otherwise, eventually receive opportunities for genuine inclusion and full dignity, so that the US–Mexican borderlands become dynamic spaces of cultural interchange free from the aerial supervision visible in both *District 9* and *Sleep Dealer.* Rivera's film suggests that only when immigrants can strengthen ties to their original hometowns, moving regularly and legally across national borders, will techno-capitalism's tendency to divide humanity from itself be significantly thwarted. It is especially insistent that the cultivation of transnational spaces—certainly including land adjacent to geopolitical border markers, but also extending much farther north and south—will be critical elements of any such reality. In this vision,

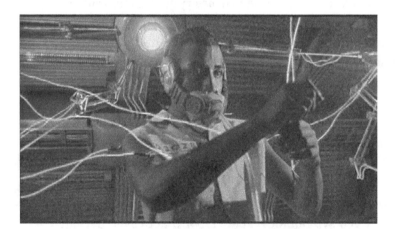

Figure 1.4.2 Cyber-capitalist marionettes control Memo in *Sleep Dealer,* but the film also imagines a subaltern repurposing of such biotechnology.

14   Ibid., 421.

15   Luis Martín-Cabrera, "The Potentiality of the Commons: A Materialist Critique of Cognitive Capitalism from the Cybracer@s to the Ley Sinde," *Hispanic Review* 80, no. 4 (Fall 2012): 590.

emerging cybernetic and biotechnology could enable not just abuses but also intercultural cooperation.

At its most basic level, *Sleep Dealer*'s plot turns on the use of cyberspace to outsource labor without importing laborers. The young adult at the film's center, Memo lives in a southern Mexico that Rivera originally located decades into the future, but during production began recognizing as closer to the present. His corn-and-bean-farming father exhausts himself hauling river water monopolized by a multinational corporation with a dam, pipelines, and high-security remote cameras, and Memo looks to cyberspace as an escape route. Inadvertently, however, his hacking draws the attention of the corporation's US-based military force, which sends a drone to destroy his home and kill his "bad guy" father, a purported "aqua-terrorist," while broadcasting the mission live on its own reality TV show. This tragedy sends Memo north toward the US border, where he acquires the implanted nodes with which to jack his nervous system into *el otro sistema*, the global economy. Working twelve-hour shifts as a cybracero, he controls—and is often controlled by—a robot welder perched dozens of stories above San Diego, though his body remains in a sleeplike trance in Tijuana. The film's sarcastic description of this arrangement, delivered by Memo's employer, is that "this is the American Dream. We give the United States what they've always wanted: all the work, without the workers. ... Your future starts today." As Memo slowly realizes, the harsher reality is that "my energy was being drained, sent far away. What happened to the river was happening to me."

The film's protest of such virtual and material exploitation is unrelenting. But there is also another science fictional novum here, the more ethically complex possibility of using nodes to upload and sell one's memories, and this is where the film's commitment to individual agency above technological formula emerges. *Sleep Dealer* not only challenges virtual power mongering, but also acknowledges the liberating potential of cybertechnology, as we see its main characters genuinely benefiting from their opportunities to participate in the larger global economy. As Luz's character especially demonstrates, everything depends on the extent to which the voluntary cyborg truly controls the biotechnology to which she is married. A young woman Memo meets on the bus north, Luz relies on a new form of immersive, hyperpersonalized journalism to pay her student loans, the creditors of which threaten to seize her possessions. In short, she sells a limited access to her own subjective experience, at least in visual and aural terms. What she saw is what her audience sees, along with her overdubbed narration of the experience, and undoubtedly this technology is using her as much as she is using it. Upon meeting Memo, she simply uses him for his story, drawing out the guilt he feels for his father's murder. However, as their relationship turns romantic, Luz has second thoughts about exploiting her unknowing source and grows frustrated with the limitations placed on her narrative. When we first watch Luz upload her memories, the software's biofeedback system refuses her the license she desires in telling the story. "Your DNA is your password," she later tells Memo, but this biological contact is also the system's means of constraining her authorial voice. The program refuses all attempts at fictional innovation or even abstract reflections upon meaning, demanding that she break the story into its most basic elements, as if there were a completely neutral and objective way it might be rendered. Gradually this effort separates the couple; as the blocking and mirrors in a bar scene suggest, Memo is caught between the actual Luz, who is falling for him, and the memory-journalist who remains the tool of techno-capitalism. When a friend tells Luz, "You can't hide anything," she notes, "Maybe that's the problem." The more powerful the technology, the more quickly and fully the tool users can become the tools.

Still, the film holds out hope that this dynamic can be reversed. Eventually, we learn that the individual buying Memo's online story installments was the drone pilot who, following orders, killed Memo's father. A second-generation Latino, Rudy is now dealing with his own guilt; he has betrayed his parents' homeland, but they share and affirm his treachery. It is thus an especially momentous decision when he travels across the border and confesses to the horrified Memo, who eventually decides to help Rudy perform some measure of penance. Rudy again pilots a drone into Mexican airspace, but this time without permission and in order to destroy the dam that had stolen Memo's livelihood, the water on which his family depended. Most crucially, Rudy's decision defies his parents' readiness to shoot first and ask questions later. His father had been a soldier too—perhaps even en route to US citizenship, as many Latino immigrants hope today—and when Rudy asked if he ever doubted his actions, he only repeats propaganda about how many lives Rudy's work has probably saved. Rivera's film thus illuminates the lasting bondage of empire, even for those who have seemingly escaped its oppression through assimilation. The first generation Latinos in *Sleep Dealer* are unable to face the steep costs they paid for success in a new land, and it is left to their offspring to decide whether those sacrifices remain acceptable.

Even in observing Rudy's abandonment of his parents' American dream and return to Mexico, though, it is equally worth considering how *Sleep Dealer* unites Latin Americans and Latinos in turning imperial technology against its invisible marionettes. Rudy's departure from his parents' values is one kind of conflict between first and second-generation immigrants, but the confrontation between Memo and Rudy yields a different sort of trust. Memo is a would-be first-generation (virtual) immigrant who simply wants to help his family survive; meanwhile, Rudy is a second-generation Latino so inured to US culture that he had not crossed the border in twelve years. When Rudy eventually uses the same technology with which his reality TV show described him as rooting out terrorists—as if his drone were flying over Afghanistan rather than Mexico—to reverse his corporation's theft of Memo's livelihood, *Sleep Dealer* demonstrates how solutions to border issues lie as much in justice for those south of the border as in new opportunities to the north. If *Monsters* recognized that US imperialism looks quite different from outside its walls, Rivera indicates that remaining inside the walls can be equally imprisoning.

As Martín-Cabrera observes, the film "proposes a much-needed transnational alliance between Chican@s and Mexicans in order to resist neocolonial capitalist exploitation and military control on both sides of the border."[16]

This vision of multigenerational, transnational cooperation comes into focus when one views *Sleep Dealer* beside Rivera's 2003 documentary, *The Sixth Section*. The earlier film follows predominately illegal immigrants from Boquerón, Mexico, in their move to Newburgh, New York, and then their integration of these cities into a single economic and cultural terrain. The "hometown association" in New York joins thousands of similarly loose, nearly invisible organizations in supporting their governmentally abandoned Latin American homelands. Yet Rivera's film resists easy answers: these border-hopping immigrants finance a new baseball stadium in Boquerón with $10 and $20 contributions that total $50,000US, then struggle to hire players because everyone young enough has migrated north. Similarly, they purchase an ambulance in New York and transport it 3,000 miles south only to lack an available driver. They are more successful in funding band instruments, a kitchen for their school's kindergarten, and a basketball court. But what they dream of most is a project their government abandoned, the repair of a massive underground well that would allow farmers at home to grow their crops again. One immigrant says, "If we had enough water, I would go back immediately." The connection to *Sleep Dealer*'s climax could not be tighter: in documentary and SF film alike, Rivera's work emphasizes the potential of multiple generations of immigrants to work across national boundaries and protect access to their homeland's natural resources.

For as *Sleep Dealer* joins several of its predecessors in insisting, borders are not the just-so stories they pretend. We see both sides of the fence repeatedly—even its endpoint some yards into the Pacific, where it extends in order to keep out terrorist surfers, as Luz jokes. The film closes with images of Memo trudging up a hill with water, just as he did near Oaxaca, but this time to nourish a small garden he has planted directly beside the fence. On the Mexican side, there is a shantytown, and on the US side, green fields, but Memo's plot extends the vegetation across the border. This is emblematic of Rivera's overall aesthetic and the increasing transnationalism of SF film: it can only do so much to resist an ideology of absolute divisions and exploitation, but at its best, it performs the very cross-generational and transnational solidarity it recommends. Celebrated by *New York Times* film critic A. O. Scott alongside other "Serious Directors/Small Films" selections, *Sleep Dealer* relied upon transnational participation and unconventional economics even at the core of its technology. Made for $2 million—by comparison, *District 9* cost $30 million and *The Phantom Menace* $115 million—it utilized more than 400 special effects shots created through volunteer labor. Rivera grouped them into twenty sets of twenty and farmed them out to friends and willing acquaintances willing to do off-hours work, and the contributions came from sources as far-flung as Anibrain India and as famous as Skywalker

---

16   Ibid., 595.

Figure 1.4.3 Laboring here without virtual reality assistance, *Sleep Dealer's* main character illustrates global SF film's concern not only with future possibilities, but also with ordinary, long-standing issues like water access.

Sound. In his DVD commentary and in interviews, Rivera refers to this pastiche approach as a means of creating "Zapatista SF" or even a "*rasquache* aesthetic" (a Chicano arts movement term that often irreverently celebrates the pragmatic achievement of maximum value from minimal resources).[17] Most significant, this approach refuses to sacrifice one side of the border to the other, a determination still evident when the credits roll first in English, then translate into Spanish as they proceed up the screen. Whichever direction one may be moving, Rivera's film insists, it cannot be toward a "future that starts today," as the Cybracero corporation promises, but toward the polytemporal hope with which Memo's narration concludes, "a future with a past." Joining earlier SF cinema in reflecting and lamenting assumptions that national borders must be incontrovertible or that power can flow in only one direction, it posits a different future in which individual and specific communal choices matter more than rhetorical abstractions or enforced patriotism and in which borderlands and other transnational spaces are characterized by dynamic interchange rather than static isolation.

BIBLIOGRAPHY

Auerbach, Jonathan. *Dark Borders: Film Noir and American Citizenship*. Durham, NC: Duke University Press, 2011.

Csicsery-Ronay, Istvan. "Empire." Essay. In *The Routledge Companion to Science Fiction*, edited by Mark Bould. London, U.K.: Routledge, 2009.

Decena, Carlos Ulises, and Margaret Gray. "Putting Transnationalism to Work: An Interview with Filmmaker Alex Rivera." *Social Text* 24, no. 3 (2006): 131–38. https://doi.org/10.1215/01642472-2006-008.

Fojas, Camilla. *Border Bandits: Hollywood on the Southern Frontier*. Austin, TX: University of Texas Press, 2008.

---

17   Carlos Ulises Decena and Margaret Gray, "Putting Transnationalism to Work: An Interview with Filmmaker Alex Rivera," *Social Text* 24, no. 3 (Fall 2006): 131.

Hairston, Andrea. "Different and Equal Together: SF Satire in District 9." *Journal of the Fantastic in the Arts* 22, no. 3 (2011): 326-346,452.

Loshitzky, Yosefa. Screening Strangers: Migration and Diaspora in Contemporary European Cinema. Bloomington, IN: Indiana University Press, 2010.

Martín-Cabrera, Luis. "The Potentiality of the Commons: A Materialist Critique of Cognitive Capitalism from the Cyberbracer@s to the Ley Sinde." *Hispanic Review* 80, no. 4 (2012): 583–605. http://www.jstor.org/stable/23275310.

Rieder, John. "Race and revenge fantasies in *Avatar, District 9* and *Inglourious Basterds*." *Science Fiction Film and Television* 4, no. 1 (2011): 41-56. muse.jhu.edu/article/427008.

Rivera, Lysa. "Future Histories and Cyborg Labor: Reading Borderlands Science Fiction after NAFTA." *Science Fiction Studies* 39, no. 3 (November 2012): 415–36. https://doi.org/10.5621/sciefictstud.39.3.0415.

Russell, John G. "Don't It Make My Black Face Blue: Race, Avatars, Albescence, and the Transnational Imaginary." *The Journal of Popular Culture* 46, no. 1 (2013): 192–217. https://doi.org/10.1111/jpcu.12021.

Smith, Eric D. *Globalization, Utopia, and Postcolonial Science Fiction: New Maps of Hope*. New York, NY: Palgrave Macmillan, 2012.

Tan, Kathy-Ann. "'If You're Not on Paper, You Don't Exist': Depictions of Illegal Immigration and Asylum in Film—on Michael Winterbottom's In This World (2002) and Code 46 (2003)." Essay. In *Multi-Ethnic Britain 2000+: New Perspectives in Literature, Film and the Arts*, edited by Barbara Korte, Lars Eckstein, Christoph Reinfandt, and Eva Ulrike Pirker. Rodopi, 2008.

POST-READING QUESTIONS/POST-SCREENING QUESTIONS

Directions: Use what you learned from reading this chapter and watching the film to respond to the questions.

1. How does the chapter situate twenty-first-century science fiction in relation to old science fiction?

2. Do you agree with the description of *District 9* and *Sleep Dealer* as challenging techno-capitalism through the science fiction genre? Explain why or why not.

3. Choose any of the twenty-first-century films discussed in this chapter and explain how they expand the science fiction genre.

4. In what ways can *Sleep Dealer* be considered a horror film?

Reading 1.5

Dark Desires

Male Masochism in the Horror Film

By Barbara Creed

KEY TERMS AND FIGURES

Third-wave feminism
Final girl
Psychoanalysis
Abjection
Masochism
Male gaze

Scopophilia
Laura Mulvey
Carol J. Clover
Barbara Creed
Julia Kristeva

RECOMMENDED FILMS

Dressed to Kill by Brian De Palma (1980)
The Brood by David Cronenberg (1979)
Silence of the Lambs by Jonathan Demme (1991)
Alien by Ridley Scott (1979)
Repulsion by Roman Polanski (1965)
Videodrome by David Cronenberg (1983)

INTRODUCTION

Right on the cusp of third-wave feminism Carol Clover published her famous examination of the slasher genre, which had become singularly pronounced in 1970s American horror films. In her book *Men, Women, and Chainsaws* (1992), Clover revisited Laura Mulvey's 1975 essay "Visual Pleasure and Narrative Cinema" to challenge the binary between scopophilia and narcissism with which female and male spectators, Mulvey argued, respectively identified in horror films. Seeing abject terror as "gendered feminine," Clover redirected our focus to the final girl trope, who other than being the last woman standing at the end of a slasher film, as well as sexually ambiguous and functioning as a double for the adolescent male viewer, is more resourceful than her male counterparts in outliving and defeating the murderous villain.

In this chapter, Barbara Creed builds on Clover's study of male anxiety and desire expressed in the slasher genre, where the suffering victim is "repeatedly figured as feminine" via projection of that suffering. But Creed focuses on male monsters and how they trouble the traditional differentiation of the sexes, implying gender ambivalence in their embodiment of feminine characteristics. She sees *Dressed to Kill* as a reworking of the theme of gender ambivalence, but where woman is the precursor to man, arguing that the film posits woman's body as the ideal body desired by a man and equates transsexuality with deviant sexuality (and therefore monstrosity). To explain this, Creed summons the Freudian concept of masochism and its three forms (erotogenic, moral, and/or feminine) and Julia Kristeva's theorization of abjection.

Creed sees two competing desires in this Freudian model—the fear of being eaten by the father (which Freud linked to masochism of the infant in the oral stage) and the desire to be beaten (which Freud linked to the sadistic phase)—as operating together to feminize the man and thus construct him as monstrous. This is because, she explains, the "very nature of horror" is an "encounter with the feminine," which is supported by Kristeva's theory of the abject that explores the "maternal bases of horror." In Kristeva's theory the abject, as Creed reminds us, is that which disturbs identity, system, and order and is linked to the feminine. But the abject is also a border and a liminal space between human and beast, good and evil, pure and impure, a concept reflected in a host of horror films from the 1970s, including *The Exorcist*, *The Omen*, *The Boys from Brazil*, *The Brood*, and *Dressed to Kill* (even though it was released in 1980). Kristeva differentiates the abject from the symbolic order in that the former is associated with the feminine and the maternal (thereby nature, reproduction, secretion of blood and milk, transformation), whereas the latter is associated with the paternal, the law, and language.

Creed explores the feminization of the male monstrous in the archetypes of the vampire and the werewolf, both of whom need to periodically replenish their blood supply, thereby sharing some parallels with menstruating women. The werewolf's cycle of feeding on blood, however, is accompanied by animal transfiguration in the form of hair, fangs, and animalistic tendencies, and is additionally distinct from vampire in that they always return to human form after being killed. Creed sees this as a form of self-reproduction: giving birth to the self in both animal and human form, the one enclosed within the other depending on which side of the lunar cycle they are on (e.g., *American Werewolf in London*). Creed then discusses murderous father/son relations and the identification with maternal power as seen in werewolf films.

In the 1941 film *The Wolf Man*, the world is split between that of the father "associated with civilization, rationality, the law, church, authority, tradition" and that of the mother associated "with nature, superstition, fate."

Creed pivots to focus on masochism in killer Buffalo Bill in *Silence of the Lambs,* for whom women are associated with nature and the animal world, and necessary to his desired (but ultimately failed) transformation, and for which reason he must wear the skin of the woman to represent the symbolic power of transformation. By contrast, Hannibal Lector, who can be seen as Buffalo Bill's alter ego, uses language and mind games to weaken his victims before eating them, thus belonging to the symbolic/paternal order, but both men are engaged with symbolic (or "totemic") actions in relation to their victims. She then discusses men's desire to experience reproduction (reflected in the character of the mad scientist and the *mise en scene* of horror films: *Alien, Videodrome, The Fly, Dead Ringers, Total Recall*), as well as castration, as further expressions of male masochism and monstrous feminization.

Creed concludes that affinities between monster and woman reside in the feminization of the monstrous, who is occasionally a sympathetic character (*Carrie, The Exorcist, The Hunger, Repulsion*). While women are typically the victims of aliens, monsters, and serial killers, the monstrous threat is feminized in the process of transformation/reproduction. In asserting that "the gaze of both male and female spectators is constructed as masochistic" and that this is built into the signifying processes of the horror film text (through characters, *mise en scene*, cinematography, and editing), Creed links the processes of signification to the pleasure of film spectators. Her argument that the origins of monstrosity are a form of abjection, speaking to the "perverse and irrational aspects of desire" of all spectators regardless of gender, reminds us of what horror has historically demonstrated: a social denigration of the feminine associated with the abject body and a social valorization of the masculine that is identified with the symbolic body. Neither *Dressed to Kill* nor *Silence of the Lambs* treat transgender characters with the nuances we would today, and to be clear, Creed is not suggesting that we should pathologize transgender characters as deviant. On the contrary, in this reading she draws attention to how films have historically aligned ideas of monstrosity with gendered femininity.

Dark Desires

Male Masochism in the Horror Film

By Barbara Creed

> *The body must bear no trace of its debt to nature: it must be clean and proper in order to be fully symbolic.*
> (Kristeva 1982)

Whenever male bodies are represented as monstrous in the horror film they assume characteristics usually associated with the female body: they experience a blood cycle, change shape, bleed, give birth, become penetrable, are castrated. Traditionally, the male body has been viewed as norm; the female body a deviation. One of the more popular medieval ideas of the difference between the sexes was that women were men turned inside out. Galen explains in careful detail how this reversal works. His discussion is part of a wider treatise justifying woman's inferiority.

> A second reason is one that appears in dissecting ... think first, please, of the man's [sexual organs] turned in and extending inward between the rectum and the bladder. If this should happen, the scrotum would necessarily take the place of the uteri [*sic*], with the testes lying outside, next to it on either side; the penis of the male would become the neck of the cavity that had been formed; and the skin at the end of the penis, now called prepuce, would become the female pudendum itself. ... In fact, you could not find a single male part left over that had not simply changed its position; for the parts that are inside in woman are outside in man.
>
> (quoted in Bullough 1973:492)

The reason Galen gives for this unusual state of affairs is body temperature. Because woman is colder than man, her bodily parts, formed when she was still a fetus, 'could not because of the defect in the heat emerge and project on the outside.' The view that women's internal organs were the reverse of man's external ones dominated medical thinking until the late eighteenth century; it even included the naming of the ovaries as female testes. One of the more novel superstitions, which sprang from this view, was that if women stood or sat with their legs spread apart their internal organs would fall out—the vagina would drop through as a penis—and women would become men! Young girls who wanted to be 'lady-like' should keep their legs crossed at all times. At the heart of this medieval view, influenced no doubt by the Platonic theory of ideal forms, is a belief that there is only one sex and that men represent its more perfect expression.

In the 1980 horror film *Dressed to Kill,* we find an unusual re-working of this ancient theme, although an interesting reversal has taken place—woman is now the prototype. Brian De Palma's *Dressed to Kill* tells the story of Dr Elliott (Michael Caine) a man who masquerades as a woman, Bobbi, and who wants to have a sex-change operation. *Dressed to Kill* belongs to a group of horror films (*Psycho,* 1960, *Homicidal,* 1961, *A Reflection of Fear,* 1973) in which the monster is seen as monstrous precisely because she or he does not have a clear gender identity. Dr Elliott/Bobbi is monstrous because of his cross-dressing/transsexuality. Towards the end of *Dressed to Kill,* two of the main characters, Liz (Nancy Allen) and Peter (Keith Gordon), sit in a restaurant discussing transsexualism. Liz, a prostitute, begins to tell Peter, who is younger and relatively naive, about the procedure for changing sex. She explains that if a man wishes to become a woman he takes female hormones which will soften his skin, cause breasts to grow and stop him from having erections. Peter, who never shows any sexual interest towards Liz, is extremely interested in this proposition. 'Instead of building a computer, I could build a woman,' he says with great delight. Liz, who loves to shock, gives Peter all the details. A lot more is involved than simply letting it all 'hang out.'

> *Liz*: 'The next step is ... penectomy.'
>
> *Peter*: 'What's that?'
>
> *Liz*: 'Well, you know. They take your penis and slice it down the middle.'
>
> *Peter*: 'Yeh, yeh. That's what I thought it was.'
>
> *Liz*: 'Then castration. Plastic reconstruction and the formation of an artificial vagina of vaginal plastics—for those in the know.'
>
> *Peter*: 'I thought Elliott just put on a dress.'
>
> *Liz*: 'Oh, he did and a wig too. But that's not good enough in bed when you've got to take everything off.'
>
> *Peter*: 'Well, I think I'm going to stick with my computer.'

Figure 1.5.1 Michael Caine in women's clothes as 'Bobbi' attacks Angie Dickinson in *Dressed to Kill*

In *Dressed to Kill,* woman's body is represented as the ideal body desired by man—and voyeuristically by the camera. On the one hand, it might be argued that we cannot accept Bobbi's desires as true for other men; Bobbi is psychotic, a monster whose desires are sick and perverted. On the other hand, the monster of the horror film is, in a sense, monstrous because he/she dares to speak the truth of repressed desire. Whether male or female, the monster speaks the unspeakable, defies order and system, flaunts morality and the law. By drawing a number of parallels between Bobbi and Peter, De Palma, in fact, makes it clear that Bobbi's desire to become a woman should not be seen simply as the desire of an insane mind. The problem with *Dressed to Kill,* and other films about the sexually ambiguous monster, is that, while they might present a critique of a culture fearful of changes in traditional sex roles, they also equate cross-dressing and transsexuality with monstrousness.

In 'The Economic Problem of Masochism,' Freud described three forms of masochism: erotogenic, moral, and feminine. Erotogenic refers to the primary experience of 'pleasure in pain' and moral masochism to the ego's need for punishment either from the super-ego or from outside powers. By 'feminine,' Freud did not mean 'masochism in women,' but rather the *feminine position* adopted by the subject in relation to masochistic desire. He proposed that what constitutes the essence of a masochistic phantasy in men is that they place the male in a 'characteristically female situation'.

> But if one has an opportunity of studying cases in which the masochistic phantasies have been especially richly elaborated, one quickly discovers that they place the subject in a characteristically female situation; they signify, that is, being castrated, or copulated with, or giving birth to a baby.
>
> (Freud 1924:162)

Freud also linked masochism to the infant's developmental phases: fear of being eaten by the totem animal (the father) originates in the primitive oral phase; the wish to be beaten by the father relates to the sadisticanal phase; and castration is a precipitate of the phallic stage. Here Freud specifies two other forms of masochism in addition to those associated with the specifically feminine position: a desire to be eaten and a desire to be beaten. Phantasies of man's masochistic desire to take up a feminine position are one of the central topics that the horror film exists to explore.

Almost all articles (Lenne 1979, Neale 1980) written on the horror film define the majority of monsters as male, the victims female. Very few writers (Williams 1984, Hollinger 1989) have attempted to qualify this opposition in any way. Yet, it seems clear that in the process of being constructed as monstrous the male is 'feminized'. This process is not simply a consequence of placing the male in a masochistic position—although this is crucial to many texts—but rather it stems from the very nature of horror as an encounter with the feminine. Julia Kristeva's theory of the abject provides us with a preliminary hypothesis for understanding the maternal bases of horror.[1] Kristeva, like Freud, also defines the 'feminine' as essential to her project.

In *Powers of Horror,* Kristeva argues that the constitution of acceptable forms of subjectivity and sociality demands the expulsion of those things defined as improper and unclean. Whatever is expelled is constituted as an abject, that which 'disturbs identity, system, order' (Kristeva 1982:4). A crucial aspect of the abject is, however, that it can never be fully removed or set apart from the subject or society; the abject both threatens and beckons. The abject constitutes the other side of seemingly stable subjectivity. 'It beseeches, worries, and fascinates desire' (ibid.: 1). The abject constitutes the gap or hole at the border of subjectivity which threatens to engulf the individual when its identity is threatened. The place of the abject is 'the place where meaning collapses' (ibid.: 2), the place where 'I' am not. Kristeva distinguishes between three main forms of abjection; these are constituted in relation to food, bodily wastes, and sexual difference. The ultimate in abjection is the corpse. The body expels its wastes so that it might continue to live. But the corpse is a body which can no longer expel its wastes. The corpse is 'the most sickening of wastes, is a border that has encroached upon everything. It is no longer I who expel, "I" is expelled' (ibid.: 3–4). The notion of the border is crucial to our understanding of the abject and the way it is represented in the horror film. The abject exists on the other side of a border which separates out the subject from all that threatens its existence. 'We may call it a border; abjection is above all ambiguity' (Kristeva 1982:9–10). It is the ambiguous side of abjection that the horror film explores, particularly in relation to the monster. The border is defined in a number of crucial ways—between human and beast (the werewolf, ape man); good and evil (*The Omen,* 1976, *The Boys From Brazil,* 1978); male and female (*Dressed to Kill,* 1980,

---

1   For a fuller discussion of Kristeva's *Powers of Horror* in relation to the horror film see my earlier article, 'Horror and the Monstrous-Feminine: an Imaginary Abjection', *Screen* 27, 1 (1986): 44–70. Also included in *Fantasy and the Cinema,* ed. James Donald, London: BFI Publishing, 1989, 63–90.

A Reflection of Fear, 1973); or between the body which is clean and proper and the body which is aligned with nature and abject wastes (*The Exorcist,* 1973, *The Brood,* 1979).

The body which is most closely aligned with the abject is the feminine, maternal body. All experiences of bodily horror, as well as those which involve a loss of subject boundaries, can be traced back to the infant's experience with the maternal entity. In her discussion of the 'clean and proper body' as defined within religious discourse, Kristeva distinguishes between the symbolic and non-symbolic body.

> The body must bear no trace of its debt to nature ... it should endure no gash other than that of circumcision, equivalent to sexual separation and/or separation from the mother. Any other mark would be the sign of belonging to the impure, the non-separate, the non-symbolic, the non-holy.
>
> (Kristeva 1982:102)

The abject is placed on the side of the feminine and the maternal in opposition to the paternal symbolic, the domain of law and language. The prototype of the abject body is the maternal body because of its link with the natural world signified in its lack of 'corporeal integrity': it secretes (blood, milk); it changes size, grows, and swells; it gives birth in 'a violent act of expulsion through which the nascent body tears itself away from the matter of maternal insides' (Kristeva 1982:101). Such actions violate the boundary of the skin which should remain smooth, taut, unblemished. As mentioned above, however, the abject does not simply repel; it also 'fascinates desire,' lures the subject to its side. The horror film explores the attraction of the abject feminized body through its graphic representation of the body-monstrous.

We can see the feminization of the monstrous male body at work in the representation of a number of archetypal figures of male monstrosity, in particular the vampire and werewolf. In the cinema, the archetypal vampire is represented by Count Dracula. He is usually depicted as a sinister but seductive heterosexual male who dwells in a Gothic castle characterized by long winding stairs, dark corridors, cobwebs, and a crypt or cellar containing his coffin. These features of the vampire film are clearly evident in John Badham's *Dracula,* a 1979 version of the classic myth. Dracula (Frank Langella) is a sleek, elegant, aristocratic figure who wears a flowing black cloak, with red lining, speaks in softly modulated tones and glides silently through the dark on his nocturnal journeys. He is linked with images of bats, spiders, rats, and the deadly *vagina dentata*—symbols usually associated with female monsters. Compared to the more rugged, masculine Van Helsing (Laurence Olivier), Dracula's arch-enemy, and a pillar of patriarchal Christian society, Dracula is a sexually ambiguous figure. In their description of the stereotypical features of the Dracula figure, Alain Silver and James Ursini draw attention to his 'dark clothes and full-flowing red-lined cape, the hair brushed back straight and flat from the forehead, the lips extraordinarily crimson and distended ...' (Silver and Ursini 1975:61).

Not only is his appearance and behavior feminized, Dracula's need to replace his blood at periodic intervals suggests he experiences a form of menstrual cycle. In *Idols of Perversity* (1986), Bram Dijkstra points out that it was popularly believed that woman became a vampire in order to replenish the blood she lost during menstruation and pregnancy. In their study of menstruation, Penelope Shuttle and Peter Redgrove argue that Count Dracula symbolizes two figures: the 'other' husband, the one who understands woman's bodies; and woman herself, 'expressed in masculine disguise' (Shuttle and Redgrove 1978:269). They see the vampire myth as a rite of passage story used to explain the onset of menstruation in girls. Before the vampire approaches, his victims—almost always young virgins—lie in bed, pale and wan. Andrew Tudor emphasizes this feature of Tod Browning's *Dracula* (1931) in which the female victims lie languidly in their beds 'unable and unwilling to resist' (Tudor 1989:164). Once bitten, their blood flows freely, and in almost all vampire films, Dracula's victims rise from their beds filled with a new energy which is both predatory and sexual. In Badham's *Dracula*, Lucy's frustration with her passive feminine role as a 'chattel' in her father's world is replaced with new energy and purpose once she joins Dracula's world. 'I despise women with no life in them, no blood,' says Dracula. The vampire always bites the neck of his victims, which Shuttle and Redgrove argue symbolizes the neck of the uterus through which menstrual blood flows.

A number of myths from ancient cultures associate woman's monthly bleeding with the full moon and the snake because all move through stages in which the old is shed and the new is born. Various myths state that a young girl begins to bleed when she is bitten by a snake—or similar creature—that lives either in the moon or on her womb. Robert Briffault refers to Rabbinical teachings which stated that the onset of menstruation was caused by copulation with a snake (Briffault 1927: 666). Lévi-Strauss points out that the Aztecs and Colombians believed menstruation was brought about by the bite of vampire bats (Lévi-Strauss 1973:382). In his essay on the virginity taboo, Freud states that some primitive people believed menstruation was caused by 'the bite of some spirit animal' (Freud 1918:197). In the light of these myths and beliefs, it is relevant to note that Dracula's teeth are like the fangs of a snake and that his bite resembles the two round puncture marks of the snake. Dracula himself is very much like a snake: in his black clothes he glides silently through the night, his fangs bared in his white moon-like face. Dracula's feminization then relates to his appearance as well as his symbolic association with the need of woman's body to release and replenish its blood at regular intervals. For just as Dracula ushers in the blood-flow, he also takes this blood into his own body. Like the menstrual cycle, Dracula's 'life' depends on this exchange.

The werewolf is another cinematic monster who, like Dracula, is a feminized figure associated with woman's menstrual cycle. According to Walter Evans, 'the werewolf's bloody attacks—which occur regularly every month—are certainly related to the menstrual cycle which suddenly and mysteriously commands the body of every adolescent girl' (Evans 1973:357). The legend of the werewolf (Douglas 1966, Twitchell 1985) is probably as old as that of Dracula and is known throughout the world; it is most common in Europe where the wolf is one of the most savage of carnivorous animals. The most heinous crime the werewolf commits is cannibalism, and in those countries where the wolf was not common, the human animal would transform into a different carnivorous beast—usually a tiger, bear, or leopard. Jacques Tourneur's classic horror film, *Cat People* (1942) deals with the transformation of a young woman into a man-eating cat.

The werewolf is recognized in a number of ways: hair growing on his palms; an index finger which is longer than any of his others; and the mark of the mystical pentagram on some part of the body. The pentagram, a five-pointed star, is an interesting symbol which appears to have been closely related to paganism. It was once worshipped by Pythagorean mystics as the birth letter interlaced five times (Hornung 1959:212). In Egypt the pentagram represented the underground womb (Walker 1983: 782). It is during the full moon that the werewolf's blood undergoes chemical changes which force him to seek the blood and flesh of humans. Whereas the vampire can roam abroad on any night (although the full moon is particularly propitious) the werewolf strikes *only* on the night of the full moon, particularly if the wolfbane is in blossom. The only reliable way of killing a werewolf is with a bullet or weapon of silver. When the werewolf is slain, he always returns to his human form. As with the vampire myth, the werewolf story also has its own symbols and motifs: the full moon, wolfbane, wounds, transformation, the pentagram, cannibalism, silver bullets, death.

Walter Evans argues that the 'horrible alterations' which afflict the transformation monster, such as the Wolfman, Frankenstein's monster, and Dracula, are associated with the changes which mark the body of the adolescent. The most significant of these is 'the monstrous transformation which is directly associated with secondary sexual characteristics and with the onset of aggressive erotic behaviour' (Evans 1973:354). In particular he associates the werewolf's sudden growth of body hair and his aggressive behavior with these changes. Evans's interpretation is interesting, but it ignores the crucial themes of menstruation, totemism, and self-rebirth in the werewolf films.

The theme of rebirth is particularly relevant to the filmic representation of the werewolf and helps to explain its feminization. In most narratives (*The Wolf Man,* 1941, *An American Werewolf in London,* 1981, *The Howling,* 1981), the victim is savagely mauled and his body covered in bloody wounds prior to his transformation into the beast. In all werewolf films, the transformation involves a series of terrifying bodily changes which signify his abject status. As he metamorphoses into a wolf, his human form remains somehow encased inside his animal exterior. When he changes back into human form, the animal remains inside. In other words the werewolf is able to give birth to himself, in either animal or human form, at the time of the full moon or once a month. Once transformed he feeds on the blood and flesh of others—presumably to replace his own blood which is at a low ebb. Like the woman with her menstrual cycle, the werewolf replenishes his blood monthly and is reborn monthly. Like the female body in the act of birth, his transformation is accompanied by a series of dramatic bodily changes.

With the revolution in special effects technology, the contemporary werewolf film is able to represent these bodily alterations in minute detail. *An American Werewolf in London* illustrates the power of this technology to challenge our disbelief. We see body and legs sprout hair, a nose extend into a snout, nostrils broaden, teeth extend into fangs, muscles bulge, hands change into paws with long pointed nails, and eyes become blood red. Insofar as man gives birth to himself in another form, he takes on the characteristics usually associated with woman when she gives birth. His body shape changes, his eyes bulge, his muscles stretch and pull. In a sense, the werewolf gives birth to himself by turning himself inside out. In his description of the transformation scene in *An American Werewolf in London,* Twitchell writes: 'And this seamless metamorphosis happens with no break-away before our unbelieving eyes, almost as if the wolf is unfolding outward *through* the skin of a man' (Twitchell 1985:217). What is most interesting about this transformation is that the inside of the human body is represented in terms of the animal. When man gives birth to himself—and hence takes up a feminine position—he is represented as an integral part of the animal world. His new body is distinguished by coarse hair, a fanged gaping mouth, and a need for blood. The border separating human from animal, the symbolic from all that threatens its integrity, is literally only skin-deep.

In some films, the world of the werewolf is clearly associated with the mother. In *The Wolf Man,* directed by George Waggner, the werewolf/son (Lon Chaney Jr.) rejects the father's world, represented by his own father, Sir Larry Talbot (Claude Rains), and returns to the world of the mother, represented by the Gypsy Queen, Malvena (Maria Ouspenskaya). The narrative establishes a series of oppositions which separate these two domains. The father's world is associated with civilization, rationality, the law, church, authority, tradition: the mother's world with nature, superstition, fate. Insofar as Malvena is the mother of the two werewolves in the film (her son is a werewolf and she calls Larry 'my son') she is also associated with orality, totemism, and taboo. Throughout the narrative the son is ill at ease in his father's world, yet is inexplicably attracted to the gypsy camp located in the forest. The carnivalesque atmosphere of the gypsy life stands in marked contrast with the sober propriety of life at Talbot castle. In the end, the father murders the son/wolf by beating him to death with a silver-headed cane. In an earlier scene, the father ties his son to a chair to prevent him from transforming. The binding and beating episodes suggest a sadistic/masochistic scenario of punishment in which the father reinforces paternal law. Through his transformation, the son transgresses against the symbolic order, retreating into a world of totemism and taboo presided over by Malvena, the mother. A murderous father-son relationship is also important to *Werewolf of London* (1935) and *Curse of the Werewolf* (1961).

A recent horror film which explores the male subject's relationship to the feminized totem animal is *The Silence of the Lambs* (Jonathan Demme, 1991). The psychotic killer, known as Buffalo Bill (Ted Levine), hunts, kills, and flays his female victims in order to make for himself a lifesize female suit from their skins. The totem animal associated with the original Buffalo Bill was the buffalo; in *The Silence of the Lambs* it is woman herself. Buffalo Bill wants to become a woman—presumably because he sees femininity as a more desirable state, possibly a superior one. In primitive cultures (Freud 1913) the totem animal was a revered creature who protected the whole group; in return human beings showed their respect by not killing the totem if it were an animal or cutting it if it were a plant. If it were necessary to kill the totem animal, various practices had to be strictly observed. To emphasize kinship with the totem, special ceremonies would be held in which people of the clan would dress up in the skin of the totem animal and imitate its behavior.

The Silence of the Lambs draws on these ancient practices in which woman is represented as a kind of totemic animal. Buffalo Bill not only wants to wear woman's skin, he also wants to be a woman. This is clearly brought out in the scene where we watch the killer preparing for his transformation; as he dances in his dark shadowy room, dressed in woman's clothes, we watch him tuck his penis up behind his legs in order to create the impression he is without a penis—'castrated' like a woman. Woman is the object of his hunt and his perverse desires. After murdering his victims, Buffalo Bill places the larvae of a rare caterpillar inside their mouths. Reborn as a beautiful butterfly, the caterpillar symbolizes the killer's own desire for rebirth. But, in order to experience a rebirth as woman, Buffalo Bill must wear the skin of woman not just to experience a physical transformation but also to acquire the *power of transformation* associated with woman's ability to give birth. As in the rituals associated with the wolf cults, the skin of the totem animal must be worn if the individual is to assume the power of the divine animal.

The other killer of *The Silence of the Lambs* is Dr Hannibal Lecter (Anthony Hopkins). Although a very different character, Lecter is represented, in a sense, as Buffalo Bill's alter ego, his other self. Lecter doesn't skin his victims; he eats their internal organs. Totemism also permitted the eating of certain parts of the sacred animal. Both men are thus engaged in totemic actions: one eats special parts of the human animal, the other wears its skin. Taken together the actions of the two men constitute a debased version of a primitive ritual in which the totem animal is human and female. Although the actions of both men are monstrous, it is Buffalo Bill who is constructed as the central or 'true' monster of the film. Lecter almost assumes the status of hero, and his relationship with the heroine, Clarice Starling (Jodie Foster), borders on a romance. Like Dracula, Lecter is an orally sadistic monster with a mesmerizing stare. He is also articulate, cultivated, and well-mannered. 'Discourtesy is unspeakably ugly to me,' says Lecter.

Part of Buffalo Bill's construction as monster involves his feminization, his desire to become a woman and his wearing of women's skins. Lecter is also associated with totemism in that when he is near people he is made to wear a mask to stop him from eating them. It transforms him into a horrifying animal-like creature. Throughout the narrative, woman is associated with the animal world (the flayed totem creature, the larvae, the lamb); even the heroine's surname, 'Starling,' locates her in the world

Figure 1.5.2 Ted Levine as Buffalo Bill at his sewing machine in *The Silence of the Lambs*

of nature. For different reasons both killers are drawn to this world, Buffalo Bill to the possibility of becoming woman, Lecter to the possibility of devouring/incorporating Clarice. When she tells Lecter about her dream of saving the lambs from slaughter, he orders lamb chops for his next meal. The incident is intended as a joke but nevertheless it points to Lecter's ambivalent attitude to Clarice.

Lecter's cannibalism also underlines a desire to devour in order to avoid being devoured. His amazing skill with words, his superior command of language also points to an obsession with the oral. In terms of abjection, Kristeva—drawing on Freud—argues that one of the infant's earlier fears is of the incorporating mother. 'Fear of the uncontrollable generative mother repels me from the body; I give up cannibalism because abjection (of the mother) leads me toward respect for the body of the other, my fellow man, my brother' (Kristeva 1982:78–9). The symbolic body, the clean and proper body, is 'non-assimilable, uneatable' (78). The subject who breaks the taboo of cannibalism signifies his alliance with the abject, his continuing identification with the devouring maternal body as well as his fear of that figure.

Dr Lecter uses his mastery of language and his ability to read human behavior to get inside the skins of his victims psychically—even driving one to commit suicide rather than listen any longer to Lecter's sadistic verbal attack. He dies by swallowing his own tongue. As Lecter's 'other self,' Buffalo Bill confronts this fear by incorporating woman literally—he physically gets 'inside woman's skin'. Both men also inhabit an underworld associated with darkness, the earth, womb-like enclosures, death: Lecter is confined underground in a cell, Buffalo Bill lives in a darkly-lit house built over a deep earthen pit in which he imprisons his victims. *The Silence of the Lambs* creates a world of horror in which the composite male monster confronts his greatest fear, woman, but in so doing is made monstrous through the processes of feminization.

In some horror films a male scientist attempts to create a new life form (*Frankenstein,* 1931) or tamper in some way with the natural order (*Altered States,* 1980, *The Fly,* 1986). Practices of couvade, a term which refers to man's desire to give birth, have been documented in the rituals of a number of peoples. The couvade is a custom in which the father, during the period when his wife is giving birth, also lies in bed where he enacts the motions of childbirth (Walker 1983:106). Myths and legends from many cultures attest to the desire of the male to give birth. Zeus gave birth to Athena from his head. In the Christian myth, Adam gives birth to Eve from his ribs. The horror film also explores the notion of the male mother/scientist, who attempts to create new life forms in his laboratory, and whose *mise-en-scène* is coded to suggest an intrauterine world. But in his bizarre attempt to usurp female reproductive powers, the male monster of science can only create monsters. Male interest in, and obsession with, birth is explored from a number of perspectives. As the scientist of *The Fly* is re-created as a Brundle fly, coded as female in the text, his genitals drop off. In *Alien* (1979), a male astronaut gives birth from his stomach whereas in *Total Recall* (1990) the baby leader of the mutant rebels lives permanently in a man's stomach. *Dead Ringers* (1988) explores male womb envy in relation to a woman who possesses a triple uterus which is described as 'fabulously rare.' In *Videodrome* (1983), the male protagonist inserts a gun into a vagina-like opening in his stomach as if impregnating himself.

While some horror films explore man's desire for castration in order to become a woman, others explore castration as part of a male death wish. We see this in rape-revenge films such as *I Spit on Your Grave* (1978) and *Naked Vengeance* (1984). In this sub-genre of the horror film, woman enacts a deadly revenge on the men who have raped her; she hunts them down and kills them in scenes of gruesome horror. In both these films, a male rapist is castrated at the very moment when he is experiencing intense sexual pleasure. In *I Spit on Your Grave,* the heroine caresses then castrates the male as he lies in a hot bath. In *Naked Vengeance,* she castrates him as they embrace in a river. In both films, the castration scenes place the male in the position of victim, and there is no doubt that the audience is intended to enjoy his savage punishment as he has earlier been portrayed as a vicious, brutal rapist.

The difference in the representation of the rape and castration scenes, however, is crucial. The rapes are represented in a more confronting manner and are depicted as violent, sadistic, and horrifying whereas the castration scenes are represented within a seduction scenario in which the atmosphere is initially romanticized. On the one hand, these scenes are romanticized because the heroine lures her victim to his doom with a promise of sexual bliss. On the other hand, the effect of this is to link man's sexual desire with a desire for death. He willingly surrenders to the woman he has previously brutalized and who has good reason to wish him dead. Dressed in a long white robe, her hair tied regally in a bun, the female avenger of *I Spit on*

Your Grave looks like a pagan goddess officiating over an ancient ritual. After she castrates the male, she locks him in the bathroom and listens to his death cries rise up against a background of classical music.

Man's desire for sex and death is clearly brought out in Brian De Palma's *Sisters* (1973). Margot Kidder plays Siamese twins, Danielle and Dominique; the former is sweet and gentle, the latter dangerous, aggressive. During an operation to separate the twins, Dominique dies. Unable to come to terms with her sister's death, Danielle takes on her sister's identity. Emile (William Finley), the doctor who performed the operation, is also Danielle's husband. He knows that Danielle has become a divided personality but is able to control 'Dominique' by keeping Danielle sedated. This is only partly effective. Emile says to Danielle that he knows whenever he makes love to her that Dominique is present. Yet Emile chooses to arouse Danielle sexually even though she has just castrated the last man with whom she made love. Predictably, Danielle/Dominique also slashes Emile's genitals, and as he dies he clasps her hand over his bleeding wound. Emile's wound parallels the one which runs down Danielle's side, a hideous reminder of her separation/castration from her sister. The image of their two hands clasped together and covered in Emile's blood reminds us of the abject nature of desire. *Sisters* presents an interesting study of male and female castration fears as well as exploring a male sexual death wish. In her interesting discussion of the male dread of woman, Karen Horney argues that perhaps the death wish for man is more closely aligned with sex.

> Is any light shed upon it by the state of lethargy—even the death—after mating, which occurs frequently in male animals? Are love and death more closely bound up with one another for the male than the female, in whom sexual union potentially produces a new life? Does man feel, side by side with his desire to conquer, a secret longing for extinction in the act of reunion with the woman (mother)? Is it perhaps this longing that underlies the 'death-instinct'?
>
> (Horney 1967:138–9)

The conventional interpretation is to argue that the male monster of the classic horror film (ape, werewolf, vampire) represents the repressed bestial desires of civilized man and that woman is almost always the object of this aggression.[2] 'Women are invariably the victims of the acts of terror unleashed by the werewolf/vampire/alien/thing' (Mercer 1986: 39). What this interpretation ignores is the extent to which the beast is also feminized through the processes of transformation. It is this aspect of male monstrousness that Linda Williams addresses in

---

2   I am not arguing that women do not constitute the majority of victims in the horror film. Rather, I am arguing that the nature of male monstrosity is itself problematic and should be given more consideration than is usually the case. The formula monster/male and victim/female is too simplistic.

'When the Woman Looks' (1984). Here she discusses the relationship between the classic monster (werewolf, ape, vampire) and the heroine. Williams argues that there is 'a surprising (and at times subversive) affinity' (85) between monster and woman in that, like woman, he is represented as 'a biological freak with impossible and threatening appetites' (87). Whereas Williams ties the monster's freakishness to its phallic status (either symbolically castrated or overly endowed), I would argue that the affinity between the monster and woman resides in the way in which all monstrous figures are constructed in terms of Kristeva's 'non-symbolic' body: the body that gives birth, secretes, changes shape, or is marked in some way. This is also Freud's masochistic, feminized body.

Williams argues that while the male spectator's look at the monster 'expresses conventional fear' (Williams 1984:87) because the monster is different, the female spectator is punished for looking because she recognizes the monster's freakishness as similar to her own. 'The woman's gaze is punished, in other words, by narrative processes that transform curiosity and desire into masochistic fantasy' (85). In my view, the gaze of *both* male and female spectators is constructed as masochistic by the signifying practices of the horror text. Although the male monster is placed in a feminine position in terms of the workings of abjection and masochistic desire, he is still male and as such elicits identification from male spectators. Furthermore, the monster is frequently represented as a sympathetic figure with whom all spectators are encouraged to identify (*King Kong*, 1933, *The Creature from the Black Lagoon*, 1954, *Psycho*, 1960, *An American Werewolf in London*). For similar reasons I would argue that female monsters (*Carrie*, 1976, *The Exorcist*, 1973, *The Hunger*, 1983, *Repulsion*, 1965) also elicit identification from both male and female spectators.

In my view, a crucial reason why the monster—regardless of its gender—draws on the masochistic aspects of looking lies with the origins of monstrosity as a form of abjection. Abjection constitutes a process by which we define the 'clean and proper body' as well as the rational, coherent, unified subject. Insofar as abjection speaks to the perverse and irrational aspects of desire it speaks to all spectators regardless of gender. It also addresses most clearly the masochistic desires of the spectator. As a consequence, the male spectator is punished, as he looks at the abject body of the other—his monstrous, feminized gender counterpart. In this way, the horror film makes a feminine position available to the male spectator—although this position is not necessarily identical to that offered to the female spectator. The problem does not lie with the horror film's appeal to the spectator's masochistic desires but rather with the fact that the abject body is identified with the feminine, which is socially denigrated, and the symbolic body with the masculine, which is socially valorized. If the horror film exists to explore our darker desires, it does so at the expense of woman's abjected body. But insofar as horror represents an encounter with the feminine body, it also points to the perversity of masculine desire and of the male imagination.

BIBLIOGRAPHY

Briffault, R. (1927) *The Mothers,* vol. 2, New York: Macmillan.

Bullough, V.L. (1973) 'Medieval Medical and Scientific Views of Women,' *Viator: Medieval and Renaissance Studies* 4: 485–501.

Dijkstra, B. (1986) *Idols of Perversity: Fantasies of Feminine Evil in Fin-de-Siècle Culture,* New York: Oxford University Press. Douglas, D. (1966) *Horrors,* London: John Baker.

Evans, W. (1973) 'Monster Movies: a Sexual Theory,' *Journal of Popular Film* 2: 353–65.

Freud, S. (1924) 'The Economic Problem of Masochism,' vol. 19 of *The Standard Edition of the Complete Psychological Works of Sigmund Freud,* trans. J. Strachey, London: Hogarth.

———. (1918) 'The Taboo of Virginity,' *Standard Edition,* vol. 11.

———. (1913) 'Totem and Taboo,' *Standard Edition,* vol. 13.

Hollinger, K. (1989) 'The Monster as Woman: Two Generations of Cat People,' *Film Criticism* 13, 2: 36–46.

Horney, K. (1967) *Feminine Psychology,* New York: Norton.

Hornung, C.P. (1959) *Hornung's Handbook of Designs and Devices,* New York: Dover.

Kristeva, J. (1982) *Powers of Horror: an Essay on Abjection,* trans. L.S. Roudiez, New York: Columbia University Press.

Lenne, G. (1979) 'Monster and Victim: Women in the Horror Film' in P. Erens (ed.) *Sexual Stratagems: the World of Women in Film,* New York: Horizon.

Lévi-Strauss, C. (1973) *From Honey to Ashes,* London: Jonathan Cape.

Mercer, K. (1986) 'Monster Metaphors—Notes on Michael Jackson's "Thriller,"' *Screen* 1, 27: 26–43.

Neale, S. (1980) *Genre,* London: British Film Institute.

Shuttle, P. and Redgrove, P. (1978) *The Wise Wound,* New York: Richard Marek.

Silver, A. and Ursini, J. (1975) *The Vampire Film,* Cranbury, NJ: A.S. Barnes.

Tudor, A. (1989) *Monsters and Mad Scientists: a Cultural History of the Horror Movie,* Oxford: Basil Blackwell.

Twitchell, J.B. (1985) *Dreadful Pleasures: an Anatomy of Modern Horror,* New York: Oxford University Press.

Walker, B.G. (1983) *The Women's Encyclopedia of Myths and Secrets,* San Francisco: Harper and Row.

Williams, L. (1984) 'When the Woman Looks' in M.A. Doane, P. Mellencamp and L. Williams (eds) *Re-Vision,* Los Angeles: American Film Institute.

POST-READING QUESTIONS/POST-SCREENING QUESTIONS

Directions: Use what you learned from reading this chapter and watching the film to respond to the questions.

1. What is third-wave feminism as it relates to horror film?

2. How do you understand Barbara Creed's definition of masochism in the male serial killer?

3. Explain how Creed uses the term *abject* in relation to gender ambivalence and monstrosity.

4. What do you think of the feminization of the monstrous as Creed explains it? Can you extend this argument to other films not discussed in her chapter?

Reading 1.6

Scream Whitey Scream

Retribution, Enduring Women, and Carnality

By Robin Means Coleman

KEY TERMS AND FIGURES

Blaxploitation horror films
SNCC
NAACP
Middle Passage
Transatlantic slave trade

Heteronormativity
Pamela Grier
Duane Jones
Enduring women

RECOMMENDED FILMS

Blackenstein by William A. Levey (1973)
Blacula by William Crain (1972)
Ganja and Hess by Bill Gunn (1973)
Get Out by Jordan Peele (2017)
Horror Noire: A History of Black Horror by Xavier Burgin (2019)
Sugar Hill by Paul Maslansky (1974)
Us by Jordan Peele (2019)

INTRODUCTION

In her book *Horror Noire: Blacks in Horror Films from the 1890s to Present*, Robin Means Coleman methodically traces a split history—that of Blacks in horror film and that of Black horror—in her examination of the representation of Black characters in American horror film, from the earliest appearances at the beginning of cinema, to the early 2000s. Her chapter, "Scream Whitey Scream: Retribution, Enduring Women, and Carnality," reprinted here, focuses on the Blaxploitation horror films of the 1970s where the critiques of Black horror films and representation of African Americans in horror films converge in interesting ways.

Coleman begins by noting that the foundation for Blaxploitation was set by George A. Romero's successful 1968 film *Night of the Living Dead,* which was the first horror film to cast a Black actor (Duane Jones) in a leading role in the wake of Hollywood's abandonment of the Hayes Code. This became an opportunity for reimagining the classic monster/horror film from the vantage point of Blackness, while injecting Black Power messaging. *Dracula* became *Blacula, Frankenstein* became *Blackenstein, Dr. Jekyl/Mr. Hyde* became *Dr. Black and Mr. Hyde.* The genre was used to critique White power structures, while cashing in on a captive audience.

Coleman recounts how these films were emboldened by Black Power ideologies of the 1970s, which embraced pride in Black history, culture, achievements, and identity, and resulted in what she describes as an avalanche of Black superheroes and anti-heroes on screen who delivered anti-establishment messages about challenging the institutional and systemic exploitation of Black communities by White agents of power. But Blaxploitation also reproduced negative stereotypes of Black people that hardly advanced the cause for Black liberation. Civil rights organizations and institutions, including the Student Non-Violent Coordinating Committee (SNCC) and the National Association for the Advancement of Colored People (NAACP), criticized the mode for the perpetuation of representations of Black people by largely White directors and producers, as separate but not equal, as well as for the highly sexualized representation of Black women—even as these films were popular among Black audiences.

One of the most well-known films from this subgenre is the 1972 *Blacula*, directed by Black filmmaker William Crain. It both repurposes the classic vampire story with modern Black Power themes and explores the effects of the loss of Black history and identity through the horror genre. Coleman discusses how the film begins with a political narrative frame that explains how African nobleman Mamawalde is turned into a vampire when he and his wife Luva visit the European Count Dracula in 1780 to request his cessation of the slave trade. Count Dracula, whose vampirism they do not suspect, rejects this request and turns Mamawalde into a vampire, leaving him to fester unquenched in a coffin, with his wife to perish next to him. Coleman mentions the way in which Mamawalde is renamed by the White vampire, as Blacula, thereby marking him as other. In spite of this political narrative, the story soon shifts to the classic and explicit "terror of Dracula's reign" that we find in the original story—in his quest for romantic love and "desired recuperation of normality"—with this romantic love, like in most vampire stories, defined as heterosexual.

Coleman also examines the hyper-sexualization of Black final girls in this subgenre, who, distinct from the sexual ambiguity of White final girls, stare down death while waging a battle against White racism and corruption. She explains that Black final girls of the 1970s are resilient and enduring because there is no closure, since the monster is systemic and institutionalized. They are in fact "enduring women" who not only fight for their own lives but also on behalf of men; their battles are ceaseless as they must deal with the ongoing battles of discrimination and societal oppression.

Coleman concludes by observing the demise of Blaxploitation films as audience tastes changed by the end of the 1970s, paralleling the rise of neoliberal economies. The Black empowerment messages of resisting "the man" and "the system" became submerged in the mounting class divisions and racially determined economic gaps of the Reagan era of the 1980s. This era, as evidenced by its horror films, associated Blackness overwhelmingly with urban decay and "White flight to the suburbs" as the horror genre "shifted more explicitly to White middle-class fears." Three decades later Black directors like Jordan Peele are redefining the genre and subverting stereotypes while powerfully critiquing systemic racism in American society.

Scream, Whitey, Scream—Retribution, Enduring Women, and Carnality

1970s

By Robin Means Coleman

> *Entirely too many "black" films have been black in name only. ... Half the time, the material not only isn't black, it isn't even original, as white material ready for the bone yard is given a hasty blackwash and sent on one last creaking go-round. ... Are these films black? I don't know the answer, but I think it's time somebody asked the question.*
> —Holly (127)[1]

In the 1970s, filmmakers took full advantage of the doors George Romero's brand of horror opened, as well as the disappearance of the Hays Code and the seemingly ever-in-flux, watered-down Motion Picture Association of America (MPAA) ratings system.[2] In just a few short years, gory, R-rated fright-fests such as *The Exorcist* (1973), *The Texas Chainsaw Massacre* (1974), and *Halloween* (1978) took hold of the genre, rendering the likes of *Dracula* (1931), *King of the Zombies* (1941), and *Creature from the Black Lagoon* (1954) bloodlessly attenuated. Though the genre saw rapid and dramatic changes in style and form, this is not to say that the classic horror films such as 1931's *Dracula* and *Frankenstein* did not continue to profoundly influence the genre. The old classics were updated with contemporary themes (and a good bit of carnage). This sort of refreshing, particularly on the heels of Romero's successful film *Night of the Living Dead*, starring a Black actor, opened up narrative space

---

1 Holly, Ellen. "Where Are the Films about Real Black Men and Women?" *New York Times*, June 2, 1974: 127. Print.

2 Motion Picture Association of America Site. Motion Picture Association, 2005. Web. April 2, 2010. The Hays Code (1930–66), which presented organizing principles for US filmmakers associated with major studios, warned against things such as: criticizing religion, showing childbirth, showing "lustful" kissing or "suggestive" dancing. These principles were replaced by a voluntary ratings system in 1968 which changed three times between 1968 and 1983: G, M, R, X; G, GP, R, X; and G, PG, R, X. There have been further revisions since the early 1980s.

for many more Black characters. Reinventing the genre from the vantage point of Blackness often meant reimagining the classics. For example, *Dracula* became *Blacula* (1972), featuring the first Black vampire in American film. *Frankenstein* became *Blackenstein* (1973),[3] with the monster being a wounded Black Vietnam War veteran put back together by a White doctor. *Dr. Jekyll and Mr. Hyde* became *Dr. Black, Mr. Hyde* (1976), with the monster taking the form of a murderous white creature, laying waste the efforts of his Black better half. A lawsuit filed by Warner Bros. film studio charged that *The Exorcist* (1973), a story about a demon from Africa possessing a White girl, was stolen by the makers of the film *Abby* (1974). *Abby* told the story of a Black woman who becomes possessed by a Yoruba sex demon. Indeed, this was a "revisionist decade"[4] for the film industry in which, for the first time, "the studios produced Black-oriented film pitched directly at pleasing Blacks."[5] Indeed, over the decade, "Black horror" would thrive, with Blacks arriving in the genre as villainous monsters, anti-heroes, and monster slayers. Black women figured prominently as strong, resilient protagonists. Whites were represented as well, but in this decade they would be victims, paying dearly for trying to victimize Blacks.

To be sure, "Black horror" films were not the first to present well-trodden movie themes. Early silent (horror) film scavenged to the point of plagiarism "preexisting formats for lucrative plots and styles of presentation that could be feasibly adopted for the moving camera" while often only minimally altering the pilfered stories with new details.[6] While Black horror filmmakers did some poaching, the genre should be credited not only with dramatically reshaping the narratives, in some cases, but also with reappropriating "generic forms for more overtly political goals [such as] to critique the white power structure."[7]

The films were emboldened by Black Power ideologies—a range of belief systems espousing an awakening of Black pride, self-sufficiency, and empowerment which were prominent during the decade. The imagistic result was "screen images of black life reflect[ing] the new confidence of black people"[8] and a "veritable avalanche" of Black super-heroes and anti-heroes found their way to the big screen.[9] However, the influx was followed by a fresh assortment of problems, as Gary Null, in *Black Hollywood*, explains:

---

3   Young, Elizabeth. *Black Frankenstein: The Making of an American Metaphor*. New York: Routledge, 2008. 219. Print. In 1977 a comic book called *Black'nstein* "featured a white Kentucky slave owner, Colonel Victah Black'nstein, who builds a black monster-slave"; 1976's *The Slave of Frankenstein* novel presents "Victor Frankenstein's son as a white abolitionist who challenges an evil pro-slavery monster"; George Clinton/Parliament released in 1977 "The Clones of Dr. Funkenstein," focusing on the creation of a Black doctor of funk.

4   Denzin, Norman K. *Reading Race*. London: Sage, 2002. 27. Print.

5   Bogle, Donald. *Toms, Coons, Mulattoes, Mammies, & Bucks*. New York: The Continuum Publishing Company, 1993. 232. Print.

6   Crane, Jonathan. *Terror and Everyday Life*. Thousand Oaks, CA: Sage Publications, 1994. 48. Print.

7   Benshoff, Harry M. "Blaxploitation Horror Films: Generic Reappropriation or Reinscription?" *Cinema Journal* 39(2) (2000): 34. JStor. Web. January 20, 2005. http://www.jstor.org/pss/1225551.

8   Null, Gary. *Black Hollywood: The Negro in Motion Pictures*. Secaucus, NJ: Citadel Press, 1975. 209. Print.

9   Leab, Daniel J. *From Sambo to Superspade: The Black Experience in Motion Pictures*. Boston, MA: Houghton Mifflin Company, 1975. 254. Print.

What emerges, in fact is an altogether new set of black stereotypes. Perhaps derived from the movement toward black power, the cool, efficient black hero seems to have more in common with James Bond than with the political ideals of any black movement. Some of these movies pay lip service to black separatism, Afro-American culture, and local control.[10]

THE HORRORS OF BLAXPLOITATION

Lamenting the representations in and quality of 1970s film featuring Blacks, Ellen Holly of the *New York Times* wrote in 1974, "one of the penalties of being black and having limited money is that we seldom control our own image. We seldom appear in media as *who we* say we are, but rather, as *who whites* say we are."[11] The economic conditions under which Black films were made gave rise to the moniker "Blaxploitation"—a portmanteau uniting the concepts of "Black" and "exploitation"[12]—to define the decade's Black films, horror and non-horror alike. Blaxploitation describes an era of Black film offerings which often drew their inspiration from Black Power ideologies while presenting themes of empowerment, self-sufficiency (though not always through legal means), and consciousness-raising. In "Black horror" specifically, mainstream or White monsters, such as Dracula or Frankenstein's the Monster, were purposefully transformed into "agents" of Black Power.[13] Blaxploitation films also often had an anti-establishment message, challenging "the Man's" or "Whitey's" exploitation of Black communities (e.g. importing drugs, running prostitution rings, rogue cops), though the critique rarely rose beyond indicting a few wicked individuals.

Blaxploitation's attempt at political engagement was not without its critics. Rhines explains:

> these films were released during the height of the Civil Rights/Black liberation movement, yet their subject matter of sex, violence, and "super cool" individualism was the antithesis of what contemporaneous Black political organizations like SNCC, the NAACP, or SCLC supported for Black people.[14]

---

10   Null (209).

11   Holly (127).

12   Exploitation films, according to Eric Shaefer in his dissertation *Bold! Daring! Shocking! True!: A History of Exploitation Films, 1919–1959*, emerged during the "classical era," 1919–1959, paralleling Hollywood cinema but also made outside of it by indie producers. The films, writes Schaefer, "were rooted in an early, exhibitionistic 'cinema of attractions' and relied on forbidden spectacle at the expense of the more costly system of narrative continuity and coherence favored by mainstream movies." Shaefer, Eric. *Bold! Daring! Shocking! True!: A History of Exploitation Films, 1919–1959*. Austin: University of Texas, 1995. Dissertation. Print.

13   Benshoff (37).

14   Rhines, Jesse Algeron. *Black Film/White Money*. New Brunswick, NJ: Rutgers University Press, 1996. 46. Print.

The films were "condemned by Black opinion leaders across the political spectrum for [their] criminal stereotypes and rightly identified as mainly the product of white studios, writers, and directors," even as the movies proved to be popular, particularly among Blacks who enjoyed seeing Black characters and communities on the big screen.[15] Moreover, the films were notoriously exploitative of women, as a hallmark of Blaxploitation films was the subjection of their female characters to misogynistic treatment, abuse, and rape. Blaxploitation later came to be thought of as a film genre in and of itself boasting drama/action classics such as *Sweet Sweetback's Baadasssss Song* (1971), *Shaft* (1971), *Super Fly* (1972), *Coffy* (1973), *Foxy Brown* (1974), *The Mack* (1973), and *Dolemite* (1975), as well as "Black horror" films such as *Blacula* (1972).

Nineteen seventy-two's *Blacula* was the decade's gold standard for recreating a (White) horror classic in the image of Blackness, while also tackling issues of Black pride and empowerment. Directed by the Black filmmaker William Crain and starring William Marshall, this "Black horror" film presents a compelling take on the vampire story while exploring the effects of racism alongside the loss of Black history and identity.

Blacula begins its story in the year 1780 with Mamuwalde (William Marshall), an African prince, traveling with his wife, Luva (Vonetta McGee), to Transylvania for a dinner meeting with Count Dracula (Charles Macaulay). In the meeting, Mamuwalde presses Dracula to renounce the slave trade, from which the enormously wealthy Dracula, seemingly, has been profiting greatly. Dracula is not only a vampire, but it turns out he is a virulent racist ("It is you who comes from the jungle") as well. *Blacula* rather self-consciously included hateful rhetoric to expose its diminishing effects and to actively rebuke such offenses. In this film, and in a great many Black horror films of this decade, "lingering racist tropes ... were now readily identified and exposed."[16]

Dracula bites Mamuwalde, thereby infecting the prince with vampirism. Mamuwalde is renamed "Blacula"—a variation of his White vampire "master's" name, which marks him as an Other, even among vampires. Given a slave name, he is robbed of his (African) identity. Dracula then entombs Mamuwalde, leaving him to suffer forever, as the undead, from blood thirst. Luva is not tainted with vampirism, though she presumably dies almost immediately.[17]

Mamuwalde-turned-Blacula remains entombed for nearly two centuries, until 1972 when Dracula's abandoned Transylvanian castle has its property put up for public sale.[18] Still in his coffin, Mamuwalde makes a much belated trip through the Middle Passage. Thus, Mamuwalde finally makes his appearance in the new world—enslaved by vampirism and auctioned off.

---

15   Worland, Rick. *The Horror Film: An Introduction*. Malden, MA: Blackwell, 2007. 97. Print.

16   Benshoff (34).

17   In the film, Luva is entombed with her prince. Her death isn't shown.

18   In the film, it is explained Dracula has been killed by his nemesis Dr. Van Helsing.

Two Los Angeles collectors, one Black, the other White, both gay men, buy some of the castle's contents, which include, unbeknownst to them, Blacula. The men, who are in a loving relationship, are depicted as stereotypically sissified, and effete in manner and dress. When Mamuwalde emerges from his coffin, ravenous for blood, he transforms from a stately man to a hairy man-monster and quickly feeds on the two men, permitting glimpses of sensuality through implications of an interracial/homosexual encounter. When Mamuwalde feeds on Billy (Rick Metzler), the White collector, he feeds on Billy's cut arm while pushing Billy's face (neck and lips) far from him. When Mamuwalde feeds on Bobby (Ted Harris), the Black collector, he first chokes him into unconsciousness and then violently bites, feeding on the lifeless body in anger. Mamuwalde's taking of the men, then, allows only a glimpse of homoerotism before quickly shifting to a homophobic, heterosexist stance signaled by rage and violence.

Mamuwalde is initially satiated, and, remarkably, does not turn his attention to avenging his own "death" or that of his beloved Luva at the hands of Whites. Instead, in spite of its politically inspired narrative beginnings, *Blacula* becomes a horror love story in which Mamuwalde begins an unrelenting pursuit of a woman, Tina (also played by McGee), who reminds him of Luva. Mamuwalde's actions, then, align with that which has "always [been] explicit in Dracula's reign of terror in England ... the search for romantic love and the desired recuperation of normality."[19]

Romantic love in *Blacula* is narrowly defined as heterosexual. In the film, the brave, savvy Dr. Gordon Thomas (Thalmus Rasulala), with the help of his medical assistant/girlfriend Michelle (Denise Nicholas), uncovers Mamuwalde's secret. Together they are a good team, and also in a loving relationship. Yet, Bobby and Billy, who are similarly doting on one another, and even equal partners in a thriving business, are reduced to "two faggot interior decorators" in the movie. Later, when Bobby's body disappears from a funeral home because he has turned into a vampire, police raise the question, "Who the hell would want a dead faggot?" And, in yet another scene, a racist stereotype, "they all look alike," is shifted to gay men, furthering the film's dismissive, heteronormative rhetorical violence.

Sharrett describes such *Dracula* films as a parody of Freud's *Totem*

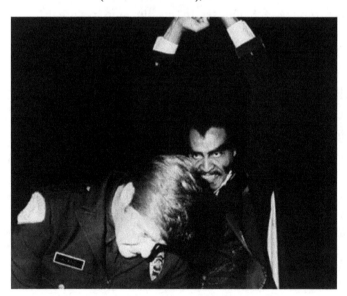

Figure 1.6.1 Blacula in full rage in *Blacula*
AIP/Photofest

---

19   Sharrett, C. "The Horror Film in Neoconservative Culture." *Journal of Popular Film and Television* 21:3 (Fall 1993): 107. Print.

and Taboo (1913), a collection of essays attending to themes such as the importance of the father-figure, obsessions with the magical realm, and illicit carnality.[20] Sharrett writes, "Dracula [is] the tyrannical father incidentally violating all sexual taboos, including those against homosexuality."[21] Though 1970s Black films (both horror and non-horror) presented characters (such as Bobby and Billy) outside the boundaries of heteronormative sexuality, their depiction was rarely with positive, innovative effect. Gays, lesbians, bisexuals, the transgendered, and others who violated "traditional" gender roles reminded audiences that sexual identities are not always stable. However, such "instability" was often severely punished. For example, a gay man is sodomized with a hot curling iron in the non-horror Blaxploitation film *Black Shampoo* (1976). Wlodarz, in "Beyond the Black Macho: Queer Blaxploitation," finds that heterosexuality anchors representations of "authentic" blackness (and heroism), while queerness gains a certain threatening representational power." This means diverse sexualities are not absent from Black film. Quite the contrary, there are a great number of, at least, queer characters. However, "the films themselves admittedly remain anxious and often phobic in their handling of these characters."[22]

Presenting an "authentic" Black, masculine ideal, Mamuwalde's amorous feelings for Tina, which she quickly reciprocates, can be viewed as motivating Afrocentric nostalgia for a complete and full Blackness. "Tina's willingness to be his partner, to become a vampire," argues Gateward in "Daywalkin' Night Stalkin' Bloodsuckas: Black Vampires in Contemporary Film," is her attempt to recuperate the nobility of African culture, during a period in American culture when the idea of Africa as a mythic homeland was prevalent in both the political and expressive cultures of Black Americans and the Diaspora as a whole."[23] Likewise, Mamuwalde's name and nobility "link him to the Afrocentric cultural politics adopted by some branches of the Black power movement."[24] Tina is persuaded to believe, by Mamuwalde, that she is the key to recuperation through a play on Africa-as-motherland rhetoric: "We are of the Abani tribe, you and I. Northeast of the Niger Delta. Our people are renowned as hunters. ... You are my Luva recreated." Even when Mamuwalde must say goodbye to Tina, he does so in Kiswahili.

However, in the film the connection between noble Africans and African Americans is (perhaps unintentionally) illusory. Mamuwalde lands in a predominately Black section of L.A. But it is clear that these are not his people. Mamuwalde is of a different time and caste. It is as if, as James Baldwin so eloquently wrote in *Notes of a Native Son* of African/American

20   Sharrett ("Neoconservative" 107).

21   Sharrett ("Neoconservative" 100–110).

22   Wlodarz, Joe. "Beyond the Black Macho: Queer Blaxploitation." *The Velvet Light Trap* 53 (Spring 2004): 11. Web. January 20, 2006. http://muse.jhu.edu/login?uri=/journals/the_velvet_light_trap/v053/53.1wlodarz.html.

23   Gateward, Frances. "Daywalkin' Night Stalkin' Bloodsuckas: Black Vampires in Contemporary Film." *Genders OnLine Journal* 40 (2004): 10. Web. June 20, 2005. http://www.genders.org/g40/g40_gateward.html.

24   Medovoi, L. "Theorizing Historicity, or the Many Meanings of Blacula." *Screen* 39 (1998): 14. Print.

relationships, "they face each other, the Negro and the African, over a gulf of three hundred years—an alienation too vast to be conquered in an evening's goodwill."[25] Certainly it does not help that Mamuwalde preys upon the Black Americans he encounters, making him little different from anyone, or thing, that had been known to victimize Blacks and their communities.

These slippages aside, *Blacula* has been credited with being revolutionary. Elizabeth Young, in *Black Frankenstein: The Making of an American Metaphor*, credits the film for capitalizing on the "freedom for political fantasy that horror films could afford."[26] Leerom Medovoi, in his article "Theorizing Historicity, or the Many Meanings of *Blacula*," observes, "the figure of Mamuwalde recalls, for instance, the eulogizing of Malcolm X throughout the late 1960s as the 'shining black prince' of African-America."[27] While Harry Benshoff, in his article "Blaxploitation Horror Films: Generic Reappropriation or Reinscription?," draws upon *Blacula* to argue that films of this period critically comment upon White racism (both institutionalized and personal) and are "steeped in African American culture of the early 1970s; references to the Black Panthers, Afrocentric style, [and] soul food."[28]

AMERICAN INTERNATIONAL PICTURES

Blacula met with enough box office success—grossing over $1 million by the end of its theatrical run[29]—that its production company, American International Pictures (AIP, 1954 to present), sought to continue to court the Black horror film. AIP had been known for their low-budget, exploitation fare targeting the youth audience, be they monster movies or "beach" films such as *Beach Party* (1963) and *Beach Blanket Bingo* (1965). AIP could not be credited with being a film trailblazer. Rather, they cautiously watched from the sidelines per their policy to "observe trends in emerging tastes."[30] Only then did they jump on bandwagons; they "always waited for someone else to test the water first."[31] In the case of Black films, one litmus test was *Sweet Sweetback's Baadasssss Song* (1971) offered through the production company Cinemation, which earned impressive box office returns grossing over $11 million.[32] The other was the film *Shaft* (1971, MGM), with its $17 million domestic gross.[33] Together, the success and acclaim of

---

25   Baldwin, J. *Notes of a Native Son.* Boston: Beacon Press, 1955/1984. 115, 122. Print.

26   Young (*Black Frankenstein* 189).

27   Medovoi (14).

28   Benshoff (36).

29   Lawrence, N. "Fear of a Blaxploitation Monster: Blackness as Generic Revision in AIP's *Blacula*." *Film International* 39 (2009): 24. Print.

30   Lawrence (18).

31   Stenger, Josh. "Mapping the Beach: Beach Movies, Exploitation Film and Geographies of Whiteness." *Classic Hollywood, Classic Whiteness.* Ed. Daniel Bernardi. Minneapolis: University of Minnesota Press, 1996. 31. Print.

32   Gent, G. "Black Films Are In, So Are Profits." *New York Times*, July 28, 1972: 22. Print.

33   Gent (22).

these films moved AIP in 1972 to release *Blacula* as well as the non-horror 1973 gangster film *Black Caesar*.[34] Theirs was an effective business strategy:

> Initially, it may seem hard to imagine two groups of films more disparate in tone, style, content and audience than AIP's beach films and blaxploitation movies; yet the studio's prioritization of the urban black audience from 1972 to 1975 serves as a compelling lesson on how the same formula employed in its exploitation of the beach a decade earlier could be updated and relocated to a new racial geography so as to produce similar results with a sharply different demographic. In its spate of films aimed at Black audiences, AIP [realized] the studio's greatest box-office returns.[35]

AIP continued to follow through with its decision to advance such niche products with horror offerings starring Black actors, such as *The Thing with Two Heads* (1972), *Scream, Blacula, Scream* (1973), *(The Zombies of) Sugar Hill* (1974), *Abby* (1974), and *J.D.'s Revenge* (1976). All were fairly low budget as it was also AIP's policy to "produce with prudence, avoiding expense for what won't show on-screen."[36] Following AIP's lead, Exclusive International released *Blackenstein*, and Dimension films offered *Dr. Black, Mr. Hyde*.

FIGHT THE POWER

Hoping to capitalize on the success of *Blacula*, Exclusive International's *Blackenstein* (1973) was "a product of White Hollywood, made by a White director, William Levey, and a White writer, Frank Saletri[; the film was] crude and sloppy, a failure even by low-budget standards.[37] *Blackenstein* evidenced a coalescence of sociopolitical concerns as it adopted an anti-(Vietnam) war stance, questioned the contribution of Blacks to what may be perceived as a colonialist war effort, and explored the continuing tensions around Black/White race relations. The film focuses on Eddie Turner (Joe De Sue), a Black man, whose body is severely damaged by a land mine during the Vietnam War.

Limbless, Eddie is essentially a head without a body. Upon being shipped back to the US, Eddie is sent to a Veterans Administration (VA) Hospital. While there, the helpless Eddie is bullied by a White orderly in an exchange which works to highlight struggles around bigotry

---

34 Stenger (31). AIP are also responsible for the distribution of an astonishing number of other "Blaxploitation-era" films, such as *Black Mama, White Mama* (1973), *The Mack* (1973), *Coffy* (1973), *Hell Up in Harlem* (1973), *Foxy Brown* (1974), *Truck Turner* (1974), *Sheba, Baby* (1975), *Cornbread, Earl, and Me* (1975), *Cooley High* (1975), and *Friday Foster* (1975).

35 Stenger (46).

36 Lawrence (18).

37 Young (*Black Frankenstein* 190).

and White supremacy. First, the orderly (Bob Brophy) taunts the armless man: "Why don't you reach over there and have a nice, cool drink of water." The scene dramatizes a racial hierarchy that is "inseparable from the setting of a VA hospital during the Vietnam War—Black Power and other activists frequently criticized the Vietnam War as a conflict run by white men but disproportionately fought by black men."[38] Next, the orderly reveals that he tried to enlist but, to his great embarrassment, was deemed unfit for service. The orderly then transfers his lack onto Eddie: "Big deal you laying there, you know it's my taxes, my friends' taxes that's gonna keep you there. We gotta take care of you." Eddie is summarily dismissed as being a fool for falling for the "scam" of patriotism, while also reduced to a welfare case—Whites must "take care" of him.

Eddie's fiancée, Dr. Winifred Walker (Ivory Stone), gets Eddie transferred out of the hospital and into the care of the kindly, White Dr. Stein (John Hart). Dr. Stein, as in the classic *Frankenstein* (1931), works out of his castle-like home, which is complete with a basement laboratory. However, Eddie is not turned monstrous by Dr. Stein; rather, his fate is sealed by Malcomb (Roosevelt Jackson), a jealous Black assistant to Dr. Stein, who wants to sabotage Eddie and Winifred's relationship. Malcomb tampers with Eddie's drugs, turning Eddie into a fully restored and mobile, but psychopathic hulking monster. Here, much like *Blacula*'s failure to directly engage White oppressions, a White country which first forced him to fight, *Blackenstein* "vitiates one of the main political contributions of the Frankenstein story: its focus on the origins of violence [thereby diffusing] the targets of its monster's anger."[39] The White orderly meets his expected gruesome demise. However, just like Mamuwalde, Eddie is also happy to kill off innocent, unsuspecting Black people. When Eddie opts to disembowel a Black woman, he does so only after the audience is provided with a lengthy "money-shot" of her jiggling, exposed breasts.

The scenes of slaughter are tempered, however, by the film's low budget. Eddie's murderous rampage is shot in poor lighting, and acted out amid shadowy darkness. As a result, the film takes on an unanticipated atmospheric, moody hue and tone. The effect is a unique one as the on-screen violence that is the hallmark of horror films takes a back seat to that which can be heard—the anguished moans of a monster moved to kill when he does not really want to, perhaps just as he (as a man) did during the war. Eddie's fate is not at all dissimilar to one narrative of disabled American war veterans. He returns to his country unaccepted and unable to fit in; impaired by (prescription) drugs, he turns to a life of crime, and is killed by law enforcement (police dogs maul Eddie to death). Though he is able to survive war in a foreign land, it is his return home that finally defeats him.

---

38   Young (*Black Frankenstein* 191).
39   Young (*Black Frankenstein* 196).

The Thing with Two Heads (1972) and *Dr. Black and Mr. Hyde* (1976) drilled down more explicitly on the themes of race relations and medical experimentation. *Heads*, named one of the 50 worst movies ever made, is a story of Black comeuppance in the face of White bigotry.[40] The film, more farcical than horror, tells the story of Dr. Maxwell Kirshner (Ray Milland), a famed surgeon and racist, who is dying and wants to live on by transplanting his head onto a healthy (White) body. The NFL football player Rosey Grier portrays "Big Jack" Moss, a Black death row inmate, who though innocent of his crimes, offers to donate his body to science rather than die in an electric chair. Unbeknownst to an unconscious Kirshner, his surgical team transplants Kirshner's head onto Jack's body. Both awaken surprised to see their heads on Jack's body—hence, the thing with two heads. The movie's premise had (ridiculous) comic consequences. "They transplanted a White Bigot's Head onto a Soul Brother's Body!" screamed the movie's ads and poster art, which perhaps served as a not so subtle metaphor for the treatment of Blackness by White image-makers.[41]

Dr. Black and Mr. Hyde, with Black director William Crain again at the image-making helm, took race and medical experimentation far more seriously, with Dr. Pryde (played by former NFL player Bernie Casey) as a caring Black doctor treating the Black poor of Watts. Dr. Pryde's name is an obvious double-entendre about Black pride (he is never called Dr. Black). In the film, Dr. Pryde is experimenting with a cure for hepatitis and cirrhosis.

Dr. Pryde develops what he believes is a promising treatment for the deadly diseases that are afflicting members of the Watts community, particularly its female prostitutes. The women are presented in gratuitous scenes of exploitation. They are frequently topless and occasionally nude. The film later reveals that the impetus

Figure 1.6.2 The Thing with Two Heads
American International/Photofest

---

40   The 2004 documentary film *The 50 Worst Movies Ever Made* cites *The Thing with Two Heads*. The DVD documentary was produced by Dante Pugliese for the studio Passport Video. *Heads* is frequently included in various fan-developed listings of horror such as Blackhorrormovies.com.

41   Worland (97).

for Dr. Pryde's search for a cure is that his own mother (though not a prostitute) died from liver damage. Indeed, this storyline is an interesting tale of achievement and commitment. Dr. Pryde has reached the heights of education and, importantly, returned "home" to do good work, despite his troubled upbringing. In fact, the film presents two "homes" for Dr. Pryde. The first is where he works, his hometown of Watts. However, he does not live in Watts. Rather, he lives in an upscale, suburban community in a sprawling mansion home. It is revealed that Dr. Pryde's boyhood home was a brothel for "ladies of the evening," in a (presumably) predominately White community.[42] There, his mother was a live-in maid in the home, where it was her responsibility to "clean up the filth." The job took its physical and emotional toll, moving Dr. Pryde's mother to drink and ultimately develop "this liver condition," which proved deadly. Hence, his residing outside of Watts is not about escape, but is a symbolic act of reclamation.

Eventually, Dr. Pryde tests his drug on himself, with the expected disastrous results. The drug turns Dr. Pryde into a "White dude"—a white, ashen-faced, blue-eyed killer monster (presumably Mr. Hyde, though he is never called this in the movie). Dr. Pryde makes his way (in his Rolls Royce) to the inner-city, making Watts his killing ground, where he unleashes his repressed hatred of prostitutes and pimps.

On the doppelgänger's hit list is Linda (Marie O'Henry), a prostitute that Dr. Pryde has fallen for. As law enforcement hunts for the killer, Linda is initially mistrustful of the police and is openly conflicted about leading them to Dr. Pryde. Here, the film is exposing a well-known tenuous relationship between law enforcement and Black communities; the film overtly addresses the issue of Blacks steering clear of police: "In the Black community, nobody knows nothing, nobody sees nothing, and nobody hears nothing." The film also speaks to the real-life quandaries Black women face when imperiled by a violent relationship—involving the police is not always an easy choice. The National Association of Black Social Workers summarizes the fears:

> Women of African ancestry often do not call the police for fear of police brutality against their mates or against themselves. ... Women of African ancestry often do not report domestic violence for fear that such reporting would be a betrayal of the race or would contribute to negative stereotypes.[43]

---

42   In the film, it is never explicitly made clear that the home is in a White neighborhood, or that the prostitutes his mother cleaned for are White. Rather, Dr. Pryde alludes to the prostitutes' race by calling them, with ironic emphasis, "ladies of the evening," while Black street prostitutes working in Watts are "hookers" and "hoes." They do not work in brothels. In addition, the film works to show the great socioeconomic distance between Watts and where Dr. Pryde lives by presenting sequences of neighborhood changes. The homes get bigger, the cars nicer, the streets cleaner, and the Black faces disappear.

43   "Domestic Violence: Domestic Violence in the African American Community." Nabsw.org. National Association of Black Social Workers, 2002. Web. April 9, 2010.

Eventually, Linda comes face to face with her tormentor. He attacks her in his monstrous state, but does not kill her, eventually releasing her (perhaps there is some of Dr. Pryde left in him). The police arrive and, as in *Blackenstein*, release police dogs on him, harking back to 1960s television images of police dogs attacking Civil Rights movement activists. Fleeing, the monster climbs to the top of the Watts Tower, with helicopters circling overhead, recalling the climactic scene of *King Kong*. Police shoot the Dr. Pryde monster—in a hail of bullets he plunges to his death. The allusion to Blacks and apes in the film's ending is a curious one, as it does not appear in the original 1886 novella *Strange Case of Dr. Jekyll and Mr. Hyde* by Robert Louis Stevenson, or in the subsequent approximately half-dozen mainstream film adaptations since the novella. However, the Black monster-ape emerges more explicitly in the 2006 film *The Strange Case of Dr. Jekyll and Mr. Hyde*, starring Black actor Tony Todd of *Candyman* (1992) fame. In the film, Dr. Jekyll first morphs into the evil Eddie Hyde. As Hyde becomes more crazed and lethal, he (oddly) transforms into a primate, attempts a rooftop escape, and is shot down like Kong, plunging to his death.

The film *Fight for Your Life* (1977) presented the "worst" of both Black and exploitation film worlds. A low-budget rip-off of *The Last House on the Left*, the film follows three sadistic escaped male convicts: an Asian, a Mexican, and a White self-appointed "boss" of the trio. Hiding from police, the men take refuge in a predominately White, small town. The home they choose to hide out in belongs to a Dr. Martin Luther King, Jr.-like Black minister, Ted Turner (Robert Judd), who preaches on themes of Black passivism, peace, patience, and the meek inheriting the Earth.

The Turners are the embodiment of an integrationist family. In addition to living in a largely White community, their recently deceased son (as a result of an earlier car accident) had a White fiancée, Karen (Bonnie Martin), who still visits the family. Karen is a friend to the family's young adult daughter Corrie (Yvonne Ross). The youngest son in the family, a pre-teen named Floyd (Reggie Rock Bythewood), has a White best friend, Joey (David Dewlow), the son of a local police officer. A central plot line in the film is whether peace or (armed) resistance is more tenable in the face of cruel racism. Ted's ideology is embraced by his wife, Louise (Catherine Peppers), but rejected by "Granny" (LeLa Small), a feisty, wheelchair bound woman who spouts Black nationalist rhetoric: "Black power is where it's at!" In the film, Jesse (William Sanderson), the White convict who refers to his partners in crime as "chink" and "spic," terrorizes the Turner family. He forces them to engage in acts of degradation—"Say, 'All us Black ass coons is hungry'"—and showers them with racial epithets. Eventually, the horrors increase as Karen and Joey are killed. Ted is beaten into unconsciousness with his own bible. Corrie is gang-raped. Finally, the family rises up by arming themselves, and killing their tormentors. However, it is Ted who is at the center of the climactic finale, in which he is not only in a showdown with Jesse, but dramatically renounces his ideology of peace and meekness for Blacks through an act of vengeance. Ted cruelly taunts Jesse, calling him a "faggot" and asserting that he is less than a real man for giving in to homosexual rape in jail. He then blows away Jesse, the last of the convicts, with a gun. *Fight for Your Life* was high on a principal message—ideologies of turn-the-other-cheek integration were no longer sustainable. However, it was also a lowly exploitation movie in which such ideologies, as well as racism, sexism, and even recidivism were cheapened, reduced to a moment in a family's life which is resolved through vigilantism.

The problem with this decade of industry exploitation of the Black film market was that occasionally a low-budget, but compelling horror film would be offered, but was unable to stand apart from the lowest dross. *Soul Vengeance* (a.k.a., *Welcome Home Brother Charles*) (1975)—directed by Black director Jamaa Fanaka—presented one of the more shocking storylines seen in horror: a Black man wills his penis to grow to abnormal lengths and to gather impossible strength so that he can use it as a weapon to kill White bigots. While *Soul Vengeance*'s horror twist may provoke incredulity, the film is possibly the most provoking response to: (1) the fear of the Black male phallus; (2) the performance of masculine gender roles; and (3) police brutality.

Soul Vengeance begins by focusing the audience on a lasting, divisive issue in race relations—White police brutality upon Black bodies. Charles Murray (Marlo Monte), a drug dealer, is picked up by "the Man"—two White Los Angeles Police Department (LAPD) officers. The officers drive Charles to an alley to beat him. One of the officers, Jim (Stan Kamber), attempts to stop his partner Harry "Free" Freeman (Ben Bigelow) from inflicting more abuse on the handcuffed Charles, but his efforts fail. Though terrorized and beaten by Harry, Charles is unbowed during the encounter and his defiance is severely punished—Harry castrates Charles with a straight razor. However, this particular punishment is motivated by something unknown to Charles: Harry's wife is having an affair with a Black man because Harry is "not enough of a man" with his "shriveled up thing." The castration, then, is a complex narrative around bigotry, penis envy, and the protection of White womanhood.

Charles is then incarcerated, with little reference made to the damage that has been done to his body. While in prison, Charles is consumed by thoughts of revenge that are played out in dreams and other visions. The depiction of Charles' mental state echoes the (in)famous writings of Black nationalist Eldridge Cleaver in *Soul on Ice*. Cleaver describes his state of mind while in jail: "I, the Black Eunuch, divested of my Balls, walked the earth with my mind locked in Cold Storage."[44] After three years in prison, Charles is released and returns to his Watts home only to discover that much of his life is unrecoverable. He is faced with the fact that recidivism looms large given his dramatic reduction in social status as an ex-con. Legitimate employers want nothing to do with him—"I can't even wash a car."

Here, the film sets aside its horror leanings to embark on an extended, dramatic exploration of the bleak life of 1970s Watts for men like Charles. Charles struggles to maintain a masculine

---

44   Cleaver, Eldridge. *Soul on Ice*. New York: Dell Publishing, 1968. 191. Print.

gender performance. He enters into a loving relationship with a woman, Carmen (Reatha Grey), but theirs is a rocky union largely because Charles laments his inability to financially support her.

Charles catches a television news report about Harry being recognized for his highly effective police work. Charles' anger over the denial of his performance of masculinity on social and economic fronts, as well as over the celebration of a rogue cop, is manifested in the film's return to horror tropes and through a focus on Charles' mutilated penis. His penis, it turns out, was not completely dismembered by Harry. Rather, it healed with aberrant musculature.

Charles talks his way into the home of the police officer who brutalized him, as well as that of the lawyer who prosecuted him. Once in their homes, Charles drops his pants, quite literally mesmerizing each man's White wife with his bewitching penis. Again, the film's narrative aligns with some of the controversial political discourse of the time:

> Many Whites flatter themselves with the idea that the Negro male's lust and desire for the White dream girl is purely an aesthetic attraction, but nothing could be farther from the truth. His motivation is often of such a bloody, hateful, bitter, and malignant nature that Whites would be hard pressed to find it flattering.[45]

In the first act of Charles' revenge, he has sex with the women while they are entranced. While they are under Charles' spell, he implants a demand into their psyche: they must open the doors to their homes for him later in the evening, when their husbands return home from work. The women do as ordered, and Charles catches the men off guard, killing them.

However, the viewer is not initially sure how the murders have been carried out, as "what lurks outside the frame or unclearly within it, generates uncertainty about what one is seeing."[46] Finally, in the murder of the lawyer, Charles' power is fully revealed. Charles is able to will his penis to grow to lengths of several feet, which he then loops around the neck of the other character, strangling him. This scene is a fascinating one as Charles' desire to have the White men choke on "it" cannot be fully realized in the literal sense, as that would require a far more homoerotic encounter than is already presented. Still, in wrapping a Black penis around White men's throats, a highly erotic, but clear visual reference to lynching is established. As such, while the White male is rendered impotent—by a cheating wife or by having to pay for sex—the Black man becomes a "super stud"[47] and the White man "a victim of his own Frankenstein monster."[48]

---

45   Cleaver (28).
46   Pinedo, Isabel Cristina. *Recreational Terror: Women and the Pleasure of Horror Film Viewing*. Albany, NY: SUNY Press, 1997. 53. Print.
47   Wallace, Michele. *Black Macho and the Myth of the Superwoman*, New York: Verso Classics, 1999. 66. Print.
48   Wallace (67).

Charles' murderous deeds are finally uncovered, he is pursued by police and, like so many Black monsters discussed earlier, he is cornered on a rooftop. The police bring Carmen to the site, asking her to talk him down. In the film's final, dramatic scene, Carmen defiantly yells to Charles, "JUMP!" The film ends abruptly. Now that Charles has molested, murdered, and has been outed as possessing an unusual physical attribute, it is expected that his life is on a very short clock. During this era, "no one wanted to see a black hero defeated";[49] hence a death in which a Black man has control of his destiny is better than handing himself—his life—over to Whites. The audience is left to assume Charles has indeed jumped.[50]

ENDURING WOMEN

Over the decades, women's roles have become increasingly central and innovative in horror. In non-Black horror films, women have triumphantly battled against monsters (e.g., Laurie Strode in *Halloween* [1978]) and have been frighteningly evil (e.g., Pamela Voorhees in *Friday the 13th* [1980]). While audiences had seen wicked women before in the form of the vamp, temptress, succubus, and Voodoo queen, the *heroic* female in horror was just beginning to make revolutionary inroads during the 1970s.

Carol Clover, in *Men, Women and Chain Saws: Gender in the Modern Horror Film*, theorizes on the form and function of the female heroine in horror, describing her as the "Final Girl." The moniker captures the meaning—she is the one who, in the end, does not die. Indeed, the Final Girl is *the* survivor—surviving the monster's attack and often the only one to do so (e.g., Ripley in *Alien* [1979]). As Clover explains, "she alone looks death in the face, [and] she alone also finds the strength either to stay the killer long enough to be rescued (ending A) or to kill him herself (ending B)."[51] The Final Girl is also *a* survivor—smart, resourceful, and a fighter in the face of evil. Again, as Clover elaborates, the films of the 1970s began to present "Final Girls who not only fight back but do so with ferocity and even kill the killer on their own, without help from outside."[52]

What is important here, in part, is the absence of a male savior. In the absence of a male savior, it is the female who gets to take on and bring down the monster. As Clover asserts, what is key is the qualities of the Final Girl, "the quality of the fight and qualities that enable her to survive."[53] For example, in *Halloween*, when Laurie Strode (Jamie Lee Curtis) is penned down

---

49 Bogle (*Toms, Coons* 240).

50 This scene is a precursor to the life-through-death decision made by the characters Thelma and Louise in the movie of the same name.

51 Clover, Carol. *Men, Women, and Chainsaws: Gender in the Modern Horror Film*. Princeton, NJ: Princeton University Press, 1992. 35. Print.

52 Clover (*Chainsaws* 37).

53 Clover (*Chainsaws* 39).

in a closet by the deadly Michael, she does not whimper and collapse, awaiting death. Instead, she moves into fight mode, even quickly fashioning a weapon out of a clothes hanger (the only thing on hand) to take on the evil. Likewise, (Ellen) Ripley (Sigourney Weaver) in *Alien* displays her tough leadership qualities when the crew is faced with the unstoppable alien monster. While a Black male, Parker (Yaphet Kotto), wants to attack headlong—"You're gonna let me kill it, right?"—it is Ripley who understands such an approach is unworkable, and takes control by screaming: "Shut up and let me think!" Final Girls tend to be White. When their fight with the monster is over, their lives return to stasis. Ripley sleeps peacefully after she ejects the alien. Laurie Stode's quiet, suburban life can return to normal.[54]

However, 1970s horror films featuring Black women handled the Final Girl with noteworthy variation. White Final Girls were generally unavailable sexually and were masculinized through their names (e.g., Ripley) and through the use of (phallic) weaponry (e.g., butcher knives or chainsaws). By contrast, Black women were often highly sexualized, with seduction serving as a principal part of their cache of armaments. Much like the White Final Girl, Black women stare down death. However, these Black women are not going up against some boogeyman; rather, often their battle is with racism and corruption. In this regard, there is no going to sleep once the "monster" is defeated, as the monster is often amorphously coded as "Whitey," and Whitey's oppressions are here to stay.

With no real way to defeat the evil (systems of inequality) that surrounds them, Black women in horror films could be described as resilient "Enduring Women." They are soldiers in ongoing battles of discrimination, in which a total victory is elusive. The Black woman's triumphant walk into the sunset promises to take her, not toward a life of peace, but back into the midst of rogue police, sexist men, and "the Man" who is exploiting her Black community.

The Enduring Woman, unlike the (asexual) Final Girl, often fights not only for her own life, but also on behalf of men. For example, in the non-horror Blaxploitation film *Foxy Brown* (1974) the character Foxy (Pam Grier) takes on "the Man," seducing her foes before killing them, while also exposing herself to beatings and rape, all because she wants to avenge her boyfriend's murder. The 1974 "Black horror" zombie film *Sugar Hill* presents a similar motivation for its Enduring Woman. The provocatively named "Sugar" (Marki Bey) wants to avenge the death of her boyfriend Langston at the hands of a "Whitey" crime boss. Sugar uses her good looks and sensuality to get close to her foes; hence she is denied the opportunity to enter into battle like other Final Girls. She does not set aside her sexuality, or have a "masculine" name or possess her own "masculine" weaponry, rather she has lips and hips, but no chainsaw. Likewise, *Scream, Blacula, Scream*'s (1973) Enduring Woman, Lisa (Pam Grier), is called into battle to save not one, but two men—one from the vampirism that is coursing through his veins, the other, a former love, from an attacking vampire.

---

54   Of course, when these movies became franchises, peace could not be had.

The acclaimed art-house movie *Ganja & Hess* (1973) (winner of the Critics' Choice prize at the Cannes Festival),[55] directed by Black director Bill Gunn, presents the story of a tormented man and a wicked Enduring Woman. The "Black horror" film centers on Dr. Hess Green (Duane Jones of *Night of the Living Dead* fame), an attractive, highly successful archeologist. The monied Hess is "an elegant and sophisticated man by his clothes, Rolls Royce, and magnificent mansion, where a servant meets his every need."[56] Hess' socioeconomic status is purposeful, as the director's strategy was "anti-stereotype" filmmaking, thereby reflecting an "earnest desire to transcend debilitating blaxploitation clichés."[57] Hence, Hess was offered as the antithesis of depictions of the urban underclass or of those securing illicit profits through underground economies as seen in a host of Blaxploitation films.

In the film, Hess is employed by the Institute of Archeology and is provided with an assistant, an older Black man, George Meda (Gunn). In a moment of privacy, while Meda is in a reception area waiting to introduce himself to Hess, he passes the time by pointing a small pistol at his reflection in a wall mirror. This is the audience's first glimpse at Meda's insanity.

Hess invites Meda back to his estate, and while there Meda reveals a crude side, offending the prim and proper Hess with vulgar jokes. Meda then sneaks away from Hess, fashions a noose, and climbs a tree on Hess' property, threatening to hang himself. Hess comes to understand that Meda is drunk and "neurotic," a volatile combination of instability. Hess asks Meda not to kill himself on his property because, as Hess reasons, "that will give the authorities the right to invade my privacy with all sorts of embarrassing questions. ... I am the only colored on the block ... and you can believe the authorities will drag me out for questioning."

Meda then attacks Hess, viciously knifing him "for the father, son, and Holy Ghost." The weapon Meda happens to use is a dagger of the Myrthia people, an ancient blood-drinking caste of Nigeria, which is part of Hess' extensive private collection of prized artifacts. Having "killed" Hess, Meda commits suicide. However, the infection from the blade means that Hess awakens undead and bloodthirsty. Hess stores Meda's body in a cellar freezer rather than call the police, thereby evidencing that even the Black elite, not just prostitutes such as *Dr. Black, Mr. Hyde*'s Linda, continue to fear (White) police.

Hess then goes blood hunting, traveling far from his sprawling estate to a ghetto to prey upon the poor. The wealthy Hess takes blood from a clinic's blood bank. He kills a prostitute and her pimp for their blood. Another prostitute, who is caring for her newborn, meets a similar fate,

55   Diawara, Manthia, and Phyllis Klotman. *"Ganja and Hess*: Vampires, Sex, and Addictions." *Black American Literature Forum* 25.2 (1991): 299. Jstor. N.p. Web. June 21, 2005. http://jstor.org/. Diawara and Klotman cited other kudos for the film. According to the authors, the film was hailed in the *Amsterdam News* as "the most important Black produced film since *Sweet Sweetback's Baadasssss Song*," as well as it being described as a "great underground class of Black film [...] If *Sweet Sweeback* is *Native Son*, *Ganja and Hess* is *Invisible Man*."

56   Diawara and Klotman (300).

57   Hasan, Mark. "Ganja & Hess [Review]." *Rue Morgue* (2007): 47. Print.

though he leaves her baby untouched and abandoned, crying near its mother's body. In this regard, *Ganja & Hess* became emblematic of films of the 1970s that were "constantly challenging the legitimacy of capitalist, patriarchal rule ..., the monster became an emblem of the upheaval in bourgeois civilization."[58]

Soon Meda's wife, Ganja (Marlene Clark), arrives in search of her husband, who has "disappeared before" during bouts of psychosis. Just as Ganja's name promises (the psychosomatic drug cannabis), Hess

Figure 1.6.3 Hess and Ganja in *Ganja & Hess*
Kelly/Jordan Ent./Photofest

becomes completely addicted to the beautiful, but uncouth woman. Ganja eventually discovers her husband's body and soon after she marries Hess. Her rationale is simple: She would rather be married to an extremely wealthy crazed man than be the widow of a poor one.

Eventually Hess reveals his secret to Ganja, transforming her by stabbing her with the knife so that they may live together "forever." Together, they represent addictive personalities—both to blood lust and to their own carnal indulgences. They work to satiate their insatiable lusts frequently—killing and having sex, sometimes simultaneously—until Hess concludes that such an existence is untenable.

Hess searches for, and discovers, a cure. He must accept Jesus as his personal savior, and then stand before a cross with the cross' shadow over his heart. Only then can Hess die, and perhaps even go to Heaven. The film concludes with Hess going to a church to cure himself. He then returns home to Ganja to die, begging her to join him in a peaceful death. However, Hess goes to his death alone.

Ganja opts to endure as infected, and as a sexy succubus, continuing on alone masquerading as high class and cultured. She stays at Hess' estate, among his wealth, while having her share of male lovers and victims. Ganja not only survives her encounter with the monster, but happily chooses to become one. Ganja is also an Enduring Woman in that she is sexy and sexual, she finds her victory in the death of her two husbands, and, now fully independent (free of husbands and flush with money), she indulges her every whim. She is no longer bound or terrorized; rather, she happily terrorizes (men) herself. She does not expect a knight in shining armor to come to her rescue; as such, she has developed ways to ensure her own survival, and even to thrive.

---

58   Sharrett ("Neoconservative Culture" 100).

Ganja & Hess was initially "suppressed" by its producers because it was far from the typical Blaxploitation fare that had become so familiar during this decade. "The producers," write Diawara and Klotman, "wanted a film that would exploit black audiences—a black version of white vampire films. However, the producers withdrew the film when Gunn went beyond the vampire genre to create an original product."[59]

PAM GRIER: EXPLOITING THE ENDURING WOMAN

Pam Grier became a Blaxploitation-era icon, starring in seven films for AIP alone.[60] She became, as Dunn describes in *"Bad Bitches" and Sassy Supermamas*, an AIP and Black cinema muse, "helping to establish Grier's sex goddess screen imagery."[61] However, Grier was not offered up by AIP as a sex goddess in the tradition of White actresses Ava Gardner, Elizabeth Taylor, Hedy Lamarr, or Lauren Bacall. Rather, she was confined to the role of a hot mamma—a "controlling image," as Hill Collins describes it, of Black female sexuality in which Black women become a symbol of deviant female sexuality, while White female heterosexuality becomes the "cult of true" womanhood.[62] Such imagery relegated Black women to the "category of sexually aggressive women," thereby providing justification and yawning narrative space for sexual abuses.[63] For example, in *Foxy Brown* (1974) Grier's character Foxy is drugged and gang-raped (by White racists). The horrific encounter is presented as a necessary hurdle as it allows Foxy to exact revenge upon those who wronged her boyfriend. In *Coffy* (1973) Grier as Coffy offers herself as an undercover prostitute—which requires her pimp to "test her out."

The hallmark of a Grier film was her partial nudity. The film camera lingered on her exposed, buxom bosom and long legs while she endured all manner of sexual exploitation. Writes Dunn:

> The exhibition of women's sexual bodies [was] enabled by the general relaxation of traditional Hollywood restrictions regarding violence, sexual content, and profane language. However, in the case of Grier, this exhibition is deeply tied to ... AIP's insistence on depicting Black female resistance and empowerment primarily through the pornographic treatment of their star.[64]

---

59   Diawara and Klotman (299).

60   *Black Mama, White Mama* (1973); *Coffy* (1973); *Scream, Blacula, Scream* (1973); *Foxy Brown* (1974); *Sheba, Baby* (1975); *Bucktown* (1975); *Friday Foster* (1975).

61   Dunn, S. *'Baad Bitches' and Sassy Supermamas: Black Power Action Films*. Urbana and Chicago: University of Illinois Press, 2008. 109. Print.

62   Hill Collins, Patricia. *Black Feminist Thought*. New York: Routledge, 2009. 91. Print.

63   Hill Collins (89).

64   Dunn (111).

Though sexual readiness does not immediately exclude a "feminist edge," the treatment of Grier and other Blaxploitation starlets was distinctly hypersexual—ever available for sex, no matter how horrifically violent.[65]

Notably, Grier is removed from these misogynistic images in the "Black horror" film *Scream, Blacula, Scream* (1973). *Scream* is the sequel to *Blacula*, which was directed by Black director William Crain and starred the acclaimed (Broadway) theater stage and screen actor, director, and jazz and opera singer William Marshall. Perhaps Grier's far-from-pornographic treatment could be attributed to Marshall's influence and earlier insistence that *Blacula* avoid stereotype. Novotny Lawrence, in *Fear of a Blaxploitation Monster: Blacks as Generic Revision in AIP's Blacula*, details Marshall's influence:

> While *Blacula* was in development, William Marshall collaborated with the producers to ensure that the image of the first black horror monster contained a level of dignity. In the original script Blacula's straight name was Andrew Brown, which is the same as Andy's in the blackface white comedy team of Amos and Andy. Marshall criticized the name commenting: "I wanted the picture to have a new framing story. A frame that would remove it completely from the stereotype of ignorant, conniving stupidity that evolved in the United States to justify slavery" ... Marshall eventually persuaded the producers to incorporate his suggestions, and the first black vampire emerged as a regal character.[66]

Marshall's demeanor, stature, and oeuvre tended to present Blacks outside of exploitative tropes (e.g., on stage he portrayed Othello, Paul Robeson, Frederick Douglass, an opera singer, and a doctor). It would seem that he would not participate in a role where he would play an (sexual) abuser. Hence, given her treatment in other films, it is perhaps worth noting that Grier's *Scream* character Lisa remains clothed, conservatively dressed even. Largely absent is the heavy makeup, revealing clothing, and large, silky wigs that were Grier's typical costume. Rather, her natural hair—a short afro—was on display in *Scream*. And, she is often seen in pantsuits with high collared tops, thereby denying the viewer the objectifying look at her cleavage and legs. Lisa strikes a serious, even professional pose in the film, bringing a rare air of dignity to the often maligned Voodoo religion. Confronted by naysayers, Lisa and others define Voodoo as an "exceedingly complex science" and as a "religion based on faith." In one scene, Lisa goes to a funeral home to pray over a deceased friend. She lights candles, assembles a small altar, and settles in to pray quietly—there is no stereotypical, frenzied dancing, drumming, or chanting. Her prayers are more akin to thoughtful meditation.

---

65   Dunn (113).

66   Lawrence (18).

Where *Scream, Blacula, Scream* is particularly innovative is its inclusion of Lisa as a smart, heroic, Enduring Woman. In the film, the vampire Blacula is resurrected through a Voodoo ritual. Blacula is resurrected by Willis (Richard Lawson), the selfish, angry brother of Lisa, his adopted sister. Willis wants to use Blacula to exact revenge on Lisa, whom he refers to as a "jive ass bitch," and other members of their Voodoo cult for failing to elect him their leader or "Papa Loa." However, Blacula is unhappy about his forced return. When he is called by his real, princely name "Mamuwalde," the anguished vampire screams, "The name is Blacula!" Tormented by his fate, Blacula asks Lisa to use her Voodoo skills to rid him of the vampire curse and send him to his death where he can rest in peace. Here, Lisa is cast as hero and savior. However, there is a key limitation to such a representation, as Clover explains: "On the face of it, the occult film is the most 'female' of horror genres, telling as it regularly does tales of women or girls in the grip of the supernatural. But behind the female 'cover' is always the story of a man in crisis."[67]

Indeed, the pressure on Lisa to heal Blacula is heightened when he threatens to kill Lisa's ex-boyfriend Justin (Don Mitchell), with whom she is still friendly. Lisa now must save both men. Unlike her male hero counterparts who "get the girl," Lisa does not get either man even as she bravely saves them both. "If anything," writes Bogle, "these action heroines pointed up the sad state of affairs for Black women in the movies. Very few films attempted to explore a Black woman's tensions or aspirations or to examine the dynamics of sexual politics within the Black community."[68] In surviving her encounter with a vampire, when others have not, protecting her ex from death, and in saving Mamuwalde's soul, Lisa possesses the foremost traits of the Final Girl: "she is the one who encounters the mutilated bodies of her friends and perceives the full extent of the preceding horror[; she will show] more courage and levelheadedness than [her] cringing male counterparts."[69] Lisa's triumph is not simply about succeeding without the intervention of a/her man. Rather, she also presents an Enduring Woman figure. Her battle is not over. For example, her struggles against sexist men and against stereotypes (Voodoo as a cult) will continue. The Enduring Woman knows that significant challenges remain for her, and for her community.

Abby (1974), too, was one of the more intriguing (copyright infringement suit with makers of *The Exorcist* notwithstanding) of the "Black horror" films due to its unique focus on sexual diversity.[70] It begins with archeology professor and theologian Garnet Williams (William Marshall) accidentally releasing an evil spirit during an archeological dig in Nigeria. The sex demon makes its way to the US and into the staunchly Christian home of Garnet's daughter-in-law, Abby Williams (Carol Speed). Abby is married to Rev. Emmett Williams (Terry

---

67   Clover (*Chainsaws* 65).

68   Bogle (*Toms, Coons* 252–253).

69   Clover (*Chainsaws* 35, 36).

70   As for *The Exorcist*, Warner Bros. thought that the film served as more than a template for the Black horror film *Abby*, and a court agreed.

Carter), and is employed at her husband's church as a marriage counselor. Where *Abby* takes a bit of a novel turn is that possessing Abby is the *male* demon Eshu (voiced by Bob Holt), a Yoruba god "steeped in a Western, sex-negative Christian ideology."[71] With the theater poster art boasting, "Abby doesn't need a man anymore," the film presents a compelling multi-sexuality narrative: a male spirit seeks sexual conquests while in a female's body. For example, through Abby the male demon asks a man, "You wanna fuck Abby, don't you?" The demon has sex with his (male) victims, and at the height of the act, he kills. The film lays bare and complicates heteronormativity as men are attracted to the outward appearance of the female Abby, who oozes sexuality and has little problem seducing her prey.

Along the way, the film capitalizes on the characterization of Garnet as a professor/theologian/minister (and the authoritative demeanor William Marshall brings to his roles) by inserting educational commentary on Eshu: (1) he claims credit for natural disasters; (2) he is one of the most powerful of all earthly deities, more than the powerful Orisha gods; and (3) Eshu is a god of sexuality, a trickster, creator of whirlwinds and chaos. Finally, through a Yoruba-informed exorcism Abby is freed of her possession. The effect is presenting a Black religion in a markedly different manner than, say, many Voodoo-themed horror films which cast the religion as singularly odd, ahistorical, and evil.

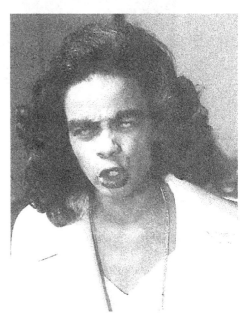

Figure 1.6.4   The monster Abby in *Abby*
American International Pictures/Photofest

Apart from these intriguing plot points, *Abby* was rather standard low-budget horror fare, with the *New York Times* calling it "silly."[72] Abby is no Final Girl or Enduring Woman as she is saved from a fanciful life of sex and partying (and killing) by her father-in-law, husband, and police officer brother while being restored to favor with her male (Western) God.

As boundary pressing as (Black) horror films are, they have not been as innovative in disrupting traditional narratives about sex and sexualities. For example, with few exceptions, films focusing on monster-apes or vampires have as their backdrop heteronormative love stories. It is not surprising, then, that Abby-as-sexual-predator must be defeated, not just because of her possession and because she kills her prey, but because "transgressive sexuality is defined as monstrous."[73]

71   Benshoff (40).

72   Weiler, A.H. (1974). "'Abby', About a Black Family and Exorcism." *New York Times*, December 26, 1974: 53. Print.

73   Sharrett, Christopher. *Mythologies of Violence in Postmodern Media*. Detroit, MI: Wayne State University Press, 1999. 103. Print.

Still, Abby's performance is (perhaps unintentionally) independent, sexually liberated, and confident. While possessed, Abby is gregarious and strong in personality as well as physical strength. Were she not a killer, she could be interesting fodder for readings of a person free of gender and sex role encumbrances.

SEXPOT SISTAS: SAME AS IT EVER WAS

Voodoo has become so expected in horror films that one periodical reported disappointment when this facet of Black culture was not presented in horror movies. The Black culture magazine *Jet* questioned why Black horror films should be based on the Christian Dracula legend "when there was Voodoo in the Black experience."[74] The "Black horror" film *Sugar Hill* (1974) attempted some reclamation of the Voodoo. If most Blaxploitation celebrated a "'bad Nigger' who challenges the oppressive White system and wins,"[75] then *Sugar Hill* celebrated the "Baad Bitch"[76] who did the same, albeit through Voodoo. In *Sugar Hill*, Blacks—specifically shackled slaves from Guinea who end up in New Orleans—are the zombie undead. The zombies are summoned by Mama Maltresse, a Voodoo queen (Zara Cully), on behalf of Sugar (Marki Bey), to exact bloody revenge on a "Whitey" crime boss, Morgan (Robert Quarry), and his thugs who have killed Sugar's boyfriend.

Figure 1.6.5 Sugar's cleavage invites more stares than her zombies in *Sugar Hill*

American International Pictures/Photofest

The silent, but lethal army of zombies has among its members a loquacious, discerning, thinking leader—Baron Semedi (Don Pedro Colley).[77] Semedi acts much like a union leader, negotiating the terms under which he and his zombie peers will work. Semedi quickly spies that his targets are irredeemably evil—

74 "Black-oriented Films Produced since Mid-1970s." *Jet* 42 (1972): 58–59. 58. Print.

75 Guerrero, E. *Framing Blackness: The African American Image in Film*. Philadelphia, PA: Temple University Press, 1993. 86. Print.

76 Dunn.

77 Semedi is a keeper of the dead, a "great lover," and a greedy spirit who values money, gifts, and women. In the film, his name is pronounced Baron Samdi.

killers, racists, and shake-down artists. As a result he and his horde happily kill Morgan and his crew. The zombies are heroes. Identifying with the monsters in *Sugar Hill* makes for "a pleasurable and a potentially empowering act"[78] as the zombies come to represent a pro-Black cadre of Black men doing away with "Whitey"—indeed, "Black heroes were winning and community identification was intense."[79] The zombies enact a particularly gruesome killing of a "sell-out" Black man, Fabulous (Charles Robinson), who permits Morgan to call him nigger and who shines Morgan's shoes.

Sugar is there nearly every step of the way as her zombie army takes on her enemies: "Hey Whitey, you and your punk friends killed my man ... I'm not accusing you, honk, I'm passing sentence and the sentence is death." However, hers is far from an image of a focused, competent leader. Sugar is still very much presented as the "Voodoo sexpot"[80] who tempts and teases her prey while clad in form-fitting, revealing outfits. Sugar's depiction presents the film's adherence to traditional gender roles. Right after her boyfriend dies, Sugar flirts with her ex-boyfriend, a policeman named Valentine (Richard Lawson). The message looms—Sugar cannot be without a man. Sugar suggests sexual availability to friend and foe alike. She even engages in the requisite sexy catfight with another (White) sexpot, Morgan's girlfriend Celeste (Betty Ann Rees). Sugar's portrayal "equivocates any change in the narrative representation of the Black woman"; she has not really usurped power from men.[81] This equivocation is best revealed when Sugar offers her soul to Semedi in return for his services, which he rejects, lustfully proclaiming, "It ain't souls I'm interested in." It is understood that she is to join his harem of "wives."

In *Sugar Hill*, the zombies fulfill their contract, and when it's time for Sugar to pay up with her own body she offers a trade. Semedi, who has been described as sexually ravenous, is offered Celeste. The acceptance of the White woman by Semedi—though he "prefers" Sugar, but Celeste "will have to do"—is likely to be read as political, the apropos punishment for a "protected" White woman. On the other hand, the trading in women is obviously sexist and objectifying; though Celeste's "White slavery" is a play on an important taboo.

Though Enduring Women were becoming scarce in this film cycle, Black women continued to figure prominently in films such as 1974's *Vampira* [a.k.a. Old Vampire] and *The Beast Must Die*. *Vampira* is a "Blacks in horror" comedy-horror film that presents the story of an "Old Dracula" (David Niven) who, too elderly to hunt for his young victims, gets them by luring them to his castle, which he has opened up to tourists. Dracula's wife, Vampira, is also out of commission, so he transfuses her with the blood of one of his victims to revitalize her. That blood happens

---

78   Benshoff (32).
79   Murray, J. "Now a Boom in Black Directors." *The New York Times*, June 8, 1972: D11. Print.
80   Harris, M. "Scary Sistas: A Brief History of Black Women in Horror Films." *Pretty-scary.net*. Pretty Scary: For Women in Horror By Women in Horror. June 4, 2006. Web. March 17, 2010.
81   Yearwood, Gladstone L. *Black Film as a Signifying Practice: Cinema, Narration and the African-American Aesthetic Tradition*. Trenton, NJ: Africa World Press, Inc., 2000. 44. Print.

to be from a Black woman, which, in Vampira, turns her young and Black—justifying (and exceeding) the mythical "one-drop rule." Vampira (Teresa Graves) is now regarded as sexy, giving unique credence to the mantra "Black is beautiful." As Null observed at the time, "if Black movies have hardly begun to elevate women to real character roles, at least the white-dominated ideas of beauty are gone.[82] Unable to "cure" his wife, whose skin color moves her to speak jive talk, Dracula unhappily joins her with Niven appearing in the film's final frames in blackface.

In the film *The Beast Must Die*, also a "Blacks in horror" film, Marlene Clark plays Caroline, the gorgeous wife of Tom (Calvin Lockhart), a wealthy big game hunter.[83] This elite Black couple, Tom and Caroline, along with their White assistant Pavel (Anton Diffring), host five White guests at an island estate in the hope of uncovering which among them is a werewolf. Tom is devastated when his beloved Caroline is accidentally infected by one of the guests, who is the real monster. In a heart-wrenching scene, he must kill his wife with a silver bullet so that she does not begin her own murderous werewolf rampage. Though very different films, *Vampira* and *Beast* share common themes of Black women as desirable and worthy, but also stricken with a taint that threatens their men.

J.D.'s Revenge (1976) echoes *Sugar Hill* in that it is similarly about possession and love denied. However, *Revenge* is also an extraordinarily sexist film, raising the ante far and above *Sugar Hill* with a startling, misogynist, anti-feminist subtext that linked the independence and sexual revolution of women with being "uppity."

J.D.'s Revenge tells the story of New Orleans resident Isaac, or "Ike" (Glynn Turman), a young, strait-laced, law school graduate studying for the bar exam. His girlfriend, Christella or "Chris" (Joan Pringle), convinces Ike to take a break from his studies for a double-date night on the town with friends. The group visits a nightclub where a hypnotist is performing. Ike is among several who volunteer to be hypnotized. Something goes wrong while he's "under," and Ike becomes possessed by the angry spirit of a 1940s' gangster J.D. Walker. Walker wants revenge for himself and for his sister Betty Jo (Alice Jubert), for their murder more than three decades earlier back in 1942.

J.D. possesses Ike's body in an attempt to reveal the true circumstances around the murders. As the violent hustler J.D. becomes more dominant in Ike's body, Chris falls victim. Chris is depicted as Isaac's complete equal. She capably quizzes Ike on legal concepts and helps him with his exam prep. She is outspoken, has a network of friends, and it is implied that she has her own money. In one scene, in a gender role reversal, Chris initiates sex while Ike opts out with "Not tonight, I got a lot on my mind tonight." The audience learns that the kindly Ike is viewed as less of a man by his friend Tony (Carl Crudup) because he is so respectful of his

---

82   Null (219).

83   Marlene Clark became a bit of a horror icon, appearing in *Ganja & Hess* and *The Beast Must Die*, as well as two other English-language, Philippines films, *Night of the Cobra Woman* (1972) and *Black Mamba* (1974).

girlfriend. When, Ike (possessed by J.D.) slaps Chris around, Ike's buddy Tony praises him for finally being a man:

> I think it's a good thing to go upside a woman's head when she starts handing you lip. I mean, believe it or not, they like that. Eh man, honest to God, you've got to go into your nigger act every once in a while. They gonna push you till you do. They want you to show 'em where the lines are. You know something, man? It's pretty encouraging that you did what you did. As long as I've know you, you always seem to be, you've been sort of repressed ... That's fantastic man.

Putting Chris in her place through a beating is particularly important because, the audience comes to learn, she likes and understands football, does not permit Ike to store his smelly sneakers in their apartment, and she is a divorcee who left her husband.

An intriguing plot point is that except for a change in style—wearing a fedora, "conking" his hair, donning a 1940s-style suit—Ike's new brutal masculine performances do not seem out of place in the 1970s (the context for the second wave of the Feminist Movement); rather, they are rewarded. As J.D., Ike is rough and dangerous—traits (certain) women find alluring. Ike picks up an attractive woman in a bar and returns to her place, providing her with "the best fuckin' I've ever had." When the woman's "old man" catches them, J.D. delights in slashing the woman's partner with a straight razor, his hyper-masculine bravado fully on display.

When Chris sees Ike come home drunk, she is angry. J.D./Ike reveals what is wrong with her kind of women (unlike those he is currently finding in bars) by calling her a "bitch" and a "bitch ho" while screaming, "How dare you talk to me like I'm some kind of common sissified nigger wimp." Eventually, Chris is completely silenced when J.D. badly beats and sexually assaults her, thereby putting an end to her uppity-ness. The film, Benshoff observes,

> suggests a man caught between two different constructions of African American maleness when Ike ... treats his girlfriend as a pimp might treat his whore. The film points out that J.D.'s style and masculine brutality are still a lingering problem in 1970s Black macho culture.[84]

Moreover, the film communicates through J.D./Ike that Chris' performance of female independence should be rejected. Chris is neither a Final Girl nor an Enduring Woman; her ex-husband comes to her aid and in the end she happily returns to Ike.

---

84 Benshoff (39).

IT HAS COME TO THIS

I walked through the graveyard like a bolt of thunder. Made the tombstones jump and put the dead on the wonder.
—Rudy Ray Moore[85]

The demise of 1970s "Black horror" was symbolized by a horror-comedy that left some entertained, but many more scratching their heads while speculating whether the inevitable decline of the Blaxploitation genre was coming none to soon. The epitome of the Blaxploitation era, stand-up comedian Rudy Ray Moore, offered the film *Petey Wheatstraw: The Devil's Son-in-Law* (1977). The jaw-dropping film opens with a pregnant Mother Wheatstraw (Rose Williams) laying in a bed inside a shack, in labor, surrounded by midwives dressed as mammies. She is experiencing a difficult labor, and a White male doctor is summoned to assist with the birth. The doctor first delivers a large watermelon and finally (as afterbirth) a fully formed, fighting and profanity-spewing boy about seven years of age. The boy, Petey Wheatstraw (Clifford Roquemore II), arrives to the beating of drums as well as to screams by the doctor of "It's alive! It's alive!," a line borrowed from *Frankenstein.*

The plot of this lowest of low-budget films is fairly indecipherable (a "pimp cane" figures prominently); however, the main narrative thrust is that the adult Petey Wheatstraw (Rudy Ray Moore), a comedian, is killed by rivals. Petey will be given a new lease on life by the Devil, provided that Petey marries the ugliest woman on Earth—the Devil's daughter. Along the way, Moore performs his trademark rhyming and signifying comedy raps.

Petey Wheatstraw was a reflexive look at 1970s films, as Moore appropriated and spoofed their most clichéd aspects of martial arts, exploitation, B movies and dumped them into his films. For example, as a boy, Petey is trained like Caine in the *Kung Fu*[86] television series by a mysterious, elderly martial arts Master. Later, as an adult, Petey would (badly) karate chop his assailants, including "demons" dressed in purple leotards and capes with red horns affixed to their heads. In between fights and other escapades, portly Wheatstraw is also presented as a sex symbol, an insatiable lover with a trove of women. Moore, in keeping with the Blaxploitation themes he perfected in his earlier films (e.g. *Dolemite* [1975]), even dropped in a revenge-against-Whitey storyline as well. For Moore, his film contributions were far from exploitative: "When we wasn't getting kicked in the ass and beat upside the head, then they termed it as 'blaxploitation,' and I think it was extremely crude to us as a people."[87] Thomas Cripps summarized Blaxploitation's

---

85   Rudy Ray Moore. "Petey Wheatstraw, the Devil's Son-in-Law," *The Cockpit.* Kent Comedy Series, 1973. CD.

86   The *Kung Fu* TV series (1972–1975) presented a young martial arts student "Grasshopper" being trained by his Shaolin Priest Master Po.

87   Rudy Ray Moore, in the documentary *Macked, Hammered, Slaughtered, and Shafted* (2004).

end, implicating Moore's film: "Predictably, such 'blaxploitation' movies soon fell from favor and were rivaled by Oriental martial arts movies, a new generation of science fiction monsters, and other arcana."[88] Not surprisingly, the genre could not sustain itself, as the exploitative nature of the films—content, investment, quality—fell from favor. In 1977, the same year *Petey Wheatstraw* was released a historically Black university "opened its spring term film series, not with one of the ephemeral Black heroes like Shaft, but with *The Texas Chainsaw Massacre*."[89]

CONCLUSION

Though many 1970s horror films were exploitative in so many ways—in budget, in quality, in the treatment of women's bodies, and in the presentation of the underclass—they should not be readily dismissed as lacking relevant discourse. The decade's "Black horror" films and "Blacks in horror" films left audiences with a clear indication of the role and function of race, gender, sexuality, culture, and class in popular culture, as well as how these identity positions may, rightly or wrongly, be reflected upon in the social world. In the films, struggles against those oppressions, and themes of (intra)racial uplift in the face of those oppressions, were in conversation with the rhetoric of non-violence and integration, as well as armed resistance and Black self-reliance, if not supremacy. The films also worked hard to reveal to audiences that for Blacks, the horror (or the monster) was located within Whiteness—Whitey, the system, the Man. Unlike mainstream horror films in which (Final Girl) heroes took on an individual evil (such as an alien with acid for blood) and fought to bring about its demise, Black horror films revealed that the evil enveloping Blackness was enduring.

While "the Black audience had always been a substantial part of the horror crowd," these 1970s films, which specifically hailed Black audiences, encouraged them to look beyond the monsters to identify with messages of Black equality through metaphorical unity (zombie armies) or through the metaphorical bullet (Voodoo potions or the penis).[90] With Black stars in these roles, even if at times exploitative, their presence and performance exploded past horror film treatments of Blacks as spooked, bug-eyed, and shuffling. Blacks of this decade were unbowed.

This period was not always purely reactionary to the kinds of racism and classism Blacks had to endure at the time. *Ganja & Hess*, by way of example, largely excluded Whiteness in an attempt to privilege stories coming out of Blackness. Here, there were no "cardboard" and "oversimplified" characters who make their reputations "by kicking white villains all over the

---

88   Cripps, Thomas. *Black Film as Genre*. Bloomington: Indiana University Press, 1978. 129. Print.
89   Cripps (*Genre* 129).
90   George, N. *Blackface: Reflections on African Americans in the Movies*. New York: HarperCollins, 1994. 87. Print.

screen."[91] Black horror films which worked to break free of such traditional Blaxploitation tropes found a tepid response among some movie-goers, as film producer Rob Cohen explained: "They want a shark marauding off the coast of a vacation spot or 'the Sting.' If there's one thing an audience doesn't want, it's a message. If there's one thing beyond that, it's a Black message."[92] In short, Blaxploitation-era films were facing a multifaceted quandary of being too culturally and politically Black, not Black enough, or not purely entertaining enough.

Blaxploitation horror films showed fairly homogeneous and confined characters—in class, gender roles, politics, and interactions with Whites. The *Washington Post* predicted the filmic trend would turn to "blacks interacting among themselves, or with whites."[93] Moreover, the newspaper expressed an optimism around the representational treatment of Blacks in which they are "portrayed as complete human beings—good and evil, rich and poor, smart and dumb."[94] Any predictions of more substantive interaction for the coming decade did not pan out. In the 1980s, Blacks become associated with dreadful urban spaces, prompting White flight to the suburbs. Blacks and their horror films were left in the cold as the genre shifted attention more exclusively to White, middle-class fears.

BIBLIOGRAPHY

Baldwin, J. *Notes of a Native Son*. Boston: Beacon Press, 1955/1984. Print.

Benshoff, Harry M. "Blaxploitation Horror Films: Generic Reappropriation or Reinscription?" *Cinema Journal* 39.2 (2000): 31–50. JStor. Web. January 20, 2005. http://www.jstor.org/pss/1225551.

Bogle, Donald. Bright Boulevards, *Bold Dreams: The Story of Black Hollywood*. New York: Ballantine One World, 2005. Print.

Cleaver, Eldridge. *Soul on Ice*. New York: Dell Publishing, 1968. Print.

Clover, Carol. *Men, Women, and Chainsaws: Gender in the Modern Horror Film*. Princeton, NJ: Princeton University Press, 1992. Print.

Crane, Jonathan. *Terror and Everyday Life*. Thousand Oaks, CA: Sage Publications, 1994. Print.

Cripps, Thomas. *Black Film as Genre*. Bloomington: Indiana University Press, 1978. Print.

Denzin, Norman K. *Reading Race*. London: Sage, 2002. Print.

Diawara, Manthia, and Phyllis Klotman. "*Ganja and Hess*: Vampires, Sex, and Addictions." *Black American Literature Forum* 25.2 (1991): 299–314. Jstor. N.p. Web. June 21, 2005. http://jsor.org/.

---

91   West, Hollie I. "Black Films: Crossovers and Beyond Blaxploitation." *Washington Post*, February 8, 1976: 119. Print.

92   West (119).

93   West (119).

94   West (119).

"Domestic Violence: Domestic Violence in the African American Community." Nabsw.org. National Association of Black Social Workers, 2002. Web. April 9, 2010.

Dunn, Stephane. *'Baad Bitches' and Sassy Supermamas: Black Power Action Films*. Urbana and Chicago: University of Illinois Press, 2008. Print.

Gateward, Frances. "Daywalkin' Night Stalkin' Bloodsuckas: Black Vampires in Contemporary Film." *Genders OnLine Journal 40* (2004). Web. June 20, 2005. http://www.genders.org/g40/g40_gateward.html.

Guerrero, Edward. *Framing Blackness: The African American Image in Film*. Philadelphia, PA: Temple University Press, 1993. Print.

Harris, Mark H. "Scary Sistas: A Brief History of Black Women in Horror Films." *Scary-Scarynet,* June 4, 2006. N.p. Web. August 13, 2010. http://www.fangirltastic.com/content/scary-sistas-brief-history-black-women-horror-films.

Hasan, Mark. "Ganja & Hess [Review]." Rue Morgue (2007): 47. Print.

Hill Collins, Patricia. *Black Feminist Thought.* New York: Routledge, 2009. Print.

Holly, Ellen. "Where Are the Films about Real Black Men and Women?" *New York Times*, June 2, 1974: 127. Print.

Lawrence, N. "Fear of a Blaxploitation Monster: Blackness as Generic Revision in AIP's Blacula." *Film International* 39 (2009): 14–26. Print.

Leab, Daniel J. *From Sambo to Superspade: The Black Experience in Motion Pictures*. Boston, MA: Houghton Miffl in Company, 1975. Print.

Medovoi, L. "Theorizing Historicity, or the Many Meanings of Blacula." *Screen* 39 (Spring 1998): 1–21. Print.

Motion Picture Association. "Motion Picture Association of America." 2005. N.p. Web. June 12, 2009. http://www.mpaa.org/ratings.

Murray, J. "Now a Boom in Black Directors." *New York Times*, June 8, 1972: D11. Print.

Muse, Clarence. "What's Going on in Hollywood." *Chicago Defender*, December 28, 1940: 21. Print.

Muse, Clarence. "When a Negro Sings a Song." *Celebrity Articles from the Screen Guild Magazine*. Ed. Anna Kate Sterling. Lanham, MD: Rowman & Littlefield, 1987. Print.

Null, Gary. *Black Hollywood: The Negro in Motion Pictures*. Secaucus, NJ: Citadel Press, 1975. Print.

Pinedo, Isabel Cristina. *Recreational Terror: Women and the Pleasure of Horror Film Viewing*. Albany, NY: SUNY Press, 1997. Print.

Rhines, Jesse Algeron. Black Film/White Money. New Brunswick, NJ: Rutgers University Press, 1996. Print.

Shaefer, Eric. *Bold! Daring! Shocking! True!: A History of Exploitation Films, 1919–1959*. Austin: University of Texas Press, 1995. Print.

Sharrett, Christopher. "The Horror Film in Neoconservative Culture." *Journal of Popular Film & Television* 21.3 (Fall 1993): 100–110. Print.

Sharrett, Christopher. *Mythologies of Violence in Postmodern Media*. Detroit, MI: Wayne State University Press, 1999. Print.

Stenger, Josh. "Mapping the Beach: Beach Movies, Exploitation Film and Geographies Whiteness." *Classic Hollywood, Classic Whiteness*. Ed. Daniel Bernardi. Minneapolis: University of Minnesota Press, 1996. 28–50. Print.

Wallace, Michele. *Black Macho and the Myth of the Superwoman*. New York: Verso Classics, 1999. Print.

Weiler, A.H. "'Abby,' about a Black Family and Exorcism." *New York Times*, December 26, 1974: 53. Print.

West, Hollie I. "Black Films: Crossovers and Beyond Blaxploitation." *Washington Post*, February 8, 1976: 119. Print.

Wlodarz, Joe. "Beyond the Black Macho: Queer Blaxploitation." *The Velvet Light Trap* 53 (Spring 2004): 10–25. Web. January 20, 2006. http://muse.jhu.edu/login?uri=/journals/the_velvet_light_trap/v053/53.1wlodarz. html.

Worland, Rick. *The Horror Film: An Introduction*. Malden, MA: Blackwell, 2007. Print.

Yearwood, Gladstone L. *Black Film as a Signifying Practice: Cinema, Narration and the African-American Aesthetic Tradition*. Trenton, NJ: Africa World Press, Inc., 2000. Print.

Young, Elizabeth. *Black Frankenstein: The Making of an American Metaphor*. New York: Routledge, 2008. Print.

POST-READING QUESTIONS/POST-SCREENING QUESTIONS

Directions: Use what you learned from reading this chapter and watching the film to respond to the questions.

1. How does Coleman define the difference between Blacks in horror cinema and Black horror cinema?

2. Why might we consider *The Night of the Living Dead* a foundational film in the history of Black horror cinema?

3. Describe some of the problems Coleman identifies around female and gay representations in a film like *Blacula* and others from the era.

4. What is the Black final girl/enduring woman trope? Use two scenes from either *Ganja and Hess* (1973) or *Sugar Hill* (1974) to illustrate this trope.

UNIT II

Newly Defined Areas

The following eight readings, composed of six original essays and two reprinted essays, illuminate cultural areas and topics that have remained largely outside canonical studies of film horror: "terrorist" horror, Arab horror, Iranian horror, Hindi horror, J-horror, Korean horror, Latin American horror, and Indigenous horror.

In reading 2.1, Madeleine Reddon explores how Indigenous North American filmmakers use the language of mainstream horror to process the historical trauma of settler colonialism through dystopian stories of zombies and residential ghosts, and figures of the rez (reservation) ghost hunter and urban Indigenous paranormal investigator. In reading 2.2, Ziad El-Bayoumi Foty discusses dual horrification as he connects the cinematic representation of the Red Scare of the 1950s to the racial inscription of the post-9/11 terrorist trope found in Hollywood films and subsequent forms of "counter-hegemonic self-representation." Gabriel Eljaiek-Rodríguez, in reading 2.3, discusses Latin American horror films as decolonial constructions that adapt and transform images originally designed to demean Latin American cultures into ones that resist the history of xenophobia from the Global North. Valentina Vitali, in reading 2.4, traces the threads of continuity and change in the development of the Hindi horror film from the 1970s films of the Ramsay brothers to its sudden popularity in the new millennium, which include notable films by women directors. Reading 2.5 is a republished essay by Elisabeth Scherer who contextualizes the historical and transcultural influences as well as the cultural impact of the avenging female ghost trope of Japanese horror film. Reading 2.6, also a republished essay, by Robert L. Cagle, connects the representation of mental illness and emotional trauma in Kim Jiwoon's 2016 film *A Tale of Two Sisters*, which is an adaptation of Korean folktale *The Story of Rose and Lotus*, to the emotional violence associated with British Victorian sensibility. In reading 2.7, Samirah Alkassim discusses Arab horror film's fluctuation between the fantastic and the real as a reflection of Arab modernity while the dominance of the Egyptian film industry wanes in the Middle East. Finally, in reading 2.8, Hadi Gharabaghi conducts a genealogical study of "horror ambiguity" in pre- and post-revolution Iranian films through a review of scholarship on and close readings of those films.

Each reading includes the following features: key terms and figures, recommended films, introduction to the reading, post-reading/post-screening questions, and bibliography. Many of the key terms can be found in the glossary at the end of the book where definitions are provided.

Paranormal Encounters

Notes on Indigenous Horror

By Madeleine Reddon

KEY TERMS AND FIGURES

Indigenous

Settler-colonialism

Lateral violence

Residential schools

Survivance

Missing and murdered Indigenous women and girls

Jeff Barnaby

Mike J. Marin

RECOMMENDED FILMS

Bearwalker by Cheechoo, Shirley (2001)

BeDevil by Tracey Moffat (1993)

Blood Quantum by Jeff Barnaby (2019)

Rhymes for Young Ghouls by Jeff Barnaby (2013)

Spout by Alex Munôz (2009)

The Dark Place by Kodie Bedford, Perun Bonser, Rob Braslin, Liam Philips, and Bjorn Stewart (2019)

The Darkside by Warwick Thornton (2013)

The Dead Can't Dance by Rodrick Pocowatchit (2013)

The Dead Lands by Toa Fraser (2015)

The Smudging by Mike J. Marin (2016)

Violet by Mark D. Williams (2015)

Paranormal Encounters

Notes on Indigenous Horror

By Madeleine Reddon

INTRODUCTION

Indigenous horror films tell stories that speak to the effects of settler-colonialism and racial capital on Indigenous life worlds.[1] Across the Americas, horror has been a continuous part of daily life for Indigenous people since contact with European colonists. Jodi Byrd (Chickasaw) asserts that the "story of the New World *is* horror."[2] It would be difficult to represent the collective experience of a genocide, protracted over five hundred years, outside the language of apocalypse. Grace Dillon (Anishinaabe) contends that "it is almost commonplace to think that the Native Apocalypse, if contemplated seriously, has already taken place."[3] Indigenous scholars, writers, and artists have routinely attested to this fact through a panoply of different forms of witnessing, testifying to the reality of this history through many mediums, and the idea is already regarded as a cliché within Indigenous studies. Filmmaker Ariel Smith (Nêhiyaw) suggests that the genre of horror resonates with Indigenous filmmakers because of this intergenerational experience of violence: "[W]e understand horror [because] we live it every

---

1 Thanks must go to Rusaba Alam, Johannah Bird, Chelsea Fritz, Sheila Giffen, Celiese Lypka, and Matthew Tétrault who read this work in advance of publication.

2 Indian is a pejorative term when used to refer to people who are native to the Americas. Indigenous is a broad term that allows scholars to talk about "people native to their lands" in a global context. By and large, Indigenous people should be referred to by their national/tribal identities. In Canada, many Indigenous people also self-identity as First Nations, Métis, or Inuit. Scholarship on Canadian issues will sometimes use the term "Indian" or "Status Indian" because those are legal terms that refer to Indigenous people registered under the *Indian Act.* In the US, Native American is considered to be a more respectful description than "Indian" unless you know the person's tribal affiliation, in which case, refer to them by tribe. In Australia, the terms "Indigenous Australians" and "First Australians" are more respectful than "aborigine and aboriginal." The same goes for New Zealand, though, where appropriate, the term "Māori" can be used. In all cases, capitalize tribal names and specific terminology as a mark of respect to these nations. Some of the writers, filmmakers, and theorists I cite self-identify in more complex ways, using multiple national and ethnic categories to describe themselves. I have chosen only to indicate tribal affiliations in this chapter for brevity's sake; Jodi Byrd, *The Transit of Empire: Indigenous Critiques of Colonialism* (Minneapolis: University of Minnesota Press, 2011), xii.

3 Grace Dillon, *Walking the Clouds: An Anthology of Indigenous Science Fiction* (Tucson: University of Arizona Press, 2012).

day."[4] As a result, horror films written and directed by Indigenous people tend to reflect and explore the daily experience of racial oppression and its unlivability rather than the novelty of the interruption of everyday life by supernatural or psychopathic forces. Horror offers Indigenous filmmakers a shared visual language to discuss experiences of global colonial violence across disparate and distinct transnational and tribal contexts. Through readings of Jeff Barnaby's (Mi'gmaw) *Rhymes for Young Ghouls (2013)* and Mike J. Marin's (Navajo/Laguna Pueblo/Washoe) *The Smudging (2016)*, I focus on a few emerging thematic frames in Indigenous filmmaking, such as the residential school story and the urban Indigenous paranormal investigator, to show how Indigenous filmmakers reinterpret the tropes and conceits of mainstream horror to process historical trauma and to negotiate ongoing community concerns regarding lateral violence, epistemological recovery, and the honoring of ancestral presences.

A BRIEF HISTORY OF INDIGENOUS HORROR MOVIES

Prior to 2010, there were only a handful of feature-length horror films directed and/or written by Indigenous artists. As handheld and other recording devices have become more affordable and accessible, Indigenous filmmaking has grown. Historically, Indigenous broadcasting, television, and films developed alongside tribal nationalist and Indigenous sovereignty movements. Throughout the 1960–1980s, many federally funded programs and nonprofit organizations emerged to help train, promote, hire, publish, and support Indigenous filmmakers and their work in their respective territories such as the Canadian National Film Board, the Inuit Broadcasting Corporation, the American Film Institute, the Santa Fe Anthropology Film Centre, Walpiri Media Association, Central Australian Aboriginal Media Association and Imparja, and Aotearoa Television Network, among others.[5] Many of these institutions and programs began in response to the lack of Indigenous representation within mainstream media in addition to the introduction of technologies like satellite television and the VCR into more remote Indigenous communities where broadcasting mainstream media threatened community arts. These new broadcasting ventures trained community members in filmmaking and production, creating Indigenous filmmakers who would go on to train other community members in media

---

4   Ariel Smith, "This Essay Was Not Built on an Ancient Indian Burial Ground," *Offscreen* 18, no. 8 (2014), n.p.

5   For more detailed histories, see Faye D. Ginsburg's, "Screen Memories: Resignifying the Traditional in Indigenous Media," in *Media Worlds: Anthropology on New Terrain* (Berkeley: University of California Press, 2019), 39–57; Emiel Martens's "Māori on the Silver Screen: The Evolution of Indigenous Feature Filmmaking in Aotearoa/New Zealand," *International Journal of Critical Indigenous Studies* 5, no. 1 (2012): 2–30; Sue Abel's, "The (Racial) Political Economy of Māori Television," *Australian Journal of Communication* 38, no. 3 (2011): 125–38; Kate Madden's "Asserting a Distinctly Inuit Concept of News: The Early Years of the Inuit Broadcasting Corporation's Qagik," *The Howard Journal of Communications* 8, no. 4 (1997): 297–313; Michael Meadows's, "Northern Exposure: Indigenous Television Developments in Northern Canada," *Media International Australia Incorporating Culture & Policy*, no. 78 (1995): 109–19; and Beverly Singer, *Native Filmmakers, Programs, and Institutions. Wiping the War Paint Off the Lens: Native American Film and Video* (Minneapolis: University of Minnesota Press, 2001).

production. Increasing self-representation through film and other multimedia often led to political momentum and cultural resurgence within communities. Due to the legacy of these institutions and the precedent they set, there have been more big-budget and independent feature-length Indigenous horror movies in the last decade (2010–2020) than ever before. The anthology film *Dark Place (2019)*, Jeff Barnaby's *Blood Quantum (2019)*, Mark D. Williams' *Violet (2015)*, Toa Fraser's *The Dead Lands (2014)*, Taika Waititi's *What We Do in the Shadows (2014)*, Rod Pocowatchit's *The Dead Can't Dance (2010)*, and Warwick Thornton's *The Darkside (2013)* are some examples in addition to the debut features from Barnaby and Marin. Tracey Moffat's *BeDevil (1993)* cleared ground for this work as the first feature-length horror film directed by an Indigenous woman. Moffat's contributions to the field can hardly be understated. Her experimental approach remains completely distinct from subsequent filmmakers, many of whom tend to stick to more conventional interpretations of the genre. These films are part of a growing transnational field that responds to the legacy of British colonialism in Canada, the United States, New Zealand, and Australia through Indigenous approaches to the genre of horror.

Though the majority of Indigenous horror movies were made in the last twenty years, Indigenous actors have been in horror films since the 1920s. "Re-crediting" these actors for their roles in these films is part of "recovering and recognizing the presence and participation" of Indigenous performers in an industry that frequently seeks to efface their existence to perpetuate "vanishing Indian" narratives.[6] Will Rogers appears to be the first Indigenous actor to star in a lead role in a horror film, playing Ichabod Crane in *The Headless Horseman (1922)*, a role that demanded comedic timing and skilled horsemanship. Fatimah Tobing Rony argues that the "racial films" of the 1920s and 1930s created a significant commercial appetite for representations of ethnographic subjects. In *The Third Eye*, Rony characterizes this market as a form of "fascinating cannibalism" that involves the "obsessive consumption" of images of primitive others.[7] When scripted ethnographies became "too predictable" for audiences, these same filmmakers turned away from realism to fantasy and horror. Known ethnographic filmmakers Merian C. Cooper and Ernest B. Shoedsack directed *King Kong (1933)*, a film that represented the return of the primitive as the ultimate threat to modern civilization. During the 1930s and 1940s, when horror films began feeding this market for images of racialized others, Indigenous actors begin appearing in Hollywood creature-features as side characters and extras, frequently uncredited for their performances. For instance, in *The Cat and the Canary (1939)*, Chief Thundercloud plays an uncredited "Indian guide." Jim Thorpe was also an uncredited extra in both *King Kong* and *The Vampire's Ghost (1945)*. Jay Silverheels plays an uncredited character in *The Feathered Serpent (1948)*.

---

6   Joanna Hearne, "Native American and Indigenous Media." *Feminist Media Histories* 4, no. 2 (2018): 123–127.

7   Fatimah Tobing Rony, *The Third Eye: Race, Cinema, and Ethnographic Spectacle* (Durham, NC: Duke University Press, 2004), 10.

From the 1970s on, Indigenous actors were given more central roles. Chief Dan George played a major character in *Shadow of the Hawk* (1976), a film about a young Native man who returns from the city to his community to fight "evil spirits" by training as a "medicine man" with his grandfather. Will Sampson stars in *Orca (1977)*, a *Jaws*-inspired thriller about a killer whale that attacks the hunter who killed his mate. *Clearcut (1991)*, starring Graham Greene, Tom Jackson, and Floyd Red Crow Westerman, is a movie about an unstable and militant Indigenous activist who kidnaps a logging company's general manager. More recently, Rodney A. Grant, Tatanka Means, Tom E. Lewis, Leon Burchill, Natasha Wanganeen, Simone Landers, and Baykali Ganambarr have starred in more mainstream horror films.[8] To some degree, these actors are in dialogue with the ethnographic trace in horror cinema. Their cinematic presence offers a powerful argument against colonial narratives seeking to misrepresent "Indians" and other racialized others as "primitives" outside of modern time as their very presence attests to their participation in and co-production of modernity through one of its most powerful technologies. This brief account is by no means exhaustive but suggests a longstanding presence of Indigenous artists in horror outside of the whitewashed tropes of Indian burial grounds, evil shamans, and skin walkers.

Indigenous horror films emerge from these complicated legacies as a part of global Indigenous cinema, what filmmaker Barry Barclay (Māori) describes as "Fourth World Cinema." To use Eric Michaels' terminology, this cinema takes an Indigenous "rhetorical stance"[9] toward the "national orthodoxy" of a first-world cinema built on colonial narratives of domination.[10] Fourth World Cinema is part of "the creative self-representation of Native American visual artists" that Michelle Raheja (Seneca) defines as a form of "visual sovereignty" that embodies the lived experience, cultural knowledge, and politics of Indigenous peoples in film to strengthen present-day communities and undermine harmful stereotypes.[11] For Jolene Rickard (Tuscarora), visual sovereignty is a method of "direct action" and "self-determination" that represents and amplifies Indigenous national struggles within art.[12] Randolph Lewis argues that Indigenous films are part of a "cinema of sovereignty" that challenges dominant political narratives about Indigenous issues by countering stereotypes through tribal self-representation.[13] Indigenous horror films express visual sovereignty through their play with genre. They construct fantasies of revenge and retribution that allow viewers to speculate about the possibility of community transformation in a fashion similar to "Indigenous Futurisms," a literature that experiments

---

8   See *Ghosts of Mars* (2001), *The Burrowers* (2008), *Red Hill* (2010), *Wyrmwood* (2014), *Cargo* (2017), and *The Nightingale* (2018).

9   Eric Michaels, *Bad Aboriginal Art: Tradition, Media and Technological Horizons* (Minneapolis: University of Minnesota Press, 1994), 12.

10   Barry Barclay, "Celebrating Fourth World Cinema," *Illusions*, July 2003, p. 6.

11   Michelle Raheja, *Reservation Reelism: Redfacing, Visual Sovereignty, and Representations of Native Americans in Film* (Lincoln: University of Nebraska Press, 2010), 9, 19.

12   Jolene Rickard, "Diversifying Sovereignty and the Reception of Indigenous Art." *Art Journal* 76, no. 2 (2017): 81–82.

13   Randolph Lewis, *Alanis Obomsawin: The Vision of a Native Filmmaker* (Lincoln: University of Nebraska Press, 2006), 192.

with genres like science fiction and speculative realism to imagine Indigenous futures and decolonized worlds.[14]

APPROACHES TO THE GENRE

To understand Indigenous approaches to horror as distinct examples of visual sovereignty, it is necessary to gloss some of the broad cultural differences between European American and Indigenous understandings of the genre. Indigenous cultural traditions take spirits and other nonhuman presences into account in ways that settler-colonial frameworks do not, an important distinction that needs to be made in order to read Indigenous films with any kind of cultural specificity.

During the rise of secularism in the Victorian period, horror became a mainstream genre in literature and other media. The turn toward empiricism, positivism, and rationalism in Europe led to the disenchantment of life that became characteristic of colonial modernity. Art became the place for re-enchantment, a socially acceptable site for exploring spiritual, sexual, and transgressive ideas and experiences outside the norms of civil society.[15] This epoch established common themes and conventions that most audiences would be familiar with today. Horror offered a set of aesthetic figures for understanding colonial modernity and critiquing its institutions. Ghouls, monsters, and deviants were used to explore socially intolerable emotions and desires and to elaborate common fantasies about women, the mother, and the Other. Frequently, these stories were morality tales that dramatized the social impact of historical crimes and represented non-normative sexuality and behaviors as destabilizing and damaging cultural forces. In the European American tradition, horror stories tend to foreground the supernatural and the deviant as uncommon and exotic experiences that interrupt ordinary life with disastrous consequences.[16]

Comparatively, traditional horror stories in Indigenous cultures—of wild men and women, sasquatches, cannibal spirits like the *wîhtikow*, and other malevolent non-/human beings—are part of longstanding oral traditions that usually represent spirits, otherworldly conflicts, and calamity as part of the everyday experience of living alongside nonhuman beings in the natural

---

14   Dillon, *Walking the Clouds*; Kristina Baudemann, "Indigenous Futurist Film: Speculation and Resistance in Jeff Barnaby's Rhymes for Young Ghouls and File Under Miscellaneous," in *Canadian Science Fiction, Fantasy, and Horror: Studies in Global Science Fiction*, edited by Amy J. Ransom and Dominick Grace (Cham: Palgrave Macmillan, 2019), 151–165; Lou Cornum, "The Space NDNs Star Map," in *Read, Listen, Tell: Indigenous Stories from Turtle Island*, edited by Sophie McCall, Deanna Reder, David Gaertner, Gabrielle L'Hirondelle Hill (Canada: Wilfrid Laurier University Press, 2017), 364–71.

15   See Gauri Viswanathan, *Masks of Conquest: Literary Study and British Rule in India* (Delhi/New York: Oxford University Press, 1998).

16   Tzvetan Todorov defines the fantastic as the experience of disruption of normative frameworks: "In a world which is indeed our world, the one we know, a world without devils, sylphides, or vampires, there occurs an event which cannot be explained by the laws of this same familiar world"; "Definition of the Fantastic," in *The Horror Reader*, edited by Ken Gelder (London: Routledge, 2000), 14.

world. These stories belong to the pedagogical traditions of Indigenous communities. When traditional horror stories are told, if it is even accurate to call them this, they remind listeners of their duty to care for the land and their communities by demonstrating what happens when human and nonhuman relationships are disrupted, become unstable, or turn malignant.[17] Stories of mischief, violence, and murder seek to provide Indigenous communities with teachings about how to survive harsh circumstances and communicate protocols for responsibility and respect. Indigenous storytellers tend to represent malevolent forces as troubled (human or nonhuman) ancestors with special and sacred powers or semi-divine animal beings. For this reason, the spiritual beings are much more commonplace in Indigenous stories than the supernatural oddities of Western horror, which are almost always coded as racial others, encroaching on settler territories (aliens) or past enemies or rivals (ghosts). Consequently, the "ghosts" and "creatures" within Indigenous cinema are usually not the villains of the story but ancestors in some kind of need or neglected spirits. Indigenous horror is a genre of storytelling that emerges from these traditions to address the history of contact with settler colonialism and the destabilization of Indigenous life and ecological relationships through forms of racial capital. This burgeoning cinema participates in longstanding aesthetic and political traditions within Native cultures regarding tribal sovereignty and its expression. For this reason, Indigenous horror cannot be reduced to mere appropriations of established Western genres.

RESIDENTIAL SCHOOL ZOMBIES

Barnaby joins a growing subset of Indigenous filmmakers whose work explores the colonial assault on children through the educational system and the institutionalization of Indigenous women. *Rhymes for Young Ghouls* takes place on a fictional Mi'gmaq reserve called Red Crow Indian Reservation. Set in the same universe as his subsequent films, *The Colony (2007)* and *Blood Quantum*, *Rhymes for Young Ghouls* is part of the filmmaker's hyperrealist foray into Indigenous horror. Barnaby's films use extreme gore, citing classic exploitation films like Tobe Hooper's *The Texas Chainsaw Massacre (1974)* and Canuxploitation films[18] like David Cronenberg's *Videodrome*

---

17   For approaches on how to read Indigenous media from this perspective see Linda Morra and Deanna Reder's *Learn, Teach, Challenge: Approaching Indigenous Literatures* (Waterloo: Wilfrid Laurier University Press, 2016). For an illustration of how Indigenous peoples understand the relationship between the land, pedagogy, and story see Jeanette Armstrong's "Land Speaking" (1988), in *Read, Listen, Tell: Indigenous Stories from Turtle Island (*Waterloo: Wilfrid Laurier University Press, 2017), 144–155.

18   The term "Canuxploitation" typically refers the B-movies during the "tax-shelter era" of the Canadian film industry in the 1970s; see Paul Corupe, "(Who's in the) Driver's Seat: The Canadian Brute Unleashed in *Death Weekend*," in *The Canadian Horror Film: Terror of the Soul* (Canada: University of Toronto Press, 2015) and Mark R. Hasan, *"Rituals:* Creating the Forest Slasher within the Canadian Tax Shelter Era," *The Canadian Horror Film: Terror of the Soul (*Canada: University of Toronto Press, 2015). However, Canadian B-movies predate this period and a short history of their production is described in Paul Corupe, "Canuxploitation: The Primer," http://www.canuxploitation.com/article/primer.html.

(1983). In this film, Aila (Kawennáhere Devery Jacobs) is a Mi'gmaw teenager who runs a drug ring on the reserve. Aila and her friends sell drugs to pay off a monthly "truancy tax" that keeps the Indian agent Popper (Mark Antony Krupa) from taking them to the nearby residential school where kids get "eaten up" by "zombie priests." On the day her father Joseph (Glen Gould) is set to be released from jail, Popper tries to entrap Aila and her friends, robbing them the day before the truancy tax is due. When she realizes they have been set up, Aila plans a heist to get their money back and to humiliate Popper as revenge for all the evils he has visited on her family and community.

Popper's entrapment is part of a broader government mandate to keep Indigenous parents from their children by any means necessary. Released near the end of Canada's *Truth and Reconciliation Commission* for residential schools (TRC), *Rhymes for Young Ghouls* can be read as a response to the Canadian government's first reckoning with the legacy of its genocidal policies. During the 1880s in Canada, Indian residential schools began to be built in large numbers as part of a federal assimilation policy that targeted the relationship between children and their parents as a way of breaking down community resistance to colonialism.[19] Indian residentials schools were church-run, state-funded institutions that tried to "kill the Indian to save the child." Frequently built far away from reserves and settler communities to minimize oversight, these schools were the site of mass Indigenous death, starvation, sexual, physical, and emotional abuse in both Canada and the United States. The film begins with title cards, based in historical fact, that condense a longer history of federal legislation into one fictional royal decree:

> The law in the Kingdom decreed that every child between the age of 5 and 16 who is physically able must attend Indian Residential School. … Her Majesty's

---

19   The Canadian federal government is obliged to provide First Nations communities with education because of treaty promises they made to secure land for settlement. Their interpretation of this duty, however, has maximized violence toward Indigenous peoples by using colonial education as method for attacking Indigenous sovereignty through family and culture. The plan to separate families to destroy Indigenous sovereignty was explicit in the political debates of the time. In 1883, Sir John A. MacDonald, then prime minister of Canada, explicitly argued in the House of Commons that taking children away from their parents was the only way to ensure "Indian" assimilation:

> When the school is on the reserve the child lives with its parents, who are savages; he is surrounded by savages, and though he may learn to read and write his habits, and training and mode of thought are Indian. He is simply a savage who can read and write. It has been strongly pressed on myself, as the head of the Department, that Indian children should be withdrawn as much as possible from the parental influence, and the only way to do that would be to put them in central training industrial schools where they will acquire the habits and modes of thought of white men. (Truth, and Reconciliation Commission Canada, "Canada's Residential Schools: The Final Report of the Truth and Reconciliation Commission of Canada: The History," *Government of Canada* 2 (2016): 576).

For more historical details on the nature of residential schools see the six volumes of the Truth and Reconciliation Commission's report on residential schooling and John S. Milloy, *A National Crime: The Canadian Government and the Residential School System, 1879 to 1986* (Winnipeg: University of Manitoba Press, 2017).

attendants, to be called truant officers, will take into custody a child whom they believe to be absent from school using as much force as the circumstance requires. ... A person caring for an Indian child who fails to cause such a child to attend school shall immediately be imprisoned, and such person arrested without warrant and said child conveyed to school by the truant officer.[20]

In 1920, an amendment to the *Indian Act* made attendance at these schools mandatory. Parents could be arrested for any number of offenses on reserves, including refusal to send their children to school. By the 1960s, Canada began decommissioning these schools due to their gross financial burden, rather than their well-documented abuse and malfeasance, but the last school did not officially close until 1996. The Canadian government did not provide a formal apology to Indigenous peoples until June 11, 2008.[21] In response to a successful 2006 class action suit, initiated by Indigenous survivors of the school, the federal government organized a TRC (2008–2015) to publicly address the violence and abuse that occurred in these institutions.

Rhymes for Young Ghouls explores issues that Indigenous communities are still facing today as a result of state crimes.[22] Barnaby asks, "What happens to a community where parents cannot parent their children either due to trauma or forcible separation? How does this re-shape family dynamics on an intergenerational basis?" The horrors that Aila's parents endured, long before she was born, remain ever present in their lives. Barnaby provides this context in the opening scenes of the film. The first frame of the film is a close-up of a weed nugget and what looks like meth. Blurry brown beer bottles are staggered throughout the frame, darkly lit and glinting in low light. In the background, we see the shadowy figure of Burner (Brandon Oakes), Aila's uncle, rolling a joint. Barnaby cuts to Aila's mother, Anna (Roseanne Supernault), who is toasting bread on the stove top. Joseph enters the kitchen with a case of bottles and tells Burner not to "smoke all their profits." Aila's parents sell and do drugs to survive. As the film progresses, these three characters appear to represent a variety of negative (and frequently pathologized) responses that Indigenous people had to residential schooling (complicity, criminality, and suicide). In comparison, the children demonstrate other survivance strategies[23] that show the resiliency of the community under the face of extreme oppressive circumstances.

---

20   Indian Act, by will of her Majesty the Queen in Right of Canada.

21   A year after, the same prime minister who made this apology, Stephen Harper, claimed that Canada has "no history of colonialism" at a G20 summit. This is one reason, among others, that many Indigenous peoples have not accepted the federal government's apology as sincere.

22   From this past year alone, 1,323 children have been found in mass and unmarked graves at former residential schools in Canada, findings that are the result of massive community efforts on the part of Indigenous communities to make the federal government accountable for their crimes.

23   "Survivance" is a term coined by Gerald Vizenor to talk about aesthetic strategies that Indigenous people have used for both survival and resistance. This term seeks to capture some of the transformative power of Indigenous communities under colonialism.

In the next scene, Burner steps outside the house. Burner pauses for a moment in the doorway before stumbling forward and vomiting all over himself, the grass, and the lawn chairs outside. Two kids are sitting on top of a black car parked in front under the starlight watching Burner make a mess of himself. Aila comforts the boy next to her, Tyler (Louis Beauvais), telling him "It's alright. It's just Burner." Trying to save face in front of the children, Burner points to a building in the far distance and tries to distract the kids with a scary story:

> Burner: You ever seen the mill up close? They cook Indian kids up there for that zombie priest.
>
> Tyler: What's a zombie?
>
> Burner: Jesus Christ, Tyler. Don't they teach you anything up at that school? Zombies are dead people who come back to life to eat brains. Dumb brains especially. Zombies will eat just about anyone. But these religified zombies …
>
> Aila: Alright, Burner. He's only joking, Ty.
>
> Burner: I wish! They throw these kids down this hole to the cooker and every time they clang off that fluted chimney. Why do you think so many kids go missing at St. Pete's huh?
>
> Tyler: You're just trying to scare me.
>
> Burner: Settle down you pussy.

Burner tries to reassert some of his authority by frightening the kids. But his story is also a lesson about why their parents are more preoccupied with partying than with their own kids. Childhood abuse has zombified the adults on the reserve. They have turned to drugs, alcohol, and other vices to escape their problems and, in the process, became the "living dead." Later in the film, Aila calls this escapism the "art of forgetfulness." She capitalizes on this desire by taking over her parents' drug operation to make money to pay the truancy tax. Burner is one of these zombies, which explains why he addresses Tyler almost as a peer, calling him a "pussy" for being scared, even though Tyler is still just a kid. Burner had to grow up before his time just as these kids will have to.

Ariel Smith writes that Barnaby's use of extreme violence is "not gratuitous" but "fitting and appropriate due to the themes he engages" such as genocide.[24] In the following scene, Aila's parents come out of the house drunk and stoned. Anna drags Joseph into the back seat of the car while Aila gets in the front seat. With Aila on her lap, Anna pulls the car out of the driveway, accidentally driving over something as she pulls out. In a horrific and deeply disturbing scene, Anna stops the car to see what she has driven over, only to discover that she has hit Tyler, crushing his head under the wheel of the car. Anna's grief causes her to hang herself the following morning.

---

24   Smith, "This Essay Was Not Built on an Ancient Indian Burial Ground."

Joseph's grief makes him take the blame for Tyler's death. Aila witnesses her father's arrest and then discovers her mother's body hanging from the trees next to their house. As Aila walks slowly toward Anna, calling out for her mother, Barnaby cuts to a shot below Anna's feet hanging from the trees, which drip with urine. Over this frame, Aila begins speaking in voiceover for the first time: "The day I found my mother dead. I aged by a thousand years."

This film is an example of how the visual language of horror offers tools for communicating, transmitting, and articulating Indigenous histories about the intergenerational violence of colonialism as well as forms of lateral violence, which demonstrate the fractal nature of abuse within a community. For people whose access to knowledge keepers has been prohibited, severed, or hindered, horror and other popular genres provide Indigenous peoples with a set of figures and visual codes for thinking through their experiences of oppression and for teaching others how to survive. Burner, for example, uses the zombie story to comment on his generation's experiences with residential schooling. The zombie is a useful metaphor for describing the violence Indigenous people underwent and understanding how those experiences continue to shape the present. Anna and Joseph, for example, had already been zombified by the priest. They were too stoned to realize what they were doing that night in 1969 and they accidentally kill Tyler. His brain is "eaten" by their car. Burner foretells this lateral violence. His story traces a link between the residential school and the dynamics of intimacy within the Indigenous family and the economic situation of the reserve.

Scattered throughout *Rhymes for Young Ghouls* are other references to horror films that provide similar commentary on the transformative effects of colonization on the community. For example, the sign for the Fish Mittens strip club features a cartoon image of the creature from the Black Lagoon carrying a topless blonde woman. Adopting Hollywood's images of monsters becomes a critical and ironic commentary on the forms of dehumanization that Indigenous people undergo under colonization. Throughout the film, there are other nods to mainstream horror such as when the children wear skeleton-like face paint and Topstone-esque creature masks or the skull mounted on Aila's bike. Real ghosts (the ghosts of Anna and Tyler) appear several times in the film, but neither the ghosts nor the other Indigenous people on the reserve are particularly malevolent or scary, even when they dress up as monsters. Ken Derry argues that Barnaby is playing with the idea of "inner" and "outer" monsters by having Indigenous people dress up as monsters but act with compassion while the Indian agents demonstrate their monstrosity.[25] Identifying with monsters, however, gives the characters access to forms of agency denied to them by state discourses. In mainstream cinema, monsters typically try to destroy the world built by white patriarchs. They are powerful, frightening, and profoundly destabilizing. Dian Million (Tanana Athabascan) argues that the TRC gave the Canadian federal government an opportunity to reaffirm the national narrative of "Indian" abjection and colonial

---

25   Ken Derry, "Myth and Monstrosity: Teaching Indigenous Films." *The Journal of Religion and Film* 22 no. 3 (2018): 1–32.

beneficence by pathologizing survivors as "trauma victim[s]" rather than colonized subjects.[26] The visual association of Indigenous children with monsters refuses this narrative of injury by appropriating these creatures as anticolonial icons.

Rhymes for Young Ghouls emphasizes the resilience of Indigenous peoples, specifically their children, against extreme forms of violence and oppression that target Indigenous families. Indigenous children are resilient, creative, and loving despite the incredible pressure on them to succumb to violence, addiction, or death. After she is abandoned by her parents, Aila uses the voiceover to periodically explain to the viewer her "rules" for survival on the reserve, which she has no doubt created to cope with her parental loss. Aila becomes her own parent. However, these rules bear witness to her protracted suffering only indirectly. Aila refuses to narrate her experiences as either trauma or redemption story and represents herself instead as an authority and critic of the zombified world. Barnaby's use of voiceover recalls Alanis Obomsawin's documentaries. Barnaby cites Obomsawin (Abenaki) as a key influence who gave him access to another language of resistance through her films on Indigenous political struggles and contemporary life.[27] Obomsawin emphasizes the political and cultural authority of Indigenous women by using her own voice to narrate her films. Likewise, the voiceover in Barnaby's film suggests that telling stories is a key survivance tool that allows Indigenous people to self-authorize their own experiences of colonialism in the wake of community fragmentation. Stories resist this fragmentation by conveying important knowledge about intergenerational relationships and political and historical contexts in the present.

As pedagogical tools, stories tell us what happened, what tools we have at our disposal, and how to resist and adapt. Besides Burner's zombie story, there are several others told to Aila over the course of the film that give her guidance. Aila's adopted grandmother, Ceres, tells Aila a story about a wolf who eats children to prepare her for going to the residential school and the "old man" on the reserve, a WWII veteran, tells Aila a story about her grandfather's courage during the war. Aila's self-made rules and these other stories offer her instruction about how to navigate issues such as loss, grief, oppression, and economic instability. Her ability to tell her own story is part of her incredible resiliency and vitality in the face of intolerable circumstances. These stories also offer us a way of reading Barnaby's own approach to horror as a genre that offers filmmakers and viewers pedagogical instruction for navigating ongoing colonial violence and internal community struggles.

---

26   Dian Million, *Therapeutic Nations: Healing in an Age of Indigenous Human Rights* (Tucson: University of Arizona Press, 2013).

27   Alex Heeney, "Jeff Barnaby on Blood Quantum and Colonialist Zombies," *Seventh Row*, April 28, 2020, https://seventh-row.com/2020/04/28/jeff-barnaby-blood-quantum-zombies/.

COMMUNITY CENTER GHOSTS

The Smudging is also a film about navigating the ghosts of the past in the present. In this movie, Marin takes up the epidemic of missing and murdered Indigenous women as a subject. The film speculates about the origins of gendered violence using traditional Indigenous horror stories and suggests that violence may not derive from criminal or social pathology but from imbalances in the spiritual world. Set in downtown Chicago, *The Smudging* is about the Night Stalkers, a group of paranormal investigators trying to get to the bottom of the strange events happening at the Native American Cultural Center (NACC). The movie begins with a series of interviews conducted by Bad (Mike J. Marin) and Danny Boy (Chris Walsh) with the NACC staff about the paranormal experiences they have been having. Four different ghosts haunt the center: a serial killer, James "Button Man" Garrison, as well as the two Indigenous women he brutally murdered, and a small girl who, reportedly, fell down the stairwell accidentally (see figure 2.1.1). In these interviews, the staff also allude to a more malicious force present in the building that viewers later discover is a semi-divine supernatural being that preys on vulnerable people, influencing them to do horrible things to themselves and to others. This evil being is almost never referred to by name and is simply called "The Dark" in the credits.

The Night Stalkers decide to stay overnight to document ghostly activity and solve the mystery behind these hauntings. When they get into trouble with The Dark, "medicine warrior" Robert Locke (Vincent Romero) steps in to help them bind this spirit, cleanse the center, and free the other spirits (see figure 2.1.2). Like many paranormal movies and television shows, this film uses low-tech cameras to achieve the illusion of realism such as hand-held camerawork, security cam footage, and night vision. Eric Michaels suggests that Indigenous people "have their own production values, distinct aesthetics, and cultural concerns,"[28] apart from high-production fidelity. Marin's decision to keep Indigenous film "local" may have been to protect the integrity of the narrative. In interviews, Marin discusses how funding structures change Indigenous stories to appeal to more mainstream audiences, negatively distorting the story in the process of monetizing Indigenous cultural knowledge.[29]

Figure 2.1.1 Bad (Mike J. Marin) looking for the Little Ghost Girl (Chaske Soto).

---

28   Eric Michaels, *Bad Aboriginal Art*, xxvii, xxix.

29   Mike J. Marin, "Cinema Red: Mike J. Marin in Conversation," November 2020, https://cineexcess.uscreen.io/programs/13-cinema-redmp4-090621.

Figure 2.1.2 Danny Boy (Chris Walsh) hides behind Medicine Warrior Robert Locke (Vincent Romero).

The Smudging is about the spiritual forces that prey on a vulnerable community. The setting for the film is important for thinking about Marin's approach to the issue of community harm through Indigenous spirituality. The American Indian Center (renamed NAAC in the film) is one of the oldest intertribal friendship centers in the United States. Historically, it was a hub for the urban Indigenous community in Chicago, a place for social and political organizing, as well as cultural resurgence amongst a displaced and dispossessed population.[30] In the late 1940s, the federal government replaced the Indian Reorganization Act with termination policies, abandoning their previous attempts to "reorganize" federal-imposed tribal governments for an explicit policy of assimilation through the termination of the "special legislative status of tribes where possible." Relocating Indigenous peoples to urban centers became part of a national program to achieve this vision. In 1953, after several unsuccessful attempts to permanently relocate Indigenous peoples to Chicago, the Bureau of Indian Affairs created a center for them in the city, a project that had been part of long-standing advocacy on the part of local Native American activists and welfare groups. The American Indian Center represents the tremendous local organizing done by Indigenous peoples to rebuild their community in the face of renewed genocidal federal policies such as termination. In press for the film, Marin writes that *The Smudging* was partly inspired by his childhood in Oakland where he spent a lot of time at the Intertribal Friendship House:

> [A]fter years of time spent there and visiting other centers around the area, I found that they all have a similar feel to them; kind of a mixture of old world comfort and concrete familiarity. Also, I noticed that they all smell like pipe tobacco and sage, the medicines of our culture. But they also have another part about them, another side to them that hides when the lights are on, that creeps out when all the living energy has gone home for the day. ... Night time at an urban Native American community center is ... scary.[31]

---

30   Grant Ardnt, "'Contrary to Our Way of Thinking': The Struggle for an American Indian Center in Chicago, 1946–1953," *American Indian Culture & Research Journal* 22, no. 4 (1998): 117.

31   Mike J. Marin, "Origin of the Story," https://sites.google.com/site/thesmudgingmovie/origin-of-the-story.

Alongside, the healing medicine exchanged at the center is knowledge of more threatening forces. For Marin, these institutions are sites of community building and Indigenous resurgence where the temporary irruption of malevolence can be addressed through shared medicines and cultural knowledge. The community center is a shared discursive space where a variety of tribally distinct Indigenous cultures, peoples, and ideas meet. Like the community center, horror films can be a meeting place where different people share knowledge and medicine to manage the darkness.

Over the course of the film, we discover that the Dark has been driving vulnerable people like Garrison to harm others and themselves. This evil force "feeds on the life of the people ... that have sought comfort and familiarity with their own culture."[32] From an Indigenous perspective, spiritual imbalances can create violence in the world. Locke tells the group:

> This entity has been here before this building was here, even before the city was here, all the natives in this area, all the different tribes ... they fought it, but they were only strong enough to drive it back. The medicine men used their most sacred elements against this thing. They knew they couldn't defeat it. The hatred that dwells within [it] creates a seed of despair that fills you with really bad energy. And it has leaked into the walls of these buildings, it's permeating this whole place, everyone that's ever been in here has felt its presence, all the in-fighting, all the violence, all the arguments. The people that were here before the natives practically worshipped it, they may have even have fed it, our people didn't bring it, their people didn't bring it, it was already here.

Different communities have different relationships to the Dark but, in each case, it is a presence that sows negative energy within groups. It is older than human life itself and extremely powerful—the only recourse for these communities is to manage the harm it causes the best they can. Locke's explanation contextualizes the violence toward Indigenous women as part of a greater spiritual imbalance. Garrison is a victim to something he could not guard himself against, and it is up to the community to draw on their strongest medicines to combat the issue, imperfect though their solutions may be. Locke appeals to the Night Stalkers to help him, explaining that "this thing it can't get out. It's contained here. But it can influence, it can injure, it can hurt. Remember James Garrison? The button man? He was a community member. He came to all the events here before he murdered those girls. ... It got to him. So how many more?" Ceremonial practices to restore balance and harmony seek to manage this primordial force and, without these renewed community practices, the Dark might hurt again. Cleansing the space and "bringing in the light" becomes imperative for halting the spread of this malicious energy.

---

32   Ibid.

CONCLUSION

The Indigenous paranormal investigator is an emerging trope in Indigenous horror that indicates a culturally distinct approach to the fantastic and supernatural.[33] Joseph Baker and Christopher Bader argue that "paranormalism ... haunts the borderlands of what is considered legitimate knowledge in numerous academic fields."[34] Paranormal investigators seek out and document phenomena that cannot be understood within the boundaries of "institutionalized knowledge," thus challenging the conventions of both empirical science and institutional religion. Ghosts, the subject of their search, "by definition ... violate a number of binaries held as central tenets of human, and especially Western, thought." Specters trouble clear distinctions between body and soul, life and death, past and present, presence and absence. Their liminality threatens established epistemological frameworks. The ghost hunter "appeals to science" by using technology to "legitimize both the activities and views of ghost believers, while also problematizing the idea that we live in a disenchanted, fully rationalized world."[35] The mediating technologies of the paranormal investigator (camera, recording equipment, the interview) were and are still used by anthropologists to document the "disappearance" of Indigenous peoples. Anthropologists obfuscated the genocidal policies of the colonial state by naturalizing the death of Indigenous peoples through a racial science that explained their deaths as evidence of their "inherent" primitivism. Marin, in the role of the paranormal investigator, negotiates the boundaries of the known world by appropriating these mediating tools to show the limits of colonial epistemes for explaining the proliferation of violence within contemporary life. Using scientific tools (recording devices, hand-held cameras, and gadgets for measuring electrical inputs), the Night Stalkers demonstrate the existence of beings that cannot be understood through Western science. While these technologies can capture proof of ghosts, they cannot contain or dispel them. Only Indigenous tech can do this. The Night Stalkers use "sage grenades" and medicine bundles to protect themselves against the Dark, preventing it from causing further harm by containing it to the NACC. The Indigenous ghost hunter challenges the assumption that traditional knowledge is no longer useful for understanding the world and supporting the community.

In this way, Marin uses the visual language of horror to undercut the master narrative of colonial modernity. Like the ghost hunter, the filmmaker questions the limits of Western epistemologies by representing absent presences whose appearance cannot be fully explained through empirical science. Indigenous cultural and epistemological traditions provide more substantive, if ambivalent, frameworks for understanding community violence and spiritual

---

33   The "rez" ghost hunter featured in Joe Singh's *Beyond the Fear* and the five feature films of the Native American Paranormal Project from Native Boy Productions correlate to the "urban" Indigenous paranormal investigator.

34   Joseph O. Baker and Christopher D. Bader, "A Social Anthropology of Ghosts in Twenty-First-Century America," *Social Compass* 61, no. 4 (2014): 585.

35   Ibid., 580.

malevolence. In an interview, Marin describes his approach to horror as bringing Native American traditions into "an urban space" where these traditional stories are "more scary" because they don't appear to belong and contradict predominant assumptions about the knowable world:

> How scary is that? Especially because we expect there to be answers for everything. There's not always answers to everything. There is always the great unknown. That's a lot of what Native mysticism is about and I can't really talk about it because, quite frankly, my elders would slap me on the back of the head.[36]

Marin is rightly concerned about protecting this knowledge. When Locke refuses to talk about the cleansing ceremony on camera or when Bad mentions he can't tell viewers what is in their medicine bundles, the film draws attention to the need to protect Indigenous knowledge from outsiders. Marin also decides to withhold giving a traditional name for The Dark, refusing to occupy the role of "native informant" by locating this character within a more specific community theology or oral history. Though Marin describes his work as "Urban Native Horror," *The Smudging* might be described as a neo-traditionalist work that understands the friendship center as a place for pan-tribal community healing through the resurgence of traditional knowledges.

Indigenous filmmakers have understood the constraints of horror as an opportunity to register the profound disruption of Indigenous life worlds and the horrors of colonialism using a visual language familiar to settler audiences. Indigenous films, however, are more than mere refutations of colonial ideology or traumatic scripts. Horror provides an occasion to demonstrate the strength and capacity of Indigenous peoples to adapt to unbearable circumstances, as both Burnaby and Marin show. Horror is a meeting place where Indigenous filmmakers can share and demonstrate survivance strategies and the continuing vitality of their communities.

BIBLIOGRAPHY

Abel, Sue. "The (Racial) Political Economy of Maori Television." *Australian Journal of Communication* 38, no. 3 (2011): 125–38.

Ardnt, Grant. "'Contrary to Our Way of Thinking': The Struggle for an American Indian Center in Chicago, 1946–1953." *American Indian Culture & Research Journal* 22, no. 4 (1998): 117–34.

---

36   Marin, "Cinema Red."

Armstrong, Jeannette. "Land Speaking." In *Read, Listen, Tell: Indigenous Stories from Turtle Island*, 141–55. Waterloo: Wilfrid Laurier University Press, 2017.

Baker, Joseph O., and Christopher D. Bader. "A Social Anthropology of Ghosts in Twenty-First-Century America." *Social Compass* 61, no. 4 (2014): 569–93.

Barclay, Barry. "Celebrating Fourth Cinema." *Illusions Magazine, New Zealand*, July 2003, 1–11.

Barnaby, Jeff. *Rhymes for Young Ghouls*, 2013.

Baudemann, Kristina. "Indigenous Futurist Film: Speculation and Resistance in Jeff Barnaby's Rhymes for Young Ghouls and File Under Miscellaneous." In *Canadian Science Fiction, Fantasy, and Horror: Studies in Global Science Fiction*, 151–165. Cham: Palgrave Macmillan, 2019.

Byrd, Jodi. *The Transit of Empire: Indigenous Critiques of Colonialism*. Minneapolis: University of Minnesota Press, 2011.

Cornum, Lou. "The Space NDNs Star Map." In *Read, Listen, Tell: Indigenous Stories from Turtle Island*, 364–71. Wilfrid Laurier University Press, 2017.

Corupe, Paul. "Canuxploitation: the Primer." Canuxploitation. http://www.canuxploitation.com/article/primer.html.

Corupe, Paul. "(Who's in the) Driver's Seat: The Canadian Brute Unleashed in *Death Weekend*." *The Canadian Horror Film: Terror of the Soul*. University of Toronto Press, 2015.

Dillon, Grace L. *Walking the Clouds: An Anthology of Indigenous Science Fiction*. Tucson: University of Arizona Press, 2012.

Ginsburg, Faye D. "Screen Memories: Resignifying the Traditional in Indigenous Media." In *Media Worlds: Anthropology on New Terrain*, 39–57. Berkeley: University of California Press, 2019.

Halfe, Louise, and David Gaertner. *Sôhkêyihta: The Poetry of Sky Dancer Louise Bernice Halfe*. Waterloo, Ontario, Canada: Wilfrid Laurier University Press, 2018.

Hasan, Mark R. "*Rituals:* Creating the Forest Slasher within the Canadian Tax Shelter Era." *The Canadian Horror Film: Terror of the Soul*. University of Toronto Press, 2015.

Hearne, Joanna. "Native American and Indigenous Media." *Feminist Media Histories* 4, no. 2 (2018): 123–127.

Heeney, Alex. "Jeff Barnaby on Blood Quantum and Colonialist Zombies." *Seventh Row*, April 28, 2020. https://seventh-row.com/2020/04/28/jeff-barnaby-blood-quantum-zombies/.

Krasowki, Sheldon. *No Surrender: The Land Remains Indigenous*. Regina: University of Regina, 2019.

Lewis, Randolph. *Alanis Obomsawin: The Vision of a Native Filmmaker*. Lincoln: University of Nebraska Press, 2006.

Madden, Kate. "Asserting a Distinctly Inuit Concept of News: The Early Years of the Inuit Broadcasting Corporation's Qagik." *The Howard Journal of Communications* 8, no. 4 (1997): 297–313.

Marin, Mike J. "Cinema Red: Mike J. Marin in Conversation," November 2020. https://cineexcess.uscreen.io/programs/13-cinema-redmp4-09062.

Marin, Mike J. "Origin of the Story." The Smudging, n.d. https://sites.google.com/site/thesmudgingmovie/origin-of-the-story.

Marin, Mike J. *The Smudging*, 2016.

Martens, E. "Maori on the Silver Screen: The Evolution of Indigenous Feature Filmmaking in Aotearoa/New Zealand." *International Journal of Critical Indigenous Studies* 5, no. 1 (2012): 2–30.

Meadows, Michael. "Northern Exposure: Indigenous Television Developments in Northern Canada." *Media International Australia Incorporating Culture & Policy*, no. 78 (1995): 109–19.

Michaels, Eric. *Bad Aboriginal Art: Tradition, Media and Technological Horizons*. Minneapolis: University of Minnesota Press, 1994.

Million, Dian. *Therapeutic Nations: Healing in an Age of Indigenous Human Rights*. Tucson: The University of Arizona Press, 2013.

Milloy, John S. *A National Crime: The Canadian Government and the Residential School System, 1879 to 1986*. Winnipeg: University of Manitoba Press, 2017.

Morra, Linda M., and Deanna Reder. *Learn, Teach, Challenge: Approaching Indigenous Literatures*. Waterloo: Wilfrid Laurier University Press, 2016.

Raheja, Michelle. *Reservation Reelism: Redfacing, Visual Sovereignty, and Representations of Native Americans in Film*. Lincoln: University of Nebraska Press, 2010.

Rickard, Jolene. "Diversifying Sovereignty and the Reception of Indigenous Art." *Art Journal* 76, no. 2 (2017): 81–84.

Rony, Fatimah Tobing. *The Third Eye: Race, Cinema, and Ethnographic Spectacle*. Durham: Duke University Press, 2004.

Singer, Beverly. *Native Filmmakers, Programs, and Institutions. Wiping the War Paint Off the Lens: Native American Film and Video*. Minneapolis: University of Minnesota Press, 2001.

Smith, Ariel. "This Essay Was Not Built on an Ancient Indian Burial Ground." *Offscreen* 18, no. 8 (2014).

Todorov, Tzvetan. "Definition of the Fantastic." In *The Horror Reader*, ed. Ken Gelder, 14–19. London: Routledge, 2000.

Truth, and Reconciliation Commission Canada. "Canada's Residential Schools: The Final Report of the Truth and Reconciliation Commission of Canada: The History." *Government of Canada* 2 (2016): 1939–2000.

Viswanathan, Gauri. *Masks of Conquest: Literary Study and British Rule in India*. Delhi/New York: Oxford University Press, 1998.

Figure Credits

POST-READING QUESTIONS/POST-SCREENING QUESTIONS

Directions: Use what you learned from reading this chapter and watching the film to respond to the questions.

1. Horror offers Indigenous filmmakers a common visual language from which to explore the specificity of their own histories and cultures. What are some of the ways that Indigenous filmmakers adapt common horror tropes and formulas for their own ends?

2. In horror, the paranormal investigator is a figure who demonstrates that we do not fully "know" the world; neither secular science nor institutional religions are able to fully explain the complexity of our lives. How does Marin use this figure to pose questions about colonialism, lateral violence, and community in *The Smudging*?

3. Summarize and explain how ghosts and other nonhuman beings are understood within Indigenous cultural traditions. How do these figures participate in the pedagogical traditions of these communities?

4. *Rhymes for Young Ghouls* examines the intergenerational impact of colonialism on the Mi'qmaq community through residential schooling. How does the system of residential schooling shape life on the reserve? How do Aila and her friends seek to break from this cycle of violence? Does Aila's "heist" disrupt business as usual on the reserve?

The Hollywood Terrorist and Counter-Hegemonic Self-Representation

By Ziad El-Bayoumi Foty

KEY TERMS AND FIGURES

Cultural apparatus

Dual horrification

State terrorism

Terrorist monster

Hegemonic power

Red Scare

McCarthyism

Hollywood ten

Arab land

Islamophobia

Counter hegemonic

RECOMMENDED FILMS

Babel by Alejandro G. Inarritu (2006)

Black Sunday by John Frankenheimer (1977)

Kiss Me Deadly by Robert Aldrich (1955)

Paradise Now by Hani Abu Assad (2005)

Ramy by Ramy Youssef (2019–), season 1, episode 4 "Strawberries"

Syriana by Stephen Gaghan (2005)

The War Within by Joseph Castelo (2005)

The Hollywood Terrorist and Counter-Hegemonic Self-Representation

By Ziad El-Bayoumi Foty

INTRODUCTION

The September 11, 2001 terrorist attack on the World Trade Center in New York City, commonly referred to as 9/11, resulted in the deaths of over three thousand people. In addition to those who perished in the horrific blast, the health of thousands of people, both first responders and those who happened to be in the vicinity during and in the aftermath, suffered adverse consequences, many with permanent damage. Outrage and condemnation came from all over the world, including Muslim and Arab countries from which the terrorists originated. The US outrage over the attack of 9/11 extended well beyond those who plotted and carried out this act, to whoever shared one or another element of their identity, whether religious, linguistic, ethnic, or racial. For many Muslims and Arabs living in the US, 9/11 marked the beginning of a long period of anxiety because of the frequency and virulence with which they were targeted, often wrongly, for being associated with terrorism. For many non-Muslims in the US, Western Europe, and Israel, the trope of the suicide bomber quickly became a symbol synonymous with an Islamic "culture of death."[1] This led to an unprecedented popular wrath against Muslims and Arabs in the US in particular. According to the FBI's annual reports at the time, hate crimes directed at mosques, Muslims, and people who were perceived to be Middle Eastern Muslims (such as Sikhs) spiked dramatically after 9/11 and continued to rise at unprecedented levels.[2] Even four years after these tragic events, horrific incidents of hate crimes and domestic terror continued to occur.

Nearly twenty years later, fear of foreign terrorism maintains its grip on the American imagination. According to a 2018 national survey by the Pew Research Center, Americans ranked addressing terrorism concerns as the top priority President Trump and Congress should

---

1 Talal Asad, *On Suicide Bombing* (New York: Columbia University Press, 2007), 1.

2 Patrick Brantlinger, *States of Emergency: Essays on Culture and Politics* (Bloomington: Indiana University Press, 2013), 128.

focus on, outranking issues of economy, health care costs, social security, and the environment. Despite estimates that the likelihood of a person living in the United States dying in a terrorist attack over the course of their lifetime is 1 in 75,000,[3] Americans are clearly concerned about the potential for terrorist attacks within the United States.[4] While this feared terrorist does not have the same physical appearance as the infamous White nationalist Timothy McVeigh who was convicted for the carnage of the 1995 Oklahoma City Bombing, they are almost always "Muslim but never white."[5] Among the many accounts of what Claire Alexander describes as "Raceing Islamophobia,"[6] a study undertaken at Georgia State University shows that the media covers "terror attacks by Muslims" 357 percent more than it covers other attacks.[7]

Scholars who have examined the American culture of fear point to the role of mass media in arousing and manipulating the public.[8] The "media-ization of emotion" can be seen in the deliberate use of fear-based reporting, where even weather reports seek to create fear.[9] In regard to the fear of terrorism, David Altheide[10] has observed that the American media operates on the "politics of fear," whereby fear creates entertainment value, generates profits, and controls audiences. Fear is thus socially constructed, and according to Altheide, when coupled with the threat of terrorism, is sufficient to create extensive fear in audiences. It is logical to then understand how cinematic representation, which enables and perpetuates societal fears, has been used as a mechanism of ideological control associated with US state policies at home and abroad, in this sense functioning as an extension of the cultural apparatus.[11]

3　John Mueller, "Inflating Terrorism" in *American foreign policy and the politics of fear: threat inflation since 9/11*, ed. A. Trevor Thrall and Jane K. Cramer (New York: Routledge, 2009), 192–209.

4　Murat Haner et al., "Public Concern about Terrorism: Fear, Worry, and Support for Anti-Muslim Policies," *Socius* 5 (2019), 1–16.

5　Caroline Mala Corbin, "Terrorists Are Always Muslim but Never White: At the Intersection of Critical Race Theory and Propaganda," *Fordham Law Review* 86, no. 455 (2017), https://ir.lawnet.fordham.edu/flr/vol86/iss2/5.

6　Claire Alexander, "Raceing Islamophobia," in *Islamophobia: Still a Challenge for Us All*, edited by Farah Elahi and Omar Khan, 13–17 (London: Runnymede Trust, 2017).

7　This may have shifted slightly since the dramatic events of 2020, in the police slayings of both Breonna Taylor in Louisville, Kentucky, and George Floyd in Minneapolis, Minnesota, revealing a more public reflection of the US's long history of terrorism against Black bodies. Erin M. Kearns et al., "Why Do Some Terrorist Attacks Receive More Media Attention Than Others?" *Justice Quarterly* 36, no. 6 (2019): 985–1022, https://doi.org/10.1080/07418825.2018.1524507.

8　David L. Altheide, *Terrorism and the Politics of Fear* (Lanham, MD: Rowman & Littlefield, 2017); Joel Best, *American Nightmares: Social Problems in an Anxious World* (Oakland: University of California Press, 2018).

9　Peter N. Stearns, "Dare to Compare: The Next Challenge in Assessing Emotional Cultures," *Emotion Review* 2, no. 3 (2010): 261–64.

10　Altheide, *Terrorism and the Politics of Fear.*

11　This construct brings into focus the politics/power relations of culture and mechanisms of its propagation. As conceptualized by C. Wright Mills, the cultural apparatus is composed of all the organizations and milieux in which artistic, intellectual, and scientific work goes on and of the means by which such work is made available. See Soheir A. Morsey, "The Bad, the Ugly, the Super⊠Rich, and the Exceptional Moderate: US Popular Images of the Arabs" in The Journal of Popular Culture (1986), Volume 20 (3), 13-29.

While the genre of horror film takes many forms, Hollywood's cinematic representations of the malevolent Arab or Muslim, which according to Britannica "cause intense repugnance, fear, or dread,"[12] participate in established cinematic codes, one expression of which is the terrorist trope: they are already part of the horror film canon. As scholarship on monster tropes predominantly focuses on what it means to be human in opposition to the monstrous, the terrorist is another iteration of monstrosity used to inspire fear in the American public imagination, in the same way that Dracula did in the 1930s. We must then ask, what are the implications of such negative representations on the American public?

In order to entertain this question, we must first look at the fluidity of the horror genre whose hybridity and adaptability have allowed for other horrific representations like that of the terrorist. Once this is established, we can then discuss the notion of dual horrification in which a film can signify a people as horrifying to the dominant White audience as a means of vilification and at the same time be representative of a horrifying experience for Arabs and Muslims who are watching the victimization of their people.

THE ELUSIVE DEFINITION OF THE HORROR GENRE AND DUAL HORRIFICATION

As Zillmann and Gibson remind us in their study of the evolution of the genre, contemporary horror films carry on traditions and tendencies which are "as old as the human capacity to tell tales."[13] While the need/desire to tell horrifying tales may be a fundamental part of the collective human experience, horror has also persisted over time and crossed into other genres and forms because of its fluidity, adaptability, and hybridity. Horror and fear have always been used as tools to control the masses by powerful state instruments and institutions, never dissociated from issues of power and control. With that in mind, we must ask, who is creating or prescribing horror and why? Who is receiving the horror? and How does this impact power relations? Anthropologist Talal Asad's book *On Suicide Bombing* underscores the importance of such questions in what he terms "death dealing," which are central to his analysis of the contrast between the suicide bomber and state terrorism.[14] Asad scrutinizes the idea of a "clash of civilizations"—the claim that "Islamic jihadism" is the essence of modern terror—and the arguments put forward to justify war in our time. In critically engaging with a range of explanations of suicide terrorism, exploring many writers' preoccupation with the motives

---

12   Encyclopædia Britannica, "Horror film," January 2, 2019, https://www.britannica.com/art/horror-film.

13   Dolf Zillmann and Rhonda Gibson, "Evolution of the Horror Genre," in *Horror Films: Current Research on Audience Preferences and Reactions,* ed. James B. Weaver, Ron Tamborini (New York: Routledge, 1996), 15.

14   Asad, *On Suicide Bombing.*

of perpetrators, he examines our emotional response to suicide (including suicide terrorism) and the horror it invokes.

In her seminal work on Black horror cinema, Robin Means Coleman discusses how the horror genre "speaks difference" and is always in conversation with the binary of the monstrous other in contrast with the ordinary citizen.[15] About this, as she notes, Hollywood has rigidified horror as a static genre with immutable rules as a marketing technique to enhance the commodity value of a given film. Beyond that, the nature of horror remains somewhat elusive, which may be the reason for its endurance over time. In the many attempts to define the genre, we all agree on the role of the uncanny to signify "that which is instantly recognizable as horrifying" and "that which meets our collective understandings and expectations of what is horrific."[16] Coleman's observations about the genre's increasing adaptability in the present day, that "purist generic boundaries are extraordinarily difficult to define," signals the changing notion of what is perceived as monstrous in a given society, and who is articulating those monstrous representations.[17] With that in mind, rather than creating a rigid definition of horror or launching a cyclical investigation of why some representations should be defined as "horror" while others not, we proceed from the very elusiveness and hybridity of the genre that open it to constantly emerging forms of horrific representation, such as the terrorist trope in Hollywood cinema. This particular trope engages a dual horrification process, similar to the trope of Blackness in horror films. As Coleman argues, in this dual horrification process, a film can at once signify a people as horrifying to the dominant [White] audience as a means of vilification, and at the same time be representative of a horrifying experience for Arabs and Muslims who are watching the victimization of their people.

Coleman's description of dual horrification for Black audiences in *Jurassic Park* (1993) resonates with Arab and Muslim audiences. She refers to the killing of Black guard #1 (Jophery C. Brown) at the beginning of the film as an "early scene of Black annihilation" that promised "a horror show." For Spielberg, there was no better way to show someone or something's extreme deadliness than "for it to secure a bloodbath victory over a Black man with a big black gun."[18] The same experience can be inverted for Arab and Muslim audiences when witnessing the killing of "terrorists" or simply enemies (see the "Arab swordsman" scene in Steven Spielberg's *Indiana Jones: Raiders of the Lost Ark*, 1981; Kathryn Bigelow's *Hurt Locker*, 2008), and sometimes innocent civilians (Clint Eastwood's *American Sniper*, 2014) as retribution for killing American citizens.

The experience of watching the savage terrorist wreak terror on Americans can produce a similar experience as that of non-male, non-heteronormative audiences when confronted with the "male gaze," as discussed in feminist film theory. Perhaps it is more accurate to utilize Kozol's

---

15   Robin R. Means Coleman, *Horror Noire: Blacks in American Horror Films from the 1890s to Present* (New York: Routledge, 2011), 2.

16   Ibid., 4.

17   Ibid., 3.

18   Ibid., 1.

notion of "the racial gaze" in which Arab and Muslim audiences hope "to see themselves as whole, full, and realized subjects rather than simply 'window dressing on the set' or human meat to up a bloody body count."[19] All of this suggests, in the same way that Coleman argues this functions for Black audiences, Arab and Muslim audiences "have a rather unique relationship with American film's presentation of [Arabs and Muslims]." Seeing the terrorist through the eyes of the dominant hegemonic power can at once push the dominant White American audience and Arab and Muslim audiences alike to see Arabs and Muslims as terrorists. The fear of being associated with the monstrous terrorist pushes some Arabs and Muslims to distance themselves from having any type of signifier that may identify them as such. This facilitates a struggle between the pressure to assimilate into the dominant American population and repress the horror of recognizing the monstrous othering with its inherent racism, or consciously reject this othering.

THE HORROR OF THE RED SCARE: McCARTHYISM AND CINEMA FROM 1948–1954

A brief overview of cinema during the McCarthy era reveals a similar government-sanctioned effort to push fear-based tactics and an "us versus them" mentality onto the American public. Attention to this period exposes a pattern of "othering" as representative of Hollywood cinema, which served as a powerful and effective arm of the state. The period in the immediate aftermath of World War II was a chilling time for most Americans and is typically referred to as the Red Scare, where the postwar society swiftly became engulfed by a wave of ardent anti-communism that consumed nearly all aspects of the culture, including cinema.[20] President Truman was under enormous pressure by the Republican right, led by Senator Joe McCarthy, to appease the public's growing unease with communism by mandating loyalty checks on all government employees to root out what he called "subversives." Being accused of having "wrong" ideas on religion, sexual orientation, race, or foreign policy were all grounds used to justify charges of treason. This led to the Loyalty Boards of 1952, where more than twenty-two thousand cases were heard and more than four thousand employees fired or resigned, culminating in one of two highly publicized hearings on communism's influence on Hollywood through the House Un-American Activities Committee (HUAC).

During this period, more than forty strongly anti-communist films were made, including *The War of the Worlds* (1953), based on H.G. Wells's novel about a Martian invasion of a small town in California, which precedes a worldwide invasion, and in which the Martians are a

---

19   Ibid.

20   Stuart J. Foster, "Red Alert!: The National Education Association Confronts the 'Red Scare' in American Public Schools, 1947–1954," *Education and Culture* 14, no. 2 (1997): 1.

clear analog for the Soviets. As the USSR and the US were antipodal world powers and nuclear armed enemies, such analogies perpetuated and reflected the collective apocalyptic paranoia of the atomic age. The film begins with Dr. Clayton Forrester (Gene Barry), a well-known atomic scientist, fishing with colleagues when a large object crashes near the town of Linda Rosa. Later that night, a round hatch on the object opens, from which a Martian weapon disintegrates the three men standing guard at the site. The invasion spreads, destroying cities all over the world, which even the US military is unable to stop. The cinematic codes of blinding red lights signifying the Martians, their blood thirsty wrath and objective to kill anything in sight, especially all things American, reinforce the film's message about threats to Western civilization in the time of atomic paranoia. The film also signals that compassion and humanity are only meant for those whom we recognize to be exactly like us; anyone who differs is exterminable,[21] and only the government/military can protect the public and obliterate the enemy. This film, among many others of its era, embodied the collective fear and paranoia cultivated in the US through cinema and other media forms in the postwar era.

Tony Magistral describes the American cinema of this period as ushering in different monsters who "embodied a range of Cold War anxieties, including our collective fear about radiation … and the general collapse of a stable and comprehensible social matrix." After the US dropping of atomic bombs on the populous Japanese cities of Hiroshima and Nagasaki in 1945, effectively ending the war, an accelerated nuclear arms race between the US and the Soviet Union defined world affairs. American domestic and foreign policy at that time reveals itself in the films. As during the war when the Supreme Court invoked a military emergency to justify displacing Japanese Americans in internment camps (because they were deemed enemy aliens or suspicious for their [cultural] ties to the enemy), during the McCarthy era, the Supreme Court repeatedly referred to the nation's security to justify the "indefinite incarceration of deportable aliens without bail or the conviction of Communist leaders for 'teaching and advocating'" their revolutionary doctrines.[22]

Robert Aldrich's *Kiss Me Deadly* (1955) is another film that reveals the paranoia and hysteria from this era. In this noire hit, private detective Mike Hammers (Ralph Meeker) becomes embroiled in a complex crime mystery linked to a mysterious box. Toward the end of the film Gabrielle (Lily Carver) shoots Dr. Soberin (Albert Dekker) because she wants all the wealth of the box to herself. In his dying last words, Dr. Soberin cries out "Listen to me as if I were Cerberus barking with all his heads at the gates of hell … don't open the box." Hammer then bursts in and Gabrielle shoots him too and then opens the box. The box emits a blinding light and piercing

---

21 Tony Magistrale, *Abject Terrors: Surveying the Modern and Postmodern Horror Film* (New York: Peter Lang, 2005), 83.

22 Carlson v. Landon, 342 US 524 (1952); Dennis v. United States 341 US 494 (1951); other films like *I Married a Communist* (1949), or the Oscar-nominated documentary *I Was a Communist for the FBI* (1951) reflected and contributed to the paranoia of communists infiltrating and blending seamlessly into American society.

sound and Gabrielle bursts into flames. It is clear that the mysterious box is a nuclear weapon, revealing the paranoia at the time about the possibility of such a world-destroying weapon getting into the wrong hands. A fictional character created by American novelist Mickey Spillane, Hammer was described by film critic J. Hoberman as "the personification of rage, a self-righteous avenger whose antagonists were gangsters and communists."[23] At the end of Spillane's fourth novel, *One Lonely Night*, Hammer exclaims, "I killed more people tonight than I have fingers on my hands. I shot them in cold blood and enjoyed every minute of it. … They were Commies." This ends-justify-the-means brutality had its contemporary political manifestation in Senator Joseph McCarthy, described by one colleague, in suitably Hammer-esque terms, as a "fighting Irish marine [who] would give the shirt off his back to anyone who needs it—except a dirty, lying, stinking Communist. That guy, he'd kill."

Despite this period being wrought with a dominating trend of anti-communist films and McCarthy-led policy decisions that together reinforced each other, there were filmmakers at the time who stood up against this double-think mentality. Tony Shaw, in his review of John Houston's *We Were Strangers* (1949), brings to light an alternative view of Hollywood's treatment of the subject of terrorism. In attempting to locate America's long history of political violence, he describes Huston's thriller as "the first Hollywood production that … depicted terrorists (Cuban Revolutionaries) as heroes."[24] The important point here is that even at that time, in the postwar period, there were some differing viewpoints that challenged the American public discourse and filmgoers to (re)think questions of power in relation to terrorism. One famous example is the Hollywood Ten blacklist in which ten producers, directors, and screenwriters refused to answer questions incriminating themselves before the HUAC, leading to their blacklisting in the American entertainment industry.[25]

THE HORROR OF THE TERRORIST IN HOLLYWOOD CINEMA PRE AND POST 9/11

The dominant representation in American cinema of the Arab homeland and its people has been overwhelmingly negative. Since the early Hollywood films to present-day attractions, the leading depiction of what Jack Shaheen has termed "Arab Land," is largely unsympathetic and includes exotic geographies inhabited by barbaric and backward people. In his book *Reel Bad Arabs: How Hollywood Vilifies a People*, Shaheen surveyed over nine hundred films that contain

---

23   J. Hoberman, "Kiss Me Deadly: The Thriller of Tomorrow," The Criterion Collection, June 10, 2011, https://www.criterion.com/current/posts/1896-kiss-me-deadly-the-thriller-of-tomorrow.

24   Tony Shaw, "Hollywood's Changing Takes on Terrorism: Re-Viewing John Huston's *We Were Strangers* (1949)," *Journal of Contemporary History* 52, no. 2 (2017): 399.

25   Richard M. Fried, *Nightmare in Red: The McCarthy Era in Perspective*, reprint ed. (New York: Oxford University Press, 1991).

Arab characters. In this study he discovered a consistent pattern of what he terms "hateful Arab stereotypes," which have become ingrained in the imaginations of Western audiences. As his book documents, there is a long and enduring history of negative representations of the Arab and Muslim homeland. It is therefore unsurprising that when Americans and others who are exposed to these films think of the Arab homeland there is a tendency to lean on the exotic images of "Arab Land" that have been established through Hollywood's cinematic codes.[26]

This consistent and enduring history of vilifying Arabs and Muslims in Hollywood cinema has come in varying iterations over the last century with multiple historical and political moments impacting the representation. The first iteration of a monster created in the silent days of Hollywood lay the ground for an accelerated manufacturing of the "terrorist monster" in post 9/11 Hollywood cinema. Similar to the cinematic codification of the communist threat during the McCarthy era, it can be argued that the terrorist trope emerging vigorously in the Hollywood films of the1980s and 90s (see Michael Singh's 2012 film *Valentino's Ghost*) was instrumental in legitimizing the post-9/11 decision to launch a war with Iraq and implement the PATRIOT Act at home in America.

A selective survey of this history of representation includes George Gene Nelson's *Harum Scarum* (1965), the Disney-produced animated film *Aladdin* (1992), and Stephen Sommer's *The Mummy* (1999). *Harum Scarum* is a musical comedy about the adventures of an American singer, Johnny Tyrone (Elvis Presley), who was recruited by an Arab tribe to assassinate an Arab king whose daughter he fell in love with. Evoking George Melford's *The Sheik* (1921), the desert landscape and its inhabitants, depicted as exotic and seductive, serve as a backdrop to Elvis's heroic quests and romantic serenading. *Aladdin* provides one of the most salient examples of "Arab Land" in its opening sequence set in the harsh desert landscape of fictional "Agraba," which according to the opening song is a land faraway "where caravan camels roam. Where they cut off your ear if they don't like your face, it's barbaric but hey, it's home." *The Mummy* portrays the Egyptian landscape as one of supernatural evil powers, inhabited by inept desert buffoons and ancient mummies. The protagonist is a White male hero on the quest to rescue his beloved from barbaric villains and lecherous Arab men. As these films demonstrate, such fantastical constructions have become part of a collective imaginary, solidified through repetition.[27]

From the late 1970s leading up to the 9/11 attacks, the terrorist trope emerged, and essentially equated the Arab and/or Muslim with a "culture of death." This terrorist trope was introduced by John Frankenheimer's *Black Sunday* (1977). Its title capitalizes on a massacre (Bloody Sunday of 1972) that precipitated actions by the militant Irish Republican Army, and a militant Middle

---

26   Jack Shaheen, "Reel Bad Arabs: How Hollywood Vilifies a People," *Annals of the Political Academy of Political and Social Science* 588, no. 1 (2003): 171–193.

27   Other films that illustrate Arabs and Muslims in a negative light include *Samson Against the Sheik* (1962), *Invitation to the Dance* (1956), and *Raiders of the Ark* (1981).

Eastern group. The film chronicles a Palestinian Black September terrorist group attempting to fly a Goodyear blimp and wipe out eighty thousand Americans, including the president, at the Super Bowl. In one scene, the lead terrorist Dahlia (Marthe Keller), in plotting her attack against America, proclaims that it is best to be "striking where it hurts them most, where they feel most at home." In another scene, she disguises herself as a Catholic nun and indiscriminately kills scores of Americans in a hotel with a silencer. One of the most famous examples of the Arab terrorist indiscriminately attacking Americans occurs in the Hollywood classic *Back to the Future* (1985), directed by Robert Zemeckis. Right at the moment where Marty McFly (Michael J. Fox) and his close friend, the eccentric scientist Doc Brown, are about to travel back in time, a group of Libyan terrorists with machine guns appear from nowhere and brutally murder Doc Brown in the mall parking lot somewhere in Middle America (see figure 2.2.1) They also attempt to kill Marty, but the inept and unnamed terrorist runs out of bullets, while he incoherently babbles in a type of Arabic gibberish as Marty escapes to the past in the time machine. Curiously, the Libyan terrorists had nothing to do with the plot of the film and were never introduced prior to the moment they randomly showed up to murder the American protagonists. In that way, they served as a quick and unchallenged plot device to advance the story, perpetuating a one-dimensional image of Arabs as an ever-present terrorist threat that was already, regrettably, familiar to the American public.

Films like Terry Leonard's *Death Before Dishonor* (1987) reflect the increasing power of the US military in the Middle East. It centers on the heroic "becoming" of Gunnery Sgt. Burns (Fred Dryer) reporting for duty at an American Embassy in an unnamed Arabic-speaking country. Armed Arab terrorists attack the compound and kidnap American hostages, leaving Sgt. Burns to become a one-man army by rescuing the hostages and wiping out the terrorists. In one scene the group of terrorists murder an American guard and indiscriminately kill an Israeli family while they are having dinner. In another scene they kidnap and torture an American marine using an electric drill, and execute another in cold blood. In a third scene, the terrorists burn the American flag in front of the embassy before dispatching a suicide bomber to blow it up. When Sgt. Burns says, "Tell your terrorist friends ... don't get us mad," the implied message is the US military is a force to be feared at the international level.

Figure 2.2.1 Libyan terrorists gun down Doc Brown in the mall parking lot in Middle America in *Back to the Future* (1985).

The majority of films from the period preceding 9/11 that deploy the terrorist trope tend to link it with Palestinians. This occurs in *The Delta Force* (1986), directed by Menahem Golan and starring Chuck Norris and Lee Marvin, where an American plane is hijacked by Palestinian terrorists and the Delta Force is sent in to resolve the crisis. James Cameron's *True Lies* (1994) similarly depicts Harry Tasker (Arnold Schwarzenegger) fighting a group of Palestinian terrorists who have smuggled nuclear weapons into the US and who are threatening to use them on innocent American civilians. The lead terrorist Aziz (Art Malik) exclaims on live television, "We are all prepared to die with one turn of that key. Two million of your people will die instantly." These harmful and misleading misrepresentations of Arab Middle Easterners reflect generalized projections produced by the mainstream US media that cast Arabs as violent, vengeful extremists at a time when the US was working to secure its interests in a region that was becoming increasingly unstable and polarized.

The immediate aftermath of the 9/11 tragedy saw an unprecedented rise in the level of public fear and paranoia that had not been felt since the McCarthy period. After President George W. Bush proclaimed to the nation, "From this day forward, any nation that continues to harbor or support terrorism will be regarded by the United States as a hostile regime," the USA PATRIOT Act was swiftly enacted. This empowered the National Security Agency to conduct warrantless wire taps and monitor citizens' emails on a massive scale similar to the Loyalty Board witch hunts of the McCarthy era, all in the name of enhancing domestic security against terrorism.[28] This period also marked what Bush called a global "war on terror" resulting in the American public being barraged with constant alerts, heightened security, and a five-tier system of color-coded terror warnings. According to the Department of Homeland Security, potential domestic terror targets jumped from 160 in 2003 to over 300,000 in the next four years. In fact, as Dalia Fahmy points out, the Islamophobia in the post 9/11 period was more far reaching and destructive than the destruction entailed by McCarthyism. In both cases, the imperialist and militaristic rhetoric, and the accompanying us-versus-them mentality worked to instill public fear and justify global wars in the preparation of international state terror. Necessary for both was the creation of the enemy, whether the "Red Scare invader" or "suicide bomber," which helped to define American identity in opposition to the monstrous other.

Films and TV shows in the post 9/11 era represent Arabs and Muslims in a more insidious way as camouflaged terrorists living amongst us, barely recognizable, innocuous yet extremely dangerous. Rolf Halse, in his study of the representation of a Muslim family in *24*, observes the limited screen time of terrorists who serve purely narrative functions such as setting in motion

---

28   Dalia F. Fahmy, "The Green Scare Is Not McCarthyism 2.0: How Islamophobia Is Redefining the Use of Propaganda in Foreign and Domestic Affairs," *Dialectical Anthropology* 39, no. 1 (2015): 63.

sequences of terror in kidnappings, threats, blackmail, and murder.[29] Director Jon Cassar noted what was most terrifying about an ordinary Muslim American family in seasons 4 (2005) and 6 (2007), who are also a terror cell:

> I remember shooting the very first scene with them sitting at the kitchen table arguing about family stuff, it wasn't even about them being terrorists, and we are watching the carnage of the train wreck they cause as they are sitting there calmly eating breakfast. ... [Y]ou think this could be my neighbor or the guy down the street. To me, that is much scarier than a nuclear bomb hitting LA, because you can't get your head around that.[30]

In Showtime's hit TV show *Sleeper Cell* (2005), a sinister network of Islamic groups operates on American street corners with homeless men and Western-looking Muslims conspiring to plot a terrorist attack. In her study on Arab and Muslim American civil rights and identity, Evelyn Alsultany discusses how prior to 9/11 most stock villains were one-dimensional bad guys who were presumed bad because of their ethnic or religious background.[31] By contrast, she observes, post 9/11 terrorist characters are "humanized," depicted as loving fathers and husbands. Often in *Sleeper Cell* what originally appears to be a normal Muslim family is revealed to be deeply tied to a terrorist cause. In one episode, Faris al-Farik (Oded Fehr) exclaims, "We are at war with America, period, and we are going to win that war by convincing enough Americans through the spread of fear, insecurity, and terror to change their ways. And the best way to teach that lesson is by attacking them where they live, work, and play." Alsultany describes the storylines in *24* and *Sleeper Cell* as reinforcing the government's justification for a war on terror by replaying the tragedy of 9/11 on a weekly basis, "keeping the trauma fresh in the collective memory" to remind us and/or make us believe that the nation is in "perpetual danger." Put another way, believing or feeling that the nation is in constant danger facilitates "support for the power of the state" while also providing "the groundwork for securing 'the nation' as a cultural and social entity."[32] This paranoia runs so deep that even during the 2008 US presidential campaign, right-wing activists accused Barack Obama of being a closet Muslim and a sleeper cell agent.

---

29 Rolf Halse, "The Muslim-American Neighbour as Terrorist: The Representation of a Muslim Family in 24," *Journal of Arab & Muslim Media Research* 5, no. 1 (2012): 3–18.

30 T. DiLullo, 24: *The Official Companion: Seasons 3 & 4* (London: Titan Books, 2007), 91.

31 Evelyn Alsultany, "Arabs and Muslims in the Media after 9/11: Representational Strategies for a 'Postrace' Era," *American Quarterly* 65, no. 1 (2013): 161–69.

32 Melani McAlister, *Epic Encounters: Culture, Media, and US Interests in the Middle East, 1945–2000* (Berkeley: University of California Press, 2001), 6.

CONFRONTING THE HOLLYWOOD ARAB TERRORIST: THE OTHER STRIKES BACK

Terrence McSweeney speaks about the absence of American films that have explicitly portrayed the war on terror and terrorism from critical perspectives and calls for creating "counter narrative(s) as opposed to the master narrative(s)." He identifies a group of films from the post 9/11 era that serves as counter narratives and oppose "America's larger post 9/11 monomyth," which include films such as Paul Greengrass's *United 93* (2006), Oliver Stone's *World Trade Center* (2006), Joseph Castelo's *The War Within* (2005), Stephen Gaghan's *Syriana* (2005), Iñárritu's *Babel* (2006), and Kathryn Bigelow's *The Hurt Locker* (2008). These films illustrate an "American will to recover and [move away] from a single-minded impression of Muslim extremism."[33]

While it is important for filmmakers to offer films that challenge negative images of "Arab Land" and the terrorist stereotype, it is perhaps even more significant for Arabs and Muslims to represent their own experiences as a counter-hegemonic form of self-expression. Both in America and in the Global South, Arab and Muslim filmmakers have confronted the representations of the Hollywood Muslim or Arab terrorist by taking control of the camera and making their own films. In so doing, they have performed what Solanas and Getino called for in their seminal manifesto, "Toward a Third Cinema," transforming film "from mere entertainment into an active means of delineation" and using the camera as means of liberation.[34] While Solanas and Gettino had more specific and militant filmmaking in mind, in this case, liberation and delineation take the form of complicating the narrative and mythology of the terrorist stereotype by constantly interrogating them. Maia Chmaissany has observed how self-representation by Arabs and Muslims, who have traditionally been on the receiving end of the media production process in mainstream media, can act as a counter-hegemonic device and help to shift the dominant discourse. She explores this in her study of the award-winning TV show *Ramy* (2019–), a comedy-drama television series that centers on the daily life and experiences of an Egyptian American character named Ramy. The show presents Arab and Muslims "not as static and one-sided caricatures, but rather as fully-fleshed characters in their living context."[35] It addresses a multiplicity of complex issues that Muslim and Arab Americans must deal with in the formation of their identity, including male and female sexuality, alcohol consumption, struggles with pornography, drug use, Muslim–Jewish relationships, difficulty adhering to Ramadan rituals, diasporic returns home, and the complex experiences with 9/11 and subsequent change in behavior from peers.[36] This show is also an example of deconstructing the Hollywood, and

---

33   Terence McSweeney, ed., *American Cinema in the Shadow of 9/11* (Edinburgh: Edinburgh University Press, 2017), 90.

34   Fernando Solanas and Octavio Getino, "Toward a Third Cinema," *Cinéaste* 4, no. 3 (1970): 1.

35   Maya Chmaissany, "Counter-Hegemonic Self-Representation of Arabs and Muslims in Ramy: A Critical Pedagogical Analysis," PhD diss. (University of Windsor, 2021), 23.

36   Ibid., 20.

by extension mainstream America, image of the Arab/Muslim "to uncover Islamophobia, ideological resistance and the limits of American exceptionalism."[37] Additionally effective in countering the dominant discourse determining the image of Arabs and Muslims is the show's inclusion of Arabs and Muslims in the production team and crew, which Chmaissany argues is crucial in creating media that is more accurately self-representative.[38]

The series follows Ramy, a first-generation American Muslim Arab who is on a spiritual journey in his politically divided New Jersey neighborhood. Season 1, episode 4, entitled "Strawberries," reveals the monster that the media and the war on terrorism has created. It directly addresses the Muslim terrorist trope by going to the root of the fear and demonstrating how self-representation on this topic can serve a counter-hegemonic purpose. The episode is a flashback to Ramy's middle school years and reflects on how his relationship with his friends changed after 9/11. After hearing the news of the attacks at school, Ramy returns home to his family who is glued to the TV as they learn of the unfolding events. He is consumed with fear as we see a close-up of his face followed by a close-up of Osama bin Laden in a cave surrounded by weapons. A news anchor exclaims, "Federal investigators are searching for any possible links between the Al-Qaeda leader and citizens of the United States." The next scene follows Ramy asking a public chat room if they believe that all Muslims are responsible for the attacks, to which a chorus of chat members emphatically affirm "yes." These scenes reveal the fear that many Muslims and Arabs at the time felt for being falsely accused as terrorists.

The next scene follows Ramy's dad Farouk (Amr Waked) inserting a large American flagpole in the front of their house and then waving to his disgruntled White neighbor, revealing the fear that Muslim and Arab communities were feeling at the time. This idea is further exacerbated during the scene where Ramy is walking to school with his friends, and one of his friends asks him, "Are you a terrorist?" Bewildered, Ramy doesn't know how to respond. His other friend tries to translate by saying, "He means, like, is your family terrorists?" Another friend chimes in saying, "We were just wondering because you are from the Middle East and everything, and we thought maybe you guys were terrorists." Ramy responds, "I am from Egypt. That is not even the Middle East. Egypt is in Africa." He continues his defense: "You don't really believe I am a terrorist, do you? You guys know me." The conversation then shifts to why Ramy has been lying to his friends about masturbating, leading to the proposal that he masturbate on a leaf to prove he is one of them, and, therefore, not a terrorist.

As Ramy goes into the woods to prove himself to his friends, he takes out a magazine with a White woman on the cover for inspiration. The scene then switches from comedy to horror as the magazine of the woman's face transforms into the face of Osama bin Landen. Ramy screams and runs off, literalizing in comedic form the horrifying effect of the terrorist stereotype on Muslims

---

37   Ibid., 90.
38   Ibid., 23.

and Arabs who are regularly in fear of persecution. This episode turns into even more of a horror film during his nightmare about Osama bin Laden. The scene begins with Ramy awoken in his bed by the sounds of his dad's scratchy walkie talkie. The ominous music and cold blue light lead him down the stairs into an encounter with Osama who is sitting in his kitchen eating strawberries and whipped cream (see figure 2.2.2). The two

Figure 2.2.2 Nightmare of Osama bin Laden in *Ramy* (2019–), season 1, episode 4, "Strawberries."

connect over the fact that Ramy doesn't feel like he belongs in New Jersey. Osama then talks about not having friends that he can trust when he says, "America was my friend, then they turned their back on me," referring to how America provided the financial backing to Al Qaeda in its formation. There is a shift when Ramy asks about why his friend's mom was killed to which Osama has little remorse. As the music swells, Ramy exclaims, "No I am not like you because I don't want to kill people. … I am not a terrorist."

As Kathryn Van Arendok observed, "Strawberries" pushes the viewer to empathize with a young Muslim American teen, for whom nothing could be more traumatizing than being called a terrorist by his friends:

> "Strawberries" is also representative of one of Ramy's most important defining ideas: representation is good, but simple mimicry is not enough. It's not enough to just put a Muslim man onscreen and show us his family. It's not enough to simply tell the story of a young Egyptian kid during 9/11, or to tell us that Ramy feels alienated from his friends. To truly mean something to its viewers and have weight beyond just "Here is the image of a person you don't usually see on TV," those stories also have to be weird and insightful and fearless about genre and form.[39]

The producers of this episode used the experience of being misrecognized and stereotyped as terrorists based on appearance and culture, with the accompanying fear of persecution, to address what appears to be a contradiction in post-9/11 America. They applied the power

39   Kathryn VanArendonk, "Ramy Isn't Telling a Universal Story. That's Why It's So Good," *Vulture*, April 18, 2019, https://www. vulture.com/2019/04/ramy-on-hulu-review.html.

of a joke and its accompanying irony to serious matters that have horrifying effects for the recipients of the stereotype, turning it into a momentarily cathartic expression. In so doing, they transformed the true horror of the terrorist trope for Muslim Arab Americans into a revealing commentary on what it is like to be Muslim, Arab, and American in a post-9/11 America, affirming through humor that one can be all of them at the same time.

CONCLUSION: CREATION OF FEAR AND HORROR AS A JUSTIFICATION TO GO TO WAR

An exemplary challenge to "flipping the script" on Hollywood portrayals of the Othered is Oliver Stone's documentary Series *The Untold History of the United States*. Inspired by Howard Zinn's book *A People's History of the United States*, the series reveals "the dark side" of American history and challenges the notion of American exceptionalism. It also provides historical contextualization of US policies that led to the wars in Iraq and Afghanistan and illuminates the political means by which the many wars of empire are sold through one or another negative imagery of the "enemy" of the time.

An example of such political means can be found in the fiction film *Rules of Engagement* (2000), where officer Colonel Terry Childers (Samuel L. Jackson) is on trial for ordering his troops to fire on civilians who stormed the US Embassy in Yemen. The film works to justify the killing of Arab "terrorists" *en masse*, and like many others of its time, revolves around legitimizing American military invasion into sovereign countries in the Middle East. Colonel Hayes Hodges (Tommy Lee Jones), the lawyer who represents Colonel Childers, goes to Yemen to investigate. At first, we are led to believe that it was armed American Marines who indiscriminately killed innocent Yemeni civilians. However, upon further investigation, the Yemeni civilians, including a girl who brought Colonel Hodges to the hospital ward, are revealed to be armed, and they fired on the Marines first. The audience is then positioned to sympathize with the Marines, after which Colonel Childers orders them to destroy the civilians. The horrific slaughter of the Yemeni civilians, including women and children, is gruesome, bloody, and a horror show. After this scene, tens of dead bodies lie on the ground as if they had been attacked by a zombie horde. As noted by Jack Shaheen, such scenes function to justify the violence, which has been determined within the narrative as "a righteous slaughter." Similar to how our Hollywood heroes justify killing the zombie, Dracula, or Frankenstein, justification of killing the terrorist monster has been codified. About this, Shaheen tells us, "the humanity is not there and if we can't see the Arab humanity what's left? If we feel nothing, if we feel that Arabs are not like us or not like anyone else, then let's kill them all ... then they deserve to die right?"[40]

---

40   Jeremy Earp and Sut Jhally, directors, *Reel Bad Arabs: How Hollywood Vilifies a People* (Media Education Foundation, 2006).

Defining events in response to 9/11, such as the 2001 invasion of Afghanistan, the 2003 invasion of Iraq, and the 2004 Abu Ghraib incidents in which Arab and Muslim terrorist suspects were tortured by American soldiers, expose how a century of vilification on screen is deeply intertwined with governmental policy decisions. Ultimately, these films mask the power asymmetry that exists between America and the fearsome "terrorist," as well as the countries they are imagined to come from. In these films the terrorists are represented as having the power to inflict death on Americans in an equal and sometimes disproportionately greater measure to that of the Americans. Conversely, examination of the terrorist trope inevitably links back to US domestic and foreign policy. Whether it is the McCarthy era or post 9/11, there is a clear pattern of using an anonymous and devious foreign enemy who lurks in the shadows as a justification to go to war. The terrorist monster, along with other dehumanizing constructs positioned as "enemies" of the state, have facilitated the creation of the largest military empire to exist in the history of the world. Hollywood's perpetuation of these monsters has aided in justifying global wars and military expansionism to American citizens and allies. But perpetual wars and militarism are ultimately unsustainable, and tropes inevitably change over time. Beyond recognizing the "Red communist," the suicide bomber, or any other monstrous enemy who inhabits the American public imaginary, we should be asking the question of why we create these monsters in the first place and examine the implications of doing so.

BIBLIOGRAPHY

Alexander, Claire. "Raceing Islamophobia." In *Islamophobia: Still a Challenge for Us All*, edited by Farah Elahi and Omar Khan, 13–17. London: Runnymede Trust, 2017.

Altheide, David L. *Terrorism and the Politics of Fear*. Lanham, MD: Rowman & Littlefield, 2017.

Alsultany, Evelyn. "Arabs and Muslims in the Media after 9/11: Representational Strategies for a "Postrace" Era." *American Quarterly* 65, no. 1 (2013): 161–69.

Asad, Talal. *On Suicide Bombing*. 1st edition. New York: Columbia University Press, 2007.

Best, Joel. *American Nightmares: Social Problems in an Anxious World*. Oakland: University of California Press, 2018.

Brantlinger, Patrick. *States of Emergency: Essays on Culture and Politics*. Bloomington: Indiana University Press, 2013.

Britannica, T. Editors of Encyclopedia. "Horror film." Encyclopedia Britannica. January 2, 2019. https://www.britannica.com/art/horror-film.

Chmaissany, Maya. "Counter-Hegemonic Self-Representation of Arabs and Muslims in Ramy: A Critical Pedagogical Analysis" (PhD diss., University of Windsor, 2021). Major Papers. 155.

Coleman, Robin R. Means. *Horror Noire: Blacks in American Horror Films from the 1890s to Present.* New York: Routledge, 2011.

Corbin, Caroline Mala. "Terrorists Are Always Muslim but Never White: At the Intersection of Critical Race Theory and Propaganda." *Fordham Law Review,* 86, iss. 2 (2017) 455. https://ir.lawnet.fordham.edu/flr/vol86/iss2/5.

DiLullo, T. *24: The Official Companion: Seasons 3 & 4.* London: Titan Books, 2007.

Earp, Jeremy, Jhally, Sut, director. *Reel Bad Arabs: How Hollywood Vilifies a People.* Media Education Foundation, 2006.

Fahmy, Dalia F. "The Green Scare Is Not McCarthyism 2.0: How Islamophobia Is Redefining the Use of Propaganda in Foreign and Domestic Affairs." *Dialectical Anthropology* 39, no. 1 (2015): 63–67.

Foster, Stuart J. "Red Alert!: The National Education Association Confronts the 'Red Scare' in American Public Schools, 1947–1954." *Education and Culture* 14, no. 2 (1997): 1–16.

Fried, Richard M. *Nightmare in Red: The McCarthy Era in Perspective.* Reprint edition. New York, NY: Oxford University Press, 1991.

Gillman, Laura. "Beyond the Shadow: Re-Scripting Race in Women's Studies." *Meridians* 7, no. 2 (2007): 117–41.

Halse, Rolf. "The Muslim-American Neighbour as Terrorist: The Representation of a Muslim Family in 24." *Journal of Arab & Muslim Media Research* 5, no 1, (2012): 3–18.

Haner, Murat, Melissa M. Sloan, Francis T. Cullen, Teresa C. Kulig, and Cheryl Lero Jonson. "Public Concern about Terrorism: Fear, Worry, and Support for Anti-Muslim Policies." Socius 5 (January), 2019: 2378023119856825. https://doi.org/10.1177/2378023119856825.

Hoberman, J. "Kiss Me Deadly: The Thriller of Tomorrow." The *Criterion Collection.* Accessed May 30, 2021. https://www.criterion.com/current/posts/1896-kiss-me-deadly-the-thriller-of-tomorrow.

Kearns, Erin M., Allison E. Betus, and Anthony F. Lemieux. "Why Do Some Terrorist Attacks Receive More Media Attention Than Others?" *Justice Quarterly* 36, no. 6, 2019): 985–1022. https://doi.org/10.1080/07418825.2018.1524507.

Magistrale, Tony. *Abject Terrors: Surveying the Modern and Postmodern Horror Film.* Illustrated edition. New York: Peter Lang Inc., International Academic Publishers, 2005.

Mueller, John. "Inflating Terrorism." In *American Foreign Policy and The Politics of Fear.* Routledge, 2009.

McAlister, Melani, and Professor Melani McAlister. *Epic Encounters: Culture, Media, and US Interests in the Middle East, 1945–2000.* University of California Press, 2001.

McSweeney, Terence, ed. *American Cinema in the Shadow of 9/11.* Edinburgh: Edinburgh University Press, 2017.

Phillips, Kendall R. *Projected Fears.* 3/31/05 edition. Westport, Conn.: Greenwood Publishing Group, 2008.

Shaheen, Jack. "Reel Bad Arabs: How Hollywood Vilifies a People." *Annals of the Political Academy of Political and Social Science* 588, no. 1 (2003): 171–193.

Shaw, Tony. "Hollywood's Changing Takes on Terrorism: Re-Viewing John Huston's We Were Strangers (1949)." *Journal of Contemporary History* 52, no. 2 (2017): 399–417.

Solanas, Fernando, and Octavio Getino. "Toward a Third Cinema." *Cinéaste* 4, no. 3 (1970): 1–10.

Stearns, Peter N. "Dare to Compare: The Next Challenge in Assessing Emotional Cultures." *Emotion Review* 2, no. 3 (2010): 261–64.

VanArendonk, Kathryn. "Ramy Isn't Telling a Universal Story. That's Why It's So Good." *Vulture*. April 18, 2019. https://www.vulture.com/2019/04/ramy-on-hulu-review.html.

Zillmann, Dolf, and Gibson, Rhonda. "Evolution of the Horror Genre." In *Horror Films: Current Research on Audience Preferences and Reactions,* ed. Lawrence Erlbaum. Routledge, 1996.

Figure Credits

POST-READING QUESTIONS/POST-SCREENING QUESTIONS

Directions: Use what you learned from reading this chapter and watching the film to respond to the questions.

1. How does the terrorist trope function within the horror genre?

2. How are the McCarthy and the post-9/11 eras similar? How was this reflected in cinematic representations in the horror genre?

3. Explain dual horrification and how it relates to the terrorist trope for many Americans.

4. What is counter-hegemonic self-representational cinema, and how does *Ramy* (2019–) challenge the "terrorist trope"?

Latin American Horror Cinema

By Gabriel Eljaiek-Rodríguez

KEY TERMS AND FIGURES

Latin America

decolonization

Andean horror

Femicide

La Llorona

Qarqacha

Pishtaco

Carlos Enrique Taboada

Guillermo del Toro

Luis Ospina

Adrián García Bogliano

RECOMMENDED FILMS

À Meia-Noite Levarei Sua Alma [At Midnight I'll Take Your Soul] by José Mujica Marins (1964)

Cronos by Guillermo del Toro (1993)

El espinazo del diablo [The Devil's Backbone] by Guillermo del Toro (2001)

El laberinto del fauno [Pan's Labyrinth] by Guillermo del Toro (2006)

El misterio de Kharisiri [Kharisiri´s Mistery] by Henry Vallejo (2005)

El páramo [The Squad] by Jaime Osorio Márquez (2011)

El vampiro [The Vampire] by Abel Salazar (1957)

Habitaciones para turistas [Rooms for Tourists] by Adrián García Bogliano (2004)

Hasta el viento tiene miedo [Even the Wind Is Afraid] by Carlos Enrique Taboada (1968)

Juan de los muertos [Juan of the Dead] by Alejandro Brugués (2011)

KM 31 by Rigoberto Castañeda (2006)

La Llorona by Jayro Bustamante (2019)

Pura sangre [Pure Blood] by Luis Ospina (1982)

Qarqacha. El demonio del incesto [The Demon of Incest] by Melitón Eusebio (2002)

Sudor frío [Cold Sweat] by Adrián García Bogliano (2011)

Vampiros en la Habana [Vampires in Havana] by Juan Padrón (1985)

Latin American Horror Cinema

By Gabriel Eljaiek-Rodríguez

INTRODUCTION: CANNIBALS AND THE AMERICAN MONSTROSITY

America as a continent (North, Central, and South America) was constructed as a place of horror by the first Europeans who invaded the continent in the 1400s. Italian explorer and conqueror Christopher Columbus was fundamental in creating this monstrous image through his journal entries and the letters written to the Spanish monarchs. Based on his knowledge of Marco Polo and John Mandeville's stories, Columbus was expecting to find cyclops, cynocephali (dog-headed humanoids), and a fantastic array of other creatures. He did not find any of these monsters in the Americas. Instead, in his writing, he created a monster that was fundamental for justifying the conquest of indigenous communities in the Caribbean. In his 1493 letter to King Ferdinand of Spain, the admiral asserted, "[T]hus I have found no monsters, nor had a report of any, except in an island 'Carib,' which is the second at the coming into the Indies, and which is inhabited by people who are regarded in all the islands as very fierce and who eat human flesh."[1] This is the first description of cannibals as Native Americans, who, despite their similarity to the other groups that the Spanish encountered, in their eyes conceal a monstrosity contrary to any form of humanity. The Caribs became the monsters that Columbus was looking for and that are going to define the imaginaries of the continent.

The image of the man-eating, naked barbarian permeated the representation of the whole continent and created a set of colonial practices that applied to the real, non-cannibalistic inhabitants of the Americas. Through such images, colonizers maintained a discourse of difference and superiority concerning the populations found, even though the "monstrous"

---

1   Christopher Columbus, "Letter to King Ferdinand of Spain, Describing the Results of the First Voyage," http://xroads. virginia.edu/~Hyper/HNS/Garden/columbus.html.

tribes were never seen. After conquest and colonization, the image of a monstrous continent and the cannibal as the tutelary monster of Latin America persisted and has continued to permeate forms of approaching and understanding the continent. Because of this colonial and postcolonial context, I describe Latin American horror cinema production as one of decolonial hybridization. Filmmakers from countries throughout the continent strategically mix colonial images of Latin America as "monstrous" on the one side, with local folklore and representations of domestic sociopolitical dynamics on the other. This process is decolonial because it displaces the colonial signifier to characterize and critique domestic processes that are themselves in part lingering consequences of Latin America's colonial position—processes such as economic instability, socioeconomic inequality, internal armed conflict, and systemic corruption. For example, in contemporary versions of the pan–Latin American legend of La Llorona, the colonial component of the myth (a Spanish man mistreating an indigenous woman) is mixed with a denouncing of Mexico's drug war and the femicides in Ciudad Juarez.

In this chapter, I document the transformation of horror cinema in the continent and analyze Latin American horror cinema landmarks as decolonial constructions that adapt and transform images initially designed to situate the American continent, from Mexico to Patagonia, in a position of inferiority. I show how Latin American horror films incorporate and modernize the continent's folkloric monstrosities, such as the Andean *Qarqachas* and the pan-Hispanic myth of *La Llorona*. In movies from all over the continent, I analyze how film directors have used horror tropes, creating cinematographic horror hybrids that serve a further political purpose of reclaiming and transforming the monstrosity as a form of historical rewriting.

PIONEERS

Latin American horror cinema has been developing and enriching itself since the first half of the twentieth century. Although it does not present the same productivity as other genres (drama or comedy), it has had significant relevance in most of the continent's film production. As in the United States, the 1930s saw the birth of the first Mexican horror films. *La llorona* by Ramón Peón, *El fantasma del convento* (The Ghost of the Convent) by Fernando de Fuentes, *Dos monjes* (Two Monks) and *El misterio del rostro pálido* (The Mystery of the Pale Face), both by Juan Bustillo Oro, are the first horror movies filmed in Mexico. In all these films, the horror is produced by supernatural beings, ghosts, vampires, demons, witches, who belong either to the European Gothic tradition or to Mexican folk myths.

Buried under ranchero comedies, musical comedies, melodramas, and police films, Mexican horror cinema did not resurface until the 1950s. This decade saw the production of quality films directed by Bustillo Oro and the prolific Chano Ureta. In 1957 Abel Salazar directed *El vampiro* (The Vampire), one of the most memorable horror films of the 1950s. Loosely based on Stoker's *Dracula,* the film features Count Karol de Lavud—the vampire Duval—a Hungarian vampire who has spent years feeding on the inhabitants of a small Mexican town under the guise of an extravagant landowner. Highly influenced by the Dracula played by Bela Lugosi in 1931, Duval became a hybrid between the image crafted by Lugosi and the Dracula that Christopher Lee embodies a year later.

These films opened the door for director Carlos Enrique Taboada's oeuvre. Initially known as a screenwriter, as director Taboada created an important tetralogy of Mexican gothic horror films: *Hasta el viento tiene miedo* (Even the Wind Is Afraid), *El libro de piedra* (The Stone Book), *Más negro que la noche* (Darker Than Night), and *Veneno para las hadas* (Poison for the Fairies). The films are essential within the cinematography of Mexican horror; nonetheless, *Hasta el viento tiene miedo* became a cinematographic milestone that revitalized the genre in the country. The movie narrates the story of a boarding school for young women, haunted by Andrea's ghost, a student who committed suicide on its grounds. The action centers on a group of students, led by the intelligent and sensitive Claudia, who, when forced to spend their vacations at the boarding school, come into contact with the ghost. This specter is a vengeful ghost who possesses Claudia to settle accounts with the strict director of the school. With a relatively simple theme, but a gothic and terrifying atmosphere comparable to the best horror films of the time, *Hasta el viento tiene miedo* made visible ghosts that haunted Mexican society during the 1960s, that is, the growing politicization of Mexican youth and the importance of the feminist movement in the country—and the repressive response of the Mexican government—horrendously expressed in the 1968 *Tlatelolco Massacre*.

In other countries of the continent, the first half of the twentieth century also brought the first horror films. Unlike what happened in Mexico, in the Southern Cone, especially in Argentina, these first productions did not focus the horror on supernatural monsters. According to Nadina Olmedo and Osvaldo Di Paolo, in Argentine horror films of this time, the monster is embodied by the "savage murderer,"[2] a man who, despite not having a monstrous façade, is monstrous in his antisocial actions. This figure is central in films such as *El hombre bestia* (The Beast Man) by Camilo Zaccaría Soprani, *El extraño caso del hombre y la bestia* (The Strange Case of Man and the Beast) by Mario Soffici, and *El vampiro negro* (The Black Vampire) by Román Viñoloy Barreto. These last two films are adaptations, the first of Robert Louis Stevenson's *Strange Case of Dr. Jekyll and Mr. Hyde* and the second of Fritz Lang's film *M*. This interest in the human monster, in the "savage," echoes the dichotomy of "civilization" and "barbarism," enunciated by the Argentine writer and president Domingo Faustino Sarmiento and fundamental in the creation of the Argentine nation.

The US American and English horror boom of the 60s and 70s occurred in parallel with a more modest (in terms of number, not quality) surge of horror films in Latin America. To the already mentioned Taboada's tetralogy in Mexico, one can add the series of films of the iconic Brazilian director and actor José Mojica Marins, better known by his artistic name *Zé do Caixão*—translated

---

2   Osvaldo Di Paolo and Nadina Olmedo, *Negrótico* (Madrid: Editorial Pliegos, 2015), 200.

as "Coffin Joe." This director created the most shocking horror character in Brazilian cinema and some of the most irreverent, violent, and hypersexualized Brazilian films of the twentieth century. His 1964 film *À Meia-Noite Levarei Sua Alma* (At Midnight I'll Take Your Soul) is considered the first Brazilian horror film, and it is part of a trilogy followed by *Esta Noite Encarnarei no Teu Cadáver* (This Night I'll Possess Your Corpse) and *Encarnação do Demônio* (Embodiment of Evil). According to Rodrigo Carreiro, Mojica was "an original and inventive author in the panorama of horror cinema made in Latin America, since he anticipated trends … and maintained an admirable stylistic consistency throughout almost six decades of career.[3]

Zé do Caixão is an entirely amoral undertaker, with the airs of a nihilist philosopher, whose only goal throughout the films is to find the perfect woman to have a child—achieving what he calls the "immortality of blood." Part metaphysical horror films, part gore-fests, and part cheap philosophical reflections, Mojica Marins populated his movies with elements borrowed from exploitation films and class B cinema. By the time Mojica Marins was creating his films, exploitation cinema was already popular in Latin America, propelled by directors such as Emilio Vieyra in Argentina and Ivan Cardoso in Brazil. The latter director created parodic horror films, part of a hybrid genre that he named *terrir* (a mixture of terror and laughter), as stated by Daniel Serravalle de Sá.

THE 80S RENAISSANCE

The 1970s and 1980s were a horrific time for many Latin American nations. Brutal dictatorial governments seized power in Chile (1973–1990), Argentina (1976–1983), Uruguay (1973–1985), Bolivia (1971–1978), Paraguay (1954–1989), and Brazil (1964–1985), controlling the lives of its citizens and regulating what kinds of cultural products were acceptable and which were punishable. Under these dictatorships, few horror films were produced, and several of them were censored, in many cases for their subtle criticism of the dictatorial regimes. According to Serravalle de Sá, Mojica Marins was one of Brazil's most censored film directors, even though his films are not considered political films from a traditional conception. However, in the short film *Ideologia* (Ideology), Mojica Marins dares to represent on-camera torture methods eerily similar to those perpetrated by the Brazilian military dictatorship: "beatings and rapes, torture using insects and animals, drowning and strangulation."[4]

On the other hand, in other countries of the region where horror was not a filmic priority, the late 70s and the early 80s saw the production of their first films. It is this case for Colombia, where film director Jario Pinilla Téllez opened the path for Colombian horror. Pinilla directed

---

3   Rodrigo Carreiro, "El problema de estilo en José Mojica Marins," in *Horrorfílmico. Aproximaciones al cine de terror en Latinoamérica y el Caribe*, ed. Rosana Díaz-Zambrana & Patricia Tomé (San Juan: Isla Negra, 2012), 356, my translation.

4   Daniel Serravalle de Sá, "Zé do Caixão: José Mojica Marins's Brazilian Gothic," *Catedral Tomada* 5, no. 8 (2017): 112–113.

the films *Funeral Siniestro* (Sinister Funeral), *Aérea maldita* (Cursed Area), *27 horas con la muerte* (27 Hours with Death) and *Extraña regresión* (Strange Regression), pioneering the genre in Colombia. As a director, Pinilla has been compared to Steven Spielberg and Ed Wood, garnering an image of cult director, not only in Colombia but in other areas of Latin America. Despite their low budgets, uneven performances, and continuity errors, many of these films drew crowds of viewers for months—a significant achievement in a country whose filmic audiences are not particularly supportive of national cinema. Pinilla opened the space for Colombian horror films that focused on using iconic monsters of European and North American horror to criticize the Colombian elites and their social vampirism.

Films such as *Pura sangre* (Pure Blood) by Luis Ospina, *Carne de tu carne* (Flesh of your Flesh), and *La mansión de Araucaíma* (The Araucaíma Mansion) by Carlos Mayolo showed that not only was it possible to make horror films in Colombia but that these films could be used for decolonial purposes. In this sense, the two Colombian filmmakers (part of a group playfully named Caliwood) directly criticize Colombian elites as exploiters seeking personal gain and as continuators of Spanish and North American forms of colonialism. Thus, *Pura sangre* and *Carne de tu carne's* monsters are landowners who literally and figuratively suck the blood and resources of their workers. In turn, they are industrialists with family and business connections to Europe and/ or the United States, who consider themselves different (and superior) to their employees.

In *Pura sangre*, the protagonist is a sugar magnate—Don Roberto Hurtado—who plays the role of a hybridized Dracula. Hurtado's hybridization is apparent because, despite being a vampire, he lives and thrives in the warm weather of Colombia's west coast. In addition, unlike Dracula or any other vampire, he is not dead, and he does not suck the blood directly from his victims' bodies. Due to a strange illness, Hurtado can barely move and requires constant blood transfusions, frequently procured by two thugs and an unscrupulous nurse who extract it from young boys from working-class neighborhoods. Despite Hurtado's apparent fragility, in *Pura sangre's* promotional poster the landowner is clearly portrayed as a terrifying monster. The blood on his beard and clawed hand informs about his vampiric nature and thirst for young blood (see figure 2.3.1).

Figure 2.3.1 Pura sangre *poster with the vampire Don Roberto Hurtado holding one of his victims. Courtesy of Luis Ospina.*

Both the tag line and the title's font choice on the poster refer to Hurtado's vampirism and his need for blood. The phrase *le dará en la vena* (you will feel it in your veins) makes the act of exsanguination explicit, intentionally transforming a Colombian saying that means "it will please you." Similarly, the film's title, written in dripping red letters, literalizes the image of blood extraction, in this case and in connection with the image, from young (and pure) victims. *Pura sangre*, along with *Carne de tu carne*, became filmic symbols of decolonial Colombian horror, criticizing domestic processes of exploitation exercised by ruling elites and connections with US forms of interventionism.

Another country in which the horror genre started to bloom in the 1980s was Cuba. Its cinema responded to the monstrification of the Caribbean with one of the most unique horror movies from the continent. *Vampiros en la Habana*, by Cuban cartoonist and animator Juan Padrón, is a horror-comedy movie that did what was supposed to be impossible: It brought sun-fearing vampires to sunny Havana. Thanks to a series of vignettes showing the historical and geographical omnipresence of vampires through history, what appears to be a transgression of the vampire figure is shown as a logical step within the multiple migratory cycles of vampires. In the film, the cause for the arrival of vampires in Havana is the deportation of Count Dracula's son—Werner von Dracula—from Europe after he accidentally kills his father. Von Dracula is a brilliant vampire scientist whose primary goal is to create a formula to protect his kind against the sun, named *Vampisol*. Von Dracula's move to Cuba is intentional since it is there where he can find the main ingredients of *Vampisol*: copious quantities of rum and *piña colada*. That the main components of the secret formula are rum and *piña colada* is a sharp criticism of the representation of the Caribbean (and Latin America) as a space that provides both exoticism and raw materials for Europe and the United States.

The film's narrative focuses on Von Dracula's nephew, Pepe—or Pepito for his closest friends. Other than a direct descendant of Count Dracula himself, Pepito is the prototypical *hombre cubano* of the 1930s: a chatty partier and womanizer male who actively participates in the resistance against Cuban dictator Gerardo Machado. His existence as a Cuban vampire is only possible because of his constant use of the perfected version of *Vampisol*, which he believes to be a vitamin supplement. As screened, Pepito contradicts all stereotypes of European or North American vampires, and nonetheless he is the keeper of Dracula's lineage. Padrón transgresses the image of the vampire while playing with historical stereotypes of both the island and Latin America in general. The director acknowledges that part of the reason vampires can adapt to the brutal environmental conditions of the tropics is that they can identify with a specific monstrous environment that preexists their arrival, that is, a "special disposition" of the Latin American continent to produce monsters, a circumstance constructed by the Europeans since the beginning of the conquest.

Despite Pepito's initial disbelief in his vampiric condition, he quickly embraces being a vampire and uses his new powers to strengthen the resistance against Machado's dictatorship.

In this sense, the Cuban vampire Pepito is presented as a bloodsucker fighting political and economic vampires. These vampires can be metaphorical, such as Machado—an exploiter of both the country and its people—or literal, as in the US and European gangs of vampires that are trying to steal the *Vampisol* formula.

LATIN AMERICAN MONSTROSITIES IN THE TWENTY-FIRST CENTURY

For the most part, Latin American horror films of the twenty-first century have focused on incorporating and modernizing some of the continent's folkloric monstrosities and their connection with global forms of horror. The 2011 film *Juan de los Muertos* (Juan of the Dead), directed by Alejandro Brugués, cleverly transforms the zombie trope (originally a Haitian construct), reappropriating some of its Caribbean roots and positioning Cuban cinema in the maps of contemporary horror. *Juan de los muertos* is at the same time horror film, black comedy, and political criticism. Due to its playful tone, it could be connected to horror comedies like *The Return of the Living Dead*, *Dead Alive*, *Shaun of the Dead*, and *Zombieland*.

As in many other zombie films, *Juan de los muertos* portrays the rapid transformation of a city and its inhabitants into zombies and the adventures that a group of survivors must endure to remain alive. Nonetheless, the film is particularly Cuban in the way their main characters react to the zombie apocalypse. The group of survivors is composed of "professional" slackers and tricksters: Juan, Lázaro, Vladi, La China, and El Primo. From the beginning, these protagonists position themselves as survivors in a pre-zombie society, as tough subjects with the ability to take advantage of social and political turmoil. Before the apparition of any zombie, Juan makes this identity clear: "I am a survivor. I survived Mariel, I survived Angola, I survived the Special Period, and that thing came later." Following Juan's logic, the fact that Cubans survived a revolution, a half a century dictatorship, and multiple periods of economic and social deprivation has prepared them to resist and find solutions in highly adverse circumstances—such as a zombie apocalypse. In this case, the downside of constant survival mode is the desensitization that makes Juan and his friends barely aware of a situation of total chaos caused by zombies. Both criticism and joke come from the difficulty of responding to what is extraordinary because it is "recognized" as familiar due to its constant presence. In this sense, Brugués praises the resilience of his compatriots while mocking the cliché that Cubans can face any difficulty and come out with poise.

As a comedic extension of Juan's survivalist skills, he and his group create an undead extermination service—aptly named "Juan de los muertos." For a preset price and going door to door, the group murders loved ones who have been turned into zombies and that their relatives do not want to or cannot kill. With this depiction, Juan is far from the self-righteous survivalist

Figure 2.3.2 Juan answers the phone that advertises his undead extermination service (Lemon Films).

at the center of many zombie narratives, tormented by his postapocalyptic actions and often military trained (Rick Grimes in *The Walking Dead*, or Scott Ward in *Army of the Dead*). Instead, Juan is an oblivious and scrawny hustler specialized in taking advantage of any circumstance (see figure 2.3.2). The creation of an undead killing service underlines a brutal, for-profit, and comedic approach to the zombie tragedy that highlights the idea of the Caribbean as the setting of the monstrous. This depiction echoes colonial and postcolonial images of the area, in effect since the European invasion and created to justify the destruction of the indigenous populations. As asserted by Persephone Braham, "[T]he zombie embodies everything that makes the Caribbean mysterious, fearful, and alluring to the imperial imagination, and all that justifies Western domination of the region by various means since the encounter."[5] In this context, the zombie represents a system of inequality sustained in the Caribbean and based on the exploitation of both the people and the natural resources of the islands.

La Llorona is another monster that has been reappropriated by Latin American horror cinema. A feared presence throughout Latin America, her story is recognized almost everywhere in and outside the continent. With multiple variants—as many as Latin American countries—the story involves a woman who has been deceived or betrayed by a man (a Spanish lover, an unfaithful husband, or the devil himself) and her son (or children), whom she eventually kills in a fit of madness (in other versions she is murdered by her husband, or by a third party). Desperate, she commits suicide, condemning herself to repeat a fruitless search for her children and to cry for them for all eternity. La Llorona has been an object of attention in Latin American horror cinema, specifically Mexican cinema. The character has been present in numerous films, from the classic *La Llorona* by Ramón Peón, to *La leyenda de la Llorona* (The Legend of La Llorona) by Alberto Rodríguez, an animated version aimed at children. Within the cinematographic variants of the story, *KM 31* by Rigoberto Castañeda stands out as a novel film, capable of recounting the

---

5   Persephone Braham, *From Amazon to Zombies. Monsters in Latin America* (Lewisburg, PA: Bucknell University Press, 2015), 156.

legend recognizably while adapting it to the twenty-first-century context and its horror audiences.

Set in contemporary Mexico City, the film narrates the story of Ágata and Catalina, sisters who develop a supernatural bond after Ágata is hit by a truck on a highway in the city's outskirts. Because of the strange circumstances of the accident, family members and friends get

Figure 2.3.3 Catalina comes face to face with La Llorona in the sewers of Mexico City (Filmax).

involved in an investigation into the crash site—the kilometer 31st—and the series of recurring female deaths occurring in the place. The search result reveals La Llorona and her son as the cause of the deaths, dragging the characters along a path of destruction and madness. In an innovative move, *KM 31* depicts La Llorona's ghost using aesthetic and technical elements taken from Japanese horror cinema. Her appearance and demeanor resemble a Yūrei, or a Japanese ghost: long black disheveled hair, white clothes, and elongated limbs that move unnaturally (see figure 2..3). This representation makes *KM 31* a hybrid film, Mexican in the use of the Llorona myth and the placement of the narrative, thematically reminiscent of US urban legends (with some nods to road films) and aesthetically and technically indebted to Japanese horror cinema.

Elements such as the excessive number of unsolved female disappearances in the highway crash site, along with the police's lack of attention and action to solve them, show the director's interest in subtly referring to the femicides occurring in Ciudad Juarez since 1993. According to Amnesty International, in Ciudad Juárez (as well as in the city of Chihuahua), "more than 370 young women and girls have been murdered ... —at least a third suffering sexual violence—without the authorities taking proper measures to investigate and address the problem."[6] In *KM 31,* Castañeda creates a horror film that responds to the enigma of the disappeared and murdered women in Ciudad Juárez, emphasizing the bizarre circularity of a violence that only produces more deaths and more ghosts. The horror film is then used as a tool to talk about what is difficult to express—the murders, torture, rapes, disappearances

6   Amnesty International, "Mexico: Justice fails in Ciudad Juarez and the city of Chihuahua," February 27, 2005, https://web.archive.org/web/20120303095740/http://www.amnestyusa.org/node/55339.

of women in Ciudad Juarez—either because it is painful or because it implies a danger for those who do it.

Even though in the film Ágata and many other women are killed by a vengeful female ghost, the director does not seem to exonerate the possible male culprits of the real-life crimes: men close to the victims, male sex traffickers, or cartel members. Through La Llorona, the film situates female abuse and disappearances as a problem that is not particular to the twenty-first century and is rooted in sexism and an inherited Spanish machismo, since, in the legend narrated in the film, La Llorona is betrayed by a Spanish man. La Llorona's unhinged revenge is a reminder of both male violence against women as well as Spanish colonial violence exercised against vulnerable populations: In several versions, La Llorona was an indigenous or mestizo woman. This cycle of suffering is circular and leaves, as a result, multiple women who cannot rest or stop suffering.

Another Latin American horror movie that had reinvigorated La Llorona's story is the Guatemalan film *La Llorona*, directed by Jayro Bustamante. In the movie, Bustamante uses the pan-Hispanic legend to openly criticize the Guatemalan elites and to denounce the horrors experienced by indigenous communities under the dictatorship of General Efrain Rios Montt (1982–1983). In power for 17 months, Rios Montt was one of Guatemala's bloodiest dictators, responsible for the genocide of almost eighteen hundred indigenous people of the Mayan Ixil ethnic group in Quiché (northern Guatemala) in 1982. According to figures from the United Nations and the International Federation for Human Rights, his regime is considered the darkest period of the Guatemalan civil war, having left forty-five thousand dead or missing. Even though Ríos Montt was sentenced to eighty years in prison for genocide and crimes against humanity in 2013, the sentence was annulled ten days later by the Constitutional Court of Guatemala after judicial maneuvers from his supporters. Because of this, the genocidal general was released and died in his house at the age of 91.

In the absence of justice for the victims of the genocide and their families, Bustamante's film is constructed as a way to correct the fact that Ríos Montt never paid for his crimes. The director reconstructs the trial in which Rios Montt was accused and found guilty (perfectly mimicking the trial recordings) and imagines an aftermath in which, instead of being exonerated, the general is killed by supernatural forces that represent the revenge of the Ixil people. In this sense, Bustamante's La Llorona and her tragedy are not lost in a pre-Hispanic past but can be traced to Ríos Montt's dictatorship. In the movie, La Llorona is a Mayan woman who General Monteverde (the name Ríos Montt is given in the film) executed years ago, after ordering the drowning of her children in the river. In this sense, her appearance in the general's house, under the guise of a young employee (Alma), is the realization of her supernatural desire for revenge. After tormenting the general and her family, Alma/La Llorona possesses Cármen, the general's wife, and forces her to murder him by breaking his neck. This possession does not occur in a violent or invasive way but instead seems to happen through dreams where Cármen takes Alma's place. In the dreams, it is revealed (to her and the audience) that Monteverde murdered her along with hundreds of others.

In a decolonial turn, the vengeful ghost that exists to memorialize the colonial abuses of the Spaniards (rapes and abandonments of indigenous women) returns in the twenty-first century to remind viewers of the indigenous genocide committed by the Guatemalan army and its mercenaries in which women and children suffered disproportionately. In addition to directing the gaze toward the murders committed by the military under the protection of the government (led by Ríos Montt/Monteverde), the film depicts the indifference of the classist and racist elites who still deny the existence of an indigenous genocide. Monteverde family's microcosm illustrates how Guatemalan mestizo elites continued the Spanish vision of the indigenous as an inferior and disposable group (which can be used as a scapegoat, either accusing them of idolatry or communism).

Mythological creatures from Andean folklore are adapted and modernized in the so-called "Andean horror" (in movies produced in Perú and Bolivia mainly). José Carlos Cano López describes these films as "territorialized productions that exhibit a cosmovision that is specific of the Andean region."[7] The Peruvian films *Qarqacha, El Demonio del incesto* (Qarqacha, Demon of Incest) by Melitón Eusebio, *Nakaq* by José Gabriel Huertas, *El misterio de Kharisiri* (The Mystery of Kharisiri) by Henry Vallejo, and *El demonio de los Andes* (The Demon of the Andes) by Palito Ortega, focus on two monsters that are central in the mythology of the region: the Qarqacha (or Jarjacha) and the Pishtaco (also known as Nakaq or Kharisiri).

The Qarqacha is a monstrous creature, sometimes described as a llama with a human face and sometimes as a llama with two or even three heads. In Quechua, its name is an onomatopoeia of the particular growling sound produced with the monster: the "qar, qar, qar." According to Andean legends, the Qarqacha was a human being, transformed into a monster by God for having committed the sin of incest. In both *Qarqacha, El demonio del incesto* and in *El demonio de los Andes*, the Qarqachas behave like werewolves and other shapeshifters of the horror traditions, nonetheless fitting perfectly in the context of the Peruvian rural towns.

On the other hand, the Pishtaco is a monster that sucks/steals humans, fat and is described in some contexts as a fat-sucking vampire. In most of the stories, the Pishtaco presents itself as a bearded White man wearing a long jacket or a cape, where he hides a knife. It is with this knife that he murders his victims and then steals their fat. This legend can be found in many rural areas of Peru and Bolivia and was originally used to represent the figure of the foreigner invader—first Spaniards and then other Europeans and White Americans. The fact that two

---

7   José Carlos Cano López, "De Transilvania a Ayacucho: Historias de vampiros y Qarqachas," in *Horrorfílmico. Aproximaciones al cine de terror en Latinoamérica y el Caribe,* ed. Rosana Díaz-Zambrana & Patricia Tomé (San Juan: Isla Negra, 2012), 183, my translation.

Peruvian films focus on this creature demonstrates its importance within the national myths, as well as its relevance when criticizing foreign interventionism in Peruvian rural communities. Although neither shows the Pishtaco as a foreigner, his presence represents an attack on the values of the community. Furthermore, in *El misterio de Kharisiri* those who fall under its influence can only be saved by healers who use ancestral indigenous knowledge, which in another context is ridiculed and looked down on.

A different group of Andean films has been reappropriating the figure of the ghost, adapting it to representations that are more recognizable in the transnational horror arena of the new millennium. For this, Colombian and Peruvian filmmakers turned their view toward Asian horror cinema and their particular way of presenting vengeful ghosts, creating films with a greater acceptance within and outside the countries of the region. The Colombian films *Al final del espectro* (At the End of the Spectra) by Juan Felipe Orozco and *El páramo* (The Moor) by Jaime Osorio Márquez, and the Peruvian films *La entidad* (The Entity) by Eduardo Schuldt and *No estamos solos* (We Are Not Alone) by Daniel Rodríguez Risco, respond to this representational trend. These films feature supernatural entities (mostly ghosts in white dresses with long black hair) and settings (using blue and green filters) that are aesthetically reminiscent of Japanese or Korean horror movies. *El páramo* uses the character of a vengeful female ghost to rightfully portray the Colombian armed conflict (1964–2016) as a meaningless and aimless confrontation, where the image of the enemy is blurred and unrecognizable. As I stated in *The Migration and Politics of Monsters in Latin American Cinema, El páramo* "offer[s] a novel and complex perspective of war and violence in Colombia, using globally recognizable horror iconography."[8] This treatment of the subject, via horror tropes and the aesthetics of Japanese horror cinema, has transformed Andean and Latin American horror cinema, opening spaces to discuss both fictional ghosts as well as the many political ghosts that besiege Latin American nations.

TWO HORROR AUTHORS

Guillermo del Toro is one of the most prolific and successful Latin American filmmakers. His compelling mix of genres (horror, fantasy, monster cinema), as well as his versatility and adaptability to different cinematographic traditions (Hollywood, Spanish, and Mexican cinema), have made him a transnational recognizable horror film author. *Cronos*, his first feature film produced and filmed in Mexico in 1993, set down the foundations for upcoming narratives and films. In the movie, Del Toro restructured the myth of the vampire, inducing the transformation through an alchemical apparatus inhabited by an insect that transforms whoever possesses it into a bloodthirsty vampire. This reinvention of one of the fundamental monsters of horror

---

8   Gabriel Eljaiek-Rodriguez, *The Migration and Politics of Monsters in Latin American Cinema* (New York: Palgrave Macmillan, 2018), 135.

opened the door to bigger budget films, such as *Mimic*, *Blade II*, *Hellboy*, *Crimson Peak*, and the Oscar winner *The Shape of Water*.

His highly praised film *El espinazo del diablo* (The Devil's Backbone) approaches the theme of the Spanish Civil War (1936–1939) from the perspective of those abandoned during the war, the orphans of families murdered during the war. A ghost story, Del Toro's film uses the idea of the ghost as a spirit doomed to grieve and repeat itself in order to delve into the theme of fratricidal warfare and loss. One of the definitions that the orphanage doctor, Dr. Casares, gives of the ghost corresponds to this idea: "What is a ghost? A terrible event doomed to repeat itself over and over again." The Spanish Civil War and its aftermath will reappear in Del Toro's work in *El laberinto del Fauno* (Pan's Labyrinth).

One of the most recognized and appreciated contemporary horror film directors in Argentina is Adrián García Bogliano. His name is synonymous with Argentine gore and with a fast and inexpensive way of filming horror films, heir to European and North American cinematographic traditions such as the *Giallo* or the *Slasher*. His intention to push the boundaries and make the viewer uncomfortable is evident in most of his films, full of blood, gore, and explicit sexual content. Despite this excess in the representation and the uneven quality of his cinematic products, films such as *Habitaciones para turistas* (Rooms for Tourists) and *Sudor frío* (Cold Sweat) effectively use horror to refer to the horrors of the Argentine dictatorship in a more or less indirect way.

The antagonists of *Sudor frío* are two former members of a far-right death squad (*Argentine Anticommunist Alliance*) who, during the 1976 dictatorship, specialized in torturing and murdering young students, considered a danger to the state. In the film's present, the two men are elderly and apparently fragile; nonetheless, they continue to torture young people they contact online and that they still see as a danger. Under a sometimes incoherent and clearly exploitative surface, García Bogliano emphasizes in *Sudor frío* the persistence in the Argentine society of fascist ideas that never ceased to exist despite the transition to democracy—and that find ways to adapt to the modern world. Similarly, *Habitaciones para turistas* also delves into dark areas of Argentine society (and specifically into the middle classes), not directly related to the dictatorship but with extreme forms of religiosity.

Del Toro and García Bogliano are only two directors of the many currently producing horror films in Latin America. I single them out for being specialists in the horror genre and because of their interest in themes that transgress the traditional horror structures: Del Toro frequently ventures into fantasy and monster cinema, and García Bogliano constantly moves between multiple subgenres of horror. In addition, the two directors are interested in expanding their own filmic work as well as the work of other filmmakers. García Bogliano is known for working in tandem with other directors—including his brother—and Del Toro has promoted the film careers of other Latin American and Spanish directors such as Argentine Andy Muschietti and Spanish J.A. Bayona.

BIBLIOGRAPHY

Amnesty International. "Mexico: Justice fails in Ciudad Juarez and the city of Chihuahua." *Wayback Machine.* February 27, 2005. https://web.archive.org/web/20120303095740/http://www.amnestyusa.org/node/55339.

Braham, Persephone. *From Amazon to Zombies: Monsters in Latin America.* Bucknell University Press, 2015.

Cano López, José Carlos. "De Transilvania a Ayacucho: historias de vampiros y Qarqachas." In *Horrorfílmico. Aproximaciones al cine de terror en Latinoamérica y el Caribe.* San Juan: Isla Negra, 2012.

Carreiro, Rodrigo. "El problema de estilo en José Mojica Marins." *Horrorfílmico. Aproximaciones al cine de terror en Latinoamérica y el Caribe.* San Juan: Isla Negra, 2012.

Columbus, Christopher. "Letter to King Ferdinand of Spain, describing the results of the first voyage." http://xroads.virginia.edu/~Hyper/HNS/Garden/columbus.html.

Di Paolo, Osvaldo. Nadina Olmedo. *Negrótico.* Madrid: Editorial Pliegos, 2015.

Eljaiek-Rodriguez, Gabriel. *The Migration and Politics of Monsters in Latin American Cinema.* Palgrave Macmillan, 2018.

Serravalle de Sá, Daniel. "Cultural Cannibalism. Gothic Parody in the Cinema of Ivan Cardoso." *Latin American Gothic in Literature and Culture.* New York: Routledge, 2018.

Serravalle de Sá, Daniel "Zé do Caixão: José Mojica Marins's Brazilian Gothic." *Catedral Tomada.* Vol. 5. No. 8. 2017.

Figure Credits

POST-READING QUESTIONS/POST-SCREENING QUESTIONS

Directions: Use what you learned from reading this chapter and watching the film to respond to the questions.

1. Explain how the first contact zones of the American continent were built as monstrous spaces (or inhabited by monsters) by the Spanish conquerors.

2. Discuss the films grouped in this chapter under the category of "Andean horror."

3. Explain the political advantages of mixing Latin American folk monsters with traditional horror film structures.

4. Analyze the different approaches to the legend of La Llorana in films like *KM 31* and *La Llorona* and movies and/or television series in the United States (like *The Curse of La Llorona*).

Reading 2.4

The Hindi Horror Film

By Valentina Vitali

KEY TERMS AND FIGURES

Female sexuality

Individuation

Religion

Communalism

Scopophilia

Hindi cinema

Women's cinema

Tulsi and Shyam Ramsay

Puja Jatinder Bedi

RECOMMENDED FILMS

1920 by Vikram Bhatt (2008)

Bhoot [The Ghost] by Ram Gopal Varma (2003)

Do Gaz Zameen Ke Neeche [Beneath Two Yards of Earth] by Tulsi Ramsay (1972)

Ghost by Puja Jatinder Bedi (2012)

Ghutan [Suffocation] by Shyam Ramsay (2007)

Haunted 3D by Vikram Bhatt (2011)

Hotel by Tulsi and Shyam Ramsay (1981)

Kaali Khuhi [The Black Well] by Terrie Samundra (2020)

Raat [The Night] by Ram Gopal Varma (1992)

Purana Mandir [The Old Temple] by Tulsi and Shyam Ramsay (1984)

Raaz [The Secret] by Vikram Bhatt (2002)

Rise of the Zombie by Devaki Singh and Luke Kenny (2013)

Shaapit [Cursed] by Vikram Bhatt (2010)

Veerana [Vengeance of the Vampire] by Tulsi and Shyam Ramsay (1988)

The Zee Horror Show by Ramsay Brothers (1993)

The Hindi Horror Film

By Valentina Vitali

INTRODUCTION

No horror film was made in India until the early 1970s, when the genre saw a period of dubious but lasting glory with the Hindi productions of the Ramsay brothers. Of course, there had been elements of horror in a range of Indian films before the 1970s. The difference between these and the Ramsay brothers' productions is that the latter were built entirely on the horror ingredient and sold explicitly as horror films. In the mid-1980s, soon after the Ramsays' most successful films, less attractive imitations began to be produced that exploited the more salacious elements of the genre, however without the Ramsays' aesthetic flair and inventiveness. Both types of production, along with the handful of higher-budget horror films released from the early 1990s, remained largely at the industry's margins. In India the horror film did not move into center ground until the new millennium, when, through significantly changed modes of distribution, it was also embraced by women directors.

The first section of this chapter focuses on the Ramsay brothers' films, for they defined the horror genre as it circulates to this day in Hindi cinema. Films such as *Purana Mandir (The Old Temple*, 1984), and *Veerana (Vengeance of the Vampire*, 1988), both by Tulsi and Shyam Ramsay, are considered classics. As we will see in the concluding section of this chapter, it is from these works, rather than from the better-financed productions of the 1990s, that women making horror films in India today draw on for their generic material and aesthetics.

DEFINING FEATURES OF THE HINDI HORROR FILM: THE RAMSAY BROTHERS

The Ramsay family consisted of the seven sons of F. U. Ramsay (1917–89), a radio engineer, manufacturer, and producer, of which Kumar, Shyam, Keshu, Tulsi, Gangu, and Kiran were actively associated with film and, from the early 1990s, with television.[1] Most of the Ramsay films were directed by Tulsi and Shyam, with Kiran, the youngest, in charge of sound. The foundational moment of the Hindi horror film is taken to be the day when, sitting in the cinema, Tulsi and Shyam Ramsay realized that night after night the opening sequence of *Ek Nanhi Munni Ladki Thi* (There Was a Young Girl, 1970), F. U. Ramsay's otherwise unsuccessful production directed by Vikram Bedekar, infallibly caused audiences to

> break out in claps. … In a world dominated by romance and thrillers and action
> and comedy and tragedy and drama and socials, often all of them in one masala
> mix "We realised that people liked being scared."[2]

Do Gaz Zameen Ke Neeche (Beneath Two Yards of Earth, 1972), the film the brothers made to monetize that realization, launched the Hindi horror genre.

From the mid-1970s the Ramsay brothers made about one horror film a year, sometimes more, each produced within the family, financed with the modest proceeds from the previous film, and targeting what was a niche at the margins of the market. Admittedly, in Hindi cinema, which was dominated by melodramas and some action films, the Ramsays' position fluctuated somewhat over the years. While early productions like *Dahshat (The Panic, 1981)* and *Sannata (The Silence, 1981)* were given a limited, district-based release, from *Hotel* onward the Ramsays' reach expanded. *Hotel (1981)* was the first film they produced with an outsider to the family, Harish Shah, who had connections with good distributors. Uncharacteristically featuring A-grade actors, *Hotel* made good money, as did *Purana Mandir*, which played to full houses in several cities across the country and became the Ramsays' biggest hit. *Veerana (Vengeance of the Vampire)* and *Bandh Darwaza (The Closed Door, 1990)*, also circulated widely.

The 1980s mark the golden age of the Ramsay banner, their presence eventually beginning to rarefy not long after *The Zee Horror Show*. Keen to attract advertising revenues by targeting specific groups, Zee TV, the first Hindi satellite channel, launched in 1992, commissioned the Ramsay brothers with a horror series. The *Zee Horror Show* (1993) was intended as a means to attract teenage viewers and was thus devoid of the mild adults-only content found in the Ramsay brothers' films. Yet the series went well beyond its target: it became Zee TV's most

---

1   For a complete filmography of the Ramsay brothers see Ashish Rajadhyaksha and Paul Willemen, *Encyclopaedia of Indian Cinema*, 2nd ed. (New Delhi: Oxford University Press and British Film Institute, 1999) and Pete Tombs, *Mondo Macabro: Weird and Wonderful Cinema Around the World* (London: Titan Books, 1997). For more information on the Ramsay brothers, see Kartik Nair, "Taste, Taboo, Trash: The Story of the Ramsay Brothers," *Bioscope: South Asian Screen Studies* 3, no. 2 (2012): 123–45; Kartik Nair, "Fear on Film: the Ramsay Brothers and Bombay's Horror Cinema," *Sarai Reader* 8 (2010): 254–261, https://sarai.net/category/publications/sarai-reader/; and Shamya Dasgupta, *Don't Disturb the Dead: the Story of the Ramsay Brothers* (New York: HarperCollins, 2017).

2   Dasgupta, *Don't Disturb the Dead*, 11–12.

popular program, drawing as much as 30.4 percent of the national audience.[3] It gave the brothers enormous publicity and, to their films, unchallenged nation-wide prominence. Even so, the Ramsays' horror never broke into the mainstream and the budgets remained always comparatively low. Ramsays' productions were, however, far more prominently placed and better regarded than the generically similar byproducts that began to proliferate as a result of their marginal success, such as *Hatyarin* (The She-Vampire) directed by Vinod Talwar (1991), or Mohan Bhakri and Kanti Shah's films, to which I return in the second part of this chapter.

The tropes of the Ramsay brothers' films are far from unique. Living corpses, graveyards, crosses, vampires and stakes, haunted Islamic mansions, tridents (god Shiva's symbol), shape-shifting females, angry, many-handed goddesses and animated objects, all of which form the basic props of these films, were inspired by Christian ritual, borrowed unashamedly from the British Hammer films while simultaneously drawing from Hindu myths and reproducing much of the iconography of Indian mythological and devotional cinema. Many of the films are set in the countryside. What story there is, is focused, as a rule, on the infringement of this world by aspects of an outside. The disrupting factors are presented as pertaining to modernity and often take the form of ruthless financial speculation. Female sexuality, either as a primary concern or as a symptom of the disruption of old values brought about by aspects of modernization, is also a regular feature.

Religious iconography and rituals play an important role in the Ramsay films, especially Christian and Hindu iconography. On the one hand, the prominence of Christian iconography is connected to the way in which Christianity reached India during the early stages (and by way) of colonialism. On the other hand, it is also associated with notions of modernization, at least to the extent that, from the mid-twentieth century, Christianity has been perceived in India as having opened up spaces where more egalitarian discourses could circulate than had been the case with other, more indigenous religions. Crucially, unlike in Indian mythological and devotional films, in the Ramsays' films religious iconography, Christian or otherwise, functions like a sales point, a customary ingredient expected of the genre, rather than as a function of the order of discourse or as a point of authority. While by the late 1970s Indian films veered to either one side or the other of the secular and religious fronts (as in the family melodrama and devotional film, respectively), Ramsay brothers' productions straddled the divide. Events, in the Ramsays' films, are neither logic nor revealed; they are strange. Rationalist notions of cause and effect are not quite barred from the narrative; rather they feature as a desirable yet no longer achievable option. The films avail themselves of religious iconography because they address a national market and a modern cultural terrain the ideological fabric of which has also been sustained by this substance. In this context, from a commercial, speculative perspective, "religious lore" not only sells; it also works generically precisely because it is deemed to require

---

3   D. Sriram and Vishnu Mohan, "Entertainment Shifts Focus," *The Economic Times*, July 20, 1994, 20.

explanation. Selling all the better for steadfastly refusing to provide closure in either (rationalist or religious) directions while registering the pressures of both vectors, the Ramsays' horror films capitalized, to use Tzvetan Todorov's terminology,[4] on hesitation. From here came the efforts, visible in the *mise en scene*, to make "strange" events look convincing, despite minimal budgets, as well as the high degree of syncretism, the borrowing from several religions at once.

Syncretism was as much a dimension of classic Ramsay brothers' horror films of the 1980s as it is of more recent work, such as *Ghutan* (Suffocation, 2007). *Ghutan* tells the story of Catherine (Heena Taslim), a young, attractive woman from Goa. She is sexually active, proud of her sexuality, and married to Ravi (Aryan Vaheed), a lazy womanizer who cheats on her, refuses to have sex with her, and drives her to drink. One day they have a fight, Ravi pushes Catherine to the floor, and she lies there, seemingly dead. In order to get rid of her body Ravi proceeds to bury Catherine in an old cemetery. When he starts digging, however, she wakes up, but Ravi decides to bury her anyway, alive. For the remaining part of the film Catherine, now dead but determined to take her killer back to her grave with her, haunts her husband and his entourage. A scene exemplary of the syncretism of the Ramsay brothers' films sees Catherine emerging from her grave. Her body marked by the ugly scars of the fight that led to her death, she decides to ask for help from the village (Catholic) priest. It is only on talking to him that Catherine (and the spectator with her) realizes that she is, in fact, dead. The terms used in their conversation to define her status include both the English word *soul* and the Hindi word *aatma* (meaning "spirit" or "self" in Hinduism, Jainism, and Buddhism). When, upon realizing that she is now dead, Catherine tells the priest that she "want[s her] body back"; the priest explains that if her "*aatma* re-enters" her dead body, she will become "an evil, a living dead." But, as horror aficionados know, a living dead, a zombie, is, by definition, a soul-less being, a dead body without a will or a self. If the term *aatma* were to be used in the generically correct sense here, Catherine would not be a zombie, or a living dead, but a *bhoot* (the Hindi word for ghost), with one difference: having reclaimed or, as the priest puts it, "re-entered" her body, Catherine becomes, somewhat paradoxically, a ghost or spirit with a body. This is to say that this scene, exemplary of the Ramsay brothers' repertoire, comprises a concoction of discourses, some (film) industrial (*Night of the Living Dead*), some religious, and some from different religions (Catholicism, or at any rate from Christianity, and Hinduism). In addition, *Ghutan* also features a police inspector with a Hindu name and Muslim surname, Shankar Khan, who keeps on invoking Allah and who, somewhat contradictorily, is the only figure in the film to speak the discourse of secular rationality, as well as a professor by the name of Siddharth Nath, who stages Victorian-style spiritualist sessions in which he acts as a medium to communicate with the afterlife, all the while being surrounded by Jewish paraphernalia

---

4   Tzvetan Todorov, *The Fantastic: A Structural Approach to a Literary Genre* (Ithaca, NY: Cornell University Press, 1973).

(such as a *menorah*) and speaking of *shakti* (the Sanskrit, Hindi, and Hindu term for "sacred force," often in a female form).

This idiosyncratic blend shows that in the Ramsay brothers' horror films goddesses, demons, crucifixes, and curses are not the objective or end of narration, but rather the means to achieve sensational narrative effects, pretexts to stage moments of fear, suspense, and surprise. Thus, they present not only the prominence of vague, syncretic figurations of magic, which often borrow from several traditions of religious and secular iconographies simultaneously, but also, importantly, the precise moment when such syncretic blend burst onto the scene. According to Shyam Ramsay, in India films like *Jaws*, where the monster is rarely seen, do not do well because in Hindi horror cinema the monster must be shown and seen.[5] At one level, this is so because the sight of the monster, or at least of some horror, as opposed to the sensation or the feeling of horror, is perceived to offer punters better value for money. And significant efforts were made by the Ramsay brothers to display sensational makeup, locations, and special effects. At another level, monsters and other horrific effects are mobilized in their films, most often in (or in connection to) scenes disclosing degrees of nudity and sexual behavior or at any rate breaking accepted notions of modesty and other social conventions. This is so in *Ghutan* as it is in earlier Ramsay productions like *Shaitani Ilaaka* (Satan's Circle, 1990) or *Veerana*.

In *Veerana* a beautiful, blood-sucking *chudail* (witch) called Nakita stalks the outskirts of a village. Every night she intercepts men and lures them to an abandoned mansion, where sex provides the occasion for the kill. Sameer, the son of the local thakur (landlord), decides to put an end to the witch's actions and, one night, accompanies her to her mansion. The two strip, slip into a bubble bath, and engage into some risqué banter. Not long into the scene, as the couple start kissing, the beautiful Nakita transforms into the ugly, animal-like witch. The timing, as in similar instances from other Ramsays' films, suggests that another way of reading Shyam Ramsay's statement would be to say that it is not so much a matter of the monster appearing to the spectator, as of the spectator finding themself in the field of vision of the monster at a particularly salient moment. It is as if in the Ramsay brothers' films the monster functions as the flipside of the pleasure of breaking a rule, the punishment, thrill, or pay-off for infringing socially sanctioned codes of modesty. In other words, sexual imagery is, of course, a customary element of such salient moments, in the Ramsays' as in other horror films. The difference is that in the Ramsays' films it is not sexuality or its representation that is the object of punishment; what triggers the appearance of the monster, and what the latter's appearance targets is, rather, the act of looking at sexual images (see figure 2.4.1).

The censors subjected *Veerana* to two extensive revisions and nearly fifty cuts.[6] What is remarkable about the list of cuts and injunctions partly listed by Nair is the censors' focus on

---

5   Interview with the author, Mumbai, May 2011.
6   Kartik Nair, "Taste, Taboo, Trash," 134.

| Figure 2.4.1 Still from *Veerana* by Tulsi and Shyam Ramsay (1988).

the act of looking itself, a fixation that explains their request to delete from the "shot of Nakita removing her clothes camera pans on Sameer looking" or "visuals of Raghu [peeping] through a hole when Jasmine is in the bathroom."[7] In this film, as in other Ramsay brothers' horror productions, the monster appears in salacious moments, and its appearance activates what Paul Willemen has called the cinema's fourth look.[8] It is a look that constitutes the spectator as subject and, what is more here, a subject whose subjectivity is grounded in their scopophilia. The censors' language and cuts lay open the operation of *Veerana's* monstrous fourth look. They act out its penalizing or shaming dimension, perhaps hoping, in this way, to contain its individuating thrust.

The Ramsays' films borrowed unashamedly from the iconography of Hinduism and Christianity as much as they borrowed from British Hammer and some US horror classics. They addressed in this way Indian audiences at a time when Hindu fundamentalism was in the ascendancy and increasingly active in all spheres of political and cultural life. Yet, although they moved within the limits set by this regressive ideology, the Ramsay brothers' horror films carve out from within the narrow margins not only a space for subjectivation and desire, but a space to say "I" in cinema. They did so at a moment when the rights of an individual irrespective of caste, class, gender, and religious persuasion came under attack on a daily basis, and as Hindi cinema came increasingly subjected to restrictions aimed at banning from the public sphere political positions and representations of behavior not conducive to social reproduction along communal and caste lines. In this climate the Ramsay brothers' exploitation of nudity and mild

---

7   Ibid., 134–135.

8   Laura Mulvey distinguished three different looks: first, the camera's look as it records the profilmic event; second, the audience's look at the image; and third, the look the characters exchange within the diegesis. See "Visual Pleasure and Narrative Cinema," *Screen* 16, no. 3 (1975): 6–18. Paul Willemen argued that "in the filmic process there are not just three looks, but four: the look *at* the viewer must be added. Jacques Lacan described this fourth look as being 'not a seen gaze, but a gaze imagined by me in the field of the Other.' It is this look which 'surprises [me] in the function of voyeur, disturbs [me] and reduces [me] to a feeling of shame.' ... In the filmic process, this look can be represented as the look which constitutes the viewer as visible subject"; "The Fourth Look," in *Looks and Frictions: Essays in Cultural Studies and Film Theory* (London: British Film Institute and Indiana University Press, 1994), 107, internal citations omitted.

sexuality foregrounding female desire sold well because it trespassed on socially unaccepted ground. As we will see in the third section of this chapter, this is why women filmmakers who have taken up the genre today, at a time when *Hindutva* is conflated with Indian culture, draw on the aesthetics of the Ramsay films rather than of later, more polished horror productions.

POLARIZATION: THE HINDI HORROR FILM BETWEEN MELODRAMA AND PORNOGRAPHY

From the mid-1990s, a few years after *The Zee Horror Show*, Ramsays' horror productions petered out. They resumed again in the early 2000s, largely under the direction of Shyam Ramsay. By then the cult status of the brothers had led others to try their hands at horror films, leading to a polarization within the genre. On the one hand productions appeared that sought to monetize the newly discovered niche market by upgrading the genre to a higher level, as a series of better financed films targeting the industry's center ground, most notably, in the 1990s, by established director Ram Gopal Varma, with *Raat* (The Night, 1992), *Kaun* (Who's There?, 1999) and *Bhoot* (The Ghost, 2003). From the early 2000s Vikram Bhatt emerged as the most prominent Hindi horror director, with *Raaz* (The Secret), its remakes, and other horror productions such as 1920, _Shaapit_ (Cursed, 2010) and *Haunted 3D* (2011).

Raat centers on a nuclear family. The only smattering of sexuality not already firmly channeled into sanctioned reproduction stems from Minnie (Revathy), the teenage daughter whose picnic with the boyfriend comes to a premature end when the young man's motorbike is punctured. Left waiting at the roadside, Minnie is promptly possessed by the invisible, revengeful spirit of a wronged and brutally murdered woman. Found to reside under the family house, in a cellar that looks like a giant vagina, the female spirit is finally annihilated by a Hindu exorcist (Om Puri). Sharji presses on a spot on the spirit's head until the poor thing disintegrates into a smudge of white slime. There are no images of nudity or sexuality as such throughout *Raat*, as it befits a production intended for the mainstream. Whatever sexuality there is, it is displaced onto innocent-looking props (the punctured tyre, cellar, spot, and slime) that are largely confined to the film's last seven minutes, the exorcism. This is the only sequence offering if not a semblance of horrific atmosphere at least a sense of the monstrous. For the preceding two hours *Raat* could just as well have been a family melodrama.

Female sexuality is also central to Vikram Bhatt's *1920*, which pins it, however, onto disturbing ideas of Hindu nationalism in ways that earlier horror films had hardly done. *1920* opens with views of a grand colonial mansion. The architect in charge of restoring it is killed by an unseen force. Some time goes by and a younger architect is called in: Arjun (Rajniesh Duggall), a devout Hindu who has abandoned Hinduism to marry Lisa (Adah Sharma), a Catholic woman. Lisa will pay for that. The young couple moves into the mansion so that Arjun can work on his commission and transform it into a hotel. Soon Lisa becomes possessed by the spirit of an Indian soldier who, having betrayed nationalist fighters during the 1857 Sepoy Rebellion, was in turn betrayed by Gayatri (Anjori Alagh), the mistress of the house at the time, who seduced him to lure the traitor into a trap and thus save Indian nationalism. For all that, the mansion is curiously devoid of spider webs and dust; it looks, from the start, like prime real estate. As the film progresses, any sense of gothic horror, arguably linked to the corrupting sexuality of the Catholic Lisa, fizzles out, to be replaced by a nationalist saga. The possession of Lisa's body by the soldier escalates, leading her to all sorts of devilish tricks, but Lisa herself is, in the end, absorbed into the gentle persona of the sacrificial mistress of the house, whose reluctant sexuality, unlike Lisa's, was expended for the nationalist cause. This catharsis is achieved by Arjun who, when all seems lost, comes to the realization that the only way to save Lisa is to reembrace Hanuman, emblem of a virulent form of Hindu fundamentalism, and to recite a prayer to the monkey god while manhandling the hapless Lisa. This ritual, which enables Arjun to regain control of his unruly wife, is played out during the closing sequence as a barely disguised brutal rape. There is, however, no sexual imagery as such here and thus no need to infuse the sequence with compensatory gothic or horrific figurations. As in *Raat*, the supernatural, indeed the religious, is tagged on at the end, to legitimate the violence proffered on the Catholic woman, and, with her purification, to restore order.

Unlike the Ramsay brothers' films, Ram Gopal Varma and Vikram Bhatt's are premised on a sturdy sense of realism. The boundary between what is real and what is not is clear-cut, an effect of the channeled, reproductive nature of the films' sexual content. No need here for defense mechanisms; all is as it should be. *Raat* and *1920* seem incapable of letting any sense of excess linger into the *mise en scene* and, confounding reality and fantasy, of luring the spectator's gaze onto the socially impermissible. The monstrous is thus restricted to the very end, when it is purged, while the special effects are polished enough to look distinctly otherworldly, pre-empting the risk of any slurring of one world into the other. We are a world away from the eerie atmosphere characteristic of the Ramsays' work, in which cheap special effects constantly trespass into strangely unglamorous, everyday locations.

Well-financed productions like *Raat* or *Raaz* were not successful in establishing the horror film as one of Hindi cinema's main genres, partly because, aiming to capture as large and diverse an audience as possible, these were barely disguised versions of Hindi cinema's staple genre, the feudal family romance or melodrama. At the other end of the spectrum, the Ramsays' success encouraged the exploitation of their films' most salacious dimensions, such as nudity, by B- and adult movie director-producers, with films like *Cheekh* (The Scream, 1985) or *Khooni Shaitan* (Bloody Devil, 2002). In sharp contrast to Ram Gopal Varma's films, Kanti Shah's were productions that let it all hang out, as it were; sexuality in these films is neither channeled into a sanctioned reproductive framework like the family nor is it suppressed. If anything, representation of "illicit" sexuality, including dubious representations of homosexuality, constitutes if not the sole selling point of Shah's films, certainly the main one. Budgets were consequentially at rock bottom and exhibition totally confined to the B&C circuit or the video market (VHS or VCD).[9] Neither energy nor money were invested in the *mise en scene*. What effect there is—frontal pantomime-like tableaux devoid of spectacularity—is very basic and barely pays lip service to horror cinema, just enough to entice spectators interested in the Ramsays' and other horror fare, providing a very thin diegetic space to display tits and bums unapologetically.[10]

THE RETURN OF THE MONSTROUS: WOMEN MAKE HORROR

These two strands of post-Ramsay Hindi horror cinema proved unsuitable to accommodate the priorities of the women filmmakers who emerged from the 2010s. Video streaming has offered films like *Kaali Khuhi* (The Black) by Terrie Samundra (2020) distribution and a degree of visibility that earlier filmmakers did not have. A case in point is Devaki Singh's *Rise of the Zombie* (2013), a film that, partly because of its low production value, would have had great difficulties circulating outside of India, or, indeed, receiving significant distribution across India. Dubiously billed "India's first zombie original film," it circulates via Netflix, from which it addresses a youth audience that is global. *Rise of the Zombie* is not, however, representative of the horror genre as it manifested itself on and off in Indian cinema. A more emblematic example is Puja Jatinder Bedi's *Ghost* (2012), a film that carries the Ramsay brothers' legacy more boldly than most recent productions.

Like the Ramsay films, *Ghost* moved at the margin of the industry, and in more ways than one. The first feature film by a woman director, *Ghost* was produced by Bharat Shah, the leading diamond merchant, real estate investor and part-time film financier arrested in 2001 for his connections with the Dubai-based gangster Chhota Shakeel. Production of the film was hampered by the scandal that engulfed its male lead, Shiney Ahuja.[11] Just prior to release the film's unorthodox use of religious iconography and splatter imagery also earned it severe cuts by the censors, while the Indian press branded it, preposterously, India's most violent film. It is impossible to say whether the same treatment would have been meted out had *Ghost* been directed by a man. Be that as it may, the actor's arrest on rape charges and the censors' heavy-handed approach helped put *Ghost* in the headlines beyond its media partner's wildest expectations.[12] Days

---

9 For more information on the B&C Circuit in Hindi cinema, see the articles in BioScope: South *Asian Screen Studies* 7, no. 2 (Dec. 2016).

10 See also Aditi Sen, "'I Wasn't Born with Enough Middle Fingers': How Low-Budget Horror Films Defy Sexual Morality and Heteronormativity in Bollywood," *Acta Orientalia Vilnensia* 12, no. 2 (2011): 75–90.

11 Ahuja, until 2008 a popular star, was arrested in June 2009 on charges of rape but released on bail in October of that year. In a country where rape investigations rarely come to trial, let alone conviction, Ahuja was tried and sent to jail for seven years.

12 Interestingly, considering the film's splatter imagery, *Ghost's* media partner was Mumbai-based Hair and Skin Clinic Berkowits.

| Figure 2.4.2 Still from *Ghost* by Puja Jatinder Bedi (2012).

before the film's release Puja Jatinder Bedi announced that, Ahuja's arrest and censorship notwithstanding (or perhaps because of it), *Ghost* could count on a large female following. She then went on to claim that the horror sequences, including much of the material censored, were directly inspired by her own dreams, by things about which "she could not think or write but which she could see."[13]

Ghost tells the story of Dr Suhani (Sayali Bhagat), a young, attractive woman doctor and devout Catholic, and Vijay (Shiney Ahuja), a detective, who, investigating brutal deaths and paranormal events at the city hospital, finds them to be caused by the vengeful spirit of Mary, an Australian woman who was brutally assaulted, raped, crucified, and left for dead, all for falling in love with a Hindu man. We learn that, taken to the hospital, Mary is declared dead but her heart continued beating. Baffled, the doctors decide that the best course of action is to chop her body into pieces and toss them into the sea. By the end we discover that the object of Mary's love was none other than detective Vijay himself, who had lost all memory of the attack. This had been orchestrated by Vijay's father to put an end to the couple's intercommunal relationship. Unlike Lisa in *1920* or the nameless female spirit in *Raat*, in *Ghost* Mary's macabre, witch-like ghost has the final say.

The perceived excess of non-reproductive female sexuality (Dr Suhani's as much as the deceased Mary's) looms large across *Ghost*. *Ghost* stands out for its highly saturated modern gothic imagery (e.g., the neon-lit hospital), a vibrantly colorful lighting palette, and a syncretic use of horror, folk, and religious imagery, some of it very imaginative but for which it was made to pay. The debut film of a woman director in a cinema where horror has historically been a marginal genre and in which women get to work behind the camera only if they are born or married into the industry, *Ghost* works with sensational and contentious ingredients both as an artifact and as a commodity. From this, *Ghost*'s emphatic deployment of anything that may pass for extreme horror, including gore, along with the low-production value of such effects. Everything in it is, as in Ramsay's productions, simultaneously overly domestic and grotesquely, violently weird. Indeed, in moments judged too disturbing to look at negative photography is used, as if to signal in a quite literal way that we are looking at the reverse side of reality (see figure 2.4.2).

---

13   Indo-Asia News Service, "Puja Bedi Says Ghost Film Consists of Scenes From My Dreams," *The Bollywood Show*, 2011, https://www.dailymotion.com/video/xm8cn6.

CONCLUSION

Ghost, like most of the Ramsay brothers' films, was dismissed, disparaged for its low production values and its "incoherent" narrative, as if aesthetic value and market value could be interchangeable, or narrative ever said to be "coherent." Such critiques reveal more about the critics' allegiances than the films themselves. For all that, the horror imagery of *Ghost*, staging uncontained outbreaks of female sexuality and desire, stands out as fiercely in conflict with dominant discourses of contemporary India. It stages the repressed—things the director "could see" but "could not think or write" about—in uncompromising ways. Isn't this what the best of horror cinema is supposed to do?

The history of Hindi horror cinema shows that low budgets impose difficult limits on filmmakers. They do not, however, limit the way filmmakers move within those limits. Large budgets, on the other hand, may afford filmmakers more polished special effects, but also impose greater ideological and aesthetic limitations, dictated by what the producer and financier are prepared to risk or not. It is distributors who tend to regulate the flow of money in the film industry in India. Historically they have controlled the chain from the financier to the producer. The arrival of streaming platforms in South Asia is also beginning to unsettle these congealed film-industrial relations. Today women directing horror films in India and elsewhere are still few and far between. Streaming may, over the years, help make niche products like women's horror cinema viable and more visible.

BIBLIOGRAPHY

BioScope: *South Asian Screen Studies* 7, no. 2 (Dec. 2016).

Dasgupta, Shamya. *Don't Disturb the Dead: The Story of the Ramsay Brothers*. Noida: HarperCollins, 2017.

Indo-Asia News Service. "Puja Bedi Says *Ghost* Film Consists of Scenes From My Dreams." *The Bollywood Show*. 2011. Accessed 22 May 2021. https://www.dailymotion.com/video/xm8cn6.

Mulvey, Laura. "Visual Pleasure and Narrative Cinema." *Screen* 16, no. 3 (1975): 6–18.

Nair, Kartik. "Fear on Film: the Ramsay Brothers and Bombay's Horror Cinema." *Sarai Reader* 8 (2010): 254–261. Accessed 22 May 2021. https://sarai.net/category/publications/sarai-reader/.

Nair, Kartik. "Taste, Taboo, Trash: The Story of the Ramsay Brothers." *Bioscope: South Asian Screen Studies* 3, no. 2 (2012): 123–45.

Rajadhyaksha, Ashish and Willemen, Paul. *Encyclopaedia of Indian Cinema,* 2nd Edition. New Delhi: Oxford University Press and British Film Institute, 1999.

Sen, Aditi. "'I wasn't born with enough middle fingers': How low-budget horror films defy sexual morality and heteronormativity in Bollywood." *Acta Orientalia Vilnensia* 12, no. 2 (2011): 75–90.

Sriram, D. and Mohan, Vishnu. "Entertainment Shifts Focus." *The Economic Times*. July 20, 1994.

Todorov, Tzvetan. *The Fantastic: A Structural Approach to a Literary Genre*. Ithaca, New York: Cornell University Press, 1973.

Tombs, Pete. *Mondo Macabro: Weird and Wonderful Cinema Around the World*. London: Titan Books, 1997.

Willemen, Paul. "The Fourth Look." In *Looks and Frictions: Essays in Cultural Studies and Film Theory*, 99–110. London and Bloomington: British Film Institute and Indiana University Press, 1994.

Figure Credits

POST-READING QUESTIONS/POST-SCREENING QUESTIONS

Directions: Use what you learned from reading this chapter and watching the films to respond to the questions.

1. Consider the timing of the appearance of the monstrous in any of these films. What triggers its appearance? What does it displace?

2. Explain how we, as spectators, are positioned vis-à-vis the horrific objects or events presented.

3. Explain the author's discussion of how monstrous or horrific elements relate to Indian history.

4. Analyze what the horrific events presented in the films say about the place and time in which the film was made.

Reading 2.5

Well-Travelled Female Avengers

The Transcultural Potential of Japanese Ghosts

By Elisabeth Scherer

KEY TERMS AND FIGURES

Revenant

Kaidan

Onryo

Lafcadio Hearn

Shinrei shashin

Hideo Nakata

J-horror

RECOMMENDED FILMS

Honogurai mizu no soko kara [Dark Water] by Hideo Nakata (2002)

Jaganrei [Psychic Vision] by Teruyoshi Ishii (1988)

Ju-On [The Grudge] by Takashi Shimizu (2002)

Kairo [Pulse] by Kiyoshi Kurosawa (2001)

Kwaidan [Ghost Stories] by Masaki Kobayashi (1965)

Ringu by Hideo Nakata (1998)

Ringu 2 by Hideo Nakata (1999)

INTRODUCTION

In this chapter, Elisabeth Scherer examines the origins and cultural influences shaping the female-avenging spirit trope in Japanese "ghost culture" and J-horror. Situating them within a nexus of foreign and local influences and observing similarly popular female-avenging spirits in nearby Asian countries, she draws our attention to the transnational nature of this trope and genre.

Scherer locates the origins of the avenging female ghost figure "dressed in white with ruffled hair" in the Edo period (1603–1867), popular in forms of entertainment from picture books to theatre performances and card games. Such ghosts always appear after the wrongful death of innocent women, taking revenge on those who wronged them, who are usually men. Other significant influences of this period were Buddhism and neo-Confucianism, and influential texts from Buddhist and neo-Confucianist doctrine equated the reproductive power of women and female sexuality with monstrosity and fear: the Buddhist Blood Pool Sutra sends the souls of all women, because of their inherent sinfulness, to swim in a lake of blood in the "blood pool hell"; and the neo-Confucianist "Great Learning for Women" text contained a set of behavior rules to tame women's inherent impulsiveness and irrationality. Scherer describes female monstrosity in the ghost stories and horror tales of this period as a "way of processing" the truly abject conditions endured by women, who were used by authors to address the "spiritual state of the unhappy dead." Due to the frequent death of women during childbirth, a common expression of this was the unhappy mother ghost with her lower body splattered with blood. Scherer observes a shared trope of the unhappy vengeful female ghost across different Asian artistic traditions and notes that these ghosts find emancipation in death from the social roles, which oppressed them in life. She also notes that important cultural differences between the Japanese O-Iwa, the Indonesian "Sundelbolong," and the Thai "Mae Nak Phra Khanong" are due to the different experiences of modernity and social change within their respective histories and social contexts.

To situate Japanese ghost culture within a more recent context, Scherer traces the influences of Chinese literature, the tales of Lafcadio Hearn (four of which were made into the 1965 film *Kwaidan* by Masaki Kobayashi), and the Western spiritualist movement of the early twentieth century. Chinese literary sources were adapted as early as the twelfth century, but it wasn't until the Edo period that Chinese ghost stories became more popular, particularly in the gothic literature known as *kaidan*. One example is the Japanese collection of supernatural tales, *Ugetsu Monogatari* (Tales of Moonlight and Rain) from 1776, based on Chinese ghost stories, in which the motivations of the female spirits derive from their inability to rest out of worry for their families. At the turn of the twentieth century, American immigrant Lafcadio Hearn, who later became a Japanese citizen, popularized Japanese ghost culture through the stories he embellished from folk tales. These tales feature the return of female spirits to find the love they missed during their lifetime or to avenge injustice. Scherer notes that Hearn's tales idealize women as perfect wives and mothers from a Western point of view, while ignoring how these women were socially oppressed. She reads this as a sign of Hearn's nostalgia for a premodern Japan mixed with a Western exoticism, as Japan crossed into the twentieth century. The Western spiritualist movement of the late nineteenth/early twentieth century is another influence on this genre, which involved rituals to contact the spirit world that had the semblance of scientific rational methodology. Scherer sees the ghost photography that became popular in Japan in the 1880s as a precursor to the figuration of haunted technologies of reproduction, and the skepticism around them, that would predominate in 1990s J-horror. She connects this skepticism to the uncanniness of liminal spaces (e.g., between life and death) that such haunted technologies signify.

While the horror genre increased in popularity after the 1950s and 60s, incorporating elements of Kabuki and Noh theatre, and monsters of Western origin (vampires, serial killers) by the end of the 1960s, J-horror did not emerge until the 1990s. Its popularity was due, Scherer argues, to its hybrid nature in combining horror cinematic conventions from Western horror with Japanese motifs, and the location of uncanny horror within highly urbanized environments. Specific motifs make J-horror appealing to an international audience living in developed countries: urban modernity in crisis, uncanny media devices, and the dissolution of the nuclear family. These take place in specific kinds of architectural spaces such as abandoned medical facilities and dark apartment buildings, which signify the economic instability of Asian countries in the 1990s. Additionally terrifying are the dark-haired female ghost, eerie noises, strange phone calls, and the idea of psychic life haunting the present, which are all part of familiar places in the home becoming signifiers of the uncanny. We see this notion of the "unhomely in the home" in *Ringu* and its sequel, which perfectly deliver this hybridity through haunted technologies of communication and reproduction (see figures. 2.5.1 and 2.5.2).

Most of the ghosts in J-horror, however, are women, which repeats the motif of monstrosity and otherness with which they have historically been associated. In these films we have families that are already broken in one way or another. This avenging spirit trope is found in tales most often about wronged female characters who return to avenge themselves not only on those who wronged them, but those who come into contact with their stories, as if the stories must be told and retold infinitely. Occasionally, however, the ghost is that of a female child, consistent with the cultural idea that children endure the most suffering from divorce and/ or broken families. Scherer observes that the trauma of broken families in J-horror is never neatly situated

Figure 2.5.1 Screengrab from *Ringu* of Reiko seeing Sadako's ghost in the reflection of the television screen.

in the past, but represented as part of the present, necessitating, as we see in *Ringu*, self-examination by the protagonists into their own subconscious motives and issues.

Since the first J-horror film, the 1988 *Psychic Vision*, haunted media devices have become stylistic conventions (as seen in *Ringu*, *The Grudge*, *Dark Water*), with uncanny effects caused by cameras, (video) tape recorders, and other haunted objects related to the home. This delivers the familiar/strange binary through the mutation of our personal spaces, emphasizing what Scherer calls "the abject horror of the mundane." In *Ringu*, however, we have not only fear of the uncanny and the return of the repressed that results in a cathartic resolution, but also a terror that reproduces itself: in order to survive one must aid in terror's reproduction, in making a copy of the tape and giving it to another person to watch. This no doubt led to *Ringu's* Hollywood remake and extended the reach of J-horror on the global stage.

Figure 2.5.2 Screengrab from *Ringu* of Sadako's ghost emerging from the television set.

Well-Travelled Female Avengers

The Transcultural Potential of Japanese Ghosts

By Elisabeth Scherer

INTRODUCTION

When Samara, the new incarnation of *Ringu*'s Sadako (dir. Hideo Nakata, 1998), crept out of the television set in Gore Verbinski's *The Ring* (2002), both the appearance and actions of the female ghost were novelties to viewers in North America and Europe. Today, the global audience is familiar with the now iconic spectral woman in white with ruffled black hair as the "poster girl for Asian horror" (Feeley, 2012: 46). The vengeance-seeking female ghost is not just native to contemporary Japanese horror cinema (J-Horror), but is also a trope found in many films throughout East and Southeast Asia including *Inner Senses/Yee do hung gaan* (dir. Chi-Leung Law, 2002), *A Tale of Two Sisters* (dir. Kim Jee-woon, 2003), *Shutter* (dir. Banjong Pisanthanakun and Parkpoom Wongpoom, 2004) and transnational co-productions like *The Eye/Gin gwai* (dir. The Pang Brothers, 2002).

   Although these ghost films share stylistic and thematic conventions, they also incorporate diverse local aesthetics and customs, as

> [...] it could be said that the New Asian ghost films were born of the confluence of the Ring-style horror films' experimental aspects and the female ghost tradition in various Asian countries.
>
> Lee Hunju, 2011: 75

As Wai-Ming Ng (2008: 143) states, local film industries 'domesticated' Japanese elements to develop innovative works and, in some cases, to also cater to a new taste for 'Asian' horror which had spread among global horror fans.

What is it that made this type of ghost such a worldwide success? Why was it so easily adapted, integrated and transformed? A comparative study of ghost films from several Asian countries is an ambitious task: aside from the difficulty of mastering a diverse range of Asian languages, one has to deal with the complex entanglement of local, Asian and global influences. Lee Hunju (2011) meets this challenge in her dissertation on what she terms "New Asian female ghost films," however her research largely remains on the surface in terms of the historical dimensions of the films she examines.

In this chapter, I have chosen to take a different approach. I will focus on Japanese 'ghost culture' and J-Horror to show how the development of stories and films about female ghosts within Japanese culture has always been influenced by the incorporation and appropriation of foreign cultural elements. By underlining the transcultural influences upon the sphere of the supernatural—such as the adaptation of Chinese literature, the popularity of Western spiritualism and the global genre of horror films—I will characterize Japanese female ghosts as nomadic entities open to transformation and transnational cooperation.

I will begin with a brief overview of the development of the female ghost figure in the Edo period, a period characterized by Buddhist and Confucian conceptions of women as sinful and irrational beings. I then explicate the way in which this stereotype was formed by Chinese literature, the stories of Lafcadio Hearn and by Western spiritualism. Finally, I will argue that J-Horror became a popular and adaptable genre by adopting conventions of Western horror cinema, before examining the notion of the uncanny within a highly urbanized environment.

THE FEMALE AVENGER IN JAPAN

The stereotype of the avenging ghost woman (*yūrei*[1]) dressed in white with ruffled hair developed during Japan's Edo period (1603–1868), a period distinguished by a lively popular culture. These revenants made their appearances in picture books, on theatre stages, in card games, and in the oral traditions of the period. Although female ghosts had existed previously in Japan—particularly in literature and *Nō* theatre—it was during the Edo period that their classic appearance developed, and the character became an eerie pre-modern pop icon. The most famous of these Edo ghosts is 'O-Iwa' in Tsuruya Nanboku's *kabuki* play "Tōkaidō Yotsuya Kaidan"/"Ghost Story of Yotsuya" (1825). In this story, the masterless samurai Iemon plans the death of his wife O-Iwa so that he can marry a rich woman. After her horrific death, O-Iwa—who

---

1   *Yūrei* is a term that can designate male as well as female ghosts. The term is most often used when discussing the stereo-typical image of a white-clothed ghost, an image that became mainstream in the Edo period. For vengeful ghosts without a concrete form, particularly in the Heian period (794–1185), the term *onryō* was used. More neutral terms for ghosts of the dead are *shinrei* and *shiryō*. For more on the terminology of ghosts, see Scherer, 2011: 35 ff.

had been submissive and self-sacrificing while alive—directs all her resentment towards her unfaithful husband and drives him insane.

The female ghosts of the Edo period appear following the death of women. As ghosts, the women have a strong presence, stand up for themselves and relentlessly pursue revenge. A woman who is so destructive towards a man and who drives the plot forward, however, was only allowed to exist in conjunction with monstrosity, as a deformed revenant that no longer belonged to human society. Characters such as O-Iwa were used in the Edo period to raise issues that were not possible to negotiate directly within the rules and laws of the feudal system.

Women in this system were of very low status—financially, and indeed within most spheres of action, they were almost completely dependent upon men. They had next to no opportunities to demand anything through appeal to the law. Ideologically, this oppression was supported by certain streams of Buddhism and Confucianism, which conceived of women as impulsive, irrational and unclean beings.

> Women as sinful beings—possessed by greed and jealousy with a strong tendency to turn into demons or ghosts—were constructed as the Other, in opposition to masculinity.
>
> Kume Yoriko, 2005: 169

Female sexuality in particular, as well as women's reproductive capacity, was viewed as a threat to male-dominated society (Ikoma Natsumi, 2006: 197). The Buddhist "Blood Pool Hell Sutra" serves as a dramatic example of the perception of female sexuality as sinful, a perception that has been widespread in Japan since the Muromachi period (1333–1573) (Shimazaki Satoko, 2011: 218–220; Árokay, 2003: 193–195). According to the *sutra*, on account of their inherent sinfulness, after death all women are consigned to the so-called 'blood pool hell', where they must swim in an enormous lake of blood. The Sōtō school of Zen Buddhism during the Edo period was particularly responsible for propagating the idea of the blood pool hell. Within Japanese Neo-Confucianism, one influential text was the "Onna Daigaku"/"Great Learning for Women," a collection of behavioral rules that characterized femininity as fundamentally impulsive and irrational.[2] In this text, "The five worst infirmities that afflict the female are indocility, discontent, slander, jealousy, and silliness" (Cranmer-Byng and Kapadia, 2010: 33).

The female monstrosity found in stories about ghosts and other female monsters was at once a worst-case scenario, in which all the supposedly malign traits of women are brought to light, while also a way of processing the repressed, miserable situation many women found

---

2   Tocco (2003), however, remarks that the text "Onna Daigaku" was just one of many texts during the Edo period that were specially directed at women. Texts about morals or education—with different intentions—appeared together with literary works and diverse illustrations. The collections also served as reading practice.

themselves in. By giving the uncanny a familiar if terrible form, the (male) authors of such stories dealt with the problem of the spiritual state of the unhappy dead.

Importantly, many women at the time still died during or after childbirth—a death which was considered especially painful, and which led to many stories of women returning from beyond the grave to care for their children.[3] These unappeased mothers, *ubume*, were generally represented in the visual arts with blood-spattered lower bodies.

While this history has formed the cultural background for the female ghosts populating Japanese cinema screens today, it is often only the outer appearance which has remained unchanged: these contemporary figures are charged with other fears. Lee, who analyzes "New Asian female ghost films" across Japan, South Korea, Hong Kong, Singapore, and Thailand (2011), identifies similar Buddhist and Confucian influences in films dealing with female ghosts from these Asian countries. Confucianism, she argues, has been the main ideology supporting Asian patriarchy since the Han Dynasty, and remained particularly recognizable in Asian ghost films of the 1950s and 1960s (Lee Hunju, 2011: 95). The women in these films conform to the role that society has assigned to them while alive, but in death they are shown as breaking out of the Confucian order and often turning against it. At the same time, Buddhism is seen to work as an effective weapon against ghosts in these earlier examples of Asian ghost films (Lee Hunju, 2011: 92). While this may often be true for ghostly figures from East Asia, I consider Lee's expansion of Confucian influence to Southeast Asian films problematic. While there are certainly similarities between female cinematic ghosts such as Japan's 'O-Iwa', Indonesia's 'Sundelbolong' and Thailand's 'Mae Nak Phra Khanong', they all are, as this volume shows, hybrid beings, which incorporate numerous influences and interpretations. Indonesian Sundelbolong movies, for example, contain aspects of politically generated gender ideology, Javenese cultural values, and Islamic morality (see Maren Wilger's contribution).

In pre-modern East Asia, and also in some cases in Southeast Asia, Buddhist and Confucian thought and values might have led to similar concepts of ideal femininity—and its monstrous downside. On the local level, however, very different visual and narrative characteristics have developed, which are permanently transformed due to societal changes. The spectral metaphors of O-Iwa, Sundelbolong and Mae Nak Phra Khanong, for example, serve other functions today than they did in the 1950s or in the 19th century.

GHOSTS AS TRANSCULTURAL WANDERERS

In addition to the major religious and intellectual currents of Buddhism and Confucianism, Chinese ghost stories, literary adaptations by Western authors and Western spiritualism were of profound influence on the formation and mythology of female ghosts in Japan.

---

3   Tanaka (1997) and Shimazaki Satoko (2011) deal with the theme of a returning mother in greater detail.

Chinese sources were adapted as early as the 12th century, such as in the collection of stories "Konjaku Monogatarishū"/"Anthology of Tales from the Past." However it was during the Edo period (1603–1868) that Chinese ghosts took on particular importance, with adaptions of Chinese ghost stories forming an important part of the highly popular gothic literature (*kaidan*) of the time (Reider, 2002: 63–66). Fueled largely by the fact travel was not allowed, there was generally a great interest in 'exotic' China throughout the Edo period. In Japan, as in Korea and Vietnam, Qu You's (1347–1433) collection of stories, "Jiandeng Xinhua"/"New stories told while trimming the wick" (1378), circulated most widely. In Korea, an adaptation of this work appeared as "Kumo shinhwa"/"Tales of the Golden Carp" in the 15th century (Cheung, 1986). An unknown Japanese author translated some of these Chinese stories into Japanese in the 1650s and published them under the title "Kii zōtanshū" (cf. Reider, 2000: 275–276). Eventually, Asai Ryōi later set these stories in Japan in "Otogi-bōko"/"Hand Puppets" (1666), which contains the well-known story of "Botan dōrō"/"Peony Lantern." In the story, a young man falls in love with a beautiful spectral woman and begins a sexual relationship with her, eventually leading to his death.

The well-known Japanese collection of supernatural stories, "Ugetsu Monogatari"/"Tales of Moonlight and Rain" (1776), was also influenced by Chinese models; within the preface alone one can find ten allusions to classical Chinese literary works (cf. Cheung, 1986: 155). For his story "House Amid the Thickets," for instance, the author Ueda Akinari drew on stories from the Japanese "Konjaku monogatarishū" and the Chinese "Jiandeng Xinhua," which both include the motif of a self-sacrificing wife, longingly awaiting the return of the husband who had abandoned her.

In Chinese literature, ghostly women mainly return to the world of the living for two reasons: either they are driven by unaccomplished passion, which must be satisfied, or they cannot find rest because they worry about their family. A romantic relationship between a living man and a spectral woman is a common theme, frequently ending in the man's death. Japanese stories dealing with supernatural affection are often based on these spectral beauties from Chinese literature.[4]

Today's Japanese 'ghost culture' has also been deeply influenced by a Western collector of ghost stories, Lafcadio Hearn. An American of Greek-Irish origin, Hearn moved to Japan in 1890 and stayed there until his death in 1904. He became famous for the ghost stories he

---

4   As Yomota Inuhiko (2009: 192) argues, the tradition of the Chinese ghost women may have also served as a model for the legend of Thailand's best-known female ghost, Mae Nak Phra Khanong. However, apart from referring to certain narrative similarities, Yomota does not provide sufficient evidence to support this supposition. As Martin Platt points out in this volume, narratives like that of Mae Nak are "a confluence of oral history, memory, and heritage"—and assumptions about unidirectional influence certainly do not do these ghost narratives justice.

adapted from Japanese sources around 1900.[5] Hearn collected traditional stories for his works and amply embellished them. His own library included many Japanese classics and *kaidan* collections.[6] However, since he could not read Japanese himself, he was dependent upon the interpretations of his wife who recounted the stories to him. He also regularly sent his wife to *kabuki* performances, which she was to describe to him afterwards (Setsuko Koizumi and Hayato Tokugawa, 2012: 29).

Hearn's works, too, exhibit a fascination for female passion. A constant motif is the return of women after death, either to find the love they missed out on during their lifetimes, or to take revenge. Hearn romanticized and dramatized his versions, as the original stories were mostly unadorned in composition and language. In Kadota's opinion, Hearn shows a tendency to characterize Japanese women as ideal wives and mothers from a Western point of view, without realizing these women's positions as victims of the feudal system (Kadota Mamoru, 2005: 210). Hearn was yearning for an 'old Japan', which he believed was disappearing in the rapid process of modernization. In his stories, he therefore constructs a version of the past which corresponds to both a nostalgic longing found among his Japanese contemporaries, and to a Western exoticist discourse on Japan. As Blouin (2013: 11) explains, American writers[7] like Hearn used "imaginary Japan as a fictive space for contemplating the limits of rationality as well as the sublime scope of modernization."

Hearn's ghost stories were and still are highly appreciated in Japan, where the author is better known by his Japanese name, Koizumi Yakumo.[8] Many stories within the old Japanese collections regained popularity only through Hearn's retellings at the beginning of the 20th century, and today his adaptations are the most common versions.

One can get an idea of the stations of this transcultural wandering through the story "The Reconciliation," which appeared in Hearn's 1904 collection "Kwaidan: Stories and Studies of Strange Things." The story first appeared in the "Konjaku Monogatarishū" (12th century). With the aid of his wife Setsuko's oral (re)telling of a 19th century edition of "Konjaku Monogatarishū," Hearn produced the 1904 English adaptation, which was first translated into Japanese in 1910.

---

5   He adapted over fifty stories, which are gathered in six collections: "In Ghostly Japan" (1899), "Shadowings" (1900), "A Japanese Miscellany" (1901), "Kotto" (1902), "Kwaidan" (1904) and "The Romance of the Milky Way" (1905) (see Perkins, 1934: 39–54).

6   Hearn's library today is part of Toyama University's library collection. A catalogue of all books is available (Toyama High School, 1927).

7   Other Western authors who adapted Japanese ghost stories in the 19th and early 20th century were A.B. Mitford (Algernon Bertram Freeman-Mitford, 1837–1916), Alice Mabel Bacon (1858–1918), William Elliot Griffis (1843–1928) and Sidney McCall (alias Mary McNeil Fenollosa, 1865–1954).

8   Lafcadio Hearn's works were translated into Japanese only a few years after their first publication in English. The ghost story collection "Kwaidan" for example, published in English in 1904, appeared in a Japanese translation by Takahama Chyōkō [sic] in 1910 (cf. Perkins, 1934: 142). Lafcadio Hearn's story collections are still available today in many editions in Japan.

In 1964, Japanese director Kobayashi Masaki picked up "The Reconciliation" as one of four of Hearn's stories for his movie *Kwaidan* (1965), adding another version to this tradition.

Hearn and Japanese cultural figures like folklorist Yanagita Kunio (1875–1962) or author Izumi Kyōka (1873–1939) understood the uncanny as a kind of anchor of Japanese identity in the face of modernity. However, with the onset of modernization in the latter half of the 19th century, belief in ghosts and other supernatural beings was more commonly regarded within intellectual discourse as backward, a pre-modern relic. Even though ghosts were still popular in literature, art and theatre, they were now labeled as 'superstition' (*meishin*), a word that found its way into Japanese language only in the Meiji period (1868–1912), in opposition to the category 'religion' (*shōkyū*), which was itself a product of the late 1850s (Josephson, 2006: 148).

A new form of dealing with ghosts that seemed more fitting for this period of renewal and departure than stories about avenging women was Western spiritualism, which gained great popularity in the late 19th and early 20th century in Japan (Takasuna Miki, 2012: 150). This was also reflected in popular culture where the game *kokkuri-san*, a practice of divination similar to Western table turning, became a mass phenomenon in the late 1880s. For this game, a small group of people gathered to invoke a spirit. *Kokkuri-san* was a cultural practice that infused everyday life with magic, and at the same time—because of its Western origin—invoked a semblance of rationality and scientific method, lending the participants with a feeling of control over the summoned ghost. According to Foster, *kokkuri* was "[...] a powerful medium, simultaneously a vestige of the ghosts that possessed the past and a portent of the spirits that would possess the future" (Foster, 2006: 273). Moreover, the first ghost photographs appeared around 1880 in Japan, which is to say examples of failed or manipulated photography, which inspired countless myths and stories (Koike, 2000). These so-called *shinrei shashin*, which are still an integral part of Japanese popular culture today (see Chalfen, 2008), were the first examples of the general skepticism towards technologies of reproduction which would become a predominant topos of J-Horror in the 1990s.

By the end of the 19th century, parapsychology had found its way to Japan through the translation of Franz Anton Mesmer's and other works. In the first decade of the 20th century, an increasing number of psychical research publications appeared, and newspapers began reporting on the findings of the Society for Psychical Research in England (Takasuna Miki, 2012: 151). One Japanese researcher in the field of parapsychology, who is still well known today, Fukurai Tomokichi, conducted experiments with *tōshi* (clairvoyance) and *nensha* (psychic photography) (Koike, 2000: 59–61). In 1913, Fukurai published his results. Lacking sufficient evidence to support his claims, he was dismissed among experts, and eventually lost his position at the Imperial University of Tokyo. Later he seems to have gained some recognition in the West, as his work was published in an English translation in 1931 entitled "Clairvoyance and Thoughtography."

The story of Fukurai and his female mediums served as a model for the events leading to Sadako's death in *Ringu* (dir. Hideo Nakata, 1998). *Shinrei shashin* are an established element of J-Horror, and even the motif of *kokkuri-san* appears in several movies. Contemporary Japanese horror cinema is thus reflective of turn of the century Japan, a period in which vigorous debates arose regarding pre-modernity and modernity, and Western science and superstition. J-Horror movies erode the foundations of modernity—a trust in technology and rationalism—creating an atmosphere of in-between, similar to the space of twilight (*tasogare*), which author Izumi Kyōka investigated in his gothic stories in the early 20th century (Figal, 1999: 6).

JAPANESE AND GLOBAL HORROR CINEMA

In Japan, stories about ghosts were adapted to film as soon as it was technically possible to do so. The new medium of cinema contributed to the shaping of the ghost figure in Japan. Though classical Japanese theatre, above all *kabuki*, had an enormous influence upon the first decade of Japanese film-making (McDonald, 1994: 23–24), the cinematic possibilities revealed through screenings of Western (mostly French) films opened up a new creative scope. Thus, by the beginning of the 20th century, ghosts had begun appearing and disappearing on screen through the use of editing techniques such as cutting, fading, and double exposure to have the illusion of ghosts appearing and disappearing on screen.

After the Second World War, Japanese audiences as well as film directors showed an increasing interest in Western (horror) movies. In the 1950s and 1960s, following the end of the American occupation, the Japanese horror film experienced a period of prosperity and retained elements of *kabuki* and *Nō* theatre. At the same time, however, directors increasingly discovered the potential of film as a medium, using an expressionist style and montage techniques to portray ghosts. According to Lee Hunju (2011: 87), the stylistic elements of Japanese *kaidan* films of the time inspired Korean ghost movie producers and directors, such as Yong-min Lee, who directed the classic *Salinma/A Devilish Homicide* (1965). In Hong Kong and the West, as Wai-ming Ng (2008: 146) states, "old-style Japanese ghost films" did not gain a significant following and thus had barely any influence on film production in other countries. However, these classic ghost stories and plays dominated Japanese horror cinema until the end of the 1960s, when studios began to turn to horrific creatures of Western origin, such as monsters, vampires and serial killers (cf. Kitajima Akihiro, 2000: 25).

Hybrid works, which featured an intense combination of stylistic conventions from Western horror film with Japanese motifs, began to emerge around 1990. An early example is Kiyoshi Kurosawa's film *Sweet Home/Suwōto Hōmu* (1989), which features a documentary filmmaker (played by Itami Juzū) and his team who are facing the perils of a haunted house. The film's style was clearly influenced by Western horror films such as *Poltergeist* (dir. Tobe Hooper, 1982), while the plot also bears resemblance to Edo period stories about haunting mothers (*ubume*). The new J-Horror boom began in the mid-1990s, when *Gakkō-no-kaidan/School Ghost Stories* reached a large audience with one television series (from 1994) and several feature films (from 1995). This series also exhibited stylistic parallels to Western movies of the 1980s. For example, the translucent pink monster that chases the children in the first *Gakkō-no-kaidan* film (dir. Hirayama Hideyuki, 1995) brings to mind 'Slimer', the green blob creature from *Ghostbusters* (dir. Evan Reitman, 1984).

The emblematic film of J-Horror, *Ringu* (1998), is also a hybrid work. Director Hideo Nakata named Western classics including *The Innocents* (dir. Jack Clayton, 1961), *The Haunting* (dir. Robert Wise, 1963) and *The Amityville Horror* (dir. Stuart Rosenberg, 1979) as inspirations (see Totaro Donato, 2000). *Ringu*'s plot and the development of suspense further reminds one of the Canadian horror movie *The Changeling* (dir. Peter Medak, 1980), where the crippled, sickly young boy Joseph, murdered by his father out of greed, returns as a ghost and haunts an old mansion. Just like Sadako, the boy's corpse is found in a forgotten old well over which a house has been built. Takahashi Hiroshi, who wrote the screenplays for *Joyū-rei/Don't look up* (dir. Hideo Nakata, 1996) and the *Ringu* series, was, as he states, deeply impressed by the film *Ghost of Sierra de Cobre* (dir. Joseph Stefano and Robert Stevens, 1964) which he had seen on television as a child (Yasushi Nakano, 2005: 127–128).

Ringu follows the principle of a discovery-plot (Carroll, 1987: 57), in the course of which the protagonists investigate strange phenomena and little by little uncover the existence of a monster or ghost, and begin to unravel the entity's motives. In classical Japanese ghost stories and films, however, the reasons for haunting are known from the outset. In *Ringu*, only at the end of the film the audience is directly confronted with Sadako's ghost when Ryūji falls prey to her. Prior to that scene, only visual fragments point to her existence. This format, which describes the danger as ever present but vague and intangible, is similar to the way in which suspense is built up in Western horror films such as Ridley Scott's *Alien* (1979). Lee Hunju (2011: 69) goes as far as to compare the female protagonists of the new Asian ghost movies, who fight against uncanny intrusions, to the 'final girls'[9] of the Western Slasher genre. According to Wai-ming Ng (2008: 147), new stylistic elements used in J-Horror films include a particular form of lighting made to evoke a dismal, depressive atmosphere, as well as the use of dull colors and metallic sound effects.[10]

---

9   Coined by Carol Clover (1993), the term 'final girls' refers to the last woman or girl alive to confront the killer in slasher films.

10   Wierzbicki (2010: 197) points out that the "sound of disembodied croaking, scraping, wheezing or bubbling" in J-Horror is directly related to the manner of death which brought the ghost into being.

Thus, the J-Horror works of the 1990s follow an established canon of stylistic elements, which has become increasingly prevalent in a globalized horror cinema today. As Klein states, genre films are particularly suitable to processes of transnationalization:

> Because of their formulaic construction and their derivation from other films, they do not demand from viewers a deep familiarity with a foreign culture or cinematic tradition, but rather a more easily acquired mastery of a recurring set of conventions.
>
> Klein, 2010: 3–4

Local features—such as female ghosts in Japan—thus meet largely neutral forms known to the global horror audience. These elements are constantly rearranged to generate new meanings. This principle is not limited to Japan, rather it can be characterized as a global phenomenon.

Local motifs and newly developed stylistic elements in turn can become part of the global circulation of horror motifs, as was the case with *Ringu*'s Sadako. US producers saw the potential of the hybridity of its material. For a Western audience, the ghost was confusingly unfamiliar, but at the same time the setting, the plot and many of the stylistic features offered enough associations to allow for the viewers to recognize the familiar within the foreign. After the first remake, rights for other J-Horror films were successfully sold to US producers, and Asian filmmakers started to make films "with an eye toward Hollywood" (Bliss Cua Lim, 2009: 198). Asian horror films thus developed "an amalgam of local, regional and global influences, citing not only from one another but also their Hollywood remakes, and vice versa" (Feeley, 2012: 46). According to Byron (2012: 374), these developments have their drawbacks, as there is a tendency to appropriate and commodify local or regional folklores for an international audience.

According to Wai-ming Ng, however, one cannot speak of a homogeneous process of globalization in the horror genre. Whereas Asian horror motifs have spread throughout Europe and the US mainly through a 'second hand globalization' in the form of remakes, the original films were circulating within Asia in both a 'direct globalization', and a 'pirated globalization' through the adopted style and plot of *Ringu* and other hit films without acquiring the rights (Wai-ming Ng, 2008: 143). The new type of horror film also became a transnational phenomenon through co-productions involving several Asian countries. The production company Applause Pictures has been highly successful in this field, producing the films *Saam gaang/Three* (dir. Kim Jee-woon, Nonzee Nimibutr and Peter Ho-Sun Chan, 2002), *Saam gaang yi/Three … Extremes* (dir. Fruit Chan, Park Chan-wook and Takashi Miike, 2004), *Gin gwai/The Eye* (dir. The Pang Brothers, 2002) and *The Maid* (dir. Kelvin Tong, 2005).[11] These co-productions are transnational in terms of financing, marketing, cast, setting, language, crew and tropes (Feeley, 2012: 45), but

---

11   Vivian Lee deals with this 'Pan-Asian Horror' in her contribution to this volume.

with a strong focus on Japan, Korea, Hong Kong, Singapore and Thailand. The global boom of 'new Asian horror' is thus actually limited to productions from several East and Southeast Asian source countries, whereas horror is produced only for the local market in most other Asian countries.[12] As such, terms like 'Asian horror' are in fact over-generalizations based on foreign expectations of 'Asian horror' from the few source markets which are globally successful.

THE SPECTERS OF URBAN MODERNITY

The transcultural flows influencing Japanese 'ghost culture' and so-called J-Horror are related to religious heritage, classical literature, and the stylistic conventions of the horror genre. However, it is not only these flows which have sparked global interest in Japanese ghost films. Most contemporary Japanese horror films generate their impact through the infiltration of the lives and worlds of those living in highly urbanized societies. In my opinion, three fundamental motifs of so-called J-Horror movies make them relevant for an international audience, which is primarily located in developed countries. These three motifs are urban modernity in crisis, uncanny media devices and the dissolution of the nuclear family. It is through these patterns that the ghosts unfold their potential to be a

> sign of something [...] that, largely ignored or repressed by the society in which it participates, refuses to be marginalized any longer, but pushes to be recognized.
>
> Kröger and Anderson, 2013: xii

The first J-Horror films were strongly influenced by urban legends, predominately the modern folk stories most widespread amongst schoolchildren in Japan. These stories deal with haunted taxis, abandoned buildings and ghosts on school toilets. Folklorist Miyata Noboru discussed such urban legends in his 1985 work "Yōkai no minzokugaku"/"Folklore of Monsters," while middle school teacher Tsunemitsu Tōru helped this modern folklore to gain nationwide attention with his 1990 collection of stories "Gakkō no kaidan"/"School Ghost Stories." This atmosphere formed the background for the emergence of J-Horror—which was confined not only to film but also manifested itself in a variety of media such as video games, manga and fantasy novels—around 1990.

Though most J-Horror films take place in Tokyo, they do not present recognizable architectural spots, but rather a familiar yet generic series of interiors, characterless apartment buildings and empty spaces. This mirrors an experience of fragmentation Reed mentions in his thesis on uncanny urban space on screen: "As the design of the city has continued to drift

---

12   The Indonesian Sundelbolong movies that Maren Wilger analyzes in this volume, for example, are largely unknown to an international audience.

outwards, and the idea of a cohesive urban center has morphed into an empty and meaningless relic, often all that remains is a void" (Reed, 2011: 96).

Whereas pre-modern Japanese haunted houses secured their uncanny atmosphere through their location far from the social life of villages and cities, and an architecture reclaimed by vegetation and torn-sliding doors, contemporary haunted houses are the corpses of modernity's dreams. Apartment blocks, built at a time of great economic growth to house citizens who in turn contributed to the financial success of the country, are slowly crumbling away. Huge medical facilities, constructed decades ago and now abandoned, become signifiers of decay, death and scientific villainy. Buildings like the creepy damp apartment building in *Honogurai mizu no soko kara/Dark Water* (dir. Hideo Nakata, 2002) are symbols of the Japan's 'lost decade' which was ushered in by the burst of the economic bubble in the early 1990s. As Lee suggests, the visual presence of economic instability in J-Horror is one factor that made it adaptable for filmmakers in other Asian countries, who were themselves facing a similar situation following the 1997 Asian financial crisis. Lee writes, "The Asian people's anxieties about Asian modernity in crisis played a significant role in constituting specific themes of the Asian female ghost films made from the late 1990s to the early 2000s" (Lee Hunju, 2011: 122).

But it is not only huge abandoned buildings that are inhabited by specters—people are anything but safe in their own houses or apartments; they are horrified by filthy black hair of unknown origin in their sink, mysterious phone calls and eerie noises. Hiding under a blanket, a strategy children use against the products of their fantasy, is of no use in *Ju-On/The Grudge* (dir. Takashi Shimizu, 2002)—the ghost is already there. As Freud (1955 [1919]) explains in his theory of the uncanny, through the process of repression something once familiar or 'homely' becomes unfamiliar, alienated from the mind and therefore 'unhomely'. In J-Horror this applies in a very literal sense, the house, the home of a family, becomes an 'un-home', an uncanny space where the lives of its inhabitants overlap with some traumatic event. This space is inscribed with memories and thus transcends temporal boundaries: "The haunted house refers to a space of recollection charged with affect: alternately fearsome, thrilling or tragic." (Bliss Cua Lim, 2009: 206). As Vidler states in his work "The Architectural Uncanny," it has become a leitmotif of postmodernism that the house is no longer a home (Vidler, 1994: 66).

In some J-Horror films, diverse settings are put into contrast to illustrate the intrusion of the (pre-modern) past into the film's present. Sadako in *Ringu* (dir. Hideo Nakata, 1998) originates from the island Izu-Ōshima, that is to say from the exterior, the marginal—from a zone where nature is rough and uncontrollable. The backdrop of Sadako's actions is the traditional Japanese *tatami* room, the so-called *washitsu*. 'Old Japan' and the idea of untamed nature are thus constructed as a source of the uncanny—which is in line with Freud's theory, where the uncanny is described as "that class of the frightening which leads back to what is known of old and long familiar" (Freud, 1955: 219). The filmic ghosts seem to confirm "primitive beliefs which have been surmounted" (Freud, 1955: 248) through the process of modernization, but which are still present, hidden under the surface. As much as the ancient grotesque figure of the *yūrei* is feared, it is at the same time the object of a longing for a time with a supposedly 'intact spirit world', when ghosts were still an accepted and effective tool to deal with loss, otherness and guilt. Through embodying social issues and individual psychic turmoil, by lending them a concrete form, ghosts act as catalysts for the ineffable while facilitating confrontation. This ambivalence of the ghost—its position between dread and desire—has always been an essential aspect in the reception of ghost stories and still accounts for J-Horror's success today.

Another particularity of the J-Horror genre is that ghosts do not simply appear in front of their victims, but rather manifest themselves through various media. The first sighting is never a direct one. Moreover, the films use multi-perspectivity to generate an atmosphere of fundamental insecurity. The movie *Jaganrei/Psychic Vision* (dir. Ishii Teruyoshi, 1988) exemplifies this style. *Jaganrei* was a low-budget movie, produced directly for the video market. It is barely known today. Nonetheless, it may be considered the first J-Horror movie, and is said to have influenced directors like *Ringu*'s (1998) Hideo Nakata.[13]

Jaganrei's narrative is construed as a 'mockumentary'. In the beginning it is declared that the film consists of original footage shot to promote pop star Satō Emi. It is also explained that the footage has never been used due to a series of peculiar incidents during the shooting, which culminate in the singer's death. The cause of these unfortunate incidents is only revealed by the footage: we see a blurred, white figure in the background, a figure people are obviously not able to perceive directly. Through the technical transformation of reality via the cinematic code, we can access a realm that is otherwise invisible. In *Jaganrei/Psychic Vision*, the bird's eye perspective implies that we even see sequences filmed by the supernatural being itself.[14]

Haunted media devices and the plurality of perspectives that results from the editing of sequences, which derive from different sources, became essential stylistic conventions of J-Horror. In *Ju-on/The Grudge* (dir. Takashi Shimizu, 2002) and *Dark Water/Honogurai mizu no soko kara* (dir. Hideo Nakata, 2002) for example, grainy images captured by surveillance cameras are the first indicators of a supernatural presence. Mobile phones become deadly devices in *Chakushin ari/The Call* (dir. Takashi Miike, 2003), and the internet is a haunted presence in *Kairo/Pulse* (dir. Kiyoshi Kurosawa, 2001). In its skepticism towards modern mass media and mediality itself, J-Horror demonstrates similarities with Western horror films. It

---

13 Japanese writer and scenarist Konaka Chiaki, who wrote the script for *Jaganrei/Psychic Vision* (dir. Ishii Teruyoshi, 1988), writes about production and reception of the film in the book "Horā eiga no miryoku"/"The Fascination of Horror Films" (2003).

14 Pinedo (1997:52–52) terms this kind of camera work, which identifies the viewer's point of view with that of the implied monster, "unclaimed point-of-view shot."

is through tape recordings that Regan's gibberish in *The Exorcist* (dir. William Friedkin, 1973) becomes comprehensible, while the ghostly voice in *The Changeling* (dir. Peter Medak, 1980) is inaudible, yet recordable. The motif of the television set as ghost portal can already be found in Tobe Hooper's *Poltergeist* (1982) and David Cronenberg's *Videodrome* (1983). The newest spin-off of the 'Ringu' series, *Sadako 3D 2* (dir. Tsutomu Hanabusa, 2013), even features a special smartphone app, which transforms the viewers' mobiles into haunted devices during the cinema screening and makes the horror experience a more personal one.

Uncanny effects caused by cameras and tape recorders are as old as these technologies of reproduction themselves. As Gunning writes in an article on spirit photography, the technology inspires an uncanny feeling through the dematerialization of reality, which undermines the unique identity of objects and people—creating 'ghostly doubles' (Gunning, 1995: 43). In spirit photography as well as J-Horror movies, the medium seems to possess a more sensitive capacity than the human eye, allowing the ghosts to be captured on film. These images cannot be traced back to a unique original. Indeed, it is this lack of tangible reference, which makes them spectral. Or, as Derrida puts it in an interview on the movie *Ghost Dance* (dir. Ken McMullen, 1983), "when the very first perception of an image is linked to a structure of reproduction, then we are dealing with the realm of phantoms" (Derrida, 1989: 61). But there is one more dimension to this phenomenon, as with the notion of the 'home' and 'un-home', it is also the position between the familiar and unfamiliar that invites ghosts to haunt media technology. Using cameras, telephones and video technology is part of our everyday life. These devices connect us to other people, collect our memories, and offer recreation and security. If a ghost conquers our television or—even worse—our mobile phone, this also represents an attack on our 'home' and our identity. When Hitomi switches on her television in *Ju-On/The Grudge* (dir. Takashi Shimizu, 2002), it should be a refuge to soothe her fears and a companion to let her forget her solitude. Instead, the familiar face of the presenter becomes distorted, the image freezes, and in so doing, the situation becomes even more uncanny through the mutation of Hitomi's personal environment.

In the Japanese ghost films of the 1950s, as in the stories of the Edo period, the ghosts often represented an attempt to confront the role of women. In contemporary J-Horror, most of the ghosts are still female, and some of the films—like *Ringu* (dir. Hideo Nakata, 1998), where Sadako and her mother Shizuko possess paranormal powers while alive—still emphasize the motif of "women's naturally-born monstrosities and otherness" (Lee Hunju, 2011: 145). A new and very remarkable development, though, is that the ghosts now also stand for the dissolution of traditional family structures.

The US classic *Poltergeist* (dir. Tobe Hooper, 1982) pictures an intact, average American family fighting against uncanny, supernatural occurrences. In Japanese films like *Ringu* and *Dark Water/Honogurai mizu no soko kara* (dir. Hideo Nakata, 2002), however, the family is already broken, with parents divorced and the mother living alone. It is perhaps then unsurprising that one of the most prolific J-Horror directors, Kiyoshi Kurosawa, turned completely to social drama in 2008 with Tokyo Sonata:

> Kurosawa is not actually departing from the J-horror tradition; rather, he is transforming the quotidian experience of Japan's working class into a discourse on the abject horror of the mundane.

Rosenbaum, 2010: 116

The scene in which Yōichi meets his father on the street in *Ringu*, for instance, is particularly striking. The two stand still for a moment and Yōichi looks at the man shrouded in darkness, but he does not recognize him as his father. Rather, the man is nothing more than a shadow crossing his path. This scene indicates that the nuclear family is no longer functioning as an influential institution offering support to its members. Relationships are shattered and family members, practically absent from one's life, can become little more than ghostly figures. The same holds true for *Dark Water/Honogurai mizu no soko kara* (dir. Hideo Nakata, 2002), where a mother struggling with her divorce is not always able to meet the needs of her daughter. The image of a little girl waiting at kindergarten for her mother to pick her up is emblematic of their situation. When the ghost of a girl the same age as the daughter haunts their apartment, the only solution the film offers is an 'adoption' of the ghost child. This may be read as an opportunity for atonement for the single mother and her failure to properly care for her own child.

Because of their low social status, single mothers are the ideal victims. In the logic of these movies, their daily struggle of coordinating work and childcare, of trying to stay afloat in the treacherous rapids of society, makes them vulnerable to attacks by supernatural forces. In Edo period ghost stories, adult women were victims mutated into horrific ghosts; in today's ghost films, they may also be the guilty party (even if the films portray them in a sympathetic way) because of their inability to sustain a 'normal' family life. Children are depicted as those who suffer the most from divorce and fragmentation of the family: A number of J-Horror ghosts are children, haunting society because of neglect or abuse. According to Nelson, in Japan children stand for hope and the future as well as for a nostalgic, traditional past. In these films then, they become "emblems of a lost past and an uncertain future, a future portrayed as so detached from tradition and national identity as to be frightening" (Nelson, 2009: 13). Kume states that these spectral children also provided a common thread that made J-Horror adaptable to Hollywood: "if children, who are supposed to be lovely, are directing strong evil forces against good people, this causes extraordinary fear and fright" (Kume Yoriko, 2005: 166).

The dysfunctionality of the traditional family appears on two levels in J-Horror, in the 'present' of the film, where family members are haunted by a ghost, and within the past, where some family tragedy lays the foundation for the present haunting. Thus, the trauma that is represented by the ghosts in J-Horror is never comfortably situated in the 'past'—it corresponds with the troubled relationships of the present, of the living. As the protagonists investigate a ghost's motives, they must, at the same time, explore their own subconscious.

CONCLUSION

Japanese female ghosts are not as unique and endemic as some people claim them to be. Although the stereotype developed in a period when Japan largely closed itself off from the world, Chinese culture still had a huge impact on stories about the supernatural. As Japan opened up again in the 19th century, the earlier figure of the ghost was largely dismissed in intellectual discourse. At the same time, Western concepts regarding the spirit world were integrated into Japanese society, thereby generating new types of ghost lore and cultural practice such as *kokkuri-san*.

J-Horror films tie in with these influences of Western spiritualism as well as with global conventions of the horror genre, yet the ghostly revenants closely resemble their 18th and 19th century predecessors. Most specters are still female, dressed in white and wearing their hair loose. What makes these ghosts successful beyond Japan is their potential to embody the actual fears of people living in urbanized societies with a high standard of living. People who encounter ghosts in J-Horror are in difficult situations marked by obscure intersections of the present and the past, of traditions and urban loneliness. The ancient figure of the female *yūrei* as the classic Japanese ghost 'par excellence' re-emerges in these movies as a signifier of a repressed past, as a pre-modern 'other', that is both an object of longing and of fear.

Be it one's own apartment, one's mobile phone or the nuclear family, in J-Horror, everything that keeps people grounded, that offers security and a feeling of 'home' breaks away. The familiar turns obscure and distorted, and the loveable (such as children) becomes destructive. Ghosts no longer point directly to one act of wrongdoing, but embody fundamental insecurity, even going so far as to affect the protagonist's identity. Frequently within J-Horror there is some connection to the ghost, some part of the protagonist is in the ghost, some part of the ghost is in the person.

It is its openness, its hybridity and its proximity to complex urban life that accounts for J-Horror's transcultural potential and success. As every transcultural artifact, Japanese ghost films have "a cosmopolitan side, but also a side of local affiliation" (Welsch, 1999: 205). Their status as 'cultural revenants' makes Japanese female ghosts a model for their companions, haunting cinemas throughout Asia and around the world.

BIBLIOGRAPHY

Árokay, Judit. "Frauen und Frauenbilder im japanischen Buddhismus (Women and Perception of Women in Japanese Buddhism)." In *Vorträge im Rahmen des weiterbildenden Studiums Buddhismus in Geschichte und Gegenwart* (Lecture Series: Buddhism in Past and Present), edited by Lambert Schmithausen and Jan-Ulrich Sobisch, 183–196. Hamburg: Hamburg University, 2003.

Bliss Cua Lim. *Translating Time: Cinema, the Fantastic, and Temporal Critique.* Durham: Duke University Press, 2009.

Blouin, Michael J. *Japan and the Cosmopolitan Gothic: Specters of Modernity.* New York: Palgrave Macmillan, 2013.

Byron, Glennis. "Global Gothic." In *A New Companion to the Gothic*, edited by David Punter, 369–378. Hoboken: Wiley, 2012.

Carroll, Noel. "The Nature of Horror." *The Journal of Aesthetics and Art Criticism* 46/1 (Autumn 1987): 51–59.

Chalfen, Richard. "Shinrei Shashin: Photographs of Ghosts in Japanese Snapshots." *Photography & Culture* 1/1 (July 2008): 51–72.

Cheung, Dominic. "With You a Part of Me: A Study of New Tales of the Trimmed Lamp, Tales of Moonlight and Rain, New Tales of the Golden Carp and the 'Ghost-Wife' Theme in China, Japan and Korea." In *Explorations: Essays in Comparative Literature*, edited by Makoto Ueda, 148–173. Lanham: University Press of America, 1986.

Clover, Carol J. *Men, Women, and Chain Saws: Gender in the Modern Horror Film.* Princeton: Princeton University Press, 1993.

Cranmer-Byng, L., and S.A. Kapadia, eds. *Onna Daigaku: A Treasure Box of Women's Learning.* Weston-super-Mare: Nezu Press, 2010.

Derrida, Jacques. "Ghost Dance Interview." *Public* 2 (1989): 60–67.

Feeley, Jennifer. "Transnational Spectres and Regional Spectators: Flexible Citizenship in new Chinese Horror Cinema." *Journal of Chinese Cinemas* 6/1 (2012): 41–64.

Foster, Michael Dylan. "Strange Games and Enchanted Science: The Mystery of Kokkuri." *The Journal of Asian Studies* 65/2 (2006): 251–275.

Freud, Sigmund. "The 'Uncanny'." In *The Standard Edition of the Complete Psychological Works of Sigmund Freud, Volume XVII (1917-1919): An Infantile Neurosis and Other Works*, edited by James Strachey, 217–256. London: Hogarth Press, 1955.

Fukurai Tomokichi. *Clairvoyance and Thoughtography.* New York: Arno Press, 1975. [Reprint of the 1931 edition, published by Rider, London].

Gunning, Tom. "Phantom Images and Modern Manifestations: Spirit Photography, Magic Theater, Trick Films and Photography's Uncanny." In *Fugitive Images from Photography to Video*, edited by Patrice Petro, 42–71. Bloomington: Indiana University Press, 1995.

_____. "Re-Newing Old Technologies." In *Rethinking Media Change: The Aesthetics of Transition*, edited by David Thorburn, Henry Jenkins and Brad Seawell, 39–60. Cambridge: MIT Press, 2004.

Ikoma Natsumi. "Why Do Japanese Ghosts Have No Legs?: Sexualized Female Ghosts and the Fear of Sexuality." In *Dark Reflections, Monstrous Reflections: Essays on the Monster in Culture*, edited by Sorcha Ni Fhlainn, 189–200. Oxford: Mansfield College, 2006.

Josephson, Jason Ānanda. "When Buddhism Became a 'Religion': Religion and Superstition in the Writings of Inoue Enryō." *Japanese Journal of Religious Studies* 33/1 (2006), 143–168.

Kadota Mamoru. "Wakai ni okeru saiwa no hōhō: Rafukadio Hān ga nozonda fūfuai no sugata (How 'The Reconciliation' Was Retold: The Conjugal Love Which Lafcadio Hearn Wished to Depict in the Story)." *Research Bulletin of Nara University of Education* 54/1 (2005): 201–210.

Kitajima Akihiro. "'Yotsuya kaidan' 'kaibyō' mono o chūshin ni kaidan eiga o ryōsan (Mass Production of Kaidan Films, mainly, Yotsuya Kaidan and 'Ghost Cat' Films)." In *Nihon horā eiga e no shōtai* (Invitation to Japanese Horror Films), edited by Tomoo Haraguchi and Hideki Murata, 24–25. Tokyo: Heibonsha, 2000.

Klein, Christina. "The American Horror Film?: Globalization and Transnational US-Asian Genres." In *American Horror Film: The Genre at the Turn of the Millennium*, edited by Steffen Hantke, 3–14. Jackson: University Press of Mississippi, 2010.

Konaka Chiaki. *Horā eiga no miryoku: Fandamentaru horā sengen* (The Fascination of Horror Films: A Fundamental Horror Manifesto). Tokyo: Iwanami shoten, 2003.

Kröger, Lisa, and Melanie R. Anderson. "Introduction." In *The Ghostly and the Ghosted in Literature and Film: Spectral Identities*, edited by Lisa Kröger and Melanie R. Anderson, ix–xvi. Lanham: Rowman & Littlefield, 2013.

Kume Yoriko. "Onna rei no inai japanīzu horā nante! (What? Japanese Horror without Female Ghosts?)" In *Horā Japanesuku no genzai* (Horror Japanesque Today), edited by Hirotaka Ichiyanagi and Morio Yoshida, 165–171. Tokyo: Seikyūsha, 2005.

Lee Hunju. "The new Asian Female Ghost Films: Modernity, Gender Politics, and Transnational Transformation." PhD diss., University of Massachusetts, 2011. Accessed January 3, 2014. http://udini.proquest.com/view/the-new-asian-female-ghost-films-pqid:2312462381/.

McDonald, Keiko. *Japanese Classical Theater in Films*. London, Toronto: Associated University Press, 1994.

Miyata Noboru. *Yōkai no minzokugaku: Nihon no mienai kūkan* (Folklore of Monsters: Japan's Invisible Space). Tokyo: Iwanami Shoten, 1985.

Perkins, Percival Densmore. *Lafcadio Hearn: A Bibliography of his Writings*. New York: Houghton Mifflin, 1934.

Pinedo, Isabel Christina. *Recreational Terror: Women and the Pleasures of Horror Film Viewing*. Albany: State University of New York Press, 1997.

Reed, Matthew. "A Public Haunted House: the Uncanny Urban Space on Screen." M.A. thesis, Concordia University Montreal, 2011. Accessed January 3, 2014. http://spectrum.library.concordia.ca/35858/1/Reed_MA_F2011.pdf.

Reider, Noriko. "The Appeal of Kaidan: Tales of the Strange." *Asian Folkore Studies* 59 (2000): 265–283.

_____. *Tales of the Supernatural in Early Modern Japan: Kaidan, Akinari, Ugetsu Monogatari*. Lewiston, N.Y. et al.: Mellen, 2002.

Rosenbaum, Roman. "From the Traditions of J-horror to the Representation of kakusa shakai in Kurosawa's Film Tokyo Sonata." *Contemporary Japan* 22 (2010): 115–136.

Scherer, Elisabeth. *Spuk der Frauenseele: Weibliche Geister im japanischen Film und ihre kulturhistorischen Ursprünge* (Haunting of the Female Soul: Female Ghosts in Japanese Cinema and their Origins in Japanese Art and Folk Beliefs). Bielefeld: Transcript, 2011.

Setsuko Koizumi, and Hayato Tokugawa, eds. *The Annotated Reminiscences of Lafcadio Hearn*. San Francisco: Shisei-Dō Publications, 2012.

Shimazaki Satoko. "'The End of the 'World': Tsuruya Nanboku IV's Female Ghosts and Late-Tokugawa Kabuki." *Monumenta Nipponica* 66/2 (2011): 209–246.

Stutterheim, Nadine. "Shinshaku Yotsuya kaidan: Kinoshita Keisukes filmische Deutung eines Kabukitheater-stückes aus dem Jahr 1825 (Shinshaku Yotsuya Kaidan: Kinoshita Keisuke's filmic interpretation of a 1825 Kabuki play)." M.A. thesis, Humboldt University Berlin, 2002. Accessed December 1, 2013. http://www.asaf.huberlin.de/seminar-fuer-ostasien-studien/japan/studium/ausgewaehlte-arbeiten/yotsuya.pdf.

Takasuna Miki. "The Fukurai Affair: Parapsychology and the History of Psychology in Japan." *History of the Human Sciences* 25/2 (2012): 149–164.

Totaro Donato. "The 'Ring' Master: Interview with Hideo Nakata." *Off Screen* 4/1 (July 2000). Accessed July 31, 2009. www.horschamp.qc.ca/new_offscreen/nakata.html.

Toyama High School. *Catalogue of the Lafcadio Hearn Library in the Toyama High School.* 1927. Accessed January 3, 2014. http://hdl.handle.net/10110/79.

Tsunemitsu Tōru. *Gakkō no kaidan* (School Ghost Stories). Tokyo: Kōdansha, 1990.

Vidler, Anthony. *The Architectural Uncanny: Essays in the Modern Unhomely*. Cambridge: MIT Press, 1994.

Wai-ming Ng, Benjamin. "When Sadako Meets Mr. Vampire: The Impact of Ringu on Hong Kong Ghost Films." *Asian Cinema* 19/1 (2008): 143–156.

Welsch, Wolfgang. "Transculturality: the Puzzling Form of Cultures Today." In *Spaces of Culture: City, Nation, World*, edited by Scott Lash and Mike Featherstone, 194–213. London et al.: Sage Publ., 1999.

Yasushi Nakano. "Joyū-rei ron: Arui wa, eiga no jikogenkyū sayō ni hisomu 'ma' ni tsuite (Discussion of Joyū-rei: Or: About the Specter Hidden in Film's Self-Referentiality)." In *Horā Japanesuku no genzai* (Horror Japanesque Today), edited by Hirotaka Ichiyanagi and Morio Yoshida, 115–130. Tokyo: Seikyūsha, 2005.

Yomota Inuhiko. "Indonesian and Thai Ghost Films." In *Asian Alternatives for a Sustainable World: Transborder Engagements in Knowledge Formation*, edited by The Work of the 2007/2008 API Fellows, 190–195. Bangkok: Nippon Foundation, 2009.

Figure Credits

Fig. 2.5.1: Copyright © 1998 by Toho.
Fig. 2.5.2: Copyright © 1998 by Toho.

POST-READING QUESTIONS/POST-SCREENING QUESTIONS

Directions: Use what you learned from reading this chapter and watching the film to respond to the questions.

1. Discuss the different cultural influences (both Japanese and foreign) that shaped Japanese ghost culture.

2. Analyze the characteristics (both visual and thematic) of the vengeance-seeking female ghost in Japanese cinema and J-horror.

3. Explore the role of haunted media technologies and how they operate in J-horror films. What do they do in the films?

4. Explain the relationship between haunted media technologies, the uncanny, broken families, and avenging female spirits in J-horror.

Reading 2.6

Diary of a Lost Girl

Victoriana, Intertextuality, and *A Tale of Two Sisters*

By Robert L. Cagle

KEY TERMS AND FIGURES

Japanese occupation	Kim Ki-young
Communism	Park Chan-wook
North and South Korea	Kim Ji-woon
Confucianism	Intertextuality
Bong Joon-ho	*Wonhon*
Yeon Sang-ho	British Victorian sensibility

RECOMMENDED FILMS

Bando [Peninsula] by Yeon Sang-ho (2020)

Busanhaeng [Train to Busan] by Yeon Sang-ho (2016)

Gisaengchung [Parasite] by Bong Joon-ho (2019)

Gokseong [The Wailing] by Na Hong-jin (2016)

Gwoemul [The Host] by Bong Joon-ho (2006)

Hanyeo [The Housemaid] by Kim Ki-young (1960)

Janghwa, Hongryeon [A Tale of Two Sisters] by Kim Ji-woon (2012)

Oldeuboi [Old Boy] by Park Chan-wook (2003)

INTRODUCTION

K orean cinema is a relatively "new" national cinema when compared to its geographic neighbors. This is largely the consequence of many years in which Korea was occupied by Japan (1910–1945), during which Korean films were propaganda vehicles for its occupier. It would not be until after 1945 and the end of WWII, and after a split between a US militarily occupied South and a communist-allied North, that Korea would develop its own film industry (see figures 2.6.1 and 2.6.2).

Korean horror, or to be more specific South Korean horror, comes into its own in the 1960s after Kim Ki-young's *The Housemaid*. A confluence of influences stemmed from American and Japanese horror genres, but equally importantly were the influences specific to Korean history, culture, and spirituality (including Confucianism). The ban on all Japanese cultural products from 1945 until 1998 resulted in an underground stream of imports from Japan, which extended to plagiarizing and copying certain Japanese cultural motifs like the ghost cat film genre or the *kaibyo eiga*. But Korean folklore also made its way into film with the animal transfigurations subgenre that became part of Korean pop culture and appears in many K horror films, like *The Thousand Year Old Fox* by Shin Sang-ok from 1969. In addition to these directions, there is a strong emphasis on hierarchies of class and gender, and relations with "outsiders" (both internal and external), which also distinguish K-horror.

Alison Peirse and Daniel Martin, in their introduction to *Korean Horror Cinema*, maintain that K-horror is a hybrid cinema, blending melodrama with folklore, science fiction, and sometimes comedy. Given the long-standing bifurcation of Korea between directions, governing ideologies, and world powers, it is not surprising that plots usually concern family relationships, dynamics, and conflicts, and that the genre of melodrama, even in its horror manifestation, holds great appeal for Korean audiences.

Figure 2.6.1 Na Woon-gyu (1902–1937), Korean actor, screenwriter, and director, is considered the first auteur director in Korean film history. Picture taken no later than 1938. Courtesy of Wikimedia.

Figure 2.6.2 Promotional poster for *Imjaeobtneun naleutbae* (1932) during the Japanese occupation, directed by Lee Gyu-Hwan and starring Na Woon-gyu. Courtesy of Wikimedia.

Although there are many films to discuss, not least of which are the recent films of Bong Joon-ho (*The Host*; *Parasite*), and Yeon Sang-ho's *Train to Busan* and *Peninsula*, the following three films mark pivotal points in the journey of K-horror from past to present. The *Housemaid* by Kim Ki-Young from 1960, considered the first Korean horror film, is a tale of seduction and family dissolution with a searing critique of class oppression that affects women most harshly in patriarchal society: a middle-class family hires a maid to assist an exhausted pregnant wife, but the maid seduces the husband and torments the family until apparently committing suicide in the end, only for us to find that this has been a cautionary tale against hiring a maid, told by the husband. *Old Boy* from 2003, a cult film by Park Chan-wook, was one of the most widely distributed and appreciated K films. Its horror resides in dark themes and violent content, which allowed it to be marketed as "extreme cinema" that uses elements of horror. By contrast, *A Tale of Two Sisters* by Kim Ji-woon, which forms the subject of this chapter, offers a more familiar tale of haunting and family trauma, and was the first K-horror film to gain mainstream theatrical distribution in the US.

In this chapter, Robert L. Cagle describes how *A Tale of Two Sisters* departs from the traditional presentation of the original Korean folktale, *The Story of Rose and Lotus*, dating from the Josean Dynasty (1392–1910) in its nonlinear adaptation. In the film the drama is centered on the traumatic mental split of Su-mi, the older sister (or Rose in the original tale) and her mourning/guilt related to Su-yeon, her younger sister (or Lotus in the original tale). Similar to the original story there is an emotionally distant widowed father and a conniving second wife. Most of the film is a flashback into the recent past that led to the opening frame. It begins (and ends) in a mental hospital, but opens with a scene of a doctor and the main character, Su-mi. She has become two people, herself and the evil stepmother, although this is only clear at the end of the film. Here the *wonhon*, the spirit of an innocent and wronged woman who has been sexually violated and/or is the victim of family drama, is the repressed secret trying to communicate and finally take revenge on the evil stepmother.

Cagle describes a British Victorian sensibility in the theme of repression, family discord, distant and ineffectual patriarchy, and the violence of angry, suppressed, and hysterical femininity. This sensibility and these themes are visualized in the way the house appears as dark heavy wood, shuttered, cavernous, and wall-papered. In other words, the mental instability and emotional trauma of the characters are reflected in the *mise en scene* (or setting). It is this power of melodrama and the codes of realism that are so often disturbed in the haunting genre (or stories of haunting), which enable this film to speak to many different global audiences. Although *A Tale of Two Sisters* belongs to a different type of horror than the other films mentioned, they have collectively placed Korea on the map of international horror and share a common concern with the importance of family unity, the loss of which is presented as one of the greatest sources of trauma.

Diary of a Lost Girl

Victoriana, Intertextuality, and *A Tale of Two Sisters*

By Robert L. Cagle

Kim Ji-woon's *A Tale of Two Sisters* (*Janghwa, Hongryeon,* 2003) is a film rent by duality and contradiction: its breathtakingly innovative narrative is constructed almost entirely out of established conventions and techniques drawn from such sources as the folktale, popular literature and the classical Hollywood film.[1] This voluntary subjugation to a stylistic strait-jacket of conventions, rules and limitations represents a key link between Kim's twenty-first-century film and a Victorian sensibility—a guiding aesthetic that manifests itself in nearly every aspect of the work, from its strikingly macabre marketing campaign to its meticulously crafted *mise-en-scène.* These visual and stylistic elements conjure up the shadowy images of a time period profoundly marked by stifling repression, obsessive morbidity and fanatical dissimulation. They provide a suitably uncanny setting for the film's unsettling storyline—a hybrid of sorts of the melodrama and the gothic, two literary forms that enjoyed immense popularity in the Victorian era, and that, like the film, make use of highly systematised and even restrictive representational strategies.

BROKEN BLOSSOMS

Kim's film takes its name from a well-known Korean folktale, *The Story of Rose and Lotus,* which dates from the Joseon Dynasty (1392–1910) and occupies a ubiquitous presence in Korean popular culture. The tale's influence is so pervasive that it has become a cultural metaphor in the same way that fairy tales such as 'Cinderella', 'Little Red Riding Hood' and 'Hansel and Gretel' have in the West. It has remained continuously in print throughout the modern era and

---

1   Critics have used terms such as 'elegant' (Lim 2009: 235), 'poignant' (Williams 2004: 85) and 'lyrical' (Elley 2003: 24) to describe the film's look, and Lim discusses its undeniable ability to stir 'passion' and 'pathos' (Lim 2009: 240) in viewers.

has been adapted to the screen no fewer than five times.[2] The tale opens as a childless couple wishes for a baby. Following a miraculous vision, the wife discovers she is pregnant, and soon afterward gives birth to a daughter. A few years later, a second girl is born. The mother dies while both children are quite young, and the father marries a younger woman who has a son of her own. The wicked stepmother becomes immensely jealous of the daughters and plots to do away with them; she accuses Rose of terminating an unwanted pregnancy, shaming the girl to suicide. Overcome with grief and loneliness, Lotus kills herself too. The restless spirits of the girls haunt the quarters of the village magistrate, until finally, armed with evidence provided by the ghosts, a young magistrate reveals the deceptions of the stepmother in a court of law and she is sentenced to death.

Lee Yoo-seop's 1972 adaptation, *Jang-Hwa and Hong-Ryeon: A Story of Two Sisters*, preserves both the traditional atmosphere (the settings, costumes and 'once upon a time' feel) and the linear, action-focused narrative of the tale. Its characters are painted in broad, almost primitive strokes. Rose and Lotus are indisputably good girls, content with their simple country lives. They are the consummate image of a particular brand of Korean femininity: subservient, pleasant and submissive—willing to suffer silently the unjust punishments demanded of them by their parents because to do otherwise would be wrong. Indeed, as is the case in the original tale, the sisters are able to articulate their grievances only through the figure of the magistrate, whose authority as a government official exceeds that of their parents. The girls' father, a highly regarded member of the community, is little more than a gruff voice and horsehair hat, iconic and yet empty symbols of inflexible patriarchal power and privilege. Their wicked stepmother, a shrewish, duplicitous woman, is similarly two-dimensional; an irredeemably corrupt being fond of exaggerated makeup and stagey histrionics, she exploits her mentally handicapped son, and plots with a bogus shaman to murder her stepdaughters and her husband to gain access to his finances and land.

The film's tableau-style framing, uniform lighting and garish colour palette flatten the image, lending it the appearance of an animated work of traditional Korean art. This is especially apparent in an early sequence in which the young magistrate comes across the two sisters playing in a field. The girls are presented as small figures against a sweeping landscape of green and blue, as they giggle and play in a tree swing. These themes—women

---

2   The story was adapted in 1924, as *The Story of Jang-hwa and Hong-ryeon* (*Janghwa Hongryeonjeon*)—although the Korean Film Archive identifies the director of the 1924 adaptation as Kim Seo-jeong, other sources (Kim 2007: 34; Lee and Choe 1998: 36; and Lee 2000: 24) give directorial credit to Park Jeong-hyeon (credited as 'Planner' in KOFA records)—again under the same title in 1936, this time in a work directed by Hong Gae-myeong; again in 1956, as *Jang-Hwa and Hong-Ryeon Story*; and in 1962, as *The Story of Jang-hwa and Hong-ryeon* (*Dae Jang-hwa Hong-ryeonjeon*), both directed by Chung Chang-wha. Finally, in 1972, the story was remade yet again as *Jang-Hwa and Hong-Ryeon: A Story of Two Sisters*, and directed by Lee Yoo-seop. Most recently, the tale surfaced again, although in title only, in Kim's 2003 feature and Lee Woon-ik's 2009 150-episode television drama, *Love and Obsession* (*Janghwa Hongryeon*), neither of which qualifies as an adaptation.

in nature, girls swinging—occur with some regularity in traditional Korean representations, perhaps most notably in Shin Yun-bok's iconic and often-reproduced painting of activities during the *Dano* holiday. Other scenes, especially those depicting characters engaged in the rituals of everyday life, could well have been lifted directly from the National Museum of Korea's collection of traditional artworks (see Cho 2008). Lee's film, thus, adheres to established literary and artistic codes, and like the story that it faithfully brings to the screen, functions unmistakably and above all else as a timeless moral tale, played out in universal and unambiguous terms; its traditional, linear trajectory moves forward from an age of innocence to one of conflict and trauma, and concludes with a conventionally happy ending.

SECRETS AND LIES

Kim's film, in contrast, eschews the linear form, facile resolution and didactic function of the earlier work, choosing instead to transform the tale into an artful meditation on loss and mourning—a project that finds its most succinct expression in the image used in the film's advertising campaign. Framed against a backdrop of deep maroon wallpaper, two wooden-looking parental figures loom ominously behind an ornate couch on which two girls, both of whom are dressed in blood-soaked nightgowns, are seated. The woman smiles coldly, and tightly grasps the shoulders of the girl on the right, who stares with a frightened look into the camera. The girl on the left slumps against the back of the seat, her eyes, half-closed, staring unfocused into the distance, her left hand draped limply over the arm of the couch, her right hand gripped tightly by her sister. The father figure rests his hand on the back of the couch, and appears to be both physically and emotionally distanced from all. The subjects have clearly assembled with the intention of posing for a family photograph, but the instant at which this photo has been taken is not the optimal one; rather than buttressing the desired image of domestic bliss, the photograph lays bare the horrific details and alarming extent of the discord that separates and alienates the members of this group from one another.

Similarly, the photo used in the *Two Sisters* marketing campaign recalls the post-mortem memorial photograph, a genre of photography widely associated with the Victorian era, and often viewed today as a symptom of the 'ghoulish and morbid' (Bown 2009: 8) nature of the Victorian sensibility. While such photos frequently depicted children who appeared to be blissfully asleep, and of whom parents had few, if any, visual representations, other family members did occasionally pose with the deceased, his or her eyes open, as if alive, in exactly the same manner in which they might pose for a 'normal' family photograph. These images embody in visual terms both a final moment of union, instantaneously frozen before an irrevocable separation, and the desire of the family members to halt time and (re)create a moment of familial happiness no longer possible.[3]

The film's eerie opening credits sequence likewise calls to mind the shuttered world of the Victorian family: titles appear superimposed over dark, floral-print wallpaper, the pattern of which suggests two faces, side by side, with one slightly obscured by shadows. The overall effect is an uncanny one, leaving uncertainty in the mind of the viewer as to what the significance of this mysterious image is. As the names of the performers (in white) appear on the screen, there is a visual disturbance that mimics waves, as if the titles were being filmed through clear water. The film's title then appears in a deep crimson as some of the flowers on the wallpaper appear to float up and away. The framing then tracks fluidly to the right, moving deeper into the shadows at the edge of the screen.

This simple opening provides a wealth of highly evocative visual material. The central motif of the wallpaper is a floral pattern, evoking at once both the flowers after which the lead characters in the folktale (Rose and Lotus) and in the film (Su-mi, Su-yeon) are named and a mode of communication that gained immense popularity during the Victorian era: the so-called 'language of flowers'. This method of symbolic exchange, according to authors of the late eighteenth and early nineteenth century, originated in the East and was introduced into Europe via Orientalist literature of the same era.[4] Authors made use of the culturally established meanings of specific flowers to provide a medium through which individuals (primarily, judging from the romantic overtones evident in works such as those by Charlotte de la Tour and Lady Mary Wortley Montagu, between persons engaged in courtships or love affairs) could conduct highly codified and therefore discreet exchanges that were, while not necessarily ambiguous, certainly inexplicit. Its system of signification—indirect and yet understandable, based, as it was, on a set of relationships that became, thanks to countless reference works published throughout the Victorian age, a kind of 'open secret'—relies upon recipients' abilities to decipher otherwise seemingly meaningless codes, much in the same way that the analyst records, rearranges and interprets the symptoms of the hysteric. The mysterious wallpaper beneath the titles, then, could be seen as an instance of the

---

3   Technologies of portrait photography in the nineteenth century required subjects to remain motionless for extended periods of time, most often in settings illuminated by strong daylight. Thus, subjects often appear uncomfortable, ill at ease; very few are shown smiling, the preferred pose for subjects of snapshots. Oh Hyeong-geun, the artist who created the poster design for the film, remarks in an interview included as part of the UK 'Asia Extreme' special edition DVD release, that he is fond of asking subjects to smile in preparation for being photographed, and then leaving them hanging for long periods of time in order to reach a moment at which comfort and happiness (however feigned) are transformed into irritation, anxiety and exasperation—thus forging an interesting representational link between past and present, Victorian and contemporary.

4   'The notion that a language of flowers existed in the Orient became known to Europe largely through the letters of Lady Mary Wortley Montagu from Turkey in the eighteenth century. Earlier travelers had referred to the use of flowers as "a mysterious language of love and gallantry ... to express the most tender and delicate of sentiments" ... But it was Lady Mary who brought it forcibly to people's attention in 1718' (Goody 1990: 2).

re-mystification of the very flowers that once held specific meanings—a breakdown of the terms of communication and a return to obscurity.

THE BEST OF EVERYTHING

The specific choice of wallpaper, John Henry Dearie's 'Blackthorn', originally produced for William Morris in 1892, represents yet another correlation between the action of the film and the Victorian era—an age, like that of late twentieth-century South Korea, of rapid modernisation, scientific and intellectual progress, and economic growth marked by a disparity in wealth made to seem even greater through the practice of conspicuous consumption (Veblen 1899), a phenomenon that cultural critics Jeongkoo Yoon and Hyeonho Seok (1996) see at work in modern-day Korea. As Barry Curtis notes:

> It was a feature of the grand houses that the income and investment that elaborated and embellished spaces and surfaces came from far away. The obscure places of the world were mined, harvested and exploited and traces or the source of wealth were displayed in eclectic patterns and ornaments. (Curtis 2008: 41)

Curtis adds that what transformed the 'grand house' from a symbol of financial privilege into something 'sinister' was the 'ways in which it drew in resources that were conspicuously lacking elsewhere' (both in the working-class homes of England and in the exploited colonies from which these exotic goods were appropriated)—a display of unconscionable greed that Beatrice and Sidney Webb found both 'oppressively unpleasant' and haunting (Curtis 2008: 41).[5]

Like the decorative elements that filled their homes, women, too, played a role in signifying a family's social standing: by denying the married woman the right to work outside the home (or, in some cases, even within the home)—a restriction that extended even to modes of dress, which hindered even basic movement, let alone any type of activity related to work—the patriarch of the bourgeois family displays the extent of his earning power (Veblen 1899: 341-2). With this in mind, parallels between Kim's film and Charlotte Perkins Gilman's 'The Yellow Wall-Paper' (1892), in which a young woman slowly loses her mind after being forced to 'rest' in a locked, upper-storey bedroom in a rented house, become startlingly apparent. Relieved of responsibilities and denied agency, the protagonist of Gilman's story, like those in other

---

5   Interestingly, it is the Victorian home that has become the preferred locus, in the popular imagination, for uncanny happenings and dark deeds, taking the place once held by the gothic castle, an earlier symbol of even more profound socio-economic privilege and the frequent setting for horror stories written during the Victorian era. See Lynch (2004) and Vidler (1994).

similar texts from the same time period—Oliphant's 'The Library Window' is another key example—personifies the mental and emotional crises of the Victorian woman who finds herself separated from intellectual stimulation or social interaction, isolated and abandoned with nothing but time on her hands, 'left alone with [her own] fears' (van Gorp 2008: 256).

SECRETS OF A SOUL

This web of intrigue opens, suitably enough, in a clinic, with a medium closeup shot of an old-fashioned white washbasin seen from above. A door slams from off camera, setting the water in the basin rippling, recalling the disturbance shown earlier in the title sequence and prefiguring, with its concentric circles, the narrative vortex into which the viewer will soon be pulled. A doctor in a white lab coat washes his hands in close-up and the image track cuts to an establishing shot of a stark examination room, furnished only with the washbasin and stand, two chairs and a small wooden desk. The doctor stands poised beside the basin and dries his hands on a towel that hangs on the chair in front of him. He glances toward the camera as the sound of a door opening repeats on the soundtrack. Although the two chairs are positioned directly under two corresponding windows, the symmetry of the shot is thrown off balance: the doctor and the washbasin form one half of the image, while the desk, windows and empty chairs form the other (unequal) half. The asymmetrical composition both suggests the unbalanced state of mind of the patient, and at the same time, sets up a dynamic in which the doctor, seen alone on the left-hand side of the screen, is separated from a space for *two* people (arguably, the two personalities that Su-mi has internalised: her own, and that of the evil stepmother). A nurse leads Su-mi (Im Soo-jeong), dressed in hospital pyjamas, into the room and helps her into the seat on the right-hand side of the screen. The doctor nods, signalling that the nurse is to leave, and he sits down, facing the patient. The image tracks then shifts, as the doctor is shown in medium close-up from the patient's point of view (her head and shoulder fill the lower right-hand portion of the screen). As the patient sits, motionless, the doctor begins asking questions. 'How was your day today? How was it?'

The doctor continues to stare fixedly at the patient as he lifts a tape recorder from the table and, as he turns it on, continues with his interrogation. 'Well, then, shall we talk?' He crosses his hands and leans forward in a move seen in countless other films. 'First tell me about yourself.' He pauses and then poses an enigmatic question: 'Who do you think you are?' When that gets no response, he produces a snapshot from a pile of papers on the desk and asks, 'Do you know who this is?' Although he makes no clear distinction as to which figure in the photograph that he wants the patient to identify, his index finger nearly obscures the face of Eun-joo. When the patient still fails to respond, he continues, 'Don't know? Hmm? It's your family.' He extends his hand, his finger still clearly placed on Eun-joo, and asks, 'Want to see it again?' His movement toward the patient is mirrored by the camera, which, static up to this point, begins to track forward. 'Fine, then. Can you tell me about that day?'

As the patient slowly begins to disappear off the right-hand side of the screen, the image track shifts from behind her to in front of her. However, unlike earlier shots of the doctor, which identified the point of view as the patient's by partially including her in the frame, the shot of Su-mi, presumably from the doctor's point of view, reduces the clinician to an arm in a white lab coat in the lower portion of the screen. 'What happened that day?' he asks again, as the camera continues the same forward-moving pattern as in the title sequence, but moving toward sunlight rather than shadow, perhaps suggesting, in visual terms, that the process of analysis will bring the shadowy secrets to light.

Again, there is a switch, as the interview is once more shown from the patient's point of view, the camera moving forward. 'You should be able to remember it clearly.' The camera draws nearer to the doctor, leaving behind any trace of the patient. 'It's okay ... Tell me what happened.' The camera switches positions one last time, continuing with its relentless forward motion, moving closer and closer to the patient, in so doing, mimicking the invasive clinical gaze, and prefiguring the move from external (reality) to internal (mental), from present to past (flashback) that is about to occur.

The association (never acknowledged, but clearly indicated by the doctor's placement of his index finger on Eun-joo's figure in the photo) between the question about the patient's identity ('Who do you think you are?') and the photographic image of the stepmother foreshadows the eventual revelation that Su-mi suffers from a post-traumatic dissociative identity disorder—a condition in which she incorporates the identity of Eun-joo, recast from nurse/mistress to the role of the wicked stepmother from the Korean folktale. The strangely archaic-looking clinical setting, the helpful doctor and the aphasic female patient, too, function as yet other links to the Victorian era, calling to mind the then-new science of psychoanalysis, which brought to light the gap between the inner (mental) and outer (everyday) life of the subject.

THE LOST MOMENT

In her study of the women's film of the 1940s, Mary Ann Doane (1987) discusses the opening sequence of Curtis Bernhardt's *Possessed* (US, 1947), which, focused as it is on the figure of a woman suffering from amnesia and aphasia, strongly resembles the one-sided clinical dialogue that opens *Two Sisters*. Louise Howell (Joan Crawford) is found wandering the streets of Los Angeles, and is taken to the psychiatric ward of a local hospital for observation. There, she is given a drug to help her recover her memories, and even more important, to induce her to recount the events that have led her to the state in which she finds herself at the film's outset. Unlike *Two Sisters,* though, the flashback that makes up the action of

Possessed is punctuated by voice-over narration provided by the female character herself. However, since the patient narrates while under the influence of psychotropic drugs, her narrative is halted, questioned, directed and analysed by the male doctors present at her examination. 'The woman's narrative', writes Doane, is 'held in check by recurrent withdrawals from her flashback account to the present tense of the doctor's diagnosis' (Doane 1987: 55). She goes on to add, 'Within the encompassing masculine medical discourse, the woman's language is granted a limited validity—it is, precisely, a point of view, and often a distorted and unbalanced one' (ibid).

In *Two Sisters,* the doctor disappears after the initial consultation and the film's narrative—a flashback—opens not over voice-over narration, but rather over musical accompaniment. Su-mi remains technically silent for most of the film; her few attempts to communicate with her father are met with disbelief. Her experiences are communicated to the spectator solely by virtue of her position as protagonist, not by way of spoken language, and thus, no opportunities for halting or redirecting her narration interrupt the story's unfolding. Indeed, the only other male figures (the individuals who, in Doane's formulation, might be able to 'rescue' the narrative and set it back on track) in the film are Moo-hyeon, the girls' emotionally distant father; Seon-gyoo, Eun-joo's younger brother, who appears in only two scenes; and Mr Jang, the gardener, who appears briefly in one shot at the opening of the film. Eun-joo's appearance in what appears to be a man's suit at the film's shocking *dénouement*—the moment at which the narrative is 'put right'—then, seems all the more significant, in that it reveals the extent to which Eun-joo, as both the father's trained assistant and as the father's mistress, is trusted and believed, while the girls and their mother (seen alternately as immature and hysterical) are not.

Yet one more aspect of the film that conforms to Doane's theories on the woman's film is that '[t]he illness of the woman is signaled by the fact that she no longer cares about her appearance' (1987: 41), as illustrated by Su-mi's ghastly appearance in the film's opening sequences. The work of the doctor, then, becomes a twofold project: the cure of the patient and the beautification of the patient. As Doane argues, 'The narratives thus trace a movement from the medical gaze to the erotic gaze in relation to the central female figure, activating a process of despecularization/respecularization' (1987: 41). Again, this is clearly the case in Kim's film, as the first shot we have of the 'healthy' or 'cured' Su-mi, arriving home from a hospital stay, is a somewhat fetishistic shot of her legs (a representational tactic notably repeated several times throughout the film) as she slides out of the back seat of her father's car.

This sudden transformation from patient to object stands in for a more significant shift that underscores the central psychic conflict between daughter and stepmother: Su-mi has matured from child to adult. This development serves to destabilise already volatile family relations, and provides the impetus for what will be the final confrontation between Su-mi's two competing identities ([step]mother and daughter)—a battle that is at the heart of the classical melodrama. As Geoffrey Nowell-Smith notes, 'the Hollywood melodrama is ... fundamentally concerned with the child's problem of growing into sexuality within the family, under the aegis of a symbolic law that the Father incarnates' (1987: 271).

Like the women's film shaped around 'the medical discourse' (Doane 1987: 38), *A Tale of Two Sisters* commences with a doctor's command that a young female patient speak—that she narrate for him the details of her illness, from its origins to the (diegetic) present. These events, given that they form the focus of the clinical analysis that opens the film, are clearly then aligned with the narrative enigma or disturbance that will drive the film to its ultimate conclusion. The 'work' of the film becomes a work of analysis, albeit an analysis in which, as Doane indicates, speech is replaced by spectacle, in which

> the 'talking cure' is translated into the terms of vision. The flashback structure is the means by which the character is depicted as apprehending his or her past ... In this mise-en-scene of memory, a matching between self and scene is accomplished and that matching generally marks the completion of the narrative. (Doane 1987: 47)

Following this logic, in *Two Sisters,* once the events of 'that day' are revealed via flashback, order should be re-established. However, despite the fact that the origin of the character's illness is revealed, its disclosure does not bring a full resolution. Rather than re-establish order (by clearly defining the difference between fantasy and reality, between pathology and wellness), this final collection of images serves to complicate further the already convoluted story that precedes it.

The series of flashbacks that set the film's final explanatory movement into motion begin immediately following the revelation that the conflicts between Su-mi and Eun-joo have all taken place in Su-mi's mind—that they have been Su-mi's own struggles with her memories and guilt. As the camera moves forward, towards Su-mi's face (from Eun-joo's point of view), and the music builds on the soundtrack, the film cuts back and forth from close-ups of Su-mi in the present to several key moments from the storyline. The film presents in explicit terms what it has hinted at in various ways throughout its running time: that Su-mi and her father have been alone in the house since her return from the hospital. With Su-mi's illness clearly established (her psychosis has taken the form of the classic Korean folktale, transforming herself, her sister and her father's mistress into the archetypal characters of victim-children and evil stepmother), the spectator is left with at least some doubts as to the validity of her claims regarding Eun-joo's mistreatment. Su-mi's father hands her two tablets of a presumably anti-psychotic drug. The image track cuts from a medium close-up of the tablets in Su-mi's hand, to an overhead shot as she pops them into her mouth. The green glass pill bottle rolls away, and the image fades to black, bringing to a close, in one economical set of images, the film's 'psychotic' passages and placing the sequences that follow clearly in the realm of diegetic reality.

But whereas *Possessed* follows up the revelation of its protagonist's guilt (and by extension, hopeless psychosis) with the intervention of a doctor who offers to work tirelessly on curing poor, lost Louise, *Two Sisters* continues to unravel and reveal more and more material, making its 'resolution' more obscure, less certain. In the sequence that follows the fade to black, Eun-joo is shown seated in the waiting room at the hospital. As a hospital staff member and Su-mi's father discuss her case, they look at Eun-joo. The forward tracking motion of the camera (closing in on Eun-joo) creates a visual suggestion that the doctor seems to believe Su-mi's claims—or at least that Eun-joo seems to think that they are talking about her in a negative way. The image cuts from Eun-joo in medium close-up to a medium shot (from behind) of Su-mi, once again equating the two women. Eun-joo (shown from shoulders to knees) walks into the room and sits next to Su-mi. A tense exchange follows, in which Eun-joo feigns concern for a seemingly unresponsive Su-mi, who stares into the distance. When Eun-joo stands to leave, Su-mi grabs her wrist, still staring straight ahead. Her verbal claims of abuse, long ignored, become a physical action that suggests a refusal to 'let Eun-joo go' unpunished.

Eun-joo and Moo-hyeon are then shown driving home together in the car. The image track cuts back to Su-mi, in close-up, who recalls the events of the day about which the doctor in the opening sequence has interrogated her. A cut from Su-mi's face to a pair of feet swinging in the air punctuates the shift from present to past, as the film slips into a final spiral into pathos: the sisters and their mother watch helplessly as the father brings his nurse/mistress into the home for a family dinner with her brother and his fiancée. For a moment, the father is shown, slightly out of focus and in the distance, trapped between the figures of the two girls, whose earlier expressions of shock and disdain seem to have provoked in him at least a slight reaction of guilt and discomfort. The sisters are shown in medium close-up again, with Su-mi looking on helplessly as Su-yeon seems on the verge of tears. Here, once again, the image track cuts back to the diegetic present as a pensive Eun-joo is shown seated alone in darkened dining room where two earlier confrontations have taken place, but now, rather than warm reds and deep burgundies, the room is lit almost entirely in cold blues. The once seemingly colourful Blackthorn wallpaper shown in the opening credits now provides a greenish-grey background to the action, imbued once again, as it was in the title sequence, with an aura of uncanniness.

Evidently triggered by Eun-joo's own memory, the film cross-cuts once again, taking the viewer back to the earlier family dinner. Su-mi slams her spoon angrily down on to the table and storms away, leaving a confused-looking Su-yeon to face Eun-joo's wrath. Eun-joo rips the spoon from Su-yeon's hand, effectively denying the child the very food she needs to survive (a classic melodramatic action), and the girl marches dutifully into the kitchen to throw her uneaten *juk* into the sink. As the mournful strains of the score rise on the soundtrack, Su-yeon walks into her bedroom and falls face down on to the bed in tears.[6] Her mother, weakened by illness and neglect, does her best to comfort the girl.

The film cuts back to the hospital and Su-mi is shown seated, from behind, as the sound of whistling is heard on the track. 'Su-yeon,' Su-mi says, as she turns toward the sound, and smiles. The whistling continues, bridging a cut from Su-mi to Eun-joo, who once again appears seated in the dining room, her hands covering her face (perhaps in shame at the recollection of her brutal mistreatment of the girls). She, too, hears the sound of whistling and goes to investigate. Eun-joo enters Soo-yeon's room and turns on the light. There, she is surrounded by a veritable riot of roses on the wallpaper and on the curtains. An audience of dolls of different shapes and sizes sits on the bench next to the window. The lights go out, the door slams shut, and Eun-joo approaches the wardrobe that has played such a prevalent role in the film thus far. She sees a tab of fabric sticking out from the folded bedding stored there and pulls on it, bringing with it what is evidently the malevolent spirit of either the mother, the younger sister, or both. As Eun-joo backs away, the dolls staring silently behind her, her mouth opens wide and the sound of the spirit fills the air. As the image track cuts to a long shot of the house from outside, we hear Eun-joo's scream fade into the night as the camera pulls away from the house and into the darkness.

Still in the present, the film cuts once more to the hospital, where Su-mi is shown lying in bed, a tear falling as she closes her eyes and says (to herself) her sister's name. The image fades to white, and returns to Su-yeon crying on the bed in her room, where she has evidently fallen asleep. As she sits up and looks toward the wardrobe, one of its doors swings open. Perplexed, Su-yeon approaches the wardrobe and discovers her mother has committed suicide and now hangs next to an emerald green *hanbok* (Korean traditional clothing).[7] The girl tries desperately to free her mother, and inadvertently pulls the wardrobe over on to herself, mortally injuring herself in the process. Here the film stops for a moment to record the reactions of Eun-joo and her brother's girlfriend, Moo-hyeon and Eun-joo's brother, and finally Su-mi, as they all turn toward the sound of the crash. A sideways tracking shot unites the reactions of Eun-joo, Su-mi and Moo-hyeon in a single motion, equating their responses and creating what, it

---

6   As I have noted in my work on the use of pop music in Korean television drama (Cagle 2013), the important (indeed, defining) role played by music has, in recent years, been undervalued, if not overlooked entirely in studies of the melodrama. The haunting score written for Kim's film by noted Korean musician and composer Lee Byeong-woo stands out as one of the best examples of how music (repetitions, variations and so on) both create a sense of cohesiveness in the work, and at the same time, inform spectatorial responses to it.

7   Su-yeon wears the *hanbok* in a photograph that falls to the ground and breaks in this sequence, and the ghost of the 'girl under the sink' wears it in the earlier 'dinner party' sequence in the film. The green dress is an explicit reference to a similar item of clothing worn by one of the sisters' ghosts in many versions of the folktale.

could be argued, functions much in the same way that the tableau does in the classical stage melodrama. Brooks (1995: 48–9; 56–7) sees these instances of action stilled as a key part of the stage melodrama, given that these moments place the moral nature of each of the play's characters into stark relief, revealing formerly hidden 'truths' about each, and allowing the spectator the opportunity to pause and reflect.

Eun-joo hurries up the stairs and discovers Su-yeon crushed under the wardrobe, but still alive. Driven either by hatred or by shock, Eun-joo backs out of the room. As she turns to go back in (and presumably save the girl), she encounters Su-mi, who has emerged from her bedroom. Su-mi insults the woman, accusing her of trying to take their mother's place. In one of the most significant and moving moments in the film, Eun-joo admonishes the young woman to speak and act with greater care, as 'one day you may regret this.' Su-mi spits a contemptuous response back at the older woman and runs down the stairs, fleeing the house that is no longer her home, and unaware of the consequences her actions have on her sister's fate. She stops mid-flight and turns to look behind her, catching a glimpse of Eun-joo standing in a balcony doorway and staring coldly out at her. As their gazes meet, Eun-joo snaps the shuttered doors closed, effectively shutting off Su-mi's last point of access to her home and everything in it, and signifying the separation from past and present, 'before' and 'after'. The camera dizzyingly circles the figure of the young woman standing alone in a field of tall grass as music swells on the track and the flow of images comes to a halt. The final image of Su-mi in the field fades from colour to black and white as the camera zooms in closer and closer to the now still photograph. Like the poster image, this shot of Su-mi takes on the symbolic value of a memorial image—a representation of the last moment of Su-mi's life before she condemns herself to an existence of maddened, self-inflicted punishment. A monochromatic image of the young woman seated on a pier replaces this still, repeating one of the first shots of the film, and colour and movement are restored once again, a little at a time. Su-mi looks to her right and the image freezes as the end credits roll.

Although the narrative significance of this series of shots is in its original context quite clear (it serves as an explanatory epilogue to a labyrinthine storyline, and translates the stepmother's earlier admonition to the girl—'One day you may regret this'—into terrifyingly literal terms), the overall effect of this final sequence extends far beyond mere exposition; as a moment of resolution, the sequence is imperfect, marred by the nagging presence of a memory trace, symbolised by the empty space to the right of the young woman in the final shot. Again, like the post-mortem photograph, this final image becomes a material representation of loss of and longing for innocence—a melancholic meditation that might equally stand in for the Victorian sensibility, the hysteric, and the melodramatic mode: a young woman, haunted by recollections, endlessly repeats a series of traumatic events, evidently with the hope of some day finding peace.

BIBLIOGRAPHY

Bernheimer, Charles and Claire Kahane (eds) (1985), *In Dora's Case: Freud, Hysteria, Feminism,* New York: Columbia University Press.

Bown, Nicola (2009), 'Empty Hands and Precious Pictures: Post-Mortem Portrait Photographs of Children', *Australasian Journal of Victorian Studies,* 14: 2, pp. 8–24.

Brooks, Peter (1995 [1976]), *The Melodramatic Imagination: Balzac, Henry James, Melodrama, and the Mode of Excess,* New Haven, CT: Yale University Press.

Cagle, Robert L. (2013), 'Don't Forget: The Musical Dimensions of South Korean Television Drama', in J. Kim (ed.), *Reading Asian Television Drama: Crossing Borders and Breaking Boundaries,* London: I. B. Tauris, forthcoming.

Cho, Insoo (2008), '*Midnight Rendezvous:* Ardent Love and Heartache of Separation', *Koreana,* 22: 3, pp. 50–3.

Curtis, Barry (2008), *Dark Places: The Haunted House in Film,* London: Reaktion.

de la Tour, Charlotte (1819), *Le Langage des fleurs,* Paris: Audot.

Doane, Mary Ann (1987), *The Desire to Desire: The Woman's Film of the 1940s,* Bloomington: Indiana University Press.

Elley, Derek (2003), 'A Tale of Two Sisters', *Variety,* 391:8, p. 24.

Freud, Sigmund with Josef Breuer (1955 [1893]), 'On the Psychical Mechanism of Hysterical Phenomena', in J. Strachey (ed. and trans.), *The Standard Edition of the Complete Psychological Works of Sigmund Freud, Volume II (1893–1895): Studies on Hysteria,* London: Hogarth, pp. 1–240.

Gilman, Charlotte Perkins (1892), 'The Yellow Wall-Paper', *New England Magazine,* 11: 5, January, pp. 647–57.

Gledhill, Christine (1987), 'The Melodramatic Field: An Investigation', in C. Gledhill (ed.), *Home Is Where the Heart Is: Studies in Melodrama and the Woman's Film,* London: BFI, pp. 5–39.

Goody, Jack (1990), 'The Secret Language of Flowers', *Yale Journal of Criticism: Interpretation in the Humanities,* 3: 2, pp. 133–52.

Ha, Tae Hung (1958), *Folk Tales of Old Korea,* Seoul: Korea Information Service.

Hustvedt, Asti (2011), *Medical Muses: Hysteria in Nineteenth-Century Paris,* New York: W. W. Norton.

Kim, Mee-hyun (ed.) (2007), *Korean Cinema from Origins to Renaissance,* Seoul: CommBooks.

Lee, Hyangjin (2000), *Contemporary Korean Cinema: Identity, Culture, and Politics,* Manchester: Manchester University Press.

Lee, Young-il and Choe Young-chol (1998), *The History of Korean Cinema: Korean Studies Series No. 12,* trans. R. Greever, Seoul: Jimoondang.

Lim, Bliss Cua (2009), *Translating Time: Cinema, the Fantastic and Temporal Critique,* Durham, NC: Duke University Press.

Lynch, Eve (2004), 'Spectral Politics: The Victorian Ghost Story and the Domestic Servant', in N. Bown et al. (eds), *The Victorian Supernatural,* Cambridge: Cambridge University Press, pp. 87–108.

Nowell-Smith, Geoffrey (1987 [1977]), 'Minnelli and Melodrama', in C. Gledhill (ed.), *Home Is Where the Heart Is: Studies in Melodrama and the Woman's Film,* London: BFI, pp. 70–4.

Oliphant, Margaret (1896), 'The Library Window', *Blackwood's Edinburgh Magazine,* 159, January, pp. 1–30.

Rousseau, G. S. (1993), '"A Strange Pathology": Hysteria in the Early Modern World, 1500–1800', in S. L. Gilman et al., *Hysteria Beyond Freud,* Berkeley: University of California Press, pp. 91–224.

Seaton, Beverly (1995), *The Language of Flowers: A History,* Charlottesville: University Press of Virginia.

van Gorp, Hendrik (2008), 'The Gothic Novel as a Romantic Narrative Genre', in G. Gillespie et al. (eds), *Romantic Prose Fiction,* Philadelphia: John Benjamins, pp. 249–61.

Veblen, Thorstein (1912 [1899]), *The Theory of the Leisure Class: An Economic Study of Institutions,* New York: Macmillan.

Vidler, Anthony (1994), *The Architectural Uncanny: Essays in the Modern Unhomely,* Cambridge, MA: MIT Press.

Williams, Linda Ruth (2004), 'A Tale of Two Sisters', *Sight and Sound,* 14:9, p. 85.

Yoon, Jeongkoo and Hyeonho Seok (1996), 'Conspicuous Consumption and Social Status in Korea: An Assessment of Reciprocal Effects', *Korea Journal of Population and Development,* 25: 2, pp. 333–54.

Zŏng In-sŏb (1952), *Folk Tales from Korea,* Westport, CT: Greenwood.

Figure Credits

Fig. 2.6.1: Source: https://commons.wikimedia.org/wiki/File:Na_Woon-gyu.jpg.

Fig. 2.6.2: Source: https://commons.wikimedia.org/wiki/File:Imjaeobtneun_naleutbae.jpg.

POST-READING QUESTIONS/POST-SCREENING QUESTIONS

Directions: Use what you learned from reading this chapter and watching the film to respond to the questions.

1. What is the history of Korea and Japan from 1910 up until the end of WWII? How did this history impact the production of Korean horror films?

2. Describe the *wonhon* and pinpoint a scene where this spirit is prominently represented in the film.

3. Why do you think *A Tale of Two Sisters* was able to appeal to many different global audiences?

4. Can you connect this film to other horror films about mental illness that we have examined in this book?

Situating the Arab Horror Film

From Djinns to Existential Horror

By Samirah Alkassim

KEY TERMS AND FIGURES

Middle East

Colonialism

Nahda

Independence

Postcolonialism

Globalization

Orientalism

Djinn

Social realism

RECOMMENDED FILMS

Anyab [Fangs] by Mohamed Shebl (1981)

Blind Sun by Joyce Nashawati (2015)

Bloodline by Rami Yasin (2020)

Al Fil al-Azraq 2 [Blue Elephant 2] by Marwan Hamed (2019)

Bab al Hadid [Cairo Station] by Yousef Chahine (1959)

Kandisha by Jerome Cohen-Olivar (2008)

Kindil al-Bahr by Damien Ounouri (2016)

Situating the Arab Horror Film

From Djinns to Existential Horror

By Samirah Alkassim

INTRODUCTION

Situating the Arab horror film involves at the outset a series of acknowledgements. The cultural diversity and geographic scope of the 22 countries spanning the Asian and African continents—united under the designation of the "Arab world" despite the diversity of ethnicity, dialect, and custom—signals that Arab identity is far from monolithic. Further complicating this is the containment of these countries within the larger geographic determination of the Middle East and North Africa (MENA), in which the Arab countries are joined by the non-Arab countries of Turkey, Iran, and Israel.[1] Sorting through these categories confronts us with their constructed nature and late nineteenth-century/early twentieth-century origins, mapped by European colonial powers in their effort to contain and limit the possible development of nationalist movements in the region.[2] The history that follows is a tumultuous procession of colonialism, national liberation struggles, neo-colonialism, wars, and globalization that extends to the early twenty-first century.

Bearing in mind such complexity, this chapter examines a few select horror films produced in the twentieth and twenty-first centuries that bear the signature of Arab horror cinema. Such a signature emerges at the intersection of established horror film codes and their adaptations, with authentic cultural codes and lore (from pre-Islamic folklore of djinn and ghouls to urban legends, and real stories of serial killers), and specific developments of modernity in the

---

1   Additionally, this region is sometimes referred to as MENASA to acknowledge both the transregional histories and connections between the Middle East and South Asia, as well as the significant populations of South Asian people living and working in the Middle East.

2   This was a project similar to the 1884–85 Berlin Conference in which European powers determined the borders of African countries, irrespective of indigenous languages, kinship ties, and cultural formations; Lizbeth Malkmus and Roy Armes, *Arab and African Film Making* (London: Zed Books, 1991).

Arab national context. It is clear when surveying recent films from the MENA countries that canonical and mostly Western horror films have left their mark in a collection of references: Moroccan film *Achoura* bears some narrative resemblance to *It; the* Emirati/American film *Djinn* mixes narrative elements and horrific affects from *Rosemary's Baby, The Shining,* and *Ringu; the* Egyptian film *Blue Elephant 2* uses a compilation of references to demonic possession that trace back to *The Exorcist* and the *Supernatural* tv series. These resemblances and references show how culture flows in unexpected ways beyond borders and corporate police as filmmakers/producers attempt to tap into global audiences, who obtain their media from a variety of sources: movie theatres, DVDs (often pirated), and, increasingly, streaming platforms such as Netflix and Shahid.

Horror, in the Arab context, is defined by everyday encounters with crushing poverty, police brutality, international economic influence of a vampiric nature, and authoritarian regimes with their institutional instruments, against the "backdrop" of decades of violence and war, in which external powers are deeply vested. Here the horror imaginary is a palimpsest: the everyday encounter is one layer concealing multiple layers of trauma and its traces that are passed down from generation to generation.

In the context of Arab cinema, we often see the confluence of social realism and horror that speaks to a collective imagination shaped by the legacies of empire, colonialism, and globalization. For example, the 2015 Jordanian film *Theeb* by Naji Abu Nowar is on the surface a "brutal coming of age story"[3] of a Bedouin boy set on the eve of the dissolution of the Ottoman Empire and the ascendancy of the British mandate in Jordan and Palestine. But the suspense and the uncannily triggered memory of David Lean's orientalizing *Lawrence of Arabia,* set in the same desert landscape and general period, delivers an existential tale of survival that relies on referencing memories and transmission of colonialism's shadow.

It is less significant to identify *when* horror film in its recognizable generic form arrived in the region because it seems only logical that horror would have its indigenous form—and more compelling to focus on various manifestations that demonstrate, as in the example of *Theeb,* the hybridity of the genre, while reflecting specific and universal concerns. While the "late arrival" of the horror genre in the Arab and North African countries has been attributed to the lack of high budgets and animation teams and the influence of Islamic clericism, the history of global horror film reveals the opposite, that it is often the low-budget, marginal, and genre-breaking film that becomes a cult classic and commands the attention of rigorous horror film scholarship. The examination of this chapter carries forward in this spirit, highlighting an emerging genre that is thriving in twenty-first century regional and global media platforms. Key to the development of the horror genre in this context is the processing of collective trauma

---

3   Stephen Holden, "Review: In 'Theeb,' a Bedouin Boy's Brutal Coming of Age," *New York Times*, November 5, 2011, https://www.nytimes.com/2015/11/06/movies/review-in-theeb-a-bedouin-boys-brutal-coming-of-age.html.

through bodily viscerality and psychological disturbance, hence the emphasis on supernatural, psychological, and existential horror in the case studies that follow.

BUT FIRST, SOME HISTORY

The Arab part of the MENA region, known as the Arab East or Mashreq, and the Arab West or Maghreb, is comprised of countries whose borders were drawn by nineteenth-century European powers (namely British and French with the support of the US) and enforced through a series of agreements (Sykes Picot of 1916,[4] Balfour Declaration of 1917[5]) in the post-WWI project of partitioning the dissolving Ottoman Empire (1918–22) and redistributing territories to benefit their strategic interests. A significant factor in the equation that would gain value over time was the discovery of oil in Iran in 1908,[6] followed by its discovery in Bahrain in 1931, Kuwait in 1938, and a few weeks later in Saudi Arabia.[7]

Ironically, these colonial powers brought new forms of media that would become instrumental in the development of the future independent nation-states: In 1798 the Napoleon campaign in Egypt, soon after its invasion, established two daily newspapers, the *Courier de l'Egypt* and *La Decade Egyptienne*, that preceded the first daily newspaper, the *Daily Mail*, to appear in Europe in 1896.[8] In 1827–1828 the first official Arabic language journals operated in Egypt under the Ottoman ruler Muhammad Ali Pasha, whose interest, shared by his son Ibrahim Pasha, was to modernize Egypt, although, like his successors, he prioritized technological modernity over intellectual modernity.[9] This period, starting under Muhammad Ali and extending until the early twentieth century, is called the *nahda* (or the Arab project of enlightenment), which brought about a cultural renaissance in the Arab world, and like its fourteenth-century European counterpart, primarily sustained existing class divisions and the authority of the state.[10] It did, however, usher in the birth of the Arabic novel and set the foundations for the twentieth-century Arab nationalist movement in which Egypt played a leading role. From 1919 onward, Egyptian nationalism and literary output grew, which mixed certain aspects of Western thought with

4   "Sykes–Picot Agreement," Britannica, https://www.britannica.com/event/Sykes-Picot-Agreement.

5   "Balfour Declaration," Britannica, https://www.britannica.com/event/Balfour-Declaration.

6   Sarah Kent, "A Brief History of the Iranian Oil Industry," *Wall Street Journal*, April 3, 2015, https://www.wsj.com/articles/a-brief-history-of-the-iranian-oil-industry-1428063016.

7   Terri Ginsberg and Chris Lippard, *Historical Dictionary of Middle Eastern Cinema*, 2nd ed. (Maryland: Rowman & Littlefield, 2020).

8   Malkmus and Armes, *Arab and African Film Making*, 7.

9   Faisal Darraj, "The Peculiar Destinies of Arab Modernity, Arab Art Histories: The Khalid Shoman Collection, 2013, translated by Anna Swank," https://daratalfunun.org/?page_id=298.

10   See Tarek Al-Ariss's overview of Arab modernity in the introduction to his book *Trials of Arab Modernity: Literary Affects and the New Political* (New York: Fordham University Press, 2013).

more traditional cultural forms, a synthesis most clearly expressed in the novels and short stories that proliferated in the 1940s and 50s.[11]

During the early twentieth century, the linguistic diversity of the Arab countries of the MENA region was somewhat unified through the spread of media technologies from Egypt, such as the gramophone by the 1930s,[12] the radio, and cinema. The post-WWII consumer boom up to the 1950s further enhanced the spread of records, and radio quickly became the media instrument of nation-state building that facilitated the spread of pan-Arabism from the eastern Mashreq countries of the Levant to the western Maghreb countries of North Africa.[13] This solidified Cairo's position as the center of the Arab world, at the critical moment when the other Arab countries were emerging from colonialism and claiming their independence: Lebanon and Syria gaining independence from France, respectively, in 1943 and 1944, Jordan from Britain in 1946, Egypt from Britain in 1950, Libya from Britain 1951, Morocco from France in 1952, Tunisia from France in 1956, and Algeria from France in 1962 (after the Algerian war of independence that raged from 1954–1962).

Although there are different ethnic minorities (Kurds, Armenians, and Amazigh/Berbers, among others) and religious minorities (Christians, Jews, Baha'i, Hindus), the dominant culture is Arab/Muslim. Although "Arab" came to mean more than ethnic designation through the *nahda* and the Arab nationalist movement of the 50s and 60s, ethnic groups currently challenge the monolithic designation (particularly among the Kurdish people of Syria and Amazigh groups in North Africa). What still binds these people is the common official language of classical Arabic (despite the many different dialects), a history of colonization by European countries from the late eighteenth to twentieth centuries, and the majority religion of Islam. At the center of these developments, from the mid-twentieth century to the present moment, stands the violent transformation of Palestine into Israel in 1947–49,[14] which symbolized the erasure of a people decided by external, non-sovereign states who happened to be former colonizers (British, French).[15] Facilitated by European powers, the establishment of Israel resulted in myriad political problems within and between countries in the region that persist to this day, including the uncertain status of descendants of the roughly seven hundred twenty thousand Palestinian refugees who constituted 80 percent of the indigenous population of pre-Israel Palestine.

---

11   Malkmus and Armes, *Arab and African Film Making*, 27.

12   Ibid., 9–10.

13   Ibid., 11.

14   Rashid Khalidi, *The 100 Years War on Palestine* (New York: Macmillan, 2020), 58.

15   After more than half of a century of waves of Jewish immigrants from Europe to Palestine fleeing persecution and the post-WWII influx of Holocaust survivors, the transformation of Palestine into Israel in 1947–49 was a traumatic experience for the Palestinians, who became refugees forced into neighboring countries. See Khalidi's *The 100 Years War on Palestine* and Illan Pappe's *The Ethnic Cleansing of Palestine* (Oxford: One World Oxford: 2006).

Egypt was and remains at the epicenter of these developments, and film/media have been the screens on which national, regional, and global politics have been projected. Egypt was also the first country in the region to develop a major film industry by the mid 1930s (on the initiative of economist Talat Harb who also founded the first Egyptian bank), even while under the unofficial British occupation that ended by 1950. It was not until independence was obtained from the colonial powers (from the 1950s and onward) that significant developments occurred in the shaping of national cinemas, namely Egyptian, Algerian, Lebanese, Syrian, and more recently Tunisian and Moroccan.[16] In these post-independence cinemas, the most prevalent genres were the melodrama, musical, epic, comedy, and crime drama, which privileged realism over fantasy and allegorized the dramas of the postcolonial nation through individual struggles of ordinary protagonists. While there was some mimicking of generic elements of Hollywood films, it was always mixed with authentic representational strategies and tropes. This tendency toward syncretism is further evidence of how Arab modernity did not simply develop in the encounter with the West and/or Western colonialism but also in response to authentic modes of thought (scientific, religious, and cultural) that were specific to the Arab world and Arab-Islamic history.[17]

The discoveries of oil in Saudi Arabia and the Gulf countries brought not only wealth, foreign investments, and skilled expatriate labor, but also an interest in the production of Arab media, which took different forms, most notably as investment in media production and later filmmaking through ventures funded by the 1981 formed Gulf Corporation Council (GCC) (composed of Bahrain, Kuwait, Oman, Qatar, Saudi Arabia, and the United Arab Emirates)[18] for which the Saudi-owned media conglomerate Middle East Broadcasting Corporation (MBC) is one example.[19] Egypt's "golden age" ended in 1952 or 1967 (depending on the scholar), but its film industry continued to produce on average fifty films per year into the 1980s,[20] and its annual output still exceeds that of the other Arab countries. Its domination over other films in the region, however, began to change with the advent of Arab satellite networks in the 1990s, the accessibility of the internet from the early 2000s, and the increasing availability of video-on-demand streaming platforms like the MBC-owned Shahid and regional branch offices of Netflix. This in turn has allowed for some expansion of genres and particularly that of horror.

---

16   Malkmus and Armes, *Arab and African Film Making*; Viola Shafik, *Arab Cinema: History and Cultural Identity* (Cairo: American University Press, 1998).

17   Faisal Daraj discusses the gap between the ideas of the intellectual class and those of the "masses" who were largely illiterate, despite the attempts during of Gamal Abdel Nasser to implement socialist reforms in the 1960s that would enhance social equity and access to education in Egypt. See "The Peculiar Destinies of Arab Modernity."

18   Iraq's discovery of oil happened in 1923, and by 2008 it was estimated to have the second largest supply after Saudi Arabia, but it is not a member of the GCC.

19   Mohammed Akhereiji, "MBC Media Group Moves to Riyadh as Saudi Arabia Seeks to 'Reinvent Itself,'" *The Arab Weekly*, February 16, 2020, https://thearabweekly.com/mbc-media-group-moves-riyadh-saudi-arabia-seeks-reinvent-itself.

20   Malkmus and Armes, *Arab and African Film Making*, 31.

A GENRE OF "FIRSTS"

In 2005, film scholar Viola Shafik described the horror genre as nonexistent in Egypt prior to the 1980s and very minimal thereafter. She attributed this to a combination of social conservatism influenced by the Arabian Gulf markets, and local Egyptian tastes among the middle class who, she claims, preferred melodramas, crime dramas, and musicals.[21] But a close examination of Egyptian cinema tells a different story, for if we consider some of the social realist films of Salah Abu Seif (who directed the 1953 *Raya and Sakina* about real-life serial killer sisters), Yousef Chahine's 1959 masterpiece *Bab al-Hadid (Cairo Station),* (about a psychologically unstable man who murders a woman), or the psychological thrillers of Kamal El-Sheikh, considered the "Egyptian Hitchcock" (*Life or Death; Last Night; Time Conqueror*), we see that horror was there at least from the 1950s. This returns us to the role of horror in expressing taboos, exploring mental instability, and entertaining audiences by inciting feelings of dread through a process of signification that is safely and clearly removed from daily life. The "first" Arab horror film may indeed have been the 1945 Egyptian film *Safir al Guhanam (Ambassador of Hell)* directed by theatre and film star Yousef Wahbi, "a classic Faustian tale about the devil showing up on a poor man's doorstep and offering him a million pounds in exchange for his soul."[22] It carries forth Arab horror's signature mixture of derivation and authenticity by combining generic elements from comedy, melodrama, and horror with influences from German expressionism found in the low camera angles, high-contrast lighting, and use of cobwebs that, according to film critic Hazem Fahmy, "emphasize the hideousness of the devil as he seduces *Abdel Khalak* and his family in their sleep."[23]

Bab al-Hadid, Yousef Chahine's 1959 film, can be considered the first Arab slasher film, although there is no gore and most of the physical violence is offscreen. The mixing of genres (melodrama, comedy, psychological horror, social realism) with the stylistic elements of Italian neorealism and French New Wave criticism[24] exemplify again Egyptian cinema's tendency to mix different cinematic styles with authentic Egyptian sensibilities. Chahine plays the main character of Qinawi, a crippled newspaper seller in Cairo's huge train station hopelessly in love with the bodacious drink seller Hannouma (played by Hind Rostum, the Brigette Bardot of Egyptian cinema). She, however, is betrothed to the virile porter Abu Sri, who is trying to unionize the other porters in the station. Upon witnessing them having sex, in an unprecedently suggestive offscreen scene, Qinawi decides to murder her (but kills another woman instead), after which he is apprehended and taken to a mental asylum. As with Chahine's previous film,

---

21   Viola Shafik, "Egypt: A Cinema without Horror?" In *Horror International*, edited by Steven Jay Schneider and Tony Williams, 273–289 (Detroit, MI: Wayne State Press, 2005).

22   Hazem Fahmy, "[Nightmares On The Nile] Ambassador Of Hell And The Horror Of Seduction," Nov 16, 2020, https://nofspodcast.com/nightmares-on-the-nile-ambassador-of-hell-and-the-horror-of-seduction.

23   Ibid.

24   Malek Khouri, *The Arab Nationalist Project in Youssef Chahine's Cinema* (Cairo: AUC Press, 2010), 28.

Baba Amin, Bab al-Hadid inhabits the world of marginalized people, focusing on the popular class at the moment when Gamal Abdel Nasser, already an anti-colonial icon by the late 1950s, was implementing reforms to lift the Egyptian people out of poverty. At the heart of the film's horror, according to Malkmus and Armes, is the disintegration of Qinawi's world view into a split subjectivity with which we spectators have uncannily become aligned, and this is what perhaps constitutes the most unsettling effect of the film.[25]

A scan of recent film festivals reveals that horror films have increased in number in the Arab world, and as of 2020 there is a film festival in Beirut, Lebanon, *Maskoon* (meaning "haunted" in Arabic), dedicated to programming horror and science fiction genres.[26] Could this be because the region, particularly post-9/11, is felt to be "dystopian to its core," as Antoine Waked suggests?[27] Might Arab horror film be an expression of Arab cultural postmodernity, even though the consensus is that Arab modernity is an "unfinished project"?[28] There are many factors pertaining to social, systemic and external threats that have afflicted the region since at least the Ottoman period, which constitute a legacy of remembered horrors passed down through the generations , but the younger generation born from the 1990s onward inherited a world greatly marked by violence and war, particularly the post-9/11 American war on terror, the Gulf War of 2003, and the fallout from the Arab Uprisings that began in 2011.[29] From these "already traumatized socio-cultural and historic" contexts,[30] what is imagined as horrifying is figured in the following tropes of unraveling and representational strategies that are specific to Arab horror: the dissolution of the family unit through the demonic possession (*Achoura*; *Al Fil al-Azraq* or *Blue Elephant 1* and *2*); the struggle to overcome crushing poverty and corrupt institutions (*122*; *Mirages*); the effects of state-sanctioned violence against women (*Kindil al-Bahr*; *Kandisha*); and the experience of xenophobia for the refugee fleeing war (*Blind Sun*).

For Egyptian horror, the most prevalent tendencies are psychological horror films, which occasionally dip into supernatural horror, from the films of Kamal El-Sheikh, to the more recent *122* and *Blue Elephant* series. *122,* directed by Yasir Al-Yasiri, centers on a working-class couple whose plan to surmount their grim financial situation via one last drug run is thwarted by

---

25   Malkmus and Armes, *Arab and African Film Making*, 117.

26   Nick Vivarelli, "Arab Genre Films Get Boost from Beirut's Maskoon Lab (Exclusive)," *Variety*, September 23, 2019, https://variety.com/2019/film/news/arab-genre-films-production-boost-beirut-maskoon-lab-1203340300/.

27   Antoine Waked, "Old World, New Horror," *Fangoria* 2, no. 11 (April 2021): 14–17.

28   Khouri, *The Arab Nationalist Project in Youssef Chahine's Cinema*.

29   These include the results of the 1967 six-day war in which Israel took the Sinai in Egypt, the Golan Heights in Syria, and the West Bank in Jordan; the Lebanese civil war from 1975–1991; the three Gulf Wars of 1980–1988 (between Iraq and Iran), 1991, and 2003; the violence of states against protestors in the Arab Uprisings/Springs of 2010–2011 (most prominently in Tunisia, Egypt, Syria, Yemen, and Libya, but throughout the region as a whole); the Syrian "civil" war that ensued from the 2011 uprisings and transformed into a series of proxy wars between world powers; the rise of ISIS from Iraq in 2014 and their spread into Syria and other countries; and the four Israeli wars on Gaza from 2009–2021.

30   Linne Blake, *The Wounds of Nations: Horror Cinema, Historical Trauma and National Identity* (Manchester: Manchester University Press, 2008), 188.

an unplanned accident and a sadistic surgeon at a nearby hospital who runs an illegal organ trafficking business. By contrast, Marwan Hamed's *Blue Elephant* centers on the demonic targeting of a debarred psychiatrist, a member of Egypt's elite professional class, who has a history of drug addiction. Other films from the Arab MENA region that concentrate on demonic spirit possession, usually gendered female for the purposes of revenge against the men who wronged them, and that are available and accessible to watch, include *Kindil al-Bahr* from Algeria, *Kandisha* from Morocco, and *Achoura* from Morocco. But there is also existential horror even when mixed with other subgenres, like dystopian futures with refugees and climate crisis in *Akher Wahed Fina* (*The Last of Us*) by Ala Eddine Slim from Morocco and *Blind Sun* by Joyce Nashawati from Lebanon; or mixed with vampire horror in Ghassan Salhab's *Atlal (The Last Man),* also from Lebanon. On the horizon sits a new interest in science fiction in recent short films (Larissa Sansour and Soren Lind's *In Vitro*; Fadi Baki's *Manivelle: The Last Days of the Man of Tomorrow*) and shorts and features in the current international film festival circuit.[31]

CASE STUDIES

The following case studies (*Blue Elephant 2, Blood Line,* and *Blind Sun*)[32] are structured around a set of questions and reflect the significance of the subgenres they represent, the prominence of the Egyptian film industry, and the rise of the horror genre in the UAE (United Arab Emirates). In supernatural horror, how does the uncanny unleash the abject, and how is the boundary between body and Other breached? In psychological horror, what happens to the destabilization of reality (via character, plot, *mise en scene*) and the blurring of boundaries? In existential horror, how are real situations of terror amplified through stylization of character, plot, and *mise en scene*? In all these categories or subgenres, how is the body shown to be "a site of rupture and signification"[33] that reflects either/both inner psychological states and external social conditions?

A sequel to Marwan Hamed's *Al Fil al-Azraq, Al Fil al-Azraq 2 (Blue Elephant* 2), also directed by Hamed, based on a novel by Ahmed Mourad, blends psychological with supernatural horror and became the highest earning Egyptian film to date.[34] Farida, a socialite (played by Hend Sabry), ends up in Ward 8 psychiatric hospital where she awaits execution for her crime after killing her children and husband while possessed by a demon named Nael. Dr. Yehya, a disgraced psychiatrist, played by Karim Abdel Aziz, is requested by the possessed Farida/Nael

---

31   Waked, "Old World, New Horror."
32   Some film titles like *Bloodline and Blind Sun* are originally in English, whereas *Blue Elephant 2* is marketed on Netflix by its English and Arabic title, *Al Fil al Azraq 2.*
33   Borrowing from Tarek Al-Ariss's project of resituating Arab modernity in nineteenth-century travel, writing with the intention of engaging with a "genealogy of symptoms and affects." See Al-Arriss, *Introduction to Trials of Arab Modernity.*
34   "The Blue Elephant 2 Becomes Highest Earning Egyptian Film, Raking in LE100mn," *Egypt Independent*, September 22, 2019, https://egyptindependent.com/the-blue-elephant-2-becomes-highest-earning-egyptian-film-raking-in-le100-mn/.

because Nael knows him from the previous *Blue Elephant*. Farida/Nael threatens to kill Yehya's family within three nights if he does not help release her from the ward. After a drug-induced hallucination where he finds himself on a deserted beach among giant framed portraits of the family he is tasked to protect (see figure 2.7.1) and the murdering of the family dog (which only he understands is due to Nael), Yehya agrees to work with her, ostensibly to save his wife (played by Nelly Karim) and children.

A signature of abject horror, Barbara Creed tells us (by way of Kristeva),[35] is the disturbing of boundaries between discretely separated things that distinguish the body from bodily waste, the patriarchal order from feminine biology, the heteronormative from the "queer,"[36] and so on. In this film, the boundary between superstition and rationality embodies this opposition, which is disturbed in a variety of ways, one of which is through (Yehya's) use of the magic square to ward off evil[37] in opposition to repeated references to "social media" (the means by which people communicate) and the high-tech toys their children play with (the daughter is shown with a VR headset; the son obsessed with his iPad). This ties into other oppositions between dream and reality, illusion and truth, past and present, loving mothers and demonically possessed women, family unity and its dissolution, as Yehya moves between these spaces, a traveler to his own story, both apart from and inseparable from it. The ending sequence fools us momentarily, offering false closure after he appears to have defeated the spirit or driven it from Farida's dying body, which triggers the awakening of his wife and children from their bedridden comas in the hospital. The apparent restoration of narrative order and closure in their tearful reunion at the hospital and return home is then unsettled by Yehya's awakening a few years later to older children, Lobna with short hair and a tattoo on his arms and back: the mark of the demon, which means that he is the new host for Nael. What seems like an unjustified moment of melodrama sets up another opposition: the misleading promise of resolution is the opposite of the ambiguity and abjection of what Yehya has become: the new host for Nael. This also allows for a future third installment in the *Blue Elephant* film series.

Although the psychiatric hospital is fairly realistically rendered (albeit via high-production values), there are very few references to the congestion and poverty of the city, save for one scene where Yehyia is in traffic and collapses on the ground after he leaves his car. Most of the time we are in very nice (though cluttered) apartments and beautiful old villas, or dream sequences, drug-induced hallucinations and visions projected by the demonic spirit. In fact, the

---

35   See Barbara Creed's *The Monstrous Feminine: Film, Feminism, Psychoanalysis* (New York: Routledge, 1993); also Rachel Gear's "All Those Nasty Womanly Things: Women Artists, Technology and the Monstrous-Feminine," *Women's Studies International Forum* 24, nos. 3–4 (May–August 2001): 321–333.

36   Here, "queer" is used to mean both the generally non-normative, and non-heteronormative sexuality and identity. See "Queer," Merriam-Webster, https://www.merriam-webster.com/dictionary/queer.

37   For an explanation of the mathematical function of the magic square, see Daryl Lynn Stephens, "Matrix Properties of Magic Squares," https://faculty.etsu.edu/stephen/matrix-magic-squares.pdf.

Figure 2.7.1 Still from *Blue Elephant 2*: Yehya and family portrait in his hallucination after taking the blue elephant pill.

mise en scene of these particular scenes reveals Marwan Hamed's mastery of the music videos medium and the visual excess they rely on. It is through them that we see Yehya's connection to the abject as a failed man of science, a disbarred psychologist due to his addictions to alcohol/drugs. He is also, it is suggested, a failed husband who brings harm to his family through his weakness to drugs and attractions to women other than his wife. Abjection and its alliance with evil/chaos appears to be gendered feminine and works to challenge our/the protagonist's hold on the rational world. But in fact it is Yehya who brings this chaos into the world: He is the husband who philanders, the father who cannot protect his children, the psychiatrist who cannot uphold the rational scientific order. Unstable, he alternates between attempting to escape these pressures through drugs and defending these boundaries through occult science, but he is ultimately emasculated by the uncontainable power of a demonic spirit who crosses time, space, and bodies.

Bloodline (2020), written and directed by Rami Yasin, was produced by Image Nation Abu Dhabi and premiered on MBC streaming channel Shahid. Pristine in its inclusion of most generic elements of the vampire film—vampires burn in daylight, must drink blook, prefer fresh kills, are initially sick when they turn, acquire superhuman strength and senses of hearing/smell, have strong emotional attachments—there is a striking absence of eros in the relations between the characters. This is perhaps why, although greatly hyped in its promotions, after an initially successful release, *Bloodline* was "met with tidal wave of derision on social media."[38] Yasin attributes this to the audience being largely unprepared to decode both (1) a film absent of melodrama, musical, or comedy numbers, to which Arab audiences have largely become habituated, and (2) a horror

---

38   William Mullaly, "'Did I Really Make Such a Bad Movie?' Rami Yasin talks 'Bloodline,'" *Arab* News, January 8, 2021, https://www.arabnews.com/node/1789231/lifestyle.

film absent of jump scares and gore. What we have instead is a "supernatural family drama," but the film being immediately released on the streaming platform during the COVID pandemic may have facilitated more criticism from viewers who, according to Yasin, tend to be more critical when viewing films from their couches rather than the immersive environment of a theater.

The central character in the story is Lamia (played by Nelly Karim), a wife and mother, whose main job is to keep her family together and protect the twins, Malik and Adam, and husband from the outside world, no matter the cost. Her husband Nader (played by Dhafer Lamidine) has become a vampire during a visit to Romania where he traveled, on her request, to obtain a "cure" that will bring their comatose son, Malik, back to life after a traumatic car accident. It is revealed that Nader has turned Malik into a vampire because it was the only way to bring him "back to life." Soon after Malik turns his twin, Adam, not only have Nader and the boys fed on the neighbor's cat and poor children in the neighborhood, but they have raised suspicions among the neighbors about the strange goings on in the house. Lamia and Nader plan to relocate the family to the countryside where they can exist more freely without arousing suspicion, with the intention of Lamia being the uninfected link between them and the outside world. However, this fails as Nader commits suicide in the sunlight to reduce his trace from suspicious police staking out their city house while Lamia and children drive to the countryside. Once there, Lamia realizes she is under-resourced to care for her sons, and she does not want to die as a mortal while they continue to live as children in perpetuity, so she sacrifices herself by allowing them to feed on her. The closing shot of the boys drinking blood from her wrists, reminiscent of mothers feeding their babies, leaves it to us to imagine whether she too becomes a vampire or simply dinner for her children.

Despite these violent plot developments, and in contrast to *Blue Elephant 2*, there is a striking absence of melodramatic flourishes: the film adheres to very stylized shot composition and color schemes in the *mise en scene*, the acting is restrained, and the dialogue is minimal. As with *Blue Elephant 2*, one hardly knows that this is Cairo, in the absence of the usual markers or realism (crowded dusty streets, lots of talkative people), and even the scenes in the countryside could have been shot anywhere. The absence of eros and the shift to "supernatural family drama" might allow one to imagine a critique of class vampirism. It is clear that people like Nader, who can extract large sums of money from bank accounts for quick real estate transactions, must belong to the elite class. This may account for what is unsettling to Arab audiences: the implicit idea that family unity can only be protected through this type of vampirism.

This particular use of the vampire trope has a history in Arab horror film. Although *Bloodline* is marketed as the "first Arab vampire film," it is at least the third Arab vampire film, preceded by Mohamed Shebl's *Anyab* (Fangs) and Salhab's *Atlal (The Last Man)*, both of which use vampirism to comment on social and economic exploitation. *Anyab* is unique as another example of a mixed-genre film (musical, horror, romcom) that mimics *The Rocky Horror Picture Show* but infuses it with uniquely Egyptian elements. The story begins with the same premise: A young couple in love envisions a rosy middle class future, but events following the breaking down of their car on a stormy night and subsequent stumbling upon a castle for refuge force upon them the realization that the world outside their dreams is anything but rosy. In *Anyab*, the transsexual from Transylvania is replaced by an alluring alpha vampire (played by Ahmed Adawiyya) who has intentions to turn Mona (played by Mona Gabr) into his mate. He is surrounded and entertained by a vampire coven which is delighted to have new guests to feast on. Although these changes allowed the film to bypass censors, vampirism is clearly an analogy for the 1980's era of privatization and corruption, brought in by the *infitah* or open-door policy of President Anwar Sadat, which is widely understood to have led to the decimation of the Egyptian middle class, thereby undoing the promises of the preceding Nasser era that had offered the hope of prosperity to a majority of the population.[39]

Blind Sun (2015) by Lebanese filmmaker Joyce Nashawati is a Greek/French co-production and a prime example of using European funding to craft an original and authentic film. It begins with Ashraf (played by Ziad Bakri) driving to an isolated villa somewhere near a seaside resort in Greece to be the caretaker during the hot summer months while its French owners are gone. On his way, he is stopped by a police officer who orders him to present his papers, step out of the car, and show the contents of the trunk, before the officer refuses to return the papers and rides off, leaving him without any proof of identity (see figure 2.7.2). When Ashraf arrives at the villa, where the wife and children are enjoying the swimming pool, the owner shows him to his quarters and gives instructions for what to attend to during their absence, including feeding the cat only refrigerated bottled water and staying away from his whiskey. When asked, Ashraf lies and says everything is in order with his papers. The wife additionally instructs him to water the garden, discretely, despite the rations on water during the dry summer months. After the family departs, Ashraf is alone with the cat, TV, and swimming pool, and soon the water is cut off. He makes his way to town only to find the local authorities and shopkeepers in a mental fog and disinclined to be of any assistance. When he goes to the police station to report his stolen papers, the sole police officer declares that the papers are not there and there is nothing to be done but return to the villa. This opening sequence sets the tone for the rest of the film, which slowly unfolds from bad to worse, highlighting the precarity of the Arab immigrant, who is reduced to irrelevance and invisibility, viewed as a threat to national homogeneity and treated as an outsider who cannot be assimilated.

Ashraf's national identity and home we never know, but it is presumed to be a place he has fled for safer shores and economic opportunity. While he attempts to manage an increasingly unendurable situation, he encounters a series of dehumanizing events through people who range

---

39   For an explanation of the consequences of the infitah or "open-door policy" initiated by Anwar Sadat and further developed by Hosni Mubarak, see Clement Henry Moore's "Money and Power: The Dilemma of the Egyptian Infitah" *Middle East Journal* 40, no. 4 (1986): 634–650.

from indifferent to predatorial and outright hostile: The French archeologist is more interested in unearthing statues of mythical relevance than offering to help him obtain water or assistance; the owners of the villa are more interested in their cat drinking bottled water and their garden being watered; the neighbor lady comes

Figure 2.7.2 Still from *Blind Sun*: Ashraf presents identity papers to police officer en route to his new job.

to borrow water and indirectly invites him to have sex with her; the intruders to the home drown the cat and paint threats ("Water Thief") on the gate of the villa. The theme of water and its scarcity, "part of a pre-apocalyptic setting,"[40] intersects with the blurring of reality and imagination which intensifies, as does the distinction between Ashraf's thirst-induced hallucinations, paranoia, and the increasingly violent threat from others. In the end, he burns the house and walks into the sea, in what Nashawati describes as deliberately open-ended because the Mediterranean has "become a tomb for so many trying to cross it to get to Europe."[41]

His bodily needs insignificant (the right to be hydrated and physically safe from violence) and source of origin undesirable, Ashraf is literally an identity-less person with no rights or recourse, caught in a Kafkaesque dilemma where he must leave Greece and re-apply for a visa in order to obtain papers. We are forced to experience this existential crisis as reality around him unravels. Having presumably survived the treacherous crossing of the Mediterranean or some other dangerous passage through predatorial human traffickers, Ashraf's dehumanization in *Blind Sun* represents the disorienting encounter with a violently unwelcome Europe for whom the Arab refugee is a creature of abjection. Such films prompt us to consider why, of all the subgenres of horror, Arab cinema perhaps does existential horror best.

CONCLUSION

This chapter begins a process of scholarship and attempts to put a few myths to rest about horror films in the Arab countries of the Middle East. The history of Arab horror film begins with certainty in Egypt in the mid-twentieth century and picks up in frequency and variation

---

40   Margaret Lenker, "Joyce A. Nashawati on *Blind Sun*, 'a Mystery Film in Daylight,'" *Variety*, January 17, 2016, https://variety.com/2016/film/global/joyce-a-nashawati-blind-sun-mystery-film-daylight-1201681884/.

41   Ibid.

of form by the beginning of the early twenty-first century, from the Mashreq countries of the Levant to the Maghreb countries of North Africa. This history is marked by a tendency to blend imitation of successful canonical horror films with authentic representational strategies, tropes, and experience. Currently, the main centers of production are in Egypt and the UAE (Abu Dhabi and Dubai) with recently established production companies like Image Nation and MAD Solutions.[42] The oil-rich UAE is now on the same level as Egypt in terms of power and influence, with Qatar as a close competitor in funding and development through a quarterly grants program for emerging regional filmmakers at the Doha Film Institute, in addition to the Aljazeera-sponsored documentary programs. Furthermore, streaming platforms have recently opened, like the regional branch office of Netflix (which produced the Egyptian series *Paranormal* and the Jordanian/Lebanese series *Djinn*). These, in combination with the MBC-owned Shahid and Shahid VP, have considerably expanded the viewing options for Arab audiences and the viewership of Arab horror films. Of additional significance, beyond the long history of Bollywood films screening on television and in theatres, is the programming of Bollywood and Hindi films on satellite channels, streaming platforms and airlines between the Gulf countries and the rest of the world. In fact, the largest number of films shot in the UAE are Indian films, where commercial cinemas screen films in the Hindi, Malayalam, Tamil, and Telegu languages, targeting the Indian communities who reside there.[43]

It is somewhat ironic that the Gulf countries are now using their petro-extractive wealth to produce and promote "indigenous" horror cinema, not least of which is the hugely hyped *Bloodline*, given the legacy of European colonialism, and the way many in the Arab countries view the American-led neo-liberal economic trade policies and globalization of the twentieth and twenty-first centuries. Beyond vampirism as an analogy for the brutal economics that have decimated the middle class across the globe, the following films also mix indigenous horror with global tropes, signaling a new wave of horror in a number of "firsts" by younger North African directors: in Damien Ounouri's *Kindil al-Bahr*, the treatment of an avenging female spirit delivers a condemnation of male authoritarianism that is linked to conservative Islam in contemporary Algerian society; in Abdelhamid Bouchnak's *Dachra*, which was both the highest grossing and the first horror film in Tunisia,[44] the transformation of a group of university students who visit a village and are besieged by cannibalistic witches functions as an allegory for a generational gap;[45] and in Sofia Alaoui's *So What if the Goats Die,* which won

42 See http://mad.film/about.php#mainbody.

43 Ginsberg and Chris Lippard, *Historical Dictionary of Middle Eastern Cinema*, 492.

44 Dennis Harvey, "'Dachra' Review: Tunisia's First Horror Movie Is Familiar but Frightening," *Variety*, July 7, 2021, https://variety.com/2021/film/reviews/dachra-review-1235013151/.

45 Nick Vivarelli. "Venice: Abdelhamid Bouchnak on How Arab Horror Film 'Dachra' Reflects Generational Conflict in Tunisia," *Variety*, September 8, 2018, https://variety.com/2018/film/news/venice-abdelhamid-bouchnak-on-bold-arab-horror-film-dachra-reflects-generational-conflict-in-tunisia-1202933152/.

the Grand Jury prize at Sundance in 2019, the encounter of a villager trying to feed his starving ghosts and alien life forms in a small Moroccan village re-articulates the familiar theme of the clash between the old and the new.

Despite the differences between old and new horror, political events and realities still find their way into narrative forms as these forms evolve. The recent increase in horror films in the region, and the increasing investment in high-production values by the companies that produce them, reflects the persistence of a genre that appeals to audience imaginations, perhaps more urgently now than ever, including the imagination of a young generation that knows the world beyond the screen has never been stable, secure, or unhaunted.

BIBLIOGRAPHY

Al-Ariss, Tarek. *Trials of Arab Modernity: Literary Affects and the New Political*. Fordham University Press, 2013, 1–19.

Alkhereiji, Mohammed. "MBC media group moves to Riyadh as Saudi Arabia seeks to 'reinvent itself.'" *The Arab Weekly*, February 16, 2020. https://thearabweekly.com/mbc-media-group-moves-riyadh-saudi-arabia-seeks-reinvent-itself.

Armes, Roy. *Roots of the New Arab Film*. Bloomington: Indiana University Press, 2018.

Blake, Linnie. *The Wounds of Nations: Horror Cinema, Historical Trauma and National Identity*. Manchester: Manchester University Press, 2008.

Britannica, T. Editors of Encyclopaedia. "Balfour Declaration." Encyclopedia Britannica. October 26, 2020. https://www.britannica.com/event/Balfour-Declaration.

Britannica, T. Editors of Encyclopaedia. "Sykes-Picot Agreement." Encyclopedia Britannica. May 22, 2020. https://www.britannica.com/event/Sykes-Picot-Agreement.

Creed, Barbara. *The Monstrous Feminine: Film, Feminism, Psychoanalysis*. Routledge, 1993.

Darraj, Faisal. "The Peculiar Destinies of Arab Modernity." In *Arab Art Histories: The Khalid Shoman Collection*. Translated by Anna Swank. 2013. https://daratalfunun.org/?page_id=298.

Fahmy, Hazem. "[Nightmares On The Nile] Ambassador Of Hell And The Horror Of Seduction." Nov. 16, 2020. https://nofspodcast.com/nightmares-on-the-nile-ambassador-of-hell-and-the-horror-of-seduction.

Gear, Rachel. "All those nasty womanly things: Women artists, technology and the monstrous-feminine." *Women's Studies International Forum* 24, Iss. 3–4 (May–August 2001): 321–333.

Ginsberg, Terri and Chris Lippard. *Historical Dictionary of Middle Eastern Cinema*, 2nd Edition. Maryland: Rowman & Littlefield, 2020.

Harvey, Dennis. "'Dachra' Review: Tunisia's First Horror Movie Is Familiar but Frightening." *Variety*. July 7, 2021. https://variety.com/2021/film/reviews/dachra-review-1235013151/.

Kent, Sarah. "A Brief History of the Iranian Oil Industry." The Wall Street Journal. April 3, 2015. https://www.wsj.com/articles/a-brief-history-of-the-iranian-oil-industry-1428063016.

Khalidi, Rashid. *The 100 Years War on Palestine*. New York: Macmillan, 2020.

Khouri, Malek. *The Arab Nationalist Project in Youssef Chahine's Cinema*. Cairo: AUC Press, 2010.

Malkmus, Lizbeth and Roy Armes. *Arab and African Film Making*. London: Zed Books Ltd, 1991.

Moore, Clement Henry. "Money and Power: The Dilemma of the Egyptian Infitah." *Middle East Journal* 40, no. 4 (Autumn, 1986): 634–650.

Mullally, William. "'Did I really make such a bad movie?' Rami Yasin talks 'Bloodline.'" *Arab News*. January 8, 2021. https://www.arabnews.com/node/1789231/lifestyle.

NA. "The Blue Elephant 2 becomes highest earning Egyptian film, raking in LE100mn." *Egypt Independent*. September 22, 2019. https://egyptindependent.com/the-blue-elephant-2-becomes-highest-earning-egyptian-film-raking-in-le100-mn/.

Nashawati, Joyce. "Joyce A. Nashawati on 'Blind Sun' 'a mystery film in daylight.'" Interview by Margaret Lenker in *Variety*, January 17, 2016. https://variety.com/2016/film/global/joyce-a-nashawati-blind-sun-mystery-film-daylight-1201681884/.

Shafik, Viola. *Arab Cinema: History and Cultural Identity*. Cairo: American University Press, 1998.

Shafik, Viola. "Egypt: A Cinema without Horror?" *In Horror International* edited by Steven Jay Schneider and Tony Williams, 273–289. Detroit: Wayne State Press, 2005.

Vivarelli, Nick. "Arab Genre Films Get Boost from Beirut's Maskoon Lab (Exclusive)." *Variety*. September 23, 2019. https://variety.com/2019/film/news/arab-genre-films-production-boost-beirut-maskoon-lab-1203340300/.

Vivarelli, Nick. "Venice: Abdelhamid Bouchnak on How Arab Horror Film 'Dachra' Reflects Generational Conflict in Tunisia." *Variety*. Sept. 8, 2018. https://variety.com/2018/film/news/venice-abdelhamid-bouchnak-on-bold-arab-horror-film-dachra-reflects-generational-conflict-in-tunisia-1202933152/.

Waked, Antoine. "Old World, New Horror." *Fangoria* 2, Iss. 11 (April 2021): 14–17.

Figure Credits

Fig. 2.7.1: Copyright © 2019 by Rotana Studios.

Fig. 2.7.2: Copyright © 2015 by Pretty Pictures.

POST-READING QUESTIONS/POST-SCREENING QUESTIONS

Directions: Use what you learned from reading this chapter and watching the film to respond to the questions.

1. Explain some historical factors shaping the development of Arab and North African horror film.

2. Many filmic treatments of vampirism allegorize the exploitation of humans. Analyze how this functions in (either of) the films *Bloodline* and *Anyab*.

3. Examine how *Blue Elephant 2* mixes references to traditional Arabic horror with the "conventional" language of horror.

4. Discuss the author's argument for existential horror and how *Blind Sun* pertains to this subgenre of Arab horror film.

Reading 2.8

Horror Ambiguity in Iranian Cinema
By Hadi Gharabaghi

KEY TERMS AND FIGURES

Synchronic

Diachronic

Postcolonialism

Iranian studies

Iranian New Wave

Neo-imperialism

Cold War containment

Māvarāi Genre

Modernization

Iranian Revolution

RECOMMENDED FILMS

A Girl Walks Home Alone at Night by Ana Lily Amirpour (2014)

Dāyereh-ye Minā [The Cycle] by Dāriush Mehrjui (1975)

Gräns [Border] by Ali Abbasi (2018, Sweden)

Hojūm [Invasion] by Shahram Mokri (2017)

Khābgāh-i Dokhtarān [Girls' Dormitory] by Mohammad Hossein Latifi (2004)

Khāneh Siāh Ast [The House Is Black] by Forough Farrokhzād (1963)

Khesht va Āyeneh [Brick and Mirror] by Ebrahim Golestan (1964)

Mādar-e Ghalb-e Atomi [Atomic Heart] by Ali Ahmadzadeh (2014)

Parināz by Bahrām Bahrāmian (2010)

Persepolis by Marjane Satrapi and Winshluss (2007, France)

Poost [Skin] by Bahman Ark and Bahram Ark (2018)

Sheitān Vojūd Nadārad [There Is No Evil] by Mohammad Rasoulof (2021)

Under the Shadow by Babak Anvari (2016, UK)

Yek Ettefāgh-i Sādeh [A Simple Event] by Sohrāb Shahid-sāles (1973)

Horror Ambiguity in Iranian Cinema

By Hadi Gharabaghi

INTRODUCTION

This chapter investigates certain inchoate elements of horror throughout Iranian cinema. A group of articles has analyzed supernatural and mythical characters appearing in recent Iranian horror movies as a case of cultural specificity. Furthermore, recent emergence of the horror genre inside Iran is theorized as a signifier of an elevated level of policing and surveillance. Another group of articles has analyzed the diasporic veiled vampire as an example of empowering representation of veiled women in the West. In turn, this project suggests some sociological perspective and genealogical continuity under an umbrella of horror ambiguity through close reading of select titles from pre- and post-revolution eras.

Horror movies and television series are on the rise in Iran. This movement emerged, mostly as a hybrid genre, initially in the early 2000s with a few movies and a wave of television series in a new *māvarāi* (supernatural) genre that tangentially employed stylistic signifiers of the genre to narrate morality tales that incorporated Qur'anically referenced supernatural beings.[1] In time, filmmakers experimented with the genre more exclusively. Artistically significant titles, such as *Poost* (Skin) by Bahman and Bahram Ark (2018), have received critical acknowledgment in the official Fajr Film Festival or have been presented by the Art and Experience Institute of Iranian Cinema, in the case of Shahram Mokri's films.[2] Besides some available bootleg and authorized copies online, horror movies appear in movie theaters, on national television, and on recently developed local platforms of online screening. Films are mostly made by first-time directors or those who have not explored the genre before. Except for a few cases, especially

---

1 Ahmad Mohammad Tabrizi, "The Iranian Supernatural Television Series: Portraying Satan and Summoning Spirit in the Most Accessible Form," *Sherkat-e Noāvarān Fanāvāzeh*, May 2, 2021, https://www.digikala.com/mag/transcendental-series-in-iran-tv/.

2 See https://www.aecinema.org.

television directors such as Behrūz Afkhami and Sirūs Moghaddam, filmmakers have rarely returned to the genre.

At a representational level, elements of horror afflict middle-class secular characters as the exclusive site of unfolding superstitious elements far more frequently than the religious working-class or rural ones. Unsettling events take place in apartment buildings, villas, and resorts. Films heavily rely on abrupt soundtracks and cuts. Plots sometimes engender class disparity within which neatly dressed characters speaking without accent may drink and use drugs and then get punished at the end. Themes of immigration, fragmented families, and pregnant women losing babies also appear in several films. A more fully articulated recent horror cinema is tolerated at the governing level of supervision and censorship only when elements of secular middle-class life stand out as the culprit, in the form of bodies that suffer and stories that function as cautionary tales.

Elements of horror, however, afflict religious working-class or rural gendered bodies differently. They rarely deconstruct, destroy, or even performatively empower women. Such films have rarely received permission at the level of script approval or have faced obstacles for public screening after their completion. For instance, The movie *Parināz* by Bahrām Bahāmian (2010), in which the high-profile actor Fātemeh Mo'tamed-āryā plays the leading role, was confiscated and barred from public screening for seven years.[3] It was finally screened in 2017 after several changes made to the film. The story depicts the life of Parināz, a young girl, who is left at the doorsteps of her aunt, Farkhondeh, after her mother passes away tragically in the aftermath of the trauma of being raped by her husband's friend. Negative reactions to the role of Farkhondeh, a religious woman with obsessive compulsive disorder, who lives in a working-class neighborhood, demonstrate the anxiety of religious conservative governing.

As for middle-age male rural characters, the horror genre has operated in a field of authorial ambiguity, leading to several artistically significant films, by building on the ethnographic *mise en scene* of rural life. The most canonical example is Dāriush Mehrjui's 1969 film, *Gāv* (The Cow). The mysterious relationship between animals or supernatural beings and rural men are explored in these works, including *Khāb-i Talkh* (Bitter Dream) by Mohsen Amir-yusefi (2003), and two films from the emerging auteurs, Ark brothers: *Heivan* (The Animal) in 2017 and *Poost*. *Gāv* and *Heivan* showcase forms of transformation of human into animal.

As Hamid Naficy demonstrates in his overarching social history, one way or other, Iranian cinema has always operated within a state-run, sometimes economically supported, and heavily censored apparatus of film production within which authorial subversion, interruption, and

---

3   I consulted Persian Wikipedia for this film and many others. An interview with Bābak Kāidan, the scriptwriter of the film, offers helpful information. "Parināz: Baziy-e Khatarnak ba Bavarhay-e Sonnati" [Dangerous Game with Traditional Beliefs], Bartarinhā, October 16, 2017, https://www.bartarinha.ir/fa/news/615114/فیلم-پریناز-بازی-خطرناک-با-باورهای-سنتی.

intervention have negotiated a range of artistic strategies.[4] Somewhat similarly, Linnie Blake also explores how horror cinema, as a cultural expression of collective trauma, finds voice within national cinemas. As she writes, horror genre "exists at the conjunction of cultural analysis and cultural policy—being the popular genre most prone to legislative regulation through censorship from above."[5] Emphasizing underlying political economy and production culture into research on the horror genre also finds amenable support in Mark Jancovich's assessment of literature on American horror films. Jancovich addresses the need to expand research on the horror genre from formulaic assumptions to broader underlying collective sentiments and cultures of production and experience.[6]

What overall characterizes the ideological makeup of the last decade of Iranian cinema, which has indirectly given rise to a recognizable horror genre, is the rise of state or conservative foundations—religiously sponsored conservative authorship that emerged after the revolution of 1979, for instance, in Mohsen Makhmalbaf's early career during the 1980s, at the expense of heavily censoring the secular voices of dissent. This pattern continued its gradual growth in the works of specific filmmakers for cinema and national television. This included producing supernatural horror series for national television, which is controlled directly by Supreme Leader appointees. Another factor was the emergence of Owj Arts and Media Organization (OAMO) in 2011 as a private entity sponsored by the cultural branch of the Islamic Revolutionary Guard Corps, Sepah.[7] The OAMO has so far produced seventeen feature films, nine television series, and over seven hundred documentary projects per year.[8] Its high value artistic output has resulted in receiving full exposure and artistic recognition in Fajr and international film festivals. While experimenting with various cinematic modes and genres, this ideologically religious conservative movement has enjoyed authorial freedom to address historically and politically sensitive subject matter unparalleled to those afforded by the private secular camp.[9] While OAMO has not directly sponsored any project in the horror genre, its experiences in action, thriller, romantic, and drama genres demonstrate a noticeable influence over popular cinematic genres in society. The horror genre, therefore, has emerged from an ideological battleground within Iranian cinema.

4   Hamid Naficy, *A Social History of Iranian Cinema*, vols. 1–4 (Durham, NC: Duke University Press, 2012).

5   Linnie Blake, *The Wounds of Nations: Horror Cinema, Historical Trauma and National Identity* (UK: Manchester University Press, 2008), 3.

6   Mark Jancovich, ed. "General Introduction," *Horror, The Film Reader* (Routledge, 2002), 1–19.

7   See http://www.owjmedia.org.

8   "A Look at Six Years of Media Works by Owj Organization," Islamic Azad University News Agency, August 9, 2017, https://www.ana.press/news/201398/نگاهی-به-فعالیت‌های-6-ساله-سازمان-اوج. Also see https://fa.wikipedia.org/wiki/سازمان_هنری_رسانه‌ای_اوج.

9   Notably, Makhmalbaf's early films carry residual elements of the horror genre stylistically through abrupt cuts, noir scenes, and depictions of psychological scars of the Iran–Iraq war: *Tobeh-i Nasūh* (Nasūh's Repentence, 1983), *Este'āzeh* (Seeking Refuge to God, 1984), *Boycott* (1985), *Dast-Forūsh* (The Peddler, 1986) and *Arūsiy-e Khūbān* (Marriage of the Blessed, 1988).

SCHOLARLY RESPONSES TO IRANIAN HORROR

The scholarly response to Iranian horror movies has been relatively slow in comparison. There is a growing literature in Persian that offers brief sketches of Western and Asian histories of horror cinema or critiques a particular film or the movement itself. Several sites also offer a ranking of Iranian horror titles. The scholarly response in English can be divided into two groups, both of which build on Noël Carroll's characterization of the horror genre "to raise certain *affect* ... a sense of suspense, a sense of mystery, and a sense of horror."[10]

The first group of articles are theoretical responses to several diasporic movies: *Persepolis* by Marjane Satrapi and Winshluss (2007, France), *A Girl Walks Home Alone at Night* by Ana Lily Amirpour 2014, USA), *Under the Shadow* by Babak Anvari (2016, UK), and *Gräns* (Border) by Ali Abbasi (2018, Sweden).[11] The first three films utilize *chādor* visually for character development and in *mise en scene* toward expressing elements of dramatic horror. In *A Girl Walks Home*, a black and white noir, a female vampire in *chādor* shatters stereotypes of Muslim women as victims of patriarchy or doomed terrorists by operating fearlessly as a feminist vigilante in dark streets of an imagined Bad City.[12] In *Under the Shadow*, a period drama depicting the rocket bombardment of Tehran during Iran–Iraq war in the mid-1980s, a formerly leftist and medical school dropout female character succumbs to superstition as she increasingly fears a jinn in *chādor* who travels on wind and enters her apartment through the hole that an unexploded rocket has left on the roof. Both films recall an earlier cinematic stylization of veiling and *chādor* in *Persepolis,* Marjane Satrapi's comic book (2000) and animation-memoir. *Persepolis* depicts Satrapi's own experience of first joy and then horror of revolution as a child in 1979, the alienation of diasporic life as an adolescent in Austria, and the post-revolution religious autocracy as a young woman returning to Iran. *Persepolis* stands out as an exceptional cinematic work that bends generic conventions as a horror-comedy feature animation and a hybrid docudrama even though the film's critique of governmentalizing women's veiling does not extend to France, where the author is based. Despite this shortcoming, collective political trauma of Iranian modernity during the twentieth century is animated in *Persepolis* through the perspective of a female persona from a leftist Iranian family;

---

10   Noël Carroll, *The Philosophy of Horror or Paradoxes of the Heart* (New York: Routledge, 1990), 14.

11   Shrabani Basu, "The Foil and the Quicksand: The Image of the 'Veil' and the Failure of Abjection in Iranian Diasporic Horror," *Cinema: Journal of Philosophy and the Moving Image* 9 (2017): 72-87, http://static1.1.sqspcdn.com/static/f/906805/27864186/1521811931250/9_Basu.pdf?token=6X1dohAsqUO4%2FRTJoQI4obd12Rs%3D; Zahra Khosroshahi, "Vampires, Jinn and the Magical in Iranian Horror Films," *Frames Cinema Journal* 16 (2019), http://framescinemajournal.com/article/vampires-jinn-and-the-magical-in-iranian-horror-films/; Allen Steven, "Persepolis: Telling Tales of Trauma," in *Scars and Wounds, edited by Nick Hodgin and Amit Thakkar* (New York: Palgrave Macmillan, 2017), 267–289.

12   Samuel Khachikian's group of hybrid thriller-horror films in late 1960s is an example of film noir. A more extensive discussion of Khachikian's films and cultural persona designate a chapter in Kaveh Askari's book, *Relaying Cinema in Midcentury Iran: Material Cultures in Transit* (Berkeley: University of California Press, 2022).

she emerges as both a national and diasporic hero. Elements of horror are peppered throughout the film.

Border stands out from other films because it maintains the least cultural connection with Iran at the audiovisual level even though the filmmaker is a first-generation diasporic Iranian. The film retells the well-known Danish fairytale story of *The Ugly Duckling* by Hans Christian Anderson, 1843, in which Tina (a Swedish customs officer) discovers herself to be not a low self-esteem human species, ostracized growing up for her "ugliness," and sexual abnormality, but a troll capable of a more empowering sexual experience after she meets Vore (another troll), who calls her beautiful. Here, Anderson's allegory of Otherness is transplanted through an Iranian filmmaker's interpretation into a live action drama set in contemporary Swedish society in which mythological characters of Scandinavian lore struggle for identity as the film crosses back and forth into emotions of disgust, horror, and humanism. Rikke Schubart's article explains genre variations in *Border* through a reading of psychological research on emotions while drawing from the story.[13]

Among the authors in this group, Sharabani Basu and Zahra Khosroshahi address horror affect in *A Girl Walks Home* and *Under the Shadow* as interventionist opportunities of veiled imagery in cinematic constructions of feminist empowerment. They address how these films, especially *A Girl Walks Home*, intervene in stereotypical demonization as well as victimization of veiled Middle Eastern and North African Muslim women that are found in many mainstream Western movies and television series after 9/11. In their analyses, they also read into cultural politics of women's rights inside Iran. Shadee Abdi and Bernadette M. Calafell also theorize this intervention via an analysis of the female vampire in *A Girl Walks Home* although through a queer reading of feminists of color.[14] The diasporic vampire is a feminist vigilante with no name. Every woman can adopt her character and power. She is the girl who walks home alone at night with no fear. She is to be feared.

The second group of articles addresses Iranian horror in films made inside Iran. The authors investigate characters and thematic elements of Iranian horror genre as a local iteration of cultural and religious difference through close analysis and sociopolitical interpretation of a few films. Pedram Partovi analyzes *Khābgāh-i Dokhtarān* (Girls' Dormitory) by Mohammad Hossein Latifi (2004) in depth as demonstrating opportunities for the agency of Iranian women in the horror genre.[15] In the film, a curious visit from Roya, a female college student, to an abandoned building nearby a temporary girls' dormitory leads to an encounter with Ghobād,

---

13   Rikke Schubart, "'I Smelled It on Him': Wonderful Trolls and Disgusting Humans in *Border*," *Kosmorama* 279, February 24, 2021, https://www.kosmorama.org/kosmorama/artikler/i-smelled-it-him-wonderful-trolls-and-disgusting-humans-border.

14   Shadee Abdi and Bernadette M. Calafell, "Queer Utopias and a (Feminist) Iranian Vampire: A Critical Analysis of Resistive Monstrosity in A Girl Walks Home Alone at Night," *Critical Studies in Media Communication* 34, no. 4 (2017): 358–370.

15   Pedram Partovi, "*Girls' Dormitory*: Women's Islam and Iranian Horror," *Visual Anthropology Review* 25, no. 2 (2009): 186–207.

a psychologically disturbed serial killer of women. Ghobād is arrested, but he escapes and subsequently takes Roya hostage. She endures physical torture and overcomes her fear. She strips her abductor from the power he acquires in the company of jinns by relating hence commanding them instead. This strategy buys her enough time until police arrive and rescue her. In the film, jinns are not just the effects of Ghobād's psychological state but exist independent of him. They shift alliance from him to Roya.

Farshid Kazemi investigates horror in *A Girl Walks Home* and *Mādar-i Ghalb-i Atomi* (Atomic Heart) by Ali Ahmadzadeh (2014).[16] In the former, Kazemi does a psychoanalytic investigation of female desire and sexuality in Shia Islam by focusing on the empowering and disruptive features of the vampire. Kazemi mentions the film's strong negative reaction from the religious conservative camp inside Iran who declared it to be "anti-Iranian," *haram* (anti-religion), and *anti-hijāb*.[17] But this reaction, which recalls a similarly strong reaction to *Parina⁻z*, only makes the phenomenon of the film more pertinent and representationally critical. The female vampire with her *chādor* and dark yet stylish costume forms a transitional hybrid who collapses the binary of class division found in most recent Iranian horror movies. In contrast to the conventional horror story of *Girls' Dormitory*, *Atomic Heart* is a formally complex film in which the story of two young female roommates driving home from an evening party in Tehran turns into a series of first adventurous then nightmarish encounters with a mysterious man who bends time and space. For instance, he brings the women into contact with Sadam Hussein, the president of Iraq during Iran-Iraq war (1980–88) who was ousted, captured, and executed after the US-led military invasion of Iraq in 2003. The mysterious man plans to take them with him to the world beyond. Kazemi interprets these post-2009 Iranian horror movies as responsive to further infringement of freedom within Iranian society.[18]

One disadvantage of the scholarly treatment of Iranian horror movies in English is the exclusiveness of the research. Despite the nearly fifty film and television series that have been proliferating inside Iran, only a few Iranian and diasporic titles have obtained the bulk of scholarly response. The irony lies in how postcolonial studies scholarship, notably Iranian studies, have become an elitist field of knowledge production in North American universities, one that hardly addresses the working-class dimension of its subject matter and barely becomes available to the readership in whose name, cultural specificity, historical suppression, and persistent misrepresentation research is conducted. A bulk of Iranian films are available on mostly unauthorized sites on the internet without subtitles, and the growing scholarship on

---

16 Farshid Kazemi, "The Interpreter of Desires: Iranian Cinema and Psychoanalysis," PhD diss. (University of Edinburgh, 2018), 146–227.

17 Ibid.

18 For further information about the 2009 disputed presidential election and the Green movement, see Negar Mottahedeh's *#iranelection: Hashtag Solidarity and the Transformation of Online Life* (Stanford, CA: Stanford University Press, 2015).

Iranian horror cinema is almost entirely available only in the English language. The discursive field of negotiation and exchange that constitute film genre, in other words, is far from democratically available to audiences, people involved in the planning, production, and access to films, and critics who become material support for the growth of genre discourse. It is important to acknowledge this problem to emphasize the invaluable contribution of the labor of producing subtitles and translations and to encourage more effort and visibility in this area toward a more meaningful diasporic engagement.

The tendency in Western analysis and the reception of Iranian cinema has been to examine generic features, synchronically, without much attention to historical and cultural context. A comparative analysis, however, can identify elements of cinematic horror, diachronically, within the plot or at the stylistic level that help to unpack the genealogical flexibility of what constitutes horror.[19] By taking a nuanced approach to examine continuities in the historical development of Iranian horror, we can move away from a group of theoretical and analytical approaches built solely on fencing in the genre, based on strict qualifications that have emerged after Carroll's conceptualization while broadly capitalizing on horror's affect. This way, we can approach horror cinema by unpacking dormant elements in hybrid genres within which horror is present not as a familiar element of horror genre or hybrid horror genre, but as a field of *horror ambiguity*. As I will demonstrate, horror ambiguity brings together different cinematic modes and eras.

Another pattern is the diasporic reading into genres of national cinema toward sociocultural and political critique. Siegfried Kracauer's investigation into German cinema during and after World War II constitutes an early example of conceptualizing a group of films as sociological clues to collective mentality, the rise of Nazism, particularly his examination of *Das Cabinet des Dr. Caligari* (The Cabinet of Dr. Caligari) by Robert Wiene (1920), an essential canon of horror cinema today.[20] Kracauer's conflicted legacy of "historical imaginary" suggests that a group of "stylistically innovative" horror movies may offer clues to a collective experience of horror in the society, as recent investigations of Iranian horror genre also imply.[21] Similarly, Adam Lowenstein asks, in his multinational investigation of the ways in which collective horrors of the twentieth century intersect with movies: "What does cinematic horror have to tell us about the horrors of history?"[22] To explain the abrupt emergence of the horror genre in the

---

19   Harry M. Benshoff's "Horror Before 'The Horror Film'" in *A Companion to the Horror Film*, ed. Harry M. Benshoff (Hoboken, NJ: Wiley, 2014), 207–224; and Kendall R. Phillips's *Darkness: The Rhetoric of Horror in Early American Cinema* (Austin: University of Texas Press, 2018).

20   Siegfried Kracauer, *From Caligari to Hitler: A Psychological History of the German Film* (Princeton, NJ: Princeton University Press, 1947).

21   See Thomas Elsaesser's critique of Kracuaer's thesis in *Weimar Cinema and After: Germany's Historical Imaginary* (New York: Routledge, 2000), 420.

22   *Shocking Representation: Historical Trauma, National Cinema, and the Modern Horror Film* (New York: Columbia University Press, 2005), 1. David J. Skal's article "The Horrors of War" addresses, similarly, connections between horror cinema's wolf monster during the Second World War, in *The Horror Film*, Stephen Prince, ed. (New Jersey: Rutgers University Press, 2004), 70–85.

last several years, therefore, generic invisibility in other eras may invite a closer investigation into horror ambiguity and help discover thematic continuity in the social struggles of pre- and post-revolution films despite drastic societal transformation. Close analysis can activate dialogic discourse between dormant cinematic horrors of pre- and post-revolutionary eras and the more crystalized recent horror genre.[23]

HORROR AMBIGUITY IN IRANIAN CINEMA

The emergence of locally produced documentary and fiction films is coterminous with violent neo-imperial suppression of democracy in Iran during the 1950s. The joint CIA–MI6 coup d'état of 1953 set in motion an era of militant suppression of political dissent and marshal law and governing followed by a large-scale modernization. What constituted modernization in this period was, in fact, an overwhelming course of Americanization—a Cold War containment project—of the society on the surface while depriving Iran of the democratic process that gave political meaning to American life. This neo-imperial influence established an official documentary style and infrastructure that ironically served the emerging top-down and central apparatus of media governance.[24]

Modernist art movements emerged in the 1950s and 60s in critical response to the American-backed Shah's top-down modernization project, which took the form of unbridled bureaucratic institutions, technocratic militancy, and a humiliating developmental rationality that suppressed political expression as too threatening for society to handle hence suppressing dissidence.[25] Forūgh Farrokhzād's *Khāneh Siāh Ast* (The House Is Black) in 1963, among the most enigmatic documentaries made during this era, stands as an example of a modernist and subversive response, in both form and content, to the horrors of the top-down modernization.[26] The film proceeds like a frightening dream, with its poetically charged montage inviting multiple viewings. But, commissioned to humanize the lives of people afflicted with leprosy in the Baba-baghi Sanatorium near Tabriz, the film does much more. Two male and female voiceovers treat documentary subjects dialectically. The male voiceover demystifies leprosy through medical

---

23   Mikhail Bakhtin's "Dialogic Discourse" explains how the work of interpretation may act as a dialogue of multiple voices influencing each other. Craig Brandist, "The Bakhtin Circle," *IEP*, accessed August 5, 2021, https://iep.utm.edu/bakhtin/.

24   For more information consult Hamid Naficy, *A Social History of Iranian Cinema*, volume 2, 71–74 and Hadi Gharabaghi, "The Syracuse Mission to Iran during the 1950s and the Rise of Documentary Diplomacy," *Journal of Cinema and Media Studies* 60, no. 4 (2021): 9–36.

25   Maria Todorova addresses the difference between modernism, modernity, and modernization in detail in "Modernism," in *Modernism: The Creation of Nation-States* (Europe: Central European University Press, 2010), 4–22.

26   While several articles have given justice to the canonic influence of this endearing film, close reading of Farrokhzād's masterpiece proves illuminating for an investigation of cinematic horror. For further research, consult Sara Saljoughi's "A New Form for a New People: Forūgh Farrokhzād's *The House Is Black*," *Camera Obscura: Feminism, Culture, and Media Studies* 32, no. 1 (2017): 1–31.

treatment. The often-discordant female voiceover, however, questions a supreme being for the devastating deformity of bodies and hopeless living conditions. Kids thank God for creation while reading from their textbook. Men in deformed bodies also praise God during prayer in mosque. Farrokhzād's lamenting voice confronts a higher being, on behalf of the people, with a poetically charged plea that references leprosy in the *Book of Job*. Farrokhzād's voice undermines a direct reading of these scenes by questioning the purpose of creation in the face of the deformity and suffering caused by leprosy.

No manifestation or visual evidence of governing welfare exists beyond the two-minute brief scene of clinical care in the film. No images of the Shah or a religious authority appear on any walls in the film. The discordance in the mosque scene is accentuated by fragmentation of deformed bodies in prayer heard by a male voiceover. The scene concludes in silence with an empty chair and metallic hands symbolizing the authority of Islamic governance without a figure head. Instead, scenes of everyday life and a marriage ceremony take precedence. This happy note, however, is undermined by images of desolate and aimless life, of waiting, symbolizing a desire for basic human welfare. The vacuum of any responsible governing, besides generic images of the clinic and a group lunch, becomes even more striking, paired with the invisibility of any signifier identifying the subjects' nationality, besides the common language, which every refugee speaks as well. The ambiguity that results from the abstraction of governing in the film is further emphasized by the abstraction of temporal and geographical markers within the text that would otherwise anchor the documented subjects to the historical world. Horror ambiguity, and the implied horror of the absence/ambiguity of governing, are further enhanced and objectified through shocking montages of disfigured subjects in the silence of the voice track. The camera lingers to the point that their discomfort becomes jarringly evident.

This abstraction of governing is compensated by Farrokhzād's voiceover, speaking on behalf of the people, while lamenting to God. Within Sufi activism, speaking with God can be a subversive critique that one otherwise cannot launch against one's own governing authority, the Shah as God's representative on Earth. In performing this, Farrokhzād articulates her authorial relation cinematically as a rising and nationally recognized passionate poet acting on behalf of the suffering rural people of Baba-baghi sanitarium. She does so, however, without offering any individuality to the documented subjects, among whom she lived for 12 days. She touched them and filmed their happiness without fear of contamination, but then she abstracted them. We do not get to know who these people are because they become abstracted images, as means of her poetry. The disfigured women in the film resemble women that carry scars on faces, bodies, and inside, scars of forced marriage and domestic violence, victims of acid attack and rape. Farrokhzād becomes the voice of all the disfigured images, reinforcing the strong bond of collective and ancient culture, and forces us to watch their abstracted images, but they are not objectified and alienated. This distinction invests a lingering experience of horror that becomes the driving force of the film. The cinematic horror proceeds from the images of atrophy and disfigurement, the documentary portrait of quarantine life with little to no welfare, and the presentation of Otherness that recalls Tina's experience of Otherness in *Border*, living among Swedish people who killed her parents and hid her orphanhood in the name of a humanizing endeavor, which she refuses to avenge. In *Border*, bodily deformity confronts us with what it means to be human by cinematically challenging body normativity from an agency that is neither animalistic nor robotic.

Among the recent output of horror films inside Iran, Shahram Mokri's genre-bending films fit best as horror ambiguity. They are formally experimental and yet suggestive of horror themes. Horror ambiguity in *Hojūm* (Invasion), 2017, invites comparison with *Khāneh Siāh Ast*. Similarly, *Hojūm* uses a linguistically Iranian space without identifiable governing and national signifiers to suggest a refugee sphere, but this time with dystopic references to a militarized border, mysterious disease, and vampiric blood consumption. Using a well-choreographed *mise en scene* and mobile framing that creates uncertainty and worrisome anticipation, it tells an open-ended story that diffuses boundaries.

The story takes place in a gray and foggy fenced territory devoid of direct sun. Afflicted with a mysterious disease, sick people are pursued by the police. The plot unfolds almost entirely in a soccer sport club involving athletic, civic, and police institutions without any concrete national signification. Ali (an athlete) is accused of murdering his friend and team leader Saman, whose body is missing. He is collaborating with the authorities to rehearse the murder scene with other teammates and Negar, Saman's twin sister (both roles played by Elāhe Bakhshi), about whom Ali had no prior knowledge. The logic of rehearsal demands that Ali is not always accompanied by an officer. After almost nine minutes into the movie, Ali starts sharing his thoughts through voiceover monologue, which offers the viewers exclusive access to his point of view. Apparently, Saman and Negar have been infected with the disease and Saman has been collecting blood secretly from his teammates for the siblings' survival. Saman, a strong leader with supernatural power, is forming an army of followers. As the second person in charge, Ali has been helping Saman with collecting blood from athletes in exchange for gaining special power. Gradually, the difference between real and rehearsed events becomes fuzzy as the viewer relies more on Ali's monologue than the increasingly absent investigative officers. This results in breaking down the objectivity of omniscient narration in rehearsal scenes as Ali joins and leaves different groups. The audience, for instance, has no way of knowing how much of the conversation between Ali and others is overheard by police authorities. This leads to a shift from omniscient to restrictive narration as the audience becomes one eavesdropping agency among potential others.

The plot unfolds another twist when Ali starts experiencing alternate states of temporality during which he goes back in time and observes earlier rehearsals that included himself. Eventually, he meets Saman. First, he thinks it is Negar, but this time it is Saman himself who has been monitoring police rehearsal on an old computer screen all along. Ali questions Saman about Negar and asks for the whole truth. In response, Saman hypnotizes Ali, who in turn experiences a different zone, a subjective monologue that recites a Rumi poem to Ali: "You are not the way I am. I am not the way you are. You are not after what I am. I am not after what you are. I am in your soul. You are in my blood. Even if I become the moon and the sun. I am still less than you." Afterward, Saman takes Ali outside the sport club to a van Ali can surveil from, through the reconditioned touchscreen car window, the lead inspector in his home watching his sick wife pass away (see figure 2.8.1). The inspector tears open his wife's pillow, and an alien form starts coming out. The observer–observed roles shift.

The movie showcases two groups of people: the old group, including the inspectors and the coach, and the young adult group of athletes. Besides their age difference, what separates them visually is their outfits. While the police agents are not in uniforms, the athletes are visually coded: They each have unifying snake tattoos on their bodies and wear black sleeveless shirts with military-style shoulder patches with an evocative large logo. The logo illustrates group think in its design of a sun dragon with head at the center, wings on the sides, sunrays on the top, a heart-shaped body, and parallel column bodies with minaret-shaped heads on the bottom.

Here, the sick are cinematically figured as transgendered bodies crossing multiple boundaries, and this is treated with great ambiguity. The result is a lingering anticipation and horror of crossing the boundaries of gender, time, territory, belonging, friendship, authority, morality,

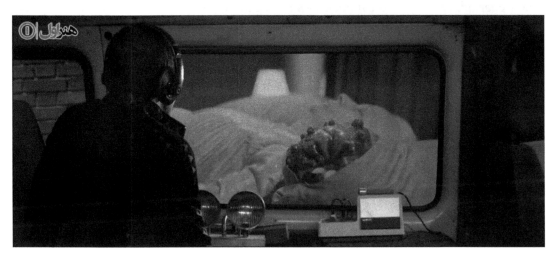

Figure 2.8.1 Ali observes, through a surveillance touchscreen technology inside a van, the emergence of an alien species from the pillow on which the wife of his inspector just passed away.

blood and skin, sickness and health, individual and collective, life and death, and body and soul in the presence of an invisible surveillance gaze enabled through the plot's narrative discourse. Despite multiple crossings, however, middle-class boundaries remain unchanged. The relativizing discourse in the film is uncannily both reductive and rewarding. On the one hand, in returning the surveilling gaze, *Hojūm* tends to relativize the hegemony of power structures as if the police and civic groups are all the same and even exchangeable. On the other, the film relativizes the binary framing of character morality that governs the Hollywood and other genre systems, into good guys versus bad guys, by constructing characters who resist fixed identification and switch roles.

Blood collecting in *Invasion* recalls Mehrjui's *Dāyereh-e Minā* (The Cycle), 1975, in which the main character, Ali, who has traveled to Tehran to admit his sick father to hospital, learns to collect blood from the poor and drug addicts in exchange for a small amount of money and then sells the blood to hospitals for a profit under the supervision of Doctor Sameri, a blood dealer. Both plots express social critique through dystopic relations that hover over spaces of disease and blood exchange. *Dāyereh-e Minā*, however, stands out for addressing class boundaries through institutional critique. Various cultural and economic classes congregate around and feed off governmental institutions through a cycle of corruption that lives a shadowy life through the invisibility of a bureaucratic order that, in turn, masks how people are connected and disconnected at the same time. Corruption in *Dāyereh-e Minā* starts with bad people and then it spreads beyond.

Despite carrying scars of leprosy, children in *Khāneh Siāh Ast* are full of life, as evident in scenes of joking, laughing, and playing. While *Khāneh Siāh Ast* cuts a balance between horror ambiguity of top-down modernization and opportunities of "radical humanism" in addressing child welfare and pedagogy, the Iranian New Wave films of the 1970s, such as *Khesht va Āyeneh* (Brick and Mirror) by Ebrahim Golestān (1965) and *Yek Ettefāgh-i Sādeh* (A Simple Event) by Sohrāb Shahid-sāles (1973) launch more bleak critiques.[27]

In *Khesht va Āyeneh*, a baby left in the car seat of a taxi brings the driver, Hāshem, closer to his girlfriend Tāji as the two experience a moment of intimacy, to which Hāshem fears committing. Manifestations of this fear pervade the entire movie both visually and thematically. Hāshem wanders in dark corners of an abandoned building in search of the baby's real mother who walked away from the cab and disappeared into the darkness. He shuts the windows and pulls the curtain of his room to hide his relationship from neighbors. He is overwhelmed with the bureaucratic maze through which the responsibility for the care of the orphan baby is tossed

---

27   The quoted phrase refers to Jonathan Rosenbaum's article, "Racial Humanism and the Coexistence of Film and Poetry in *The House Is Black*," *The House Is Black* (Facets Cine-Notes, Facets Multi-Media, Inc., 2005), 12–19. For an analysis of the Iranian New Wave movement consult with Hamid Naficy, *A Social History, volume 2*, 325-431 and Farbod Honarpisheh, "Fragmented Allegories of National Authenticity: Art and Politics of the Iranian New Wave Cinema, 1960–79," PhD diss. (Columbia University, 2016).

around. Perhaps, the most horrific scene happens when Tāji experiences her own doubts after visiting kids in an orphanage. The soundscape of kids' cries enters her space first while walking through long alienating hallway. She finally meets the kids at the end of the hallway. The scene is cold and uninviting. She encounters about twenty toddler boys strapped on their buckets in sitting position for potty training. Upon seeing her, kids start dragging themselves toward Tāji in small steps. They are framed only as a group. Tāji first smiles and then becomes sad. As she sits down, the corresponding eye-line match shot of kids changes to ground level, capturing an unsettling moment of toddlers pulling themselves toward the camera. This alienating group frame on the visual track is emphasized by kids' vague and somewhat noisy soundtrack that denies any opportunity for recognizable utterance and individuality.

Yek Ettefāgh-i Sādeh captures the horror of technocratic modernization that has pushed an otherwise deeply collective culture into its frontiers of alienation, isolation, and bureaucratic fragmentation. Mohammad, an elementary student, lives a simple life in the port city of Bandar-e Torkman in Caspian region in the north. His mother is sick and his father fishes illegally. Mohammad does not speak much or relate to anyone throughout the film. He does not get attention from anyone either. Conversation is reduced to minimal expression, and a minimally moving mobile camera follows the boy walking during his daily chores around the town through a series of long shots in long takes. The film is attentive more to the movement of the subject within the frame than the movement of camera itself. This strategy, in turn, demands the viewer become trained in a methodical and patient viewing, to discover the space as it is navigated by Mohammad, the main and silent protagonist of the film.

As we watch the boy walking his way in the expanding landscape, we start discovering the desolate space and feeling the listless rhythm of life in the small town. In face of little expression by Mohammad, the emotionally crushing *mise en scene* forms an interior subjectivity of the schoolboy for the viewer. We begin to feel the boy, and it becomes increasingly devastating. We never see relatives show up. Of course, there are people in the *mise en scene* and places where people gather and do things. The town seems lifeless. While people gather in places, conduct business and commute in streets, they hardly interact emotionally and meaningfully. Something is deeply wrong in the coastal town in *Yek Ettefāgh-i Sādeh* in ways that individuals do not relate to each other as people and an elementary school boy observes and belabors the horror of this alienation throughout the film. While *Khāneh Siāh Ast* also addresses isolation, due to public safety quarantine, people still relate to each other, and children play. In *Yek Ettefāgh-i Sādeh*, however, the wrath of fragmentation has left no lively space even among the children. Mohammad is a silent observer who transforms this horror poetically in the film once we make ourselves available to the film as attentive audiences. To read into the film through Jonathan Kahana's interpretation of Hannah Arendt's theory of public as a space not just shared by people but a space within which people act to relate to each other, *Yek Ettefāgh-i Sādeh* captures cinematically, through the everyday life of a young boy, a town devoid of public.[28]

The subtlety of unfolding horror in *Yek Ettefāgh-i Sādeh* cinematically resurrects in a disempowering bureaucratic nightmare Mohammad Rasoulof's recent episodic film *Sheitān Vojūd Nadārad* (There Is No Evil), 2021.[29] The first episode stands out as a towering work that confronts the viewer with one of the most challenging moments of horror in Iranian and world cinema. It depicts a quintessentially post-revolution middle-class family that feels ideologically neutral. In 32 minutes, a middle-class global viewer can find themself in the cinematic mirror that characters perform, especially after Asghar Farhadi's *Jodayi-i Nāder az Simin* (A Separation), 2011, in which daily needs, chores, and aspirations of a middle-class family transcend national and cultural boundaries in an era of global neoliberalism marked increasingly by the automation of life.

There is little to dislike about this family and the familial character roles it carves out: a caring husband, father, and son; a caring teacher, wife, mother, and daughter-in-law; and a beautiful young daughter and student. Multiple chores and needs govern this family, such as picking up one's partner from work, depositing a salary check, picking up children from school and a dress from tailor shop, shopping, eating out, and visiting and caring for the elderly. The husband role in the film pushes against patriarchal limitations. He is calm and considerate in the face of others losing their temper. He vacuums his mother's apartment and colors his wife's hair (see figure 2.8.2). He is good at executing a task and remaining focused on it against many distractions. His character recalls the father in *Father Knows Best*, the early Cold War American television series. He is the exemplary bureaucrat and an ideal personality for many governments and corporate careers. The film offers a few clues before the last revelatory shot. He wakes up at 3:00 a.m. and goes to work. He stops before traffic lights and stares at colors as they change. The light turns green, but he is not driving. He does not look sleepy, but rather frozen while staring at infinity. Upon arrival, his work seems fully solitary. He walks through a long hallway and enters a small room with basic amenities. He boils water for tea and washes fruit to eat. Two rows of color-coded light spots next to a small opening on the wall recall traffic lights and draw attention.

A series of orange spots light up followed by a series of green ones. He is paying attention to the lights and seems to be counting the time. Then he presses a single switch on the wall and stares through the small opening. A cut takes us to a still frame. The switch has released pedestals

---

28   Jonathan Kahana, "Arendt in Jerusalem: Documentary, Theatricality and the Echo of Irony," *World Records, Vol. 4: At the Presence of Others* 4, no. 5 (2020), https://vols.worldrecordsjournal.org/04/05?fbclid=IwAR3SIQZ4Q31lLFdxPzJGQraSYyzt RJgoa4cezpgJcyspuKSNWEPaoQntZQY#ref12.

29   The title of the film references Hannah Arendt's journalistic report of the trial of Adolf Eichmann in Israel, titled "Eichmann in Jerusalem," for *The New Yorker* in 1963, which was later published as a book with the added phrase: *A Report on the Banality of Evil* (Viking Press).

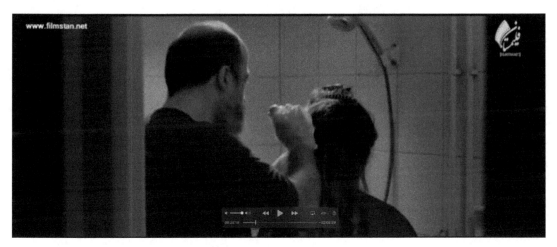

| Figure 2.8.2 The husband/executioner is helping his wife color her hair.

on which four humans stood hence letting go of suspended and now shaking bodies hanging in the air. The still frame only shows the lower body from the knees down. Four men have just been executed by hanging and their identities are anonymous to their executioner, the family man, and, of course, to the viewers. Four pairs of adult male legs agonize in space in an static long take that feels eternal. A few slippers fall to the ground and bodily fluid discharges from shaking bodies until they become completely motionless, suspended in the air. A still camera lingers on the bodies, capturing every subtle movement within the frame. Four people were executed anonymously through a disembodied and efficient process of automation. The family man performs his duty at the right moment and efficiently through releasing the pedestals. His job offers no access to faces of executed people. Our model caring character is an executioner! Restricted narration only offers us access to his actions as they unfold and reveal one step at a time in the course of the episode. His caring character and patient routine establishes strong identification, which in turn, leaves the viewers devastated at the end.

Sheitān Vojūd Nadārad reconnects cinematically the bureaucratic order of things that breaks down an otherwise unbearable, ethically challenging, or questionable experience that connects small daily chores of busy urban life to the quiet sphere of efficient killing machines. This then connects acts of state violence to people in whose name those acts are carried out. The anonymity of faces and invisibility of the process are key features of modern forms of discipline, as Michel Foucault has discussed. This anonymity also maintains the bureaucratic order of fragmentation.

A confrontational diasporic reaction to dysfunctional pedagogies in *Khāneh Siāh Ast* and *Yek Ettefāgh-i Sādeh* happens in Babak Anvari's short film *Two and Two (2010).*[30] A foreboding

---

30   Abbas Kiarostami's *Ghazieh Shekl-e Aval, Shekl-e Dovvom* (First Case, Second Case) and *Mashgh-e Shab* (Homework) also offer great examples for analysis.

teacher shows up one day in a classroom and announces that the result of two plus two is no longer four but five. Students quietly acquiesce. One student, however, objects this result and refuses to back down. Three older students/guards show up with red armbands to enforce the teacher's claim with actual threats. Everything is now at stake. The student still resists. The guards aim at the student symbolically and execute him. Blood splashes on the blackboard, however, and the sonic track fully registers the impact of the bullets even in the absence of visual evidence of actual guns. The student falls dead in the classroom. Students seem fearful and silent. A close-up of one notebook, however, demonstrates that resistance continues: A hand first writes the number five as the result of the equation and then crosses it out with the number four.

CONCLUSION

This chapter discusses the mostly synchronic scholarly attention to the recent wave of Iranian horror film that has addressed cultural specificity through investigation of select themes and characters. It does so by taking a diachronic approach to comparatively investigate, through close analysis of select films from pre- and post-revolution Iran, elements of horror ambiguity that serve as authorial responses to top-down modernization and increased surveillance, bureaucratic automation, and militarization of public life.

This recent appearance of horror film and television series departs abruptly from the more established patterns of neorealist social drama and comedy, documentary, and arthouse projects. This is evident at both narrative and formal levels where mysterious tales are often expressed through abrupt cuts and ominous soundtracks. As with horror film in general, Iranian horror invests heavily in middle-class family life as the site of unfolding crisis through the disruption by supernatural beings.

Historically, two events in the last decade have marked major ideological influences in Iranian cinema, which have affected the new wave of horror: the rise of a religiously conservative hybrid supernatural genre in the form of mostly television series since the early 2000s and cinematic works sponsored by the private foundation, Owj Arts and Media Organization, which is supported by the Islamic Revolutionary Guard Corps, Sepah. Within this milieu of the increasing influence of religiously conservative foundations and state support, the horror genre appears to be a major testing ground for popularity as experimented by first-time directors, seasoned ones, and a few who have returned to the genre.[31]

---

31   Thanks to Bret Vukoder for his insightful comments on the draft version of this chapter.

BIBLIOGRAPHY

Abdi, Shadee and Bernadette M. Calafell. "Queer Utopias and a (Feminist) Iranian Vampire: A Critical Analysis of Resistive Monstrosity in *A Girl Walks Home Alone at Night*." *Critical Studies in Media Communication* 34, no. 4 (2017): 358–370.

"A Look at Six Years of Media Works by Owj Organization." *Islamic Azad University News Agency*. August 9, 2017. Accessed August 2, 2021. https://www.ana.press/news/201398/نگاه‌به‌فعالیت‌های‌6-ساله‌-اسازمان‌-اجو.

Arendt, Hannah. *Eichmann in Jerusalem: A Report on the Banality of Evil*. New York: Viking Press, 1963.

Basu, Shrabani. "The Foil and the Quicksand: The Image of the 'Veil' and the Failure of Abjection in Iranian Diasporic Horror." *Cinema: Journal of Philosophy and the Moving Image* 9 (2017): 72–87. Accessed August 2, 2021. http://static1.1.sqspcdn.com/static/f/906805/27864186/1521811931250/9_Basu.pdf?token=QGfDFFXcSJuiyqrFqjPXPQ85rgM%3D.

Benshoff, Harry M. "Horror Before 'The Horror Film.'" In *A Companion to the Horror Film*, ed. Harry M. Benshoff, 207-224. New York: Wiley Blackwell, 2014.

Blake, Linnie. *The Wounds of Nations: Horror Cinema, Historical Trauma and National Identity*. Manchester: Manchester University Press, 2008.

Carroll, Noël. *The Philosophy of Horror or Paradoxes of the Heart*. New York: Routledge, 1990.

Elsaesser, Thomas. *Weimar Cinema and After: Germany's Historical Imaginary*. New York: Routledge, 2000.

Gharabaghi, Hadi. "The Syracuse Mission to Iran during the 1950s and the Rise of Documentary Diplomacy." *Journal of Cinema and Media Studies* 60, no. 4 (Summer 2021): 9–36.

Honarpisheh, Farbod. Fragmented Allegories of National Authenticity: Art and Politics of the Iranian New Wave Cinema, 1960–79. PhD diss. New York: Columbia University, 2016.

Jancovich, Mark. ed. *Horror, The Film Reader*. New York: Routledge, 2002.

Kahana, Jonathan. "Arendt in Jerusalem: Documentary, Theatricality and the Echo of Irony," in *World Records, Vol. 4: At the Presence of Others*, Fall 2020. Accessed August 3, 2021. https://vols.worldrecordsjournal.org/04/05?fbclid=IwAR3SIQZ4Q31lLFdxPzJGQraSYyztRJgoa4cezpgJcyspuKSNWEPaoQntZQY#ref12.

Kazemi, Farshid. The Interpreter of Desires: Iranian Cinema and Psychoanalysis. PhD diss. The University of Edinburgh, 2018.

Khosroshahi, Zahra. "Vampires, Jinn and the Magical in Iranian Horror Films." *Frames Cinema Journal* 16 (2019). Accessed August 2, 2021. https://framescinemajournal.com/article/vampires-jinn-and-the-magical-in-iranian-horror-films/.

Kracauer, Siegfried. *From Caligari to Hitler: A Psychological History of the German Film*. Princeton: Princeton University Press, 1947.

Kracauer, Siegfried. "Propaganda and the Nazi War Film." Folder 1367A, Box 139, Series 900, RG 4-1114L. Rockefeller Archive Center. Sleepy Hollow, NY.

Lowenstein, Adam. *Shocking Representation: Historical Trauma, National Cinema, and the Modern Horror Film*. New York: Columbia University Press, 2005.

Mottahedeh, Negar. *#iranelection: Hashtag Solidarity and the Transformation of Online Life*. Palo Alto: Standford University Press, 2015.

Naficy, Hamid. *A Social History of Iranian Cinema, volumes 1–4*. Durham: Duke University Press, 2012.

"Parināz: Dangerous Game with Traditional Beliefs." Interview with Bābak Kāidan. Iran. Oct. 16, 2017. *Bartarinhā*. Accessed August 2, 2021. https://www.bartarinha.ir/fa/news/615114/فیلم-پریان-باز-خطرناک-بازی-باورهای-سنتی.

Partovi, Pedram. "Girls' Dormitory: Women's Islam and Iranian Horror." *Visual Anthropology Review* 25, No. 2 (2009): 186–207.

Phillips, Kendall R. *Darkness: The Rhetoric of Horror in Early American Cinema*. Austin: University of Texas Press, 2018.

Picart, Caroline Joan S. "The Documentary Impulse and Reel/Real Horror." In *A Companion to the Horror Film*, ed. Harry M. Benshoff, 536–553. New York: Wiley-Blackwell, 2014.

Rosenbaum, Jonathan. "Racial Humanism and the Coexistence of Film and Poetry." In *The Documentary Film Reader: History, Theory, Criticism*, ed. Jonahtan Kahana, 473–477. New York: Oxford University Press, 2016.

Saljoughi, Sara. "A New Form for a New People: Forāgh Farrokhzād's *The House Is Black*." *Camera Obscura: Feminism, Culture, and Media Studies* 32, no. 1 (2017): 1–31.

Schubart, Rikke. "'I Smelled It on Him'—Wonderful Trolls and Disgusting Humans in *Border*," *Kosmorama*. Feb. 24, 2021. Accessed August 2, 2021. https://www.kosmorama.org/kosmorama/artikler/i-smelled-it-him-wonderful-trolls-and-disgusting-humans-border.

Skal, David J. "The Horrors of War." In *The Horror Film*, ed. Stephen Prince, 70–85. New Brunswick: Rutgers University Press, 2004.

Steven, Allen. "Persepolis: Telling Tales of Trauma." In *Scars and Wounds*, 267–289. New York: Palgrave Macmillan, 2017.

Tabrizi, Ahmad Mohammad. "The Iranian Supernatural Television Series: Portraying Satan and Summoning Spirit in the Most Accessible Form." DigikalaMAG. *Sherkat-e Noāvarān Fanāvāzeh*. May 2, 2021. Accessed August 2, 2021. https://www.digikala.com/mag/transcendental-series-in-iran-tv/.

Todorova, Mona. "Modernism." In *Modernism—The Creation of Nation-States*. eds. Ahmet Ersoy, Maciej Górny and Vangelis Kechriotis, 4–22. Budapest: Central European University Press, 2010.

Figure Credits

POST-READING QUESTIONS/POST-SCREENING QUESTIONS

Directions: Use what you learned from reading this chapter and watching the film to respond to the questions below.

1. Explain how the 1963 film, *Khāneh Siāh Ast [The House Is Black]* by Forough Farrokhzād relates to horror cinema.

2. Discuss some of the representational characteristics of the new movement of horror genre in Iran.

3. Analyze the Hadi Gharabaghi's argument about horror ambiguity.

4. Explain the distinction between synchronic and diachronic studies of film and how it relates to this examination of Iranian horror film.

About the Contributors

Samirah Alkassim is an experimental documentary filmmaker and assistant professor of film theory at George Mason University. She is the co-editor of *Palgrave Studies in Arab Cinema*, and her publications include the co-authored book *The Cinema of Muhammad Malas* (Palgrave, 2018), contributions to *The Historical Dictionary of Middle Eastern Cinema*, 2nd edition (Rowman and Littlefield, 2020), chapters in *Cinema of the Arab World: Contemporary Directions in Theory and Practice* (Palgrave, 2020), *Refocus: The Films of Jocelyne Saab* (Edinburgh University Press, 2021) and *Gaza on Screen* (Duke University Press, forthcoming 2023). She is currently researching for her forthcoming book *A Journey of Screens in 21st Century Arab Film and Media* (Bloomsbury, 2024).

Ziad El-Bayoumi Foty is an independent film director/producer, lecturer at Howard University, and entrepreneur. He holds his bachelor's in English literature and film from Lafayette College, a master's from Trinity College Dublin in film history and theory, and a master's in fine arts in film production from Howard University. His research interests focus on Palestinian American identity, Arab cinema, and the politics of memory. Foty has taught film studies and production at George Mason University and Catholic University. He is the founder of a web design firm, Design in DC, and film production company, Foty Fusion Films, where he produces films that focus on underrepresented stories with strong social justice themes. (See https://www.linkedin.com/in/ziad-foty-74393446/ and https://filmfreeway.com/ZiadFoty.)

Gabriel Eljaiek-Rodríguez is a Colombian writer and academic. He teaches at Spelman College in Atlanta and has written extensively on the Latin American Gothic, horror cinema, and cultural migration. He is the author of *Selva de fantasmas: El gótico en la literatura y el cine latinoamericanos* (Pontificia Universidad Javeriana, 2017), *The Migration and Politics of Monsters in Latin American Cinema* (Palgrave Macmillan, 2018), *Colombian Gothic in Cinema and Literature* (Anthem Press, 2021), and *Baroque Aesthetic in Contemporary American Horror* (Palgrave Macmillan, 2021).

Hadi Gharabaghi has a PhD in cinema studies from New York University. His archival research makes a case for the emergence of documentary diplomacy during the early history of the United States Information Service (USIS)/Iran relations. His publications include a chapter in the edited volume *Cinema of the Arab World: Contemporary Directions in Theory and Practice* (Palgrave, 2020), essays in the summer 2021 print issue and the winter 2022 online teaching dossier section of the *Journal of Cinema and Media Studies*, a special issue of the *Journal of e-Media Studies* (co-edited with Bret Vukoder, 2022), and the edited volume, *Governing Genealogies of Film Education* (co-edited with Terri Ginsberg, forthcoming 2022).

Madeleine Reddon is a member of the Métis Nation of Alberta and an assistant professor in English literature at Loyola University of Chicago. She has recently published an article in *Canada and Beyond: A Journal of Literary and Cultural Studies:* "Indigenous Modernism: Dehabituating Reading Practices." Her research interests include global avant-garde and modernist literatures, Indigenous studies, critical nationalisms, and psychoanalysis.

Valentina Vitali is professor of film studies at the University of East London, director of the Moving Image Research Centre (UEL), and independent film programmer. Her research explores, from a comparative perspective, the relation between history, economics, and film aesthetics. She has published on South and East Asian cinemas, on the relation between cinema and nation, on image-based work by women, and on aspects of Indian visual cultural production. Vitali's publications include *Capital and Popular Cinema* (Manchester University Press, 2016), *Hindi Action Cinema* (Oxford University Press, 2008), and *Theorising National Cinema* (Bloomsbury, 2006, with Paul Willemen). Her curated events include *Contemporary Women Filmmakers in South Asia* (FACT, Liverpool, 2019), and *Alia Syed* (Whitechapel Gallery, London, 2017). (See https://www.uel.ac.uk/staff/v/valentina-vitali.)

Glossary

Abjection: Julia Kristeva explained abjection in her 1980 book *The Powers of Horror* as the human reaction of extreme disgust to a potential breakdown in meaning caused by the loss of the distinction between self and other. This is primarily triggered by the sight of dead bodies, but other signifiers can bring about the same response: menstruation, the open wound, excrement, sewage, and objects that physically resemble all the above. In horror, the abject pertains to bodily horror, madness, and utter misery.

Andean horror: A subgenre of horror films specific to the Andes region of Peru and Bolivia featuring the mythological creatures of the Qarqacha and Pishtaco.

Biopower: A term coined by French philosopher Michel Foucault that centers on the power of populations rather than individuals, and on the administration and caring of life within society, rather than an individual's power.

Biotechnology: An area of biology that involves the use of living systems and organisms to develop or make technological products.

Blaxploitation horror films: Films made in the period of 1969 to 1976 targeting Black American audiences and capitalizing on the contemporaneous Black Power consciousness that arose from the civil rights movement of the 1960s. These films were almost exclusively produced by White producers, directors, and crew members, but cast Black actors in predominantly crime dramas set in urban environments.

British Empire: Originating in 1497, its power was solidified between the sixteenth and eighteenth centuries with overseas colonies and trading posts in the Americas, South Asia, and China, and by the nineteenth century it was the largest empire in the history of the world. After its dissolution in the early twentieth century, it still had a large and enduring cultural, legal, and linguistic legacy throughout all of its former colonies.

British Victorian sensibility: Associated with the period during the rule of British Queen Victoria (1837–1901), a sensibility and culture characterized by emotional/sexual repression, family discord, distant and ineffectual patriarchy, and the violence of suppressed, angry, and hysterical femininity.

Cold War containment: An American geopolitical strategy whereby the US instituted a policy of containment to prevent the spread of communism after the end of WWII.

Colonialism: The process by which one state dominates the government, economy, communications, and the administration of civic life of another state. This results in the control by the colonizing force of all aspects of life for the colonized subject, as well as, in some cases, that of international commerce.

Communalism: Belonging to a social group based on ethnic or religious affiliation.

Communism: A theory and system of social organization created by German philosopher Karl Marx. This system sees all property as owned by the community and each person must contribute and receive according to their needs and abilities. This system is often viewed in direct opposition to capitalism in its advocation of a classless system where the means of production are communally owned and private property is nonexistent.

Confucianism: An ethical belief system/religion from ancient China, named after the Chinese philosopher Confucius (551–479 BC), based on respect for others, particularly elders, and four main principles: respect for autonomy, beneficence, nonmaleficence, and justice.

Corrective science: A type of science that has tinkered with humanity to create monsters and that features frequently in horror films.

Counter hegemonic: The attempt to critique or dismantle large systems of hegemonic power.

Cyborgification: The process by which human physical abilities are extended beyond the normal biological limitations by placing mechanical elements into the body.

Decolonization: The process of dismantling and/or challenging colonialism with the objective of gaining independence, through collective and individual acts, primarily experienced in the territories that were occupied by dominant powers, such as the Spanish colonies in Latin America, the British and French colonies in Asia, the Middle East, Africa, and the Japanese colonies in East Asia.

Djinn: Also spelled as "jinn," supernatural creatures, usually in the form of spirits or demons dating back to pre-Islamic Arabian folklore and Islamic mythology and theology.

Dual horrification: The process of signification by which a group of people are represented, through their vilification, as horrifying to a dominant audience, while at the same time this signification is experienced as horrifying for the oppressed group who are watching the vilification of their people.

Enduring woman: A type of Black final girl theorized by Robin Means Coleman, the enduring woman never gets to enjoy closure because as soon as she has survived one monster there are more to come due to institutional sexism and racism.

Femicide: The murdering of women, associated with systemic practices of violence (economic, social, psychological) against women.

Final girl: A term coined by Carol J. Clover to describe the central female character in slasher, occult, and rape-revenge films, who, despite being degraded and the object of violent bodily harm by a male perpetrator, manages to save herself and sometimes others in the end, by which time audience identification has shifted to her perspective.

German expressionism: An early twentieth-century German art movement that focused on extreme distortion to express inner emotional reality characterized by stylized sets, distorted buildings, and non-realistic performances. This movement was influenced by Germany's crushing defeat in WWI.

Global South: A term used to identify countries in Latin America, Africa, and most of South Asia that are economically "underdeveloped" and dependent on asymmetrical trade agreements with the more affluent countries of the Global North.

Globalization: The process of international trade in goods and services, technology, and flows of people, investment, and information, promoted by dominant economic powers as benefiting the common good, with the idea that the more the world is intertwined economically, politically, and culturally, the more interconnected it is. This idea, however, does not take into account how globalization is shaped by economic trade agreements that benefit large corporations and dominant world economic powers more than workers and poor countries.

Gothic folklore: A genre of European literature dating back to the late eighteenth century that stressed themes of mortality, terror, decay, death, and the battle between humanity and unnatural forces of evil. Gothic tales are often set in large ancient houses, which are occasionally haunted or characterized by harboring frightening figures.

Haitian voodoo: A syncretic religion practiced in Africa, Haiti, and South America that combines elements and practices of Catholicism with Central African spirituality. Cinematic references to voodoo usually connote dark magic and the history of slavery, as well as slave rebellion in Haiti.

Hegemonic power: A term coined by Marxist philosopher Antonio Gramsci originally referring to the political, economic, or military domination of one state over other states; it can also apply to the power of institutions and systems over individuals within and beyond states.

Heteronormativity: The assumption that all people are heterosexual and the belief/enforcement of the idea that such assumptions are held as natural and normal.

Hindi cinema: The Indian or Hindi language "Bollywood" film industry located in Mumbai, India, which produces the largest number of feature films annually.

Indigenous: A group of people native to a specific region who retain social, cultural, economic, and political characteristics that are distinct from those of the dominant societies in which they live.

Individuation: The process, in psychoanalysis, by which an individual establishes a sense of identity separate from that of other determining figures, such as one's parents or one's society.

Iran: The second largest country in the Middle East and officially known as the Islamic republic of Iran, it is one of the world's oldest civilizations beginning with the formation of the Elamite kingdoms in the fourth millennium BC and known for the Persian Empire, which spanned from the sixth century to the twentieth century.

Iranian new wave: A movement in Iranian cinema of auteur films that emerged in the 1960s and 70s and actively responded to the cultural, political, and social conditions of the time. Its beginning dates back to Hajir Darioush's 1964 *Serpent's Skin*, followed by three signature films from 1969: Dariush Mehrjuyee's *The Cow*, Massoud Kimyayee's *Qaysar*, and Naser Taqvale's *Calm In Front of Others*. It is not to be confused with the post-revolutionary auteur-driven "second new wave" of new Iranian cinema, including Abbas Kiarostami, Mohsen Makhmalbaf, and Jafar Panahi, among other directors.

Iranian revolution: A mass popular, and relatively nonviolent movement in Iran initially led by students, leftist groups, and Islamist organizations in response to the authoritarian rule of the US-backed leader Mohamed Reza Shah Pahlavi. This ultimately resulted in overthrowing the Shah, after which the revolution was appropriated by the Islamic clerics who enabled the exiled Ayatollah Ruhollah Khomeini to return and assume authority as the supreme leader of what then became the Islamic Republic of Iran.

Iranian studies: An interdisciplinary field that studies the history, literature, art, and culture of Iranian peoples and is seen as part of the wider field of Oriental and/or Middle Eastern studies.

Islamophobia: The hatred or prejudice against Muslims and the Muslim religion.

Japanese occupation: The period between 1910–1945 in which the Korean Empire (of the Josean Dynasty) was annexed by the Empire of Japan and subjected to a harsh Japanization project on both the cultural and industrial fronts. This included forbidding the speaking of Korean in universities, the production of propaganda films for the Japanese, the usurping of homes and land, and the enforcement of Korean labor in Japan and for the Japanese settlers in Korea, among other things.

Julia Kristeva: A Bulgarian French author and professor who blends Freudian and Lacanian psychoanalysis with post-structuralist criticism and developed her own theory about the symbolic and semiotic in relation to the subject's identity formation. She argued that the child constantly moves between the symbolic realm (of shared cultural meanings which the child arrives at during the mirror stage and the semiotic realm (connected to music, poetry and the feminine), never arriving at a fixed identity.

Kaidan: A ghost story with roots in Japanese folktales of the Edo period (1683–1867).

La Llorona: Featuring prominently in Mexican cinema, she is the spirit of a woman who commits suicide after being wronged by both a man (a lover, an unfaithful husband, or the devil himself) and her son (or children), whom she eventually kills in a fit of madness. The spirit then conducts a search for the children she has murdered and cries for them for all eternity.

Lafcadio Hearn: An American writer of Greek/Irish origin who emigrated to Japan in 1890 where he lived the rest of his life and become a Japanese citizen. His 1904 book, *Kwaidan: Stories and Studies of Strange Things*, based on Japanese ghost stories, was selectively adapted to screen in Masaki Kobayashi's 1965 film *Kwaidan*.

Lateral violence: A cyclical form of abuse perpetrated on an oppressed person by another oppressed person, which is the reproduction of the violence enacted on them directed toward others within the same community or others recognized as being oppressed. As it pertains to Indigenous and Aboriginal persons it is understood to be the effect of the violence of colonialism and intergenerational trauma and can take the form of workplace bullying, internalized colonialism, and relational aggression.

Latin America: A geographic region encompassing the Spanish and Portuguese-speaking countries of Central America and South America, from Mexico to Patagonia.

Male gaze: A theory developed by Laura Mulvey in the 1970s as the masculinist perspective privileged by the cinematic apparatus with which spectators are "automatically" aligned. This is produced by the voyeuristic relationship between viewers and the screen, which works in coordination with the institutionalized male gaze and its sexualized representations of women. Many other feminist film scholars have argued that while this male gaze is institutionalized, this pleasure can pertain to all genders and does not automatically align women viewers with that of the male protagonist.

Māvarāi genre: A type of Iranian horror film and television series privileging the supernatural that became a hybrid genre in the early 2000s.

Middle East: A term coined in the early twentieth century to define a region spanning western Asia and Egypt. It has changed over time to reflect the geopolitical interests of European and American powers and is presently composed of the countries of Algeria, Azerbaijan, Bahrain, Cyprus (northern), Egypt, Iran, Iraq, Israel, Jordan, Kuwait, Lebanon, Libya, Morocco, Oman, Qatar, Saudi Arabia, Somalia, Sudan, Syria, Tunisia, Turkey, United Arab Emirates, West Bank and Gaza (Palestine), and Yemen.

Middle Passage: The area of the Atlantic Ocean that the slave-bearing ships had to cross between Africa and the Americas during the transatlantic slave trade between 1514 and 1866.

Migratory vampires: These are vampires who like immigrants are suspected of multiple allegiances and diminished patriotism. As a result, these figures are ones of resistance and empowerment as they navigate multiple borders.

Missing and Murdered Indigenous Women, Girls and Two Spirit: MMIWG2S is shorthand in Canada, for the epidemic death and disappearance of Indigenous women, girls, and Two-Spirit peoples across the Americas. Since the 1980s, Indigenous feminists, activists, and political leaders have called for investigations into the MMIWG2S. By the mid 2000s, they finally received mainstream attention after the publication of multiple reports by nonprofit organizations like

Amnesty International, which led to a national inquiry into missing and murdered Indigenous women in 2016.

Modernization: The process of progressive transition from a pre-modern to a modern society. While typically referencing urbanization, industrialization, and social progress, this term has often been used as a justification for colonial, neo-colonial, and neo-imperial expansion by powerful states.

Nahda: The period of Arab modernity beginning under Ottoman ruler Muhammad Ali Pasha's reign in Egypt, starting in the middle of the nineteenth century to the early twentieth century. It set the foundations for the twentieth-century Arab nationalist movement, which emerged from the ashes of European colonialism.

National Association for the Advancement of Colored People (NAACP): An American interracial organization formed in 1909 to abolish segregation and discrimination based on race, housing, employment, voting, and transportation, and with the aim of countering systemic racism in America.

Neo-imperialism: The first use of this term pertains to the period from the mid-nineteenth century until the outbreak of WWI in 1914, when the dominant Western European, American, Russian, and Japanese powers sought to acquire new territories, but it also applies to the post-WWII global power of the US, which is solidified through informal legal agreements, economic relations, and cultural influence as opposed to outright colonialism. The contemporary use of the term applies to the neo-liberal global economic systems that define advanced capitalism.

North and South Korea: The splitting of Korea at the end of WWII in 1945 after the Japanese surrender, into a communist-allied North and a US-allied South. The failure of the two powers to agree on how to unify the country led to the eventual 1950–53 Korean War and a clash between Cold War powers.

Onryo: The "vengeful spirit" in Japanese folklore believed to be capable of causing harm in the world of the living to redress the wrongs it received while alive.

Orientalism: A perception of "the Orient" (or the East) and "the Occident" (or the West) as diametrically opposed, where the West is perceived as the rational, modern world of historical progress and the East as an inferior, uncivilized territory. Historically, in European cultural work, academia, and political affairs, Orientalism entailed an essentialized image of a typical Oriental represented as culturally and biologically inferior. Critical theorist Edward Said's 1978 book *Orientalism* shifted the academic discourse such that the term "Orientalism" now refers to a generally patronizing Western attitude toward Middle Eastern, Asian, and North African societies.

Ottoman Empire: An empire based out of modern-day Turkey that reigned from 1299 until 1922, by the end of which it controlled much of southeast Europe, west Asia, and North Africa.

Pishtaco: A creature in Andean folklore who, once a human being, was transformed by God into a monster after committing incest, and who can shapeshift into other creatures.

Postcolonialism: A body of literary work and critical theory that examines the economic, political, cultural, and social impact of eighteenth- to twentieth-century European colonialism/imperialism on African, Asian, Middle Eastern, and Latin American nations.

Post-Enlightenment individualism: This term arose after the seventeenth- and eighteenth-century period of Enlightenment in Europe, based on the notion of the individual conceived as self-made, independent, and autonomous.

Psychoanalysis: In film theory, psychoanalysis has brought two waves, the second of which, in the 1980s and 90s, embraced feminist theory, which critically expanded on the foundations established by Laura Mulvey, incorporating Freudian and Lacanian psychoanalytic theories of gendered identity formation.

Qarqacha: A monstrous creature in Andean folklore who sometimes appears as a llama with a human face or as a llama with two or three heads.

Red Scare: A period in American society from 1947–1957 marked by paranoia and hysteria over the perceived threat of communism during the Cold War. This resulted in the persecution of many innocent people by the House Un-American Activities Committee under the direction of Senator Joseph R. McCarthy, who specifically targeted individuals working in the federal government and the Hollywood film industry.

Religion: An organized system of beliefs entailing the worship of one or more all-powerful deities, which involves adhering to a set of rules and activities by which to worship and live a virtuous life.

Residential schools: A state-sponsored Christian boarding school system that forcibly separated Indigenous children from their parents and families to enforce Christian culture, education, and the dominant language (English in the US and Canada, Spanish in Central/South America), while training them to work in domestic and vocational trades. This resulted in widespread abuse, cultural erasure, and trauma for the children and their communities.

Revenant: A person who has returned from the dead, particularly significant in horror literature and folklore, including Japanese horror.

Scopophilia: Based on the psychoanalytic term to refer to the pleasure in looking, Laura Mulvey theorized it as the voyeuristic nature of spectatorship based on the pleasure in looking, in reference to the predominantly male gaze of Hollywood cinema, which has historically objectified women.

Settler colonialism: A form of colonialism that works to replace the Indigenous people of a given land (e.g., the Indigenous tribes of North America) through a variety of violent means, by a new settler community that benefits from the occupation and usurpation of lands that were native to the Indigenous population, often resulting in genocide and ethnic cleansing.

Shinrei shashin: Japanese term for "spirit or ghost photography," where a ghost is believed to be recorded, usually accidentally, in a photograph or other media form. This connects to the skepticism around technologies of reproduction that predominate in 1990s J-horror.

Slavery: The condition of being enslaved by a person or group of peoples, in which the enslaved person is treated as property, has no rights, and is forbidden to quit service. Slavery in recent history frequently refers to the European and American trade in the kidnapped people of African descent in the Americas.

Social realism: A style of representation in painting, photography, literature, and film, where realist depiction delivers social commentary and often political critique while addressing the struggles of working-class people who, especially after WWI, were predominantly the audience of cinema.

State terrorism: The act of terrorism conducted by one state toward another state or by the state toward its own citizens. In the dominant media, terrorism is often elicited to describe individual acts of terror but rarely the actions of state terrorism, which often inflict a much higher death rate.

Student Nonviolent Coordinating Committee (SNCC): An American civil rights group formed in 1960 by young people dedicated to nonviolent, direct action tactics in the effort to gain civil rights for Black people in America.

Survivance: A term meaning both "survival" and "resistance" that was coined by Anishinaabe writer Gerald Vizenor to describe the dynamic ways in which the Indigenous peoples of North America participate in their societies and contribute to the world, beyond the determinations of absence, tragedy, powerlessness by which they have historically been defined.

Techno-capitalism: A new version of capitalism, coined by Luis Suraez-Villa, that generates new forms of corporate organization and exploits creativity and new knowledge. These organizations are deeply rooted in technological research as opposed to the production of manufacturing and services.

Terrorist monster: The depiction in American cinema and television of terrorists, who are frequently Arabs and Muslims, and who are monstrous and evil.

Third-wave feminism: A wave of feminist theory and activism that began in the early 1990s, in part to address the blind sights of second-wave feminism. The term *intersectionality* was coined during this wave to describe the intersecting layers of oppression experienced by women across the categories of race, class, and gender.

Transatlantic slave trade: The oceanic trade in African men, women, and children, mostly from West and Central Africa, who were sold into slavery. This resulted in the kidnapping of approximately 12.5 million persons over the duration of 366 years, from 1514 to 1866.

Transnational borders: Borders between countries and nation-states that are fluid, dynamic, and mobile, contrary to the idea that their borders are discrete and impermeable.

Uncanny: Translated from the German *unheimlich*, it generally means a sense of unease, of a creepy, atmosphere intruding into daily life, and has figured prominently in the horror genre. (See *unheimlich*.)

Unheimlich: A term that translates from German as "strange" and often as "the uncanny" in English, it was coined by Sigmund Freud as a psychoanalytic term that locates the strangeness in the ordinary and that is encountered in an unsettling or taboo context relating to "the return of the repressed."

Veiling: The Muslim practice of women veiling their hair as a form of modesty. According to the Quran, the Islamic holy book, this practice is not mandatory and should be the woman's choice. The Persian word for the veil is *chador*.

Virtual immigrants: The migration of skills and labor that are extracted from the Global South to the West in which laborers physically remain in their own country but create transnational virtual spaces where vast amounts of data and code are virtually passed across borders.

Women's cinema: A film genre primarily designed for female audiences that centers on the travails of female protagonists and has allowed space to contest patriarchal systems of power.

Wonhon: The ghost of an innocent woman who has been sexually violated and/or is the victim of family drama who has returned to avenge her untimely death.

Zombie: Undead creatures produced by reanimated corpses that frequently accompany a film's critique of consumer culture and militarism. Romero's zombie was originally based on the monstrous "ghoul," a pre-Islamic monster who eats on the flesh of others, but zombies also evoke the spirituality of voodoo and the history of slavery in Haiti.

Index

U

Uncanny / *unheimlich*, 5–6, 8, 10, 14, 19, 309
Under the Shadow (2016), 278, 282, 283
United 93 (2006), 179

V

Vampiros en la Habana (1985), 188, 194
VanArendonk, Kathryn, 181, 185
Varma, Ram Gopal, 204, 211–212
Veerana / Vengeance of the Vampire (1988), 204, 206
Veiling, 20, 22, 40–41, 282, 309
Vengeful spirit, 214, 306
Videodrome (1983), 91, 93, 104, 153, 235
Violet (2015), 147, 150
Virtual immigrants, 73, 76, 309

W

Waked, Antoine, 267
War on terror, 177–180, 267
Wegner, Paul, 3
Wells, H.G., 172

What We Do in the Shadows (2014), 150
White nationalist, 169
Wiene, Robert, 3, 285
Willemen, Paul, 206, 210, 215, 300
Winterbottom, Michael, 73, 77, 79–80
Wonhon, 242, 244, 259, 309
World Trade Center (2006), 168, 179
World War 1, 67
World War II, 55, 62, 67, 68, 172, 285
WWII, 52, 158, 243, 259, 264, 302, 306

Y

Yek Ettefāgh-i Sādeh [A Simple Event] (1973), 278, 290
Yeon Sang-ho, 242, 244
Youssef, Ramy, 167

Z

Zee TV, 206
Zillmann, Dolf, 170, 185
Zinn, Howard, 182
Zombie, 1, 22, 25, 47, 51–54

CPSIA information can be obtained
at www.ICGtesting.com
Printed in the USA
LVHW052114211222
735722LV00004B/24